POLITICAL THEORY

To Canberra friends

POLITICAL THEORY

Tradition and Diversity

edited by
ANDREW VINCENT

CAMBRIDGE
UNIVERSITY PRESS

PUBLISHED BY THE PRESS SYNDICATE OF THE UNIVERSITY OF CAMBRIDGE
The Pitt Building, Trumpington Street, Cambridge CB2 1RP, United Kingdom

CAMBRIDGE UNIVERSITY PRESS
The Edinburgh Building, Cambridge CB2 2RU, United Kingdom
40 West 20th Street, New York, NY 10011–4211, USA
10 Stamford Road, Oakleigh, Melbourne 3166, Australia

First published 1997

Printed in Hong Kong by Colorcraft

Typeset in New Baskerville 10/12 pt

National Library of Australia Cataloguing in Publication data

Political theory: tradition and diversity.
Bibliography.
Includes index.
ISBN 0 521 57358 0
ISBN 0 521 57500 1 (pbk.)
1. Political science – Philosophy. 2. Political science –
History – 20th century. I. Vincent, Andrew.
320.011

Library of Congress Cataloguing in Publication data

Political theory: tradition and diversity/edited by Andrew Vincent.
       p.   cm.
Chiefly papers derived from a seminar series in 1995, in the
Political Science Program of the Research School of the Social
Sciences at the Australian National University on the theme Whither
political theory.
Includes bibliographical references and index.
ISBN 0 521 57358 0 (alk. paper). – ISBN 0 521 57500 1 (pbk. alk. paper)
1. Political science. I. Vincent, Andrew. II. Australian
National University. Political Science Program.
JA71.P6335 1997
320'.01'1–dc21   97–19623

A catalogue record for this book is available from the British Library

ISBN 0 521 57358 0 hardback
ISBN 0 521 57500 1 paperback

Contents

CONTENTS

Preface

Many, but not all of the chapters in this volume derive from a seminar series organized in 1995, in the Political Science Program of the Research School of the Social Sciences at the Australian National University, on the theme 'Whither Political Theory?'. Having taught versions of political theory for many years, I had some background expectation of what I would encounter. Gradually, as the seminars proceeded, I found the ground shifting underneath me. A wide range of distinct preoccupations characterized what was going under the rubric of theory. Different, at times incommensurable, normative, historical, methodological and ontological approaches were canvassed. The chapters in this volume, although in no way encompassing the breadth of what is actually taking place in political theory, nonetheless illustrate this restless diversity of perspectives. The chapters were not meant to focus directly on the nature of the discipline of theory, unless the author wished to; rather, the authors were encouraged to concentrate on their research at that time. In this sense, the reader can focus on individual arguments without having to deal with the underlying questions the book is designed to raise. Thus, the essays presented here can function at a number of levels.

My thanks go to the School of European Studies in the University of Wales, Cardiff, for enabling my leave of absence; and also to the Research School of the Social Sciences of the Australian National University, not only for offering me a research fellowship in the first place and providing such a congenial environment for research and writing, but also for contributing in such a supportive and active manner to the seminar series in 1995. I found that I learnt a great deal during the long series of discussions, both in and outside the seminar rooms. My thanks also go to the wider community of political theory scholars in the Australian National University. However, I would like to particularly acknowledge

vii

Geoffrey Brennan, the former director of the Research School, and also Philip Pettit, for their kindness and support during my two years in Canberra. My gratitude also goes to Barry Hindess, head of the Political Science Program in the Research School, for providing such an intellectually stimulating, friendly and humorous atmosphere to work in. Thanks must also go to my political theory colleagues and friends in Wales, particularly to Lewis Allan, Graeme Garrard and David Boucher for their advice and help. Finally, my thanks to Phillipa McGuinness of Cambridge University Press, Melbourne, for her patient encouragement.

Andrew Vincent
University of Wales, Cardiff

Contributors

TERENCE BALL: Professor of Political Science at the University of Minnesota. He has held visiting appointments at Oxford and U.C. – San Diego. His most recent book is *Reappraising Political Theory* (1995). He is currently coediting (with Joyce Appleby) *Thomas Jefferson: Political Writings* for the Cambridge Texts series.

DAVID BOUCHER: Reader in Political Theory at the University of Wales, Swansea. Among his recent publications are *A Radical Hegelian* (1993) with Andrew Vincent, and an edited collection, *The British Idealists* (1997), for the Cambridge Texts series. Forthcoming is *The Political Theory of International Relations*.

GEOFFREY BRENNAN: Professor of Economics, Research School of the Social Sciences, Australian National University. He was Director of the Research School 1991–96. Recent publications include *Democracy and Decision* (1993) with Loren Lomasky. Currently continuing research on rational choice theory.

TOM CAMPBELL: Professor of Law, Australian National University. Formerly Professor of Jurisprudence, University of Glasgow (1980–90); Fellow of the Royal Society of Edinburgh. Author of *The Legal Theory of Ethical Positivism* (1996). Researching on freedom of communication and legal positivism.

CONAL CONDREN: Professor of Political Science and Director of the Humanities Research Program, University of New South Wales; Fellow of the Australian Academy of the Humanities. Recent publications: *The Language of Politics in Seventeenth-Century England* (1994); *Satire, Lies and*

Politics: The Case of Dr Arbuthnot (1997). Research interests: political semantics in early modern Britain and the presuppositions informing semantic change; metaphor and concept formation.

ELIZABETH FRAZER: Fellow and Tutor, and University Lecturer in Politics, New College Oxford. She is author, with Nicola Lacey, of *The Politics of Community: A Feminist Critique of the Liberal-Communitarian Debate* (1993), and editor, with Jennifer Hornsby and Sabina Lovibond, of *Ethics: A Feminist Reader* (1992). Currently working on feminist political theory.

ROBERT E. GOODIN: Professor of Philosophy in the Research School of Social Sciences at the Australian National University. Founding editor of the *Journal of Political Philosophy* and author of, most recently, *Utilitarianism as a Public Philosophy* (1996); he is currently working on two books for Cambridge University Press, one exploring the moral foundations and the other the empirical dynamics of the welfare state.

BARRY HINDESS: Professor of Political Science in the Research School of Social Sciences at the Australian National University. His most recent book is *Discourses of Power: from Hobbes to Foucault* (1996). *Governing Australia* (jointly edited with Mitchell Dean) and *Democracy* will be published in 1998. Research interests cover a variety of issues in social and political theory and in contemporary politics. At present he is working on problems associated with influential conceptions of political community in Western political discourse, with particular reference to such ideas as democracy, equality, liberty, power and rationality.

DUNCAN IVISON: Lecturer in Political Theory at the University of York. He was previously Post-Doctoral Fellow at the Research School of Social Sciences, Australian National University. He has published articles in the *Canadian Journal of Political Science, History of Political Thought* and the *Oxford Journal of Legal Studies*. His book *The Self at Liberty* was published in 1997.

CHANDRAN KUKATHAS: Senior Lecturer in Politics in the School of Politics, University College, University of New South Wales, at the Australian Defence Force Academy. He is the author of *Hayek and Modern Liberalism* (1989), and several books and papers on topics in Australian politics, and on political philosophy. He is presently completing a book on liberalism and cultural diversity entitled *The Liberal Archipelago*.

PAUL PATTON: Paul Patton is Associate Professor in Philosophy at the University of Sydney. He recently edited *Deleuze: A Critical Reader* (1996), and is also completing a book on *Deleuze and the Political*.

PHILIP PETTIT: Professor of Social and Political Theory at the Australian National University and also holds a part-time position as Professor of Philosophy at Columbia University, New York. His books include *Not Just Deserts: A Republican Theory of Criminal Justice*, with John Braithwaite, (1990); *The Common Mind: An Essay on Psychology, Society and Politics* (1993 and 1996), and a recently completed book entitled *Republicanism: A Theory of Freedom and Government* (1997).

ANDREW VINCENT: Professor of Political Theory, School of European Studies, University of Wales, Cardiff. Former Fellow at the Research School of the Social Sciences, Australian National University. Associate editor of the *Journal of Political Ideologies*. Recent books include *Theories of the State* (1994 reprint); *Modern Political Ideologies* (1992 and 2nd edition 1995); *A Radical Hegelian* (with David Boucher, 1993). Currently completing a book on twentieth-century political theory.

Introduction

Many political theorists remain untroubled about the nature of the subject. The important thing in political theory is to get on and do it. In this reading, it is a form of thought with a direct practical orientation, and always has been since the ancient Greeks. It is concerned with logical coherence, rigour in argument, empirical accuracy, moral seriousness and practical efficacy. However, political theory, as a subject of academic study, is in a peculiar situation at present. In the anglophone world it has gone through a number of subtle transformations in the twentieth century – tracked in part in Terence Ball's opening chapter. After a period of doldrums during the 1950s, it has grown in significance. Despite times of travail in universities, there is no shortage of interest in the subject, if this is measured in terms of demand for journals and books. However, what does the average student of politics think they are entering into when starting a course on political theory? Are there any clear expectations as to what is being engaged in? In the period from 1945 up to the 1970s, a course entitled 'political theory', 'political philosophy' or, more nebulously, 'political ideas', could have entailed any of the following: the history of political theory – a text-based course relating to the purported canon of theorists; analytical political theory, a concept-based course; or a refinement of the concepts course which focused on one hyper-concept or hyper-theorist. Justice and equality have been the most favoured hyper-concepts, John Rawls being the most favoured hyper-theorist since the 1970s. Further, such a course could concentrate on moral stances within political theory, usually focusing on utilitarian consequentialism and Kantianism, or teleological as against deontic theories, or theories of the right and good. Finally, it could be a hybrid of historical and conceptual concerns, under the rubric of political ideologies (although this has, oddly, grown in popularity only in the last

1

decade).[1] These formats have shaped the structure of political theory in many university environments.

This is not to say that there was no contention; there were even dire mutterings about 'death', and 'putrefaction' in some cases, of political theory. However, by and large, there was an approximate agreement, from the 1950s to the 1970s, on the structure of political theory. The dominant types were the history of political thought and forms of analytic conceptual theory. With the advent of Rawls's work, normative political theory began to form the dominant motif from the later 1970s up to the late 1980s. Despite the post-1945 dominance of a particular analytic style of philosophy, the last two decades have also seen a gradual influx of different modes of philosophical thinking, like hermeneutics and poststructuralism, often loosely grouped under the title 'Continental philosophy'. This volume is not intended as a joust between any of these components. Rather, it allows some of the different styles to address their concerns.

It is one of the themes of this introduction that there is now, in the 1990s, more hesitancy at the core of political theory, a hesitancy which has become more apparent in the last few years. Even the term 'political theory' is itself porous (see Rengger 1995: xiii). Words like 'theory', 'political', 'ideology' and 'philosophy' resonate with symbolic signifi-cance and diverse usage. Yet, each is sufficiently contested to generate overlaps and problems of identification. Is political theory different from philosophy? Is political philosophy the same as ideology? What is the relation of political and moral philosophy? Is political theory a sub-branch of political science or synonymous with it? Alternatively, is politi-cal theory just an aspect of the history of ideas? Is it a hybrid subject, involving elements from other disciplines? There are now clearly over-laps between political theory, history, moral philosophy, psychology, international relations, law and economics. What is the precise relation of political theory to these areas? Does political theory benefit, for example, from the importation of economic theory? Do such disciplines enrich or impoverish it? I am not suggesting there are any definitive answers to these questions; rather, they indicate areas of concern. The claim that political theory has become more hesitant in the last few years does *not* imply that there was any golden age of consensus. Far from it: all that is being asserted is that, within anglophone political theory, there simply *was* more of a pragmatic consensus between 1945 and the 1970s. The surge of justice-based theories during the 1970s and 1980s could be said to have established another partial consensus, where theory had purportedly returned to its heartland of grand normative theory (although others have implied that it never left that heartland).

The hesitancy over political theory is related in complex ways to the manner in which the substantive issues of politics are debated. The nature of theory and the conception of the task of the theorist establish complex theoretical webs within which the substantive issues of the discipline are caught. The restless diversity of theoretical preoccupations goes some way to explain what, at first glance, might appear as a disparate group of papers in this volume. No doubt some legal theorists, poststructuralists or international relations theorists might want a more fulsome commitment to their own intellectual niche. There might, in that sense, be an element of frustration that the contents are so apparently broad-ranging. This volume is distinctive in so far as it indirectly raises the question 'What is political theory?' via the diversity of approaches.

This volume of essays can thus be used by readers on a number of levels. First, if the student of political theory is seeking an up-to-date summary discussion, in a manageable compass, of issues like rational choice theory (Geoffrey Brennan), utilitarian political theory (Robert Goodin), republican theory (Philip Pettit), international relations theory (David Boucher), and the like, then there are chapters which address these questions quite directly. In this sense, the essays function on a basic, informative level for both students and scholars of political theory. Second, they can also be read in a more collective sense, to raise questions about the present status, character, role and future of political theory as a discipline. The plan of this introduction is *not* to follow the arguments of the various chapters, but rather to examine certain broad themes in contemporary political theory.[2]

'Politics' and 'Theory'

The compound term 'political theory' is a comparatively late development – certainly in the manner that we now employ it. In the nineteenth century, the word 'theory' often had pejorative connotations, being equivalent to speculation, conjecture or untested fact. The ancient association of theory with philosophy[3] has meant, though, that theory has been tied, and still is, to the changing fortunes and nature of claims to knowledge and philosophical thought – whether the style of philosophy be idealist, phenomenological, existential, hermeneutic, poststructuralist, Marxist or analytic. Thus, political theory has tended to mirror the fragmented character of philosophical thought.

One overt facet of political theory is that it inhabits both an abstracted philosophical realm and the more immediately practical domain of politics. There is an implicit tension between these realms. As Michael Sandel comments, 'philosophy may indulge our moral aspirations, but politics deals in recalcitrant facts' (1996: xi). However, there is an assumption, in some forms of political theory, that it must, in some way, address itself consistently to the practice of politics, that is, institutions, policies and processes. Political institutions and policies, in this reading, would be the embodiment of ideas: literally, living theory. This is certainly one important way in which the canon of political theorists and classic texts has been viewed. However, there are profound ambiguities on this issue. One problem is the hard distinction which has often been driven through theory and practice in some Western philosophy. Another is the epistemological problem of what theory is doing. Is it representing, explaining, interpreting, justifying or creating politics?

The distinction between theory and practice has a long history in European thought. Aristotle, Kant, Hegel and Marx all distinguished the spheres of theoretical and practical reason (see Lobkowitz 1967). Aspects of the distinction reappear in various forms of twentieth-century political philosophy. Thus, for Michael Oakeshott (1933), practice is distinct from philosophy. There is no way, categorially, that philosophy could involve itself in political practice without ceasing to be philosophy.[4] Political activity, for Oakeshott, is not something which arises from worked-out, rational belief. Rather, it is rooted in an existing tradition of behaviour. A tradition, for Oakeshott, is a 'multi-voiced' entity which does not constitute a creed, set of maxims, rules or propositions. Practical knowledge is assimilated in the 'doing' within a tradition (see Oakeshott 1991). The rationalist in politics selects and abstracts to make a self-consistent creed. A body of maxims, rules and precise concepts is then seen to encapsulate reality. Yet it is the day-to-day practical decisions which change the world, not the conclusions of theories. The theorist should not therefore try to see any link between 'political theory' and 'practice'. Politics can be discussed historically or philosophically. Such discussion would involve the interpretation of explanatory languages. Given that such languages are either philosophical or historical, they cannot, for Oakeshott, provide rational principles on how to act in the political world. In this sense, political theory paints its grey on grey. A cognate distinction appeared in Leo Strauss's writings. He argued that political philosophy needed to recover a realm of transcendental truths and move away from both the messy, self-interested domain of political science, policy and ideology, as well as the dangerous reefs of relativism, nihilism and historicism (Strauss 1959). In one sense, this demand for a transcendental ahistorical realm of political philosophy is not without some modern adherents, not just in the writings of a Straussian like Allan Bloom, but also in the initial writings of John Rawls, Robert Nozick and Ronald Dworkin.[5] There is a difference, however, between Nozick, Dworkin, the early Rawls and Oakeshott on this question: the first three theorists would like their abstract theories to have an impact on day-to-day politics and policy-making, even if at one or two removes. Oakeshott, though, makes a virtue of distance from practice, a theme which is echoed, in a different philosophical format, in T. D. Weldon's work and Wittgenstein's later writings. The obverse of Oakeshott's position is where political theory links closely with practice. In much contemporary political philosophy, rigour in argument, consistency with formally stated normative principles and clear lines of rational inference to practice take definite priority. A consistent political theory will lead to good politics and policy. On one level, there is indeed something rather obvious about the relation of theory to political practice. As Fred Dallmayr notes, 'To the extent that it seeks to render political life intelligible, political theory has to remain attentive to the concrete sufferings and predicaments of people' (1978: 2). Theories do not therefore arise *in vacuo*.[6] Rather they originate in practice, provide maps of the political realm, and offer us normative guidance on where to proceed.

There are, though, what might be termed *inclusive* and *exclusive* readings of the theory–practice link. The latter brings pristine theory *to* politics, the former finds or retrieves theory *from* political practice. The exclusive reading, which pervades a great deal of literature, maintains that a good political theory can be applied to, and can modify and improve, political practice. This usually implies a more technical solution to political practice. The exclusive reading has a number of subtle variations. Two distinct forms of exclusive theory exist in current literature. On the first account, theory is formulated, *sub specie aeternitatis*, as a body of systematic ideas and values which can be applied to politics. This was certainly characteristic of the *early* Rawlsian enterprise (Rawls 1971). It is also characteristic of rational choice theory, much late twentieth-century utilitarian theory and contractarian thought.[7] For some theorists it has led to the demand for closer linkage between political theory and empiricism, political science and policy-making: in sum, *applied* political theory.[8] The second account of exclusive theory has developed from the most recent developments in liberal theory. In Rawls's current work (Rawls 1993), theory is not formulated externally, like David Gauthier's contractualism (Gauthier 1986), and applied to the world. It is deliberately more non-univeralist and non-transcendental in intent. It is drawn *from* and addressed *to* a particular public culture and public reason. Theory – despite being free-standing – is seen to draw its sustenance and validity from the ordinary 'considered convictions' of the mass of the citizenry of particular political cultures. For some, this move in Rawls gives up everything that is worthwhile in his political theory (Barry 1995: xi, 3, 5). Rawls is thus often seen as partially capitulating to his communitarian critics (Hampton 1989: 792ff.) or drifting towards a partial Hegelianism. For others, correctly understood, Rawls has made a definite advance in political theory (Larmore 1990: 356–7).

In the inclusive account, however, theory is seen as neither an instrumental adaptation of politics or policy, nor an adjustment to an external reality; rather, it has a constitutive and interpretive role to play in politics. There are, thus, no brute facts which are not permeated with interpretive assumptions and beliefs. The practices and institutions which result from this find their sense (or nonsense) in such beliefs. Forms of communitarianism, multicultural theory, feminism and some recent liberal nationalist theory have developed this mode of analysis. Such theory moves, in some cases, with great ease into a hermeneutic perspective – Charles Taylor is the prime example. For modern communitarians, it is a core thesis that the self is embedded in the community. In Michael Sandel's phraseology, there are no 'unencumbered selves' standing outside a community frame. Thus, for Sandel, we cannot adopt the stance of Rawls's original position, because it makes the unwarranted metaphysical assumption of the unencumbered self (see Sandel 1982: 175). If we cannot accept this unanchored, insubstantial Rawlsian self, then it follows that we have no grounds for accepting the two principles of justice. Thus, in the Sandelian view, Rawls presupposes an implausible account of the moral subject, which is the logical prerequisite for the impartiality of justice. Life in the polis and citizenship precede any sense we might have of our unique human individuality. This argument is also echoed in Alasdair MacIntyre's narrative conception of the self, a self which is constituted, in part, from the history and telos of the community (MacIntyre 1981). Similarly, for Michael Walzer, we read off existing traditions of discourse. We do not need external theoretical foundations for a practical life; rather, we draw upon the interpretations of a tradition or form of life. We cannot totally step back to assess communities, morality or justice with a view from nowhere, although we can criticize them from within using internal standards of rationality (Walzer 1987: 6–7). From one perspective, communitarianism should have no link with normative theory at all. It works at an interpretive level, citing the philosophical conditions for the use of concepts like the self and human rationality (see Taylor in Rosenblum 1989: 159). It thus might be considered a category mistake to see it *recommending* a particular substantive view of society.[9] Political theory rather provides an articulate rendering and interpretation of the unarticulated beliefs of a community (see, for example, MacIntyre in Miller and Seidentrop 1983).

Turning briefly to the concept of politics: the term developed from a unique vocabulary in Greek thought concerned with the city-state – *polis*. This vocabulary was, in a sense, rediscovered in the thirteenth century with William of Moerbecke's translation of Aristotle's *Politics*; it was used by Aquinas and later Aristotelianism until the fifteenth century, when it became more closely associated with a republican form of government (see Rubinstein 1987: 42ff.). Theoretical political knowledge was often seen to be *intertwined* with political practice. To use a contemporary vocabulary, the thickly textured consensual goods of the ancient polis or republic could be 'read off' from the institutions.

Politics, in the above sense, largely focused on the state and cognate terms like government, legislatures or public policy. The modern polis (state), and its unity of purpose, became the point of convergence for many modern political theories until comparatively recently. As Will Kymlicka notes, 'most Western political theorists have operated with an idealized model of the polis in which fellow citizens share a common descent, language and culture' (1995: 2; Vincent 1987: 4ff.). The state, despite its profound conceptual ambiguity, forms an unproblematic, consensual backdrop for such theorizing. The current claimants for this approach, with often much thinner notions of consensual goods, incorporate a conception of politics premised on, for example, shared notions of equality, rationality, impartiality and justice. In Rawls's most recent work (1993), for example, justice is seen as offering neither a *modus vivendi* thesis premised on rational choice, nor a comprehensive, morally based outlook. For Rawls, practical reason achieves an over-lapping consensus through the embeddedness of liberal values, like freedom and equality, within the institutions of liberal democratic societies. Politics, in this reading – given that we are dealing with justice which is political, not metaphysical – is a description of a situated public reason or shared consensus which resolves matters impartially. This bears little or no relation to a politics of power, class, gender, colonial or elite manipulation, which is the more immediate intuition about politics within other areas of political theory. It also bears little relation to the more diffuse and contested vision of politics that has arisen in recent years.[10]

One major problem for contemporary political theory is that the dominant liberal notion of the 'political' as a site of consensual, if minimal, public norms and institutions (whether viewed from a universalist or partial communitarian standpoint) is now deeply contested from a range of theoretical perspectives. Feminist theorists have challenged this more orthodox concept of the political as embodying patriarchal power (Pateman 1988; Okin 1992). It is a cardinal point of feminist political theory that politics is a much broader phenomenon than can be encompassed in the state, government or centralized demands for distributive justice. For poststructural (and indeed many feminist) writers like Michel Foucault or Judith Butler, the language of public reason is not viewed as a transparent conveyor of meaning. Political theory cannot stand back from social conflict. It is the medium of expression and experience of such conflict. In other words, political theory is enmeshed itself in complex relations of power. Foucault, amongst others, therefore suggests genealogical explanation, which examines how certain 'regimes of truth' concerning politics – including forms of political theory – come about (see Foucault 1980). The notion of the individual, rational, choosing subject is itself seen as the *product* of a regime of truth, which itself needs genealogical explanation. Similarly, ideas of justice, rights or freedom, do not stand above power relations or politics, they are part of power relations. For Foucault, knowledge, of all forms, is neither external to the world nor a way out of the world. Knowledge is intimately bound to power and politics.

Twentieth-century Marxism has also impacted strongly on the idea of politics. The primary schools of Marxism have been the critical 'humanistic' theory of the Frankfurt school, the anti-humanist structuralist Marxism of Louis Althusser, and analytical and rational choice Marxism. Structuralist Marxism was of fairly short duration – from the late 1960s to the early 1970s – and had the least impact on anglophone political theory. If anything, it is now interesting only in relation to the more general concerns of structuralism as an intellectual movement. The more recent ideas of analytical and rational choice Marxism have utilized the resources of analytic philosophy, methodological individualism and rational choice to construct their idiosyncratic positions (see Elster 1985; Roemer 1986; Carver and Thomas 1995), downplaying the more historical aspects of traditional Marxism. Out of all of these, Critical Theory has had the most significant impact. Its most prestigious exponent – although some would deny that he is now so clearly identified with the aims of Critical Theory – is Habermas. The broad aims of Critical Theory have been concerned with a historically based critique of reason and the critical exposure of ideologies for the purposes of political and moral emancipation (see Jay 1973; Held 1980). Politics, like reason, is seen as a contingent historical idea. Habermas's work has been the most systematic, optimistic and developed project of Critical Theory to date, culminating in the last few decades with his attempt to construct a general theory of communicative rationality. Habermas endorses a more critical dialectical-hermeneutic approach to politics. He envisages the 'political' as tied to a search for a rational public consensus, through an ideal speech situation of unconstrained deliberative rationality (1984; 1987). Minimally, in all these spheres of Marxist thought (with the possible exception of Habermas whose ideas are more complex and nuanced), politics is seen as a sphere of historical contingency and conflict. More recent discourse analysis blends Foucaultian poststucturalism, deconstruction theory and late Marxist thought.[11] It identifies the political with discursive struggles to fix, hegemonically, the meaning or configuration of key terms in political discourse for the sake of power (see Laclau 1990; Laclau and Mouffe 1985).

Further, the nation-state form – which has been so intimately connected to one sense of politics in Western thought – has also been subject to intense challenges in the last few decades from both globalism and localism.[12] The recent restless debates over communitarianism, nationalism, multiculturalism, difference theory, interculturalism and postcolonialism, have raised further searching questions over the precise location and character of politics, often outside the boundaries of the state.[13] Finally, there are growing numbers of theorists who argue that much modern political theory has actually displaced politics. Thus, Bonnie Honig comments that many modern political theorists are 'hostile to the disruption of politics', confining it to the 'juridical, administrative, or regulative tasks of stabilizing moral and political subjects' (1993: 2; also Barber 1988). This latter view sees many political theorists as unwilling to come to grips with the conflictual, messy and agonistic character of politics. Alternatively, theorists are seen as engaging in an 'effete' self-justifying activity which is distant from the 'hurly-burly' of the political world (see Gunnell 1986).[14]

In summary, politics moves across a spectrum of ideas, sometimes intersecting with, sometimes veering away from, systematic theory. Politics, in this sense, is not simply an object to be explained, but is, rather, the site of a multiplicity of contesting theories, languages and vocabularies. Theory, in this format, is no longer so unambiguously linked to practice. We are often in a double-bind here. In a pre-modern sense we still expect to see political theory intimately linked with a consensual practice. Yet, in a (post)modernist frame, theories often contest and skate over the surface of politics.

Political Theory: History and Tradition

There is a deep-rooted assumption within political theory that the study of the canon of classic texts is *the* defining aspect of the discipline of politics. The development of the academic discipline of politics in the nineteenth century began, in fact, with the historically based study of such texts. In this sense, the history of political thought became an established part of the discipline into the twentieth century. However, not all of those with interests in political theory in the late twentieth century have been so struck with its importance. For some, focusing on the history of political theory is in fact debilitating. As one critic notes, 'the study of the history of political thought should not be the core of the discipline of political theory . . . by treating it as the foundation of our study we have corrupted it and incapacitated ourselves as creative thinkers' (Spence 1980: 699; see also Freeman and Robertson 1980: 3). Spence compares the classic texts to Rorschach's inkblots 'on which

contemporary political theorists can project their aspirations and values'
(1980: 705). For recent theorists, like John Dunn, this mistrust of history
– which he sees more broadly within the recent Anglo-American tradition, particularly in the hegemony of liberal contractarian thought – is a
matter of irritation (Dunn 1995: 13).[15] However, it is worth noting something of the genealogy of the relation of political theory and history
before jumping to any conclusion on this issue.

History, like politics, is comparatively recent as an independent
academic discipline, though we commonly trace its ancestry to remote
antiquity. In fact, in the anglophone world, both history and the history
of political theory, as self-conscious academic disciplines, are the product
of the nineteenth century (see Boucher 1989; Condren 1985).[16] However, the history of political theory has served different roles in its comparatively short academic history since the nineteenth century, many of
them, directly or indirectly, tied to politics. Some of these roles bear
upon the function of history itself as a discipline. From its first inception,
the history of political theory was viewed as part of the education of
the citizen, teaching virtue through the great classic books and providing
sustenance for character development. It was also, by the later
nineteenth century, perceived to be an important aspect of the training
in civic awareness and national consciousness. Universities had in mind
particular professional citizens (civil servants), enabling them to see the
'development' of ideas which led to their own society. The history of
political theory embodied the morally uplifting story of the nation. Thus
'historians believed that in their teaching and writing they were
continuing a tradition which, by cultivating character and mental abilities, led to a discovery of truth proven by historical events' (Soffer 1994:
5). This process also functioned in the institutional interests of universities. Progressively, over the nineteenth and early twentieth centuries,
universities 'successfully transformed a set of values encoded in the
concept of "liberal education" into a licensing system for a national elite'
(Soffer 1994: 5), a process which has continued into the twentieth
century. In Britain, it was thus overtly nationalist and institutional concerns which impinged upon the construction of both the disciplines of
history and the history of political theory. The same process was echoed
in the creation of history in both North American and European
universities.[17]

Further, the history of political theory, from a more directly academic
perspective, was seen to embody the fundamental and perennial *ideas* of
political science from the ancient Greeks to the present. This was one
predominant sense of 'political science' in the early part of the twentieth
century (and has not lost support to the present). The first modern
usage of the term 'political science' dates back to thinkers like

Montesquieu, Adam Smith, Adam Ferguson and David Hume, where it was understood as the 'science of the legislator' (see Collini et al. 1983).[18] However, in the nineteenth and early twentieth centuries, many academic lawyers and historians tended to use the term 'political science' to denote, *qua* Aristotle and the predominant classicism of the time, the ideas and ideals associated with politics, particularly via the state. This theme is reflected in ideas of one of the first professors of political science in Cambridge University.[19] Ernest Barker noted, in his inaugural lecture in 1928: 'I am not altogether happy about the term "science". It has been vindicated so largely, and almost exclusively, for exact and experimental study of natural phenomena . . . I shall use it, as Aristotle . . . to signify a method or form of inquiry by the name of Political Theory' (1978: 18).[20] Political science indicated, in this context, a systematic structuring of ideas about politics which blended empirical, historical and more abstract normative considerations.

The above point is not unrelated to interests within late-nineteenth-century institutional, jurisprudential and constitutional theory in German *Staatslehre*. In fact, for some commentators, like John Gunnell, the manner in which 'theory' entered politics more self-consciously as a discipline, particularly in America, developed from interests in *Staatslehre* (Gunnell 1993: 20ff.; see also Dyson 1980: 174ff.). Many of the academic writers on politics in the nineteenth and early twentieth centuries, like F. W. Maitland, were trained in either law or history, and often focused on legal and constitutional description and institutional taxonomy (Maitland 1920). Political science combined, without any difficulties, systematic institutional theory with the history of political theory. It is also important here to bear in mind that, at the turn of the century, academic disciplines were less sharply defined and were consequently more fluid in character. Philosophy, history, law, sociology, international relations, and even evolutionary biology, were often blended together in (what now would be taken as) political theories. It is at this juncture, however, that we see the beginnings of the development of the academic discipline of politics in universities. The discipline began to develop its own distinctive institutional character in the United States first, and then Britain, particularly during the period 1890 to 1930. Further, there was a gradual effort to separate it from other disciplines like law, history and philosophy.[21] The historical side of politics began to lose ground to more direct institutional description. The historical side was then either demarcated into the history of political thought and institutional history, or integrated as a preface to comparative institutional study. In the late twentieth century we are still dealing with this odd legacy.

In the late nineteenth century another powerful impetus for the historical study of political theory derived from Idealist philosophers.

The history of philosophy, for Idealists, embodied a teleological concern with the realization of certain ideas like freedom and self-realization. The history of ideas thus took on a deep purposive significance. Certainly this is the manner in which thinkers like T. H. Green approached the history of moral and political philosophy, and his perspective was powerfully influential into the early twentieth century (Vincent and Plant 1984; Boucher 1985). This concern with the development of philosophy also influenced twentieth-century historical methodology, particularly in the writings of one of the last of the major philosophical Idealists in Britain – R. G. Collingwood.

In the 1930s, the study of the history of political theory took on more urgency in the face of ideologies like fascism and Marxist–Leninism. The history of political theory at that time can be said to have embodied, quite directly, the beliefs and aspirations of Western liberalism. It enabled citizens of democratic states to understand the operative ideas implicit within their own institutions and thus to confront totalitarianism. This was particularly the case in much of the literature on political thought produced during the 1930s and 1940s, reaching its summation in G. H. Sabine's *A History of Political Theory* in 1937. As one of the writers of the period concluded his history of political theory: 'A mere century and a half, though fraught with fateful and tremendous change, has not diverted the fundamental lines of political thought . . . The great European tradition of intellectual liberty and power . . . of self-government under the Law . . . of originality and enterprise is unlikely to be swamped in the convulsions of the new Mass Society' (Bowle 1947: 451; see also Doyle 1949: 296ff.).

All these elements helped establish, for the twentieth century, the canonical tradition of political thinkers, which has been criticized as an academic artifice by theorists like Gunnell (1986; 1987; 1993) and defended, to the present day, from slightly unexpected quarters, by John Dunn (1995). There have been differing views, though, of what this canonical tradition represents. One perspective, formed in the 1930s, often by German émigrés, read the canon in cosmic terms. For Leo Strauss, the history of political theory is concerned with a search for the ultimate knowledge of the right order. History reveals a process of decline in modernity. (Strauss saw three waves of modernity, represented in the writings of Machiavelli, Hobbes, Nietzsche.) For Straussians, there is a dire need to unravel modernity and rediscover the universal virtues of the great classics (even if it is a secret doctrine for the initiated). This entails reopening old questions, like that between the ancients and the moderns. Similar cosmic themes are explored in writers like Eric Voegelin, Dante Germino, Hannah Arendt and Yves Simon, amongst many others. Allan Bloom revived these themes again in the 1980s in popular books like *The Closing of the American Mind* (1987).

In the 1960s, a more tempered vision appeared in theorists like Sheldon Wolin. He proposed that the canon of political theory is best understood by 'analyzing the many ways that the acknowledged masters have practised it. No single philosopher and no one historical age can be said to have defined it conclusively' (1960: 2). Yet it can be of therapeutic value in both diagnosing and addressing modern ills. Thus, it has direct normative significance. However, a third strand of interpretation, filtered through interests in the analytic style of philosophy, saw the canon as a resource of ideas and conceptual conundrums. This resource is something that can be mined for present concerns. We can thus pick up Machiavelli or Locke and debate with them and consider whether they offered sound arguments. This approach was more characteristic of thinkers like John Plamenatz.

Partly as a reaction to this latter view, the 1970s saw a new preoccupation focused on the contextually sensitive reconstruction of texts. The work of Quentin Skinner and J. G. A. Pocock and the German *Begriffsgeschichte* (critical conceptual history) are the best-known contributions (see Ball 1988; Tully 1988).[22] Skinner argued for the need to examine painstakingly the conventions that govern the language of political theory. The aim was to construct 'a history of political theory with a genuinely historical character' (1978, vol. 1: xi).[23] Some see this move as the real transformation of the history of political theory, although from what remains slightly indeterminate. In the early enthusiastic phase of this movement, John Dunn could write, 'I simply cannot conceive of constructing an analysis of any issue in contemporary political theory around the affirmation or negation of anything which Locke says about political matters' (quoted in Tuck 1995: 82), thus confirming the worst fears of some analytical critics. Dunn, however, is more chastened on this issue now, commenting in a recent essay that 'the history of political theory is still a key aid in understanding politics (yesterday, today and tomorrow)' (1995: 2). However, his earlier views are still not without some support (Wootton 1993: 9). Others, like James Tully and Richard Tuck in their recent writings, have also forced some distance on this issue; Tuck remarks that 'the better our historical sense of what those [seventeenth-century] conflicts were, the more often they seem to resemble modern ones' (1993: xii). In addition, despite his initial worries about using the past as an anachronistic conceptual resource, Skinner has made significant contributions to current debates about republicanism and freedom, utilizing his considerable historical knowledge (1984; 1991).

Overall, therefore, it is clear that there have been diverse responses to both the nature of history and the role of the history of political theory, some of which have strong normative characteristics. The historical dimension of the subject is no clear demarcator from other dimensions of political theory. In fact, in Marxian Critical Theory or Foucaultian genealogy the close relation of theory and history has been pretty much the norm. It is, largely, in anglophone political theory that problems arise. However even here, as Conal Condren indicates in his chapter, political theory still wends a precarious path in a penumbral region between history and philosophy (see, for example, Rorty et al. 1984).

Normative Political Theory

The most conventional approach to recent political theory focuses on normative theory. As a generic category, this covers theories whose primary focus has been concerned with evaluating standards, prescribing forms of conduct and recommending forms of life and institutional structures. Thus, John Plamenatz defined political theory as 'systematic thinking about the purposes of government' (Plamenatz 1960: 37; see also Hacker 1961: 20; Gewirth 1965: 1; Kateb 1968:15; Blackstone 1973: 25; Held 1991: 20; Pettit 1993: 284–5). In this sense, political theory is closely related to moral theory, although this is not a settled debate by any means. For some theorists, we should clearly distinguish moral and political theory (Barry 1995: 71); for others, there is a close interdependence between political and moral argument (Kymlicka 1990: 7; Gewirth 1965: 1ff.; Shklar 1991: 16; Raz 1994).[24] Normative theory also embodies what some modern commentators have called 'the return of grand theory' (Skinner 1985). The significance of the idea of 'return' is due to the fact that it had been bitterly resisted from within other sectors of political theory in the 1945–70 period. However, normative theory is a complex category, due to the range of substantive argumentation over the last three decades.[25]

There are certain regulative concerns in normative political theory which are interpreted differently by substantive theories. The main normative theories in contention at the present moment are a diversity of forms of liberalism and libertarianism, communitarianism, feminism, neo-Aristotelianism, humanistic and analytical Marxism and republicanism.

The broad regulative themes are, first, a concern with the premises or foundations on which a theory can be built. Although thinkers like Rawls have tried to relegate metaphysics to the private realm, it is none too clear whether Rawls has been successful, certainly not as a description of what has often driven normative theory. Metaphysics is not the same as prejudice or blind faith. It is concerned with plausible assumptions, which are tied to argument and inference. Such assumptions are fundamental in the sense that they, as Collingwood put it, are absolutely presupposed. They are presupposed by the question to which they are related. They are not propositions about which one seeks truth or falsity (Collingwood 1940: 21–33). Such foundational assumptions in political theory are, in an important sense, extra-political. They 'support a particular form of political order, without . . . depending on any substantive assumptions about the legitimacy of particular forms of human interaction' (Ripstein 1987: 115). They are thus seen to be undeniable by reasonable individuals and also immune to revision (see Herzog 1985). Thus, the arguments of Thomas Hobbes or Gauthier, for example, for particular political arrangements – whether convincing or not – rest on absolute assumptions concerning human rationality and motivation which claim to be extra-political in character. In sum, as Jean Hampton has argued, 'the activity of philosophy is itself based upon substantive metaphysical beliefs about the nature of human beings' (1989: 814). Metaphysics is not therefore to be so easily avoided or brushed aside.

Having established certain foundational assumptions, normative theory attempts to ascertain how a political order should be established in accordance with the foundational values. In other words, it shows how the institutions and political processes can be derived from and justified by the foundational assumptions. The associated political life should be a more rational, just or desirable form of existence. This latter theme is often accompanied by a concern with institutional design, namely, an interest in the character and type of public institutions, associations and the rules which have some determinative effect on the lives of human beings. Various devices for realizing, justifying or drawing attention to consensual values have been utilized by contemporary theorists: for example, procedural devices like the Rawlsian veil of ignorance; forms of contractarianism; trading on minimal ethical commitments like human agency; using basic elements of practical reason premised upon human desires; reading off and interpreting existing situated community commitments or the ethos of a society; or, alternatively, premising arguments on human needs, equality or human rights. The prevalent discourse in this domain is liberal justice theory. Justice, as mentioned earlier, has been the most significant concept in normative discourse over the last three decades. Its dominant mode of operation has been via contractarianism – which is concerned primarily with the conditions in which individuals come to a decision or agreement about the manner of distribution in society. The contractarian claims can be further subdivided into what Brian Barry has called 'justice as mutual advantage' and 'justice as impartiality' (1989). In the former, justice is seen as the outcome of a mutual bargaining process among individuals (James Buchanan and David Gauthier). In the latter, justice is seen to be the process and outcome of rational agreement (John Rawls, Brian Barry, Thomas Scanlon).

According to one interpretation, this general pattern of normative theorizing has continued unabated – with minor hitches – from the ancient Greeks to the late twentieth century. The practice of being a political theorist is commonplace enough now. The only question in this interpretation lies in the debates mentioned earlier in the history and tradition section, questioning the synonymity between past and present political philosophy and raising the spectre of the invention of a canon in the twentieth century. Indeed, in thinking about the present state of political theory, it is worth considering whether it has a coherent past. Did Aristotle, Augustine, Aquinas, Montesquieu – let alone Adam Smith, David Hume, Kant, Herder or Hegel – have any conception of themselves as political theorists? Did they all clearly separate the realms of moral philosophy, political economy, history and psychology into discrete disciplines? Did they even have the same notion of politics? The invention of the canon or tradition of political theory legitimizes a selective language which picks out what is required from thinkers and isolates their contribution as 'political theory', yet traditional theory is a creature from a diverse set of historical and intellectual environments. What we have now is a mesh, constructed in the twentieth century, that we have cast over a wide range of different thinkers and times in order to make those thinkers speak to us coherently. It is clear, though, that we cannot have a dialogue or conversation with the dead. This does not undermine the enterprise of historical judgment, but it raises scepticism concerning some of the more optimistic claims for the canon. Hegel and Adam Smith were philosophers who addressed an area called politics – which might not be the present understanding of politics; this area was intimately linked with morality, political economy and psychology. The highly discrete sense of political theory appears to be a modern invention which coincides with the professionalization of the discipline in the twentieth century. Thus, the vision of an articulate consistent enterprise which was lost and then refound, or died and then was resurrected, is not particularly convincing. The distinct venture of political philosophy, as it arose in the 1970s, is a comparatively novel enterprise.

There is, therefore, a difference between, on the one hand, the aggregation of concerns, loosely grouped under the heading political philosophy or theory in the pre-modern and early modern era, and, on the other hand, the twentieth-century university-based academic profession and specialism called political philosophy. Political philosophers now largely address other political philosophers; as Michael Walzer puts it, 'professors writing for other professors' (see Walzer 1989: 337). Not many think, except in rare and consciously simplified and apologetic moments, of addressing themselves to the populace, let alone pragmatic state bureaucracies.[26] What might unselfconsciously have been political theory, before this institutionalization process, often addressed itself, if not directly to the populace, then to more immediate perceptions of urgency. This is by no means a hard-and-fast distinction. However, it is clear that political philosophy now is not so crucially motivated by urgency in the world of practice as by the endemic problems of highly specialized languages and the intrinsic pressures of an institutionalized profession. For some commentators, this would partially explain the silence of anglophone political theory over enormous historical and political upheavals, like those of 1989, namely, the collapse of the Soviet hegemony and the unifying of Germany (see Isaacs 1995 and the ensuing debate).

Ideology and Political Theory

Ideology is a comparatively new word dating from the early 1800s; its use was not recognizable until the 1840s, and not popular till the late nineteenth century (see Vincent 1995: ch. 1). It comes into its own in the twentieth century. There is little consensus on the issue of ideology in contemporary political theory. Ideology still remains a deeply contested notion with, at the present moment, a very wide range of possible uses and referents. It can, for example, denote an individual's particular political perspective, the ideas implicit within a political party or movement, or a total encompassing world-view. There is still a deep ambiguity concerning the sense and reference of the concept, even within profoundly sophisticated academic debate. One prevalent interpretation of ideology (however the substantive idea is viewed) is that it is a debased product which lacks the virtues of political philosophy. In this latter interpretation, political philosophy is marked by a reflective openness, critical distance, and an awareness of human experience which transcends political struggles. Ideology, on the other hand, would be viewed as the opposite. It closes reflection and throws itself into partisan struggle; its ideas are designed instrumentally to persuade and manipulate actors and ultimately to achieve political power. Despite what its promoters say, the above view is not a time-honoured immemorial position, but an artifice of nineteenth- and twentieth-century thought.

In the nineteenth century one of the first to use the term ideology, in the above pejorative manner, was Karl Marx. Ideology was seen as a form of distortion or illusion, as distinct from authentic philosophical anthropology. In Marx's later writings, the distinction becomes (especially via Engels) one of ideology as distinct from the truths of science. Another theorist, in this century, who upheld vigorously the distinction of political philosophy and ideology (and the pejorative use of the latter), was Strauss. For Strauss, philosophy was an ancient quest for wisdom and universal knowledge – 'the knowledge of God, the world and man' (1959: 11). Political ideology, though, is indifferent to the distinction between knowledge and opinion and is concerned with the uncritical espousal of myths. The modern era has seen a decline of political philosophy into ideology.[27]

The above concern is reflected, indirectly, in some expositions of the twentieth-century analytic style of philosophy, particularly via the dismissal of normative theory. In logical positivism, for example, the pervasive distinction was drawn between the types of meaningful propositions. Analytic propositions were *a priori* claims to be found in mathematics, logical and lexical definitions. Synthetic empirical propositions were those characteristically found in the natural sciences, which could be empirically verified. Philosophy was a second-order activity. It did not contribute any first-order knowledge – which was largely the domain of the natural sciences.[28] Other types of proposition, which might loosely be grouped under the label 'normative', did not tell us about the world; rather, they revealed the emotional and psychological states of individuals. In this sense, ideology – via such analysis – moved directly into the obfuscatory normative realm of emotional 'hurrahs'.

In early, ordinary-language philosophy the task of philosophy was perceived to be the close attention to the ordinary uses of words and concepts. The philosopher was engaged in the neutral elucidation of concepts. Philosophical problems were seen to be a combination of syntactical and semantic issues. Whereas logical positivism saw meaning as dependent upon the categories of the analytic and synthetic, combined with verification, ordinary-language philosophy viewed meaning as common usage. The diverse usage of normative language could not be simply swept aside. The emphasis therefore shifted from the precise meaningful definition of words towards elucidating concepts in their diverse senses. However, ordinary language was still in agreement with logical positivism that philosophy did not include justification or prescription. The same point would hold for the philosophy of the later Wittgenstein. Political philosophy had more of a role to play – as a form of linguistic therapy – but it was still a second-order activity distinct from direct normative claims, as might be found in ideology.

One important facet of these portrayals of political philosophy is again the separation from political practice and ideology. Ideology, in this case, looked deeply suspect. It was this kind of analysis which formed the backdrop to the bulk of Anglo-American political philosophy up to the 1980s. Thus David Raphael (in a popular textbook of 1976) noted that ideology is 'a prescriptive doctrine that is not supported by argument' (1976: 17; see also, for similar judgments, Hacker 1961: 6; Kateb 1968: 8; Gewirth 1965: 2; Quinton 1967: 1; Germino 1976: 42ff.; Copleston 1983: 23).

Richard Ashcraft, directing his fire at both historians of political theory and analytical political theorists, argues that 'some of the responsibility for the divorce of traditional political theory from present concerns of political life rests squarely with those teachers of political theory who have encapsulated the meaning of politics within the frozen worlds of "analysis" or "history"' (1975: 19; 1980). Ashcraft suggests that most theorists in the past *were* concerned about problems in society. Locke and Hobbes, for example, were not offering abstracted treatises to delight later generations of academic political philosophers. Using ideology to denote some sense of political activism, Ashcraft comments, 'only an ideologically grounded approach with respect to current political problems can provide a bridge between the traditions of political philosophy and the perception of what counts as "political" phenomena' (1975: 20). In effect, political philosophers are political ideologists. Ashcraft has little time for the idea that philosophy is something higher, more saintly, than ideology.[29]

The major problem with Ashcraft's position is what happens to the purported 'universality' of political philosophy/ideology, if the enterprise is so circumstance-bound? Thus, for many political philosophers, the title ideologist denotes 'the original sin' (Ashcraft 1980: 695). For Ashcraft, this universality seems worth losing. Putting this question to one side, Ashcraft's analysis also makes ideology and political philosophy into one featureless entity. It might be more perspicuous to see ideology as an internally complex idea which moves through many levels, from simple-minded rhetoric up to philosophical concerns. This would at least encompass the wide theoretical ambit of the term ideology in practice.

Another dimension of this question, which links fortuitously with Ashcraft's view, is provided by communitarians of the 1980s. They also tended to associate theory with 'situated' communal practice. Virtues cannot be defined independent of the human relationships which constitute them. Thus, communitarians often argue that political and moral goods cannot be determined by abstract reasoning *sub specie aeternitatis*. Such 'goods' arise from particular historical communities. There are no absolute external rational foundations for ethics or the good life. John Rawls's 'original position', Ronald Dworkin's 'insurance game', Bruce Ackerman's 'perfect technology of justice', and the like, cannot redeem the world via theory since there is no theory which stands apart from a social context (see Walzer 1987: 6–7). As in Ashcraft, theorists become expositors and, possibly, ideologists of their own communities. This, however, does not solve the problem for those who wish to separate the claims of ideology and philosophy. Overall, the question of ideology and its relation to political theory remains both inconclusive and deeply perplexing.

Some recent communitarian writings have complicated this issue further. They have shifted their focus from the conception of unified communities to diversity and difference – what Charles Taylor has called the problem of 'deep diversity' (Taylor in Tully 1994: 254). Writers like Michael Walzer and Taylor have noted a plurality of spheres within the modern polis, although others, like William Connolly (1995), think that they have not gone far enough.[30] Many modern states have to accept, minimally, aspects of the politics of radical pluralization and difference (see Young 1990; Connolly 1995).[31] Many theorists still argue that there is a dire need for some method to adjudicate between rival rationalities, although it is becoming more difficult to know how to do this. Much contemporary political theory has been drifting in a similar direction to communitarianism. The political and historical embeddedness and pluralism arguments characterize a great deal of recent work: Rawls's political liberalism is just one significant example. This has been one way that the Rawlsian generation has overcome the charge that their theories are abstracted from actual practices, although it has spawned, in turn, a range of new problems.

A Professional Discipline at the Crossroads?

One way of conceptualizing this current problem of pluralism, diversity and contingency is through James Tully's recently articulated idea of 'strange multiplicity'. Tully's central question is: 'Can a modern constitution recognize and accommodate cultural diversity?' (1995: 1).[32] The problem he identifies is that modern constitutionalism embodies a Western 'imperial' legacy of language and values. There is thus an implicit, if deeply veiled, monologic character to modern constitutionalism. In sum, for Tully, 'the politics of modern constitutionalism and the politics of recognition face an impasse. How can proponents of recognition bring forth their claims in a public forum in which their cultures have been excluded or demeaned for centuries?' (1995: 56). Imperial constitutionalists 'comprehend' different perspectives by incorporating them into the inclusive language of constitutionalism. If one language is dominant, there can be no true dialogue. A post-imperial injunction, for Tully, is to listen to other voices. Any new constitutionalism would have to be a multi-voiced creature in which each voice was given a clear hearing, negotiation was integral, and no one culture was dominant.

There is a connection between Tully's argument on strange multiplicity and the present state of political theory. Many contemporary theorists argue that modern constitutionalism, liberalism and justice theory can cope with the problem of difference and multiplicity (see Kukathas's chapter in this volume). However, this issue can be read more broadly. If one considers Tully's argument and recent postcolonial literature, one important point is stressed, namely, that the language of constitutionalism, liberalism and justice theory – in sum, the language of much modern Western political theory – is not a language which necessarily invites deep-rooted dialogue, unless one debates *within* the language itself. There are parallels here between the postcolonial debates and the recent radical pluralization arguments. Extending Tully's point one step, political theory may itself now be a creature subject to 'strange multiplicity'. The difficulty now is how to accommodate the diverse voices of political theory.

Political theory still bridges a gap between ways of being in the political world, although part of the tragedy of current political theory is that either it has nothing to say, or it has a surfeit of things to say, on what we ought to do. The nostalgia that normative theory plays upon is premised on the conception of a definite order to the world – an order that possibly existed in a pre-modern and early modern setting, but is no longer so clear. We are aware of the past order from the canon of classic texts, but it is continually disappearing and has to be resurrected and, in some cases, fabricated in the unusual environment of the university. There is, thus, little apparent solace in politics (Jacobson 1978: xiii–xiv). Political theory, in this sense, exists as a tense interstice, continually committed to describing, explaining, interpreting and re-evaluating normative alternatives; and yet, no single work or task captures the richness and diversity of our social, political or personal existence.

A final word concerning the ordering of the chapters. As mentioned earlier, there is no reason why they cannot be read, with profit, individually. In fact, the reader who is directly interested in the majority of the topics in this volume could peruse all the chapters in a random sequence. There is, though, an implicit order, although the reader does not have to follow it. First, the chapters by Terence Ball and Conal Condren deal with the history of political theory in different ways. Second, the chapters by Robert Goodin and Geoffrey Brennan propound specific methods for dealing with political theory as a more applied discipline. Third, Philip Pettit offers arguments for a specific normative theory of republicanism. Fourth, Duncan Ivison and Chandran Kukathas examine, from different perspectives, the current problems of difference, multiculturalism and postcolonial theory in the light of contemporary liberal political theory. This might be viewed as a different mode of applied political theory. Next, the chapters by Tom Campbell and David Boucher examine substantive debates in legal theory and international relations through the eyes of political theorists, illustrating, in one sense, the reach of political theory. Finally, the chapters by Elizabeth Frazer, Paul Patton and Barry Hindess cover a range of issues – hermeneutics, feminism, communitarianism and post-structuralism – which question the status, character and role of political theory and offer alternative perspectives.

Notes

1 The year 1996, for example, saw the founding of a new journal – the *Journal of Political Ideologies* – devoted to this theme.

2 Although a distinction is made occasionally between political theory and political philosophy, this is not one which will be used in this introduction.

3 The word theory, from its earliest use in European thought, was imbricated with reflective thought in general and philosophy in particular. Theory was, characteristically, in Greek thought, associated with *observation* (a *thea* was a spectacle; the one who observed the spectacle was a *theoros*). Theory was the intermediary between the event and the observer 'representing' the event or practice. In Aristotle, *theoria* denoted intellectual observation and contemplation in accordance with *sophia*. The friend or lover (*philia*) of wisdom (*sophia*) had the ability to observe (*theoria*) through the eye of the mind. *Theoria* virtually became the act of knowing itself, although, as distinct from practice, it pursued such knowing for its own sake. Theory *was* a pursuit of the real, not an abstract hypothetical fiction. It was the attempt to grasp the central realities of what is most valuable and most divine and therefore also human.

4 The term 'categorially' is Oakeshott's usage.

5 As Barber argues, politics takes skills which might bear little relation to the demands of formal abstract political theory. Theorists like Rawls and Nozick are seen to be squeezing politics out in their formal abstractions. Thus, for Barber, 'politics is what men do when metaphysics fails; it is not metaphysics reified' (1988: 209).

6 As Hannah Arendt commented, 'thought itself arises out of incidents of lived experience and must remain bound to them as the only guideposts by which to take its bearings' (1968: 14)

7 See Brennan's chapter in this volume; on contractarianism, see Boucher and Kelly 1994.

8 See Goodin's chapter in this volume; also Miller 1990; 1992.

9 It is clearly possibly to distinguish types of communitarian theory. There are, ironically, liberal universalist forms (Taylor and Walzer) and more relativist and reactionary forms. Many of the latter are traced in minute critical detail by Stephen Holmes 1993.

10 As in the work of theorists like Michel Foucault, Iris Marion Young or William Connolly.

11 In this sense, discourse analysis in the writings of Ernesto Laclau and Chantal Mouffe might be described as post-Marxist.

12 David Boucher's chapter in this volume touches upon this theme.

13 See the contrasting views in chapters by Kukathas and Ivison.

14 John Gunnell (1986) sees Habermas's theory as the very epitome of the alienation of theory from the political realm. Nevertheless, as Barry Hindess points out in his chapter in this volume, Gunnell has his own, partially obscured, suppositions about what constitutes politics, which are equally contestable.

15 Oddly, some of the critique of Rawls's later work (and communitarianism) could be allied to this unease with the history of political theory. Once you situate a theory within a particular culture, it immediately raises the question as to whether it has any application above and beyond that culture, which, of course, is one of the characteristic criticisms of the history of political theory by some normative theorists.

16 History first became an honours degree in Britain in Oxford in 1872 and Cambridge in 1873. The first chair of history – the Regius Chair – although set up in 1724, was first filled by a historian in 1866. The Oxford Chichele Chair of Modern History was created in 1862. Like most such disciplines, the origin outside the university environment remains more obscure. As Michael Oakeshott commented, 'Activities emerge naively, like games that children invent themselves. Each appears, first, not in response to a premeditated achievement, but as a direction of attention pursued without premonition of what it will lead to. How should our artless ancestor have known what (as it has turned out) it is to be an astronomer, an accountant, or an historian' (1991: 151).

17 'The satisfaction of national pride and culture, and the rendezvous with destiny that it often implied, whether in England, Germany, or America, reflected the distinctive meaning of government education, and history in each country' (Soffer, 1994: 6).

18 In fact, other areas, like political economy, were also often viewed as a subset of political science. Thus, Adam Smith in his *Wealth of Nations* described political economy as a 'branch of the science of a statesman or legislator' (1979: 428). There was little or no demarcation of what might now be regarded as separate disciplines. Smith's *Wealth of Nations*, for example, blends economics, moral philosophy, political theory and history as part of a unified social scientific enterprise.

19 The first chair of politics in Britain was the Gladstone Professorship of Political Theory and Institutions, established in Oxford University in 1912.

20 Barker's successor at Cambridge University, Dennis Brogan (whose tenure lasted until 1967), was happier just talking about history and institutions, and seems to have been genuinely puzzled at being in a chair of politics.

21 Achieved first in America in the 1920s with the beginnings of behavioural political science, particularly under the auspices of Charles Merriam in Chicago University.

22 Besides Terence Ball's work, a recent exposition and comparison of the *Begriffsgeschichte* movement with Skinner and Pocock, well worth consulting is Richter 1995, especially ch. 6.

23 The best recent work on Skinner is Tully 1988. For more critical commentary, see Boucher 1985.

24 Another dimension on this issue is the complex relation between morality, politics and law, discussed in Tom Campbell's chapter.

25 Normative political theory also includes empirical and institutional elements, together with detailed strategies to enable the realization of values. Philip Pettit neatly summarizes some these dimensions as the valuable, eligible and feasible (1993: 285).

26 Although, as Walzer (1981) notes, judges make good audiences for political philosophers.

27 Oakeshott (1991) also expounded a similar distinction between philosophy and ideology. Another reformulation of Oakeshott's position can be found in Ken Minogue's *Alien Powers* (1986). Oddly, a similar dismissal of ideology was made in some political science circles in the context of the 'end of

ideology' movement, see Vincent 1995: 10ff. However, in this latter case, the crucial contrast was between 'social science' and 'ideology'.
28 As T. D. Weldon remarked, 'It is not the job of philosophy to provide new information about politics . . . or any other matters of fact. Philosophical problems are entirely second-order problems. They are problems, that is, which are generated by the language in which facts are described and explained by those whose function it is to construct and defend scientific, historical, or other types of theory' (1957: 22).
29 Ashcraft asks, 'How is it even possible for . . . epistemological presuppositions to stand apart from the very conflict they propose to "study" and are assumed to transcend' (1975: 26).
30 Thus, for MacIntyre, 'we are the inheritors . . . of a number of rival and incompatible traditions and there is no way of either selecting a list of books to be read . . . interpreted, and elucidated which does not involve taking a partisan stand in the conflict of traditions' (1990: 228).
31 Thinkers like Rorty have concluded that philosophy should thus give up the lofty universalist path altogether, accept radical contingency and adopt irony and literary criticism (Rorty 1989).
32 For an interesting background to Tully's concerns, particularly in relation to Wittgenstein, see Tully 1989.

References

Arendt, Hannah. 1968. *Between Past and Future*. New York: Viking Press.
Ashcraft, R. 1975. 'On the Problem of Methodology and the Nature of Political Theory', *Political Theory*, 3, no. 1.
Ashcraft, R. 1980. 'Political Theory and the Problem of Ideology', *Journal of Politics*, 80.
Ball, Terence. 1988. *Transforming Political Discourse: Political Theory and Critical Conceptual History*. Oxford: Blackwell.
Barber, B. 1988. *The Conquest of Politics: Liberal Political Philosophy in Democratic Times*. Princeton, NJ: Princeton University Press.
Barker, Ernest. 1978. 'The Study of the Science of Politics', in Preston King (ed.), *The Study of Politics*. New York and London: Frank Cass.
Barry, Brian. 1989. *Theories of Justice*. London: Harvester Wheatsheaf.
Barry, Brian. 1995. *Justice as Impartiality*. Oxford: Clarendon Press.
Blackstone, W. 1973. *Political Philosophy: An Introduction*. New York: Thomas Y. Crowell Company.
Bloom, A. 1987. *The Closing of the American Mind: How Higher Education has Failed Democracy and Impoverished the Souls of Today's Students*. London: Penguin.
Boucher, David. 1985. *Texts in Context*. The Hague: Martinus Nijhoff.
Boucher, David. 1989. 'Philosophy, History and Practical Life: The Emergence of the History of Political Thought in England', *Australian Journal of Politics and History*, 35.
Boucher, D. and Kelly, P., eds. 1994. *The Social Contract from Hobbes to Rawls*. London: Routledge.
Bowle, John. 1947. *Western Political Thought*. London: Jonathan Cape.
Carver, Terrell, and Thomas, Paul, eds. 1995. *Rational Choice Marxism*. London: Macmillan.
Collingwood, R .G. 1940. *An Essay on Metaphysics*. Oxford: Clarendon.

Collini, Stefan, Winch, Donald, and Burrow, John. 1983. *That Noble Science of Politics: A Study of Nineteenth-Century Intellectual History.* Cambridge: Cambridge University Press.

Condren, C. 1985. *The Status and Appraisal of Classic Texts.* Princeton: Princeton University Press.

Connolly, W. E. 1995. *The Ethos of Pluralization.* Minneapolis: University of Minnesota Press.

Copleston, F. C. 1983. 'Philosophy and Ideology', in A. Parel, ed., *Ideology, Philosophy and Politics.* Waterloo, Ontario: Wilfrid Laurier University Press.

Dallmayr, Fred R., ed. 1978. *From Contract to Community: Political Theory at the Crossroads.* New York and Basel: Marcel Dekker Inc.

Doyle, Phyllis. 1949. *A History of Political Thought.* London: Jonathan Cape.

Dunn, John. 1995. *The History of Political Theory.* Cambridge: Cambridge University Press.

Dyson, Kenneth. 1980. *The State Tradition in Western Europe.* Oxford: Martin Robertson.

Elster, J. 1985. *Making Sense of Marx.* Cambridge: Cambridge University Press.

Foucault, M. 1980. *Power/Knowledge,* ed. by Colin Gordon. Brighton: Harvester Wheatsheaf.

Freeman, M., and Robertson, D., eds. 1980. *The Frontiers of Political Theory: Essays in a Revitalised Discipline.* Brighton: Harvester Press.

Gauthier, D. 1986. *Morals by Agreement.* Oxford, Clarendon Press.

Germino, D. 1976. *Beyond Ideology: The Revival of Political Theory.* Chicago: Chicago University Press.

Gewirth, A. 1965. *Political Philosophy.* New York and London: Macmillan Collier.

Gunnell, John C. 1986. *Between Philosophy and Politics.* Amherst: University of Massachusetts Press.

Gunnell, John C. 1987. *Political Theory: Tradition and Interpretation.* New York: University Press of America.

Gunnell, John C. 1993. *The Descent of Political Theory: The Genealogy of an American Vocation.* Chicago: Chicago University Press.

Habermas, J. 1984. *The Theory of Communicative Rationality, vol. 1: Reason and the Rationaliation of Society.* Boston: Beacon Press.

Habermas, J. 1987. *The Theory of Communicative Rationality, vol. 2: The Critique of Functionalist Reason.* Boston: Beacon Press.

Hacker, Andrew. 1961. *Political Theory: Philosophy, Ideology, Science.* New York: Macmillan.

Hampton, Jean. 1989. 'Should Political Philosophy be Done without Metaphysics', *Ethics,* 99.

Held, D. 1980. *Introduction to Critical Theory.* London: Hutchinson.

Held, D., ed. 1991. *Political Theory Today.* Stanford: Stanford University Press.

Herzog, Don. 1985. *Without Foundations: Justification in Political Theory.* Ithaca, NY: Cornell University Press.

Holmes, S. 1993. *The Anatomy of Antiliberalism.* Cambridge, Mass.: Harvard University Press.

Honig, Bonnie. 1993. *Political Theory and the Displacement of Politics.* London and Ithaca, NY: Cornell University Press.

Isaacs, Jeffrey C. 1995. 'The Strange Silence of Political Theory', *Political Theory,* 23, no. 4.

Jacobson, Norman. 1978. *Pride and Solace: The Functions and Limits of Political Theory.* London: Methuen.

Jay, M. 1973. *The Dialectical Imagination.* Boston: Little Brown.

Kateb, G. 1968. *Political Theory: Its Nature and Uses.* New York: St Martin's Press.

Kymlicka, W. 1989. *Liberalism, Community and Culture*. Oxford: Clarendon Press.
Kymlicka, W. 1990. *Contemporary Political Philosophy: An Introduction*. Oxford: Clarendon Press.
Kymlicka, W. 1995. *Multicultural Citizens: A Liberal Theory of Minority Rights*. Oxford: Clarendon Press.
Laclau, E. 1990. *Reflections on the Revolution of Our Time*. London: Verso.
Laclau, E., and Mouffe, C. 1985. *Hegemony and Socialist Strategy: Towards a Radical Democratic Politics*. London: Verso.
Larmore, Charles. 1990. 'Political Liberalism', *Political Theory*, 18, no. 3.
Lobkowitz, N. 1967. *Theory and Practice: The History of a Concept from Aristotle to Marx*. Indiana: University of Notre Dame Press.
Locke, John. 1993. *Political Writings*, ed. David Wootton. Harmondsworth, Mddx: Penguin.
MacIntyre, A. 1981. *After Virtue: A Study in Moral Theory*. London: Duckworth.
MacIntyre, A. 1990. *Three Rival Versions of Moral Enquiry*. London: Duckworth.
Maitland, F. W. 1920. *The Constitutional History of England*. Cambridge: Cambridge University Press.
Miller, David. 1990. 'The Resurgence of Political Theory', *Political Studies*, 38.
Miller, David. 1992. 'Distributive Justice: What the People Think', *Ethics*, 102, no. 2.
Miller, David, and Seidentrop, L., eds. 1983. *The Nature of Political Theory*. Oxford: Clarendon Press.
Minogue, K. 1986. *Alien Powers: The Pure Theory of Ideology*. London: Weidenfeld and Nicholson.
Mouffe, C. 1993. *The Return of the Political*. London: Verso.
Nelson, Alan. 1986. 'Explanation and Justification in Political Philosophy', *Ethics*, 97.
Oakeshott, Michael. 1933. *Experience and its Modes*. Cambridge: Cambridge University Press.
Oakeshott, Michael. 1991. *Rationalism in Politics and Other Essays*. Indianapolis: Liberty Press.
Okin, S. M. 1992. *Women in Western Political Thought*. Princeton: Princeton University Press.
Pateman, Carole. 1988. *The Sexual Contract*. Stanford: Stanford University Press.
Pettit, Philip. 1993. *The Common Mind: An Essay on Psychology, Society and Politics*. Oxford: Oxford University Press.
Plamenatz, John. 1960. 'The Use of Political Theory', *Political Studies*, 8.
Quinton, A. 1967. *Political Philosophy*. Oxford: Oxford University Press.
Raphael, D. D. 1976. *Problems of Political Philosophy*, rev. edn. London: Macmillan.
Rawls, John. 1971. *A Theory of Justice*. Oxford: Oxford University Press.
Rawls, John. 1993. *Political Liberalism*. New York: Columbia University Press.
Raz, J. 1994. *Ethics in the Public Domain: Essays in the Morality of Law*. Oxford: Clarendon Press.
Rengger, N. 1995. *Political Theory, Modernity and Postmodernity*. Oxford: Blackwell.
Richter, Melvin. 1995. *The History of Political and Social Concepts*. Oxford: Oxford University Press.
Ripstein, Arthur. 1987. 'Foundationalism in Political Theory', *Philosophy and Public Affairs*. 16, no. 2.
Roemer, J., ed. 1986. *Analytical Marxism*. Cambridge: Cambridge University Press.
Rorty, R. 1989. *Contingency, Irony and Solidarity*. Cambridge: Cambridge University Press.

Rorty, R., Schneewind, J. B., and Skinner, Q. eds. 1984. *Philosophy in History.* Cambridge: Cambridge University Press.

Rosenblum, N. L., ed. 1989. *Liberalism and the Moral Life.* Cambridge Mass.: Harvard University Press.

Rubinstein, N. 1987. 'The History of the Word *Politicus* in Early Modern Europe', in Anthony Pagden, ed., *The Languages of Political Theory in Early Modern Europe.* Cambridge: Cambridge University Press.

Sandel, M. J. 1982. *Liberalism and the Limits of Justice.* Cambridge: Cambridge University Press.

Sandel, M. J. 1996. *Democracy's Discontents: America in Search of a Public Philosophy.* Cambridge, Mass.: Belknap Press of Harvard University Press.

Shklar, J. 1991. *Faces of Injustice.* New Haven: Yale University Press.

Skinner, Q. 1978. *The Foundations of Modern Political Thought,* 2 vols. Cambridge: Cambridge University Press.

Skinner, Q. 1984. 'The Idea of Negative Liberty: Philosophical and Historical Perspectives', in Rorty, Schneewind and Skinner, eds, *Philosophy in History.*

Skinner, Q. 1991. 'The Paradoxes of Political Liberty', in David Miller, ed., *Liberty.* Oxford: Oxford University Press.

Skinner, Q., ed. 1985. *The Return of Grand Theory in the Human Sciences.* Cambridge: Cambridge University Press.

Smith, Adam. 1979. *An Enquiry into the Nature and Causes of the Wealth of Nations.* Oxford: Clarendon Press.

Soffer, Reba. 1994. *Discipline and Power: The University and the Making of an English Elite, 1870–1930.* Stanford: Stanford University Press.

Spence, Larry D. 1980. 'Political Theory as a Vacation', *Polity,* 12, no. 4.

Strauss, Leo. 1959. *What is Political Philosophy?* Glencoe, Ill.: Free Press.

Tuck, Richard. 1993. *Philosophy and Government, 1572–1651.* Cambridge: Cambridge University Press.

Tuck, Richard. 1995. 'The Contribution of History', in R. E. Goodin and P. Pettit, eds, *A Companion to Contemporary Political Philosophy,* Oxford: Blackwell.

Tully, James. 1989. 'Wittgenstein and Political Philosophy: Understanding Practices of Critical Reflection', *Political Theory,* 17, no. 2.

Tully, James. 1995. *Strange Multiplicity: Constitutionalism in an Age of Diversity.* Cambridge: Cambridge University Press.

Tully, James, ed. 1988. *Meaning and Context: Quentin Skinner and his Critics.* Oxford: Polity Press.

Tully, James, ed. 1994. *Philosophy in an Age of Pluralism.* Cambridge: Cambridge University Press.

Vincent, Andrew. 1987. *Theories of the State.* Oxford: Blackwell.

Vincent, Andrew. 1995. *Modern Political Ideologies.* 2nd edn. Oxford: Blackwell.

Vincent, Andrew, and Plant, Raymond. 1984. *Philosophy Politics and Citizenship: The Life and Times of the British Idealists.* Oxford: Blackwell.

Walzer, Michael. 1981. 'Philosophy and Democracy', *Political Theory,* 9.

Walzer, Michael. 1987. *Interpretation and Social Criticism.* Cambridge, Mass.: Harvard University Press.

Walzer, Michael. 1989. 'The State of Political Theory', *Dissent,* Summer.

Weldon, T. D. 1953. *The Vocabulary of Politics.* Harmondsworth: Penguin.

Weldon, T. D. 1957. 'Political Principles', in P. Laslett, ed., *Politics Philosophy and Society.* Oxford: Blackwell.

Wolin, Sheldon. 1960. *Politics and Vision: Continuity and Innovation in Western Political Thought.* Toronto: Little, Brown and Co.

Young, Iris Marion. 1990. *Justice and the Politics of Difference.* Princeton: Princeton University Press.

CHAPTER 1

Political Theory and Conceptual Change

Terence Ball

The end of a century, and more especially the end of a millennium, is surely a propitious time to look back, to take stock: to see where political theory has been, where it is now, and where it might be headed. This is obviously too tall an order to fill in a single chapter, and I happily leave that daunting task to my fellow contributors to the present volume. My task here is the much more modest one of tracing a number of twists and kinks in the 'linguistic turn' in political theory. Over the last half-century or so, the study of political theory in Britain and North America has moved away from 'linguistic (or conceptual) analysis' and toward 'conceptual history', amongst other approaches. A re-viewing of these developments from the vantage-point of the present might shed some light on the problems and prospects of political theory on the eve of the third millennium.

I plan to proceed in the following way. First I shall sketch, with as few strokes as possible, a potted (and partial) history of the 'linguistic turn' in twentieth-century political theory. That story is, in part and very roughly, a tale about the transition from 'conceptual analysis' to 'conceptual history'. Then I shall outline what one might (with some slight exaggeration) call two 'schools' of, or 'approaches' to, conceptual history – the German *Begriffsgeschichte* and its Anglo-American counterpart, with particular emphasis on the latter. Next I shall try to delineate what I take to be the distinguishing or defining features of *political* discourse as a field of investigation. Then I shall say something about what I call 'critical conceptual history' as an approach to the investigation of political innovation and conceptual change. And finally I shall conclude with a brief defence of the place of conceptual history in contemporary political theory.

28

The 'Linguistic Turn'

To begin by stating the obvious, an interest in language (often, but not always, under the heading of 'rhetoric') is as old as philosophy, and political philosophy in particular. The twin topics of conceptual confusion and political corruption can be found in Thucydides' *History*, in Plato's dialogues, in Roman and later Renaissance writers, in the work of Thomas Hobbes (Thucydides' first English translator), and many others. But if the interest in language is not new, the twentieth century has seen new approaches to the language of politics. The 'linguistic turn' – a phrase coined by Gustav Bergman and popularized by Richard Rorty (1967) – is a relatively recent development.

The first phase of the linguistic turn, in the late 1920s, was broadly positivist. The central place accorded to language by Logical Positivism can be seen in the title (and the text) of A. J. Ayer's *Language, Truth, and Logic* (1936; 2nd edn 1946). Ayer's aspiration to purge and reform the language of philosophy – so as to eliminate the bugbear of 'metaphysics' (and meaninglessness) – soon found a sympathetic audience among political theorists. Their aim was to purge the language of politics and political theory so as to make it more meaningful, less muddled, and more precise. But this was, by Logical Positivist lights, an exceedingly difficult, if not foredoomed, task. For, viewed through positivist lenses, the language of political theory is a rather peculiar hybrid. According to Logical Positivism's classificatory scheme, statements are of three types. There are, first, 'synthetic' statements of empirical fact ('The cat is on the mat' was a perennial favourite). Next are 'analytic' statements about necessary truths-by-convention ('All bachelors are unmarried males' was another favourite). Thirdly, there is a large catch-all category of 'emotive' utterances which are, strictly speaking, cognitively meaningless – mere 'ejaculations', in Ayer's slightly salacious term. To say, for example, that 'Stealing money is wrong', says nothing about theft; it merely expresses or signals the negative 'feelings' or 'attitudes' of the speaker toward that form of activity (Ayer 1946: 107–12).

Political theory, it appeared, is an odd, not to say incoherent, admixture of the analytic, the synthetic and the emotive (or evaluative). From Plato to the present, the 'classics' of political theory are marked – and indeed marred – by muddle: 'facts' and 'values' are jumbled together; persuasive definitions are misleadingly made to appear in value-neutral guise; and fictions, metaphors and other tropes abound – states of nature, social contracts, and (we might now add) ideal speech situations (Macdonald 1951). The critical and reforming spirit of Logical Positivism was much in evidence at mid-century. At an American symposium on 'The Semantics of Social Science', for example, critics charged that the advance of the social sciences, and political science in particular, has been retarded by the pernicious presence of political theory, with its 'teleological, normative, or even moralistic terms'. Many, if not most, of 'the propositions of political theory have a character of "unreality" and futility'. As long as political theory exerts its pernicious influence, political science will consist 'mostly [of] history and ethics'. Political theory 'belong[s] to a subjective or fictitious universe of discourse quite inappropriate to a general science of society' (Perry 1950: 401).

The only hope for political theory lay in purging its language to make its concepts cognitively meaningful. This approach was notoriously well-represented by T. D. Weldon's *The Vocabulary of Politics* (1953) and a host of imitators. Weldon claimed that political theory was deficient to the degree that its practitioners attempted the impossible task of finding rock-bottom 'foundations' and, worse, attempted to do so by reasoning with imprecise or 'muddled' terms and concepts. The first task of political theory must therefore be to clean this Augean stable; it must abandon the search for foundations and be content with the humbler and more austere task of clarifying, refining and redefining the very vocabulary of politics.

Once we cut through the cant, the muddle, and the metaphysics of our inherited vocabulary, we can at last engage in meaningful debates about power, justice, equality, liberty, and the like. We therefore must, at the very least, sort out the different statement-types and keep them separate: 'This is a (persuasive) definition.' 'That is a statement of (presumed) fact.' 'That is an emotive (or hortatory, or prescriptive) utterance.' And so on. Not surprisingly, this sort of 'linguistic analysis' made for minute – and (if I might register my own emotive response) dreadfully dry – dissections of Plato's *Republic*, amongst many other 'classics' of political theory (see, for example, Murphy 1968). The language of political theory should be purged, whipped into shape, and made to aspire to the transparent clarity of the language of science – at least as the natural sciences were (mis)conceived and idealized by the Logical Positivists. Thus the political theorist was to be like Locke's under-labourer, charged with the task of clearing the brush, and not an ambitious 'master-builder':

> The commonwealth of learning is not at this time without master-builders, whose mighty designs, in advancing the sciences, will leave lasting monuments to the admiration of posterity: but everyone must not hope to be a Boyle or a Sydenham; and in an age that produces such masters as the great Huygenius and the incomparable Mr Newton, . . . it is ambition enough to be employed as an under-labourer in clearing the ground a little, and removing some of the rubbish that lies in the way to knowledge.

Whether read as winningly modest or Uriah Heepish, Locke's Epistle to the Reader of the *Essay Concerning Human Understanding* was often quoted as an antidote to pride and vaulting philosophical ambition. In the natural sciences there are master-builders; in philosophy the would-be master-builders – from Plato to Hegel – were to be exposed for the metaphysical frauds they were, taken down ten notches, and put in their place by hard-working under-labourers (Alasdair MacIntyre once likened this task to taking Aristotle out behind the woodshed for a good thrashing). This under-labourer view reduced the tasks of philosophy to criticism and clarification, and nothing more.

And what of political theory? The humble theorists were now to occupy themselves with two modest but important tasks: on the one hand they were to take their long-dead elders and betters out to the woodshed; and, on the other, they were to perform the semantic scut-work of clarifying the terms employed by empirically minded political scientists. The primary purpose of political theory, as a committee of the American Political Science Association once put it, was to 'define the concepts of political science' and provide precise 'definitions of political terms' that political scientists could use (Wilson et al. 1944: 726, 729; cf. Plamenatz 1968: vii). Not a noble calling, perhaps, but a useful one. In the 1950s and early 1960s a number of political theorists attempted to redefine the terms of 'traditional' or 'normative' theory so as to make them useful for the empirical-scientific analysis and explanation of political behaviour. For example, 'the idea of freedom', wrote Felix Oppenheim, 'has not yet been subjected to . . . behavioral analysis'. This is an unfortunate omission, for it has retarded the development of empirical social science. 'Whether freedom can become a subject of empirical science depends on whether "freedom" can become a concept of empirical science' (Oppenheim 1961: 4). And, as for freedom, so for all the other concepts of a scientized political discourse: power, influence, authority, control, and so on.

The reforming spirit of Logical Positivism proved to be remarkably short-lived, amongst political theorists if perhaps not amongst their colleagues in political science. The latter were rather slower to recognize that Logical Positivism was passé in philosophy, including the philosophy of science, and that many of the most influential positivists had recanted. When asked by an interviewer in 1977 what had been the main defects of Logical Positivism, A. J. Ayer, with admirable candour, replied: 'Well, I suppose the most important of the defects was that nearly all of it was false' (Magee 1978: 131).

The next ratchet in the linguistic turn – so-called 'ordinary-language' philosophy – was highly critical of its positivist predecessor and decidedly less critical of political theory, past and present. The language of the natural sciences was no longer to serve as a standard of precision and cognitive meaningfulness (see, for example, Chappell 1964). We use language, as J. L. Austin famously put it, to *do* things – to describe, explain, excuse, endorse, appraise, warn, and hundreds of other 'speech acts' (Austin 1970; Searle 1969). None of these utterance types is privileged, much less paradigmatic. We analyse words and concepts, not by looking for their meaning *per se*, but for their use – they are meaningful only in the context of the uses to which they are put. Even the most 'empirical' of the concepts employed in ordinary discourse are not amenable to strictly drawn definitions; they are 'porous' or 'open-textured' (Waismann 1951). To the degree that their porosity is ordinarily no hindrance to communication, concepts do not need to be reformed, redefined, or made more rigorous than such communication requires. We achieve as much clarity as we need by noting 'what we [i.e. ordinary speakers] say' in certain situations and contexts.

Ordinary-language philosophers took a kindlier and more tolerant view of political theory than their positivist predecessors did. In the spirit of Aristotle they seemed almost to say that one should look for only as much precision as the subject admits of – and that if the language of politics often seems vague and imprecise, then so be it: that is a characteristic feature of political discourse. Ordinary-language philosophy, as Wittgenstein remarked in one of his more oracular utterances, 'leaves everything as it is'. In a reversal of Marx's Eleventh Thesis, ordinary-language philosophy aims to understand the world, not to change it. This led, unsurprisingly, to the charge that ordinary-language philosophy, especially when applied to the analysis of political concepts, was not normatively neutral but in fact deeply if covertly conservative. The language ordinarily used to describe and legitimize unjust social institutions and arrangements can hardly suffice for a critical philosophy, since that very language serves as an ideological mask to conceal such injustice and inhibit radical criticism (Gellner 1959: ch. 8). Linguistic analysis of this sort 'contributes to enclosing thought in the circle of the mutilated universe of ordinary discourse' (Marcuse 1964: 199).

The charge of 'conservatism' proved to be partly right and partly wrong (Wertheimer 1976). It is certainly true that ordinary-language analysis *per se* advanced no political prescriptions or morally charged injunctions that would lead its advocates (or anyone else) to take to the streets or mount the barricades. To be interested in the concept of justice is not identical with being concerned to expose injustices and to see justice prevail. The political theorist, *qua* ordinary-language analyst, aims only to clarify what people mean when they employ the concept to criticize or commend social and civic arrangements. Not exactly inspirational work, perhaps, but a humble task that can clear up at least some of the confusion that deepens political divisions. If we all agree about what we mean by 'justice', then we can move more confidently toward rectifying actions and practices that we can all agree are unjust. (The fallacy of this aspiration is deftly exposed by David Miller, 1983.)

In so far as one can speak of the 'politics' of ordinary-language analysis, it was more meliorist than conservative. But the adjectives that are more readily applicable are 'naive', 'parochial', and 'ahistorical'. For in emphasizing the minute analysis and clarification of 'the' meaning and use of particular concepts, 'linguistic' or 'ordinary-language' philosophy or 'conceptual analysis', as formerly practised in Britain and the United States, tended to focus upon the language of one age and culture, namely our own. This narrowing not only blinded political theorists to the fact that meaning and usage change from one age and generation to the next, but it also led them to believe their enterprise to be a politically neutral one. The task was to clarify and analyse what 'we' say, as though 'we' were a single speaking subject, undivided by partisan and perspectival differences (having to do with race, ethnicity, social class, gender, etc.), and employing concepts whose meanings did not change over time. In thus assuming that there is a unified, or at any rate undifferentiated, 'we', ordinary-language philosophy largely ignored the twin issues of political conflict and conceptual contestation. Which is to say, with only slight exaggeration, that linguistic analysis largely ignored or was blind or indifferent to politics itself.

It also bears mentioning that previous political philosophers almost never took 'what we say' as sufficient or satisfactory in settling conceptual quarrels; indeed, they typically took issue with the ordinary language of their day, attempting to alter or reform the vocabulary of politics by criticizing commonly held views about 'power', 'property', 'liberty', and the like. To take only one of many examples: 'It may perhaps be censured as an impertinent Criticism in a discourse of this nature, to find fault with words and names that have obtained in the World: And yet possibly it may not be amiss to offer new ones when the old are apt to lead Men into mistakes.' The writer is John Locke, the text is his *Second Treatise*, and the concept in question is 'paternal power' – a concept by which Sir Robert Filmer set great store in *Patriarcha* (1680), and which Locke had either to redefine or to reveal to be bereft of meaning if his argument against royal absolutism was to persuade his audience. The criticism and attempted reform of 'ordinary language' has long been the stock-in-trade of philosophers and political theorists.

Despite their differences, both positivistic and ordinary-language variants of linguistic philosophy were agreed that conceptual contests could be settled – either (as the former held) by purging the muddle and rigorously redefining key concepts, or (as the latter would have it) by attending closely to what 'we' say. Either way, conceptual contestation can, in principle, come to an end, and agreement can be reached.

This rather sanguine view was challenged in a path-breaking paper by W. B. Gallie (1956). Some concepts – those that figure in aesthetic and political discourse in particular – are, Gallie argued, '*essentially* contested'; that is, continuing disagreement over their meaning and application is an essential and ineliminable feature of their functioning in the discourses in which they figure. A concept is essentially contested if it has no single definition, range of reference, and/or criteria of application upon which all competent speakers can agree. The hope of arriving at such agreement is the will-o'-the-wisp in certain domains and discourses, and perhaps particularly in aesthetics and politics. In these discourses there are – and in principle can be – no agreed-upon criteria according to which we can classify, categorize, discuss and debate certain sorts of questions.

Consider the concept of 'art', for example. What distinguishes a work of art from a piece of non-art? We might all agree that Leonardo's 'Last Supper' is a work of art, but disagree over whether Andy Warhol's picture of row upon row of identical soup tins qualifies as 'art'. As with art, so with 'music': do atonal compositions consisting of silences punctuated by coughs and car-horns qualify as music – or are they merely noise? And so too with politics. There appear to be few, if any, 'political' concepts that are not 'essentially contested'. One needs only think of the concept of rights, or of democracy, freedom, justice, equality, obligation, power, authority, and many others as well: clearly, all have been, and still are, hotly contested, their meanings the stuff of endless dispute and continuing disagreement.

With political theorists' somewhat belated discovery and appreciation of the thesis of essential contestability came the next ratcheting of the linguistic turn in political theory. Gallie's thesis seemed admirably attuned and attentive to what is surely a, or perhaps *the*, central feature of *political* life – deep-seated conflict and disagreement. Gallie duly recognizes and honours conflict in a non-judgmental and even-handed way: there is no single 'correct' conception of power or any other political concept. There are merely disagreements and differences that, once argued and articulated, will not – and indeed cannot – be rationally resolved.

The essential contestability thesis was put to interesting and illuminating use by a number of political theorists in the 1970s. Among the most notable and influential invocations of the thesis were William Connolly's *The Terms of Political Discourse* (1974) and Steven Lukes's *Power: A Radical View* (1974). Both accepted without argument the validity of Gallie's thesis, which they then applied in illuminating ways to key concepts in political theory and political science. Both openly advanced explicitly 'radical' political aims and agendas. 'Indeed,' Lukes wrote, 'to engage in such [conceptual] disputes is itself to engage in politics' (1974: 26). Genteel and gentlemanly talk of what 'we' say was replaced by openly partisan conceptual combat. One was left with the liberating sense that 'linguistic' political philosophy had abandoned the sheltered environs of an Oxbridge senior common room for the rougher setting of a Soho street corner. Polite conversation was to be replaced with open confrontation and, absent rational argument, attempts to convert others to one's own views.

The linguistic turn in political theory was ratcheted yet another notch as the essential contestability thesis came under scrutiny and then open attack. Some critics argued that the thesis was internally inconsistent and incoherent, and that any theory of (say) power that relied on the essential contestability thesis was 'a theory divided against itself' (Gray 1983: 78). On the one hand, Lukes and Connolly claim that 'power' and other political concepts are forever in dispute, their meanings both unsettled and undecidable – *a priori* and in principle – by rational argument, evidence, etc. But, on the other hand, both advance telling criticisms of rival conceptions; they also construct rational arguments and employ sociological and other evidence in support of their conceptions of power. Lukes boasts that his conception of power is 'superior' to rival views, which are of 'less value' than his own (1974: 9, 30). What is this, critics charged, if not a demonstration that the essential contestability thesis is both incoherent and indefensible, not to say politically pernicious? For surely politics is not only about conflict and disagreement, but also and no less importantly about anticipated agreement in language and life.

Politics and political theory rest upon the hope (all too rarely realized, to be sure) that the pen is mightier than the sword and that the force of argument will win out over, or perhaps preclude, the force of arms. In aim and aspiration, then, political discourse anticipates agreement and consensus even as its speakers disagree among themselves. This discursive ideal is as old as Socratic dialogue and as recent as Habermas's ideal speech situation. The essential contestability thesis rightly sensitizes us to the persistence of conceptual-cum-political disagreement, but desensitizes us to the possibility and importance of anticipated agreement (Ball 1993).

There is, in addition to this immanent critique, another way of challenging the essential contestability thesis. And that is to turn to the history of political theory and practice. Very briefly and crudely, that argument proceeds in the following way. Proponents of the essential contestability thesis are correct in claiming that conceptual contestation is so persistent and recurrent a feature of political discourse that it amounts almost to a defining feature of that domain. But to claim that a particular concept is essentially contested is to take a timeless and ahistorical view of the character and function of political concepts. Not all concepts have been, or could be, contested at all times. Conceptual contestation remains a permanent possibility, even though it is, in practice, actualized only intermittently. The now-ubiquitous disputes about the meaning of 'democracy', for instance, are of relatively recent vintage, whilst the once-heated arguments about 'republic' have cooled considerably since the late eighteenth century – indeed they now rage only amongst historians of political thought, and not amongst political actors or agents (Ball 1988: ch. 3).

The essential contestability thesis holds true, then, not as a thesis about individual concepts but as a valid generalization about political language as a species of discourse. The language of political discourse is essentially contestable, but the individual concepts comprising any political language are contingently contestable. Which concepts are believed to be worth disputing and revising is more often a political than a philosophical matter. In some situations it becomes important for political agents to take issue with their opponents' and/or audience's understanding of 'party' or 'power' or 'authority' or 'democracy'. What one might, at a stretch, call the contingent contestability thesis is less dramatic than its essentialist predecessor; but its fit with the facts is a good deal tighter.

The thesis of contingent contestability also marks a further phase of the linguistic turn and opens the door to another approach to the study of political thought – 'the history of political concepts,' or 'conceptual history', for short. Either phrase is misleading, if one imagines that there might be a history of concepts wholly set apart from a history of political disagreement and argument. The history of political theory is in no small part the story of political arguments, which often (though not always) take the form of conceptual contests in which older meanings are challenged and arguments are advanced in favour of new understandings. Political innovation and conceptual change are two sides of the same old and still circulating coin.

Two Approaches to Conceptual History

There is now a noticeable move away from the static and ahistorical enterprise of 'conceptual analysis' to a more dynamic and historically oriented emphasis on 'conceptual history' – that is, a concern with conceptual change and the construction of conceptual histories. There are at present two 'schools' of, or approaches to, conceptual history. These proceed along roughly parallel tracks. On one track is the modern

German genre known as *Begriffsgeschichte*; on the other, Anglo-American 'conceptual history' or what I call 'critical conceptual history' (Ball 1988). Let me offer, by way of introduction to these two approaches, a broad-brush and somewhat crude characterization of each.

Reinhart Koselleck, a leading defender and practitioner of *Begriffsgeschichte*, observes that 'Without common concepts there is no society, and above all, no political field of action.' But which concepts are to be the common coin of discourse – and what they mean – becomes, at crucial historical junctures, a veritable field of battle. 'The struggle over the "correct" concepts', says Koselleck, 'becomes socially and politically explosive' (Koselleck 1985: 74, 77). The conceptual historian attempts to map the minefield, as it were, by examining the various historical turning-points or watersheds in the history of the concepts constituting modern political discourse. This involves not only noting when and for what purposes and at what political sites new and now-familiar words were coined – 'ideology', 'industrialism', 'liberalism', 'conservatism', 'socialism' and 'altruism', among many others – but tracing marked changes in the meaning of older terms such as 'constitution' and 'revolution'. This is just the task outlined and given theoretical justification by Koselleck and undertaken in painstaking detail by the contributors to the massive *Geschichtliche Grundbegriffe* (Brunner et al. 1972–) and the *Handbuch politische-sozialer Grundbegriffe in Frankreich 1680–1820* (Reichardt and Schmitt 1985).

In these and other works, the German conceptual historians are attempting to test a number of hypotheses. One is that the eighteenth century was a period of unprecedented conceptual shifts. Another is that these shifts involved not only the minting of new terms and the reminting of older ones, but that they point to an increased tendency toward ideological abstraction. Thus the late eighteenth and early nineteenth centuries saw the rise of the various 'isms' – socialism, communism, industrialism, etc. – which, by supplying speakers with a new means of locating themselves in social and political space, actually reconstituted that very space. Political conflict accordingly became more overtly ideological, more concerned with questions of principle (or even first principles) than was previously the case. Concepts that had previously had concrete class and geographic referents became free-floating abstractions about which one could speak in the ostensibly universal voice valued by thinkers of the Enlightenment. 'Rights', for example, ceased to refer to the rights of Englishmen and other national or legal groups, becoming instead 'the rights of man' or, as we are apt to say nowadays, 'human rights'. The studies undertaken by Koselleck and his colleagues have, on the whole, tended to confirm these conjectures (see Richter 1986; 1987).

The Anglo-American conceptual historians differ from their Continental counterparts both in method and emphasis. First, as one would expect, the German conceptual historians have so far concentrated their considerable learning largely (though by no means exclusively) on mapping conceptual changes in earlier German and Francophone political and philosophical discourse. Their English-speaking colleagues have focused largely on the history of anglophone political discourse. Second, the German conceptual historians have employed a unified method, have worked collaboratively, and have been remarkably encyclopaedic in range and scope. Their English-speaking cousins have for the most part worked individually, have subscribed to no single method, and have been more selective than encyclopaedic in their ambitions and choice of concepts. Even so, their respective conjectures about conceptual change do occasionally overlap and complement one another. In a very limited way some of my own work amounts, in effect, to a comparative test of several of the hypotheses about conceptual change advanced by the German conceptual historians. For example, several of my enquiries suggest that the eighteenth century was indeed a period of profound and unprecedented conceptual transformation in anglophone political discourse, at least as regards the concepts of 'party' and 'republic' (Ball 1988: chs 2, 3).

Earlier, and especially eighteenth-century, shifts were significant, but conceptual change is not safely confined to the past: it is continuing even as, and because, we speak. My own view, which may be more a suspicion than a testable hypothesis, is that we are living through and participating in a period of profound, exhilarating, and in some ways deeply disturbing conceptual shifts. (I have attempted in *Transforming Political Discourse* and with my colleagues in two collaborative works – *Political Innovation and Conceptual Change* (1989) and *Conceptual Change and the Constitution* (1988) – to give voice and substance to this suspicion.)

The Nature of Political Discourse

If we are to take a 'conceptual-historical' approach to the study of political phenomena, then we need to be clear about the concepts comprising our own discourse. And we need to identify the defining or distinguishing features of political discourse as a field of investigation. So I should perhaps say that, in speaking of this or that 'language', I do not refer to the natural languages analysed by linguists – Attic Greek, for example, or medieval German – but instead to what one might at a first cut call a moral or political language. A language of this sort includes those 'shared conceptions of the world, shared manners and values, shared resources and expectations and procedures for speech and thought' through which 'communities are in fact defined and con-stituted' (White 1984: 6). This is immediately complicated, however, by a second consideration. A community's language is not a seamless web or a single structurally unified whole, but consists instead of a series of sub-languages or idioms which I call discourses.

A 'discourse', as I use the term, is the sub-language spoken in and constitutive of a particular discipline, domain, sphere or sub-community. Examples of such sub-languages might include the discourse of eco-nomics, of the law, of medicine, of computer programming, and a score of other disciplines or domains.

But what of *political* discourse? Is it merely one discourse amongst many, or does it have unique distinguishing features of its own? Here matters become much more complicated. One of the key features of political discourse is to be found in its central tension, which may be described in the following way. Political discourse employs the language that we supposedly share, not as speakers of specialized sub-languages, but in our common capacity as citizens. But, at the same time, this ideal is undermined in two ways.

First, political discourse borrows from and draws upon more special-ized discourses; it is compounded, as it were, out of lesser languages. When the concepts and metaphors constituting the discourse of eco-nomics, for example – or of computer programming or law or religion or medicine or any other discipline – enter the field of political meanings, they alter the shape and structure of that field by altering its speakers' terms of discourse. This process of transgressing, of leaking across discursive boundaries, is a prime source of conceptual change.

Second, political discourse characteristically consists of concepts whose meanings are not always agreed upon but are often heatedly con-tested by citizen-speakers. The possibility of communicative breakdown is an ever-present feature, if not indeed a defining characteristic, of political discourse. As the late Bertrand de Jouvenel once observed:

> The elementary political process is the action of mind upon mind through speech. Communication by speech completely depends upon the existence in the memories of both parties of a common stock of words to which they attach much the same meanings . . . Even as people belong to the same culture by the use of the same language, so they belong to the same society by the under-standing of the same moral language. As this common moral language ex-tends, so does society; as it breaks up, so does society. [de Jouvenel 1957: 304]

Passing this observation through a finer (and less 'mentalistic') mesh, one should add that the elementary political process is the action of speaker upon speaker about matters of public or common concern. But of course what is and is not 'public' – and therefore presumably political

– is itself a subject of political dispute and argument. Disagreements about the scope and domain of 'the political' are themselves constitutive features of political discourse.

Critical Conceptual Histories

The task of the critical conceptual historian is to chart changes in the concepts constituting the discourses of political agents, living and dead. The kinds of questions to be asked about the transformation of political discourses typically include the following. How might one identify or describe these discourses and the specific changes made in them? Which concepts, in particular, had their meanings altered? How and why did these changes come about? Who brought them about, for what reasons, and what rhetorical strategies did they use? And, not least, what difference did (or does) it make?

These questions are often, though not always, answered in some part by pointing to a particular political tradition or, if one prefers, a tradition of discourse. Examples of such traditions might include republicanism, liberalism and Marxism, amongst many others. These can in turn be further divided into sub-traditions such as classical and Renaissance republicanism, Soviet Marxism, Manchester liberalism, and the like.

Political discourses, and the concepts that constitute them, have histories that can be narratively reconstructed in any number of ways. Such histories would show where these discourses functioned and how they changed. These changes may, moreover, be traced to the problems perceived by particular (classes of) historical agents in particular political situations. Conceptual changes are brought about by political agents occupying specific sites, and working under the identifiable linguistic constraints of a particular tradition as it exists at a particular time. The vocabularies within and upon which these agents work are to some degree flexible, although not infinitely malleable. They can to some extent transform their language; but, conversely, their language also subtly transforms them, helping to make them the kinds of creatures they are. The ways in which speakers shape, and are in turn shaped by, their language are the subject matter of critical conceptual history.

But – a critic might ask – why speak of concepts instead of words, of 'conceptual' change rather than 'linguistic' change, and of conceptual history rather than linguistic history (White 1987)? And what – my critic might continue – is *critical* about 'critical conceptual histories'?

The first question is easily answered. A political vocabulary consists not simply of words but of concepts. To have a word for X is to be in possession of the concept of X. Yet one may possess a concept without having a word to express it. It is, for instance, clear that Milton knew about, and valued, 'originality'; otherwise he would not have thought it important to try to do 'things unattempted yet in prose or rhyme'. But although Milton quite clearly possessed the *concept* of originality, he had no word with which to express it, for 'originality' did not enter the English language until a century after his death (Skinner 1989a). Or, to take another example, a child who says 'I love my country' possesses the concept of patriotism, even if she does not (yet) know the word (Farr 1989: 31). Much the same is true of moral and political concepts. For example, the concept of rights long predated the word (Dagger 1989). Moreover, the same word can, in different periods, stand for quite different concepts. The 'rights' of Englishmen, for example, were quite unlike the 'rights' of man or the 'human rights' defended or violated by modern regimes. Nor did 'the state', or at any rate *lo stato*, mean for Machiavelli what it means for us (Skinner 1989b). Nor did 'revolution' mean for Locke and his contemporaries what it means for us. They understood a revolution to be a coming full circle, a restoration of some earlier uncorrupted condition; we understand it to be the collective overthrow of an old regime and the creation of an entirely new one (Dunn 1989). 'Corruption' has decidedly different meanings in the discourses of classical republicanism and modern liberalism (Euben 1989). 'Ideology' was originally, in the eighteenth century, the systematic scientific study of the origins of ideas; now it refers to a more or less tightly constrained set of political ideas and ideals (Goldie 1989). A 'patriot' – nowadays an uncritical supporter of his country's government – was once one who for the sake of his *patria* dared to be an opponent and critic of his government (Dietz 1989). These and many other examples suggest that words do not change, but concepts and meanings do. In an important sense, then, words do not have histories but concepts do.

The history of *political* concepts (or more precisely, concepts used in political discourse) cannot, however, be narrated apart from the political conflicts in which they figure. Political concepts are weapons of war, tools of persuasion and legitimation, badges of identity and solidarity. They are (to reinvoke a Cold War cliché) in the thick of partisan battles for 'the hearts and minds of men'. To study the history of political concepts is to revisit old battlefields and reconstruct the positions and strategies of the opposing forces. What concepts were on this occasion available, for what purposes and with what effect(s) were they used? How were their meanings altered in the course of their deployment? To put my point less dramatically, what distinguishes critical conceptual history from philology or etymology is its attention to the *arguments* in which concepts appear and are used to perform particular kinds of actions at particular times and at particular political sites. Histories of political concepts are, in short, histories of political arguments, and of the conceptual contests and disputes on which they turned and to which they gave rise.

A second and more complicated question still remains to be answered: what, exactly, is critical about 'critical conceptual histories'? Several answers can be given. The first is that these are histories written with a critical intention of showing that conceptual change is not only possible but is virtually a defining feature of political discourse. Second, such histories will, if successful, show how particular political agents became aware of the subtle and heretofore unrecognized ways in which their discourses had transformed them (and their contemporaries) before setting about the task of transforming political discourse. Third, a critical conceptual history shows in some detail how these agents actually transformed the discourse of their day. This requires that the historian identify the processes and mechanisms by means of which specific agents brought about particular changes. These include, pre-eminently, the discovery, exposure and criticism of ostensible contradictions and incoherences in dominant discourses, and the arguments and rhetorical stratagems employed for that critical purpose and for the more positive purpose of constructing an alternative discourse (Farr 1989). Far from being the domain of detached armchair philosophers, this kind of critical activity affects the ways in which political agents themselves think and act. What Alasdair MacIntyre says of the role of criticism in changing moral concepts is no less true of its role in changing political ones:

> philosophical inquiry itself plays a part in changing moral concepts. It is not that we have first a straightforward history of moral concepts and then a separate and secondary history of philosophical comment. For to analyze a concept philosophically may often be to assist in its transformation by suggesting that it needs revision, or that it is discredited in some way. Philosophy leaves everything as it is – except concepts. And since to possess a concept involves behaving or being able to behave in certain ways in certain circumstances, to alter concepts, whether by modifying existing concepts or by making new concepts available or by destroying old ones, is to alter behavior. A history which takes this point seriously, which is concerned with the role of philosophy in relation to actual conduct, cannot be philosophically neutral. [MacIntyre 1966: 2–3]

Nor, by the same token, can conceptual histories be politically neutral. This is not to say that they are necessarily partisan in any narrow sense, but rather that they are critical, inasmuch as they alert their audience to the ways in which, and the means by which, their communicatively constituted world has transformed them, and how they in their turn may yet transform it.

As one among many approaches to the study of political theory, conceptual history serves to alert us to features of our world that familiarity has obscured. It supplies us with the distant mirror of past practices and beliefs that seem strange and alien to our modern (or perhaps post-modern) eyes. To encounter and attempt to understand these beliefs and practices in all their strangeness requires the stretching of our own concepts and categories. The conceptual historian aims to address this sense of strangeness, of difference: not to make it less strange or different, but to make it more comprehensible. The aim is to shed light on past practices and beliefs, and in so doing to stretch the linguistic limits of present-day political discourse.

References

Austin, J. L. 1970. *Philosophical Papers*, 2nd edn. Oxford: Oxford University Press.

Ayer, A. J. 1946. *Language, Truth and Logic*, 2nd edn. New York: Dover.

Ball, T. 1988. *Transforming Political Discourse: Political Theory and Critical Conceptual History*. Oxford: Blackwell.

Ball, T. 1993. 'Power', in Robert E. Goodin and Philip Pettit, eds, *A Companion to Contemporary Political Philosophy*. Oxford: Blackwell.

Ball, T., Farr, J., and Hanson, R. L., eds. 1989. *Political Innovation and Conceptual Change*. Cambridge: Cambridge University Press.

Ball, T., and Pocock, J. G. A., eds. 1988. *Conceptual Change and the Constitution*. Lawrence, Kansas: University Press of Kansas.

Brunner, O., Conze, W., and Koselleck, R., eds. 1972–92. *Geschichtliche Grundbegriffe. Historisches Lexikon zur Politisch-Sozialer Sprache in Deutschland*. Stuttgart: Klett-Cotta, 7 vols.

Chappell, V. C., ed. 1964. *Ordinary Language*. Englewood Cliffs, NJ: Prentice Hall.

Connolly, W. E. 1983. *The Terms of Political Discourse*, 2nd rev. edn. Princeton, NJ: Princeton University Press.

Dagger, R. 1989. 'Rights', in Ball, Farr and Hanson, 1989, ch. 14.

de Jouvenel, B. 1957. *Sovereignty*, trans. J. F. Huntington, Chicago: University of Chicago Press.

Dietz, M. G. 1989. 'Patriotism', in Ball, Farr and Hanson, 1989, ch. 8.

Dunn, J. 1989. 'Revolution', in Ball, Farr and Hanson, 1989, ch. 16.

Euben, J. P. 1989. 'Corruption', in Ball, Farr and Hanson, 1989, ch. 11.

Farr, J. 1989. 'Understanding Conceptual Change Politically', in Ball, Farr and Hanson, 1989, ch. 2.

Gallie, W. B. 1956. 'Essentially Contested Concepts', *Proceedings of the Aristotelian Society*, 56.

Gellner, E. 1959. *Words and Things*. London: Gollancz.

Goldie, M. 1989. 'Ideology', in Ball, Farr and Hanson, 1989, ch. 13.

Gray, J. 1983. 'Political Power, Social Theory, and Essential Contestability', in D. Miller and L. Siedentop, eds, *The Nature of Political Theory*. Oxford: Clarendon Press.

Koselleck, R. 1985. *Futures Past: On the Semantics of Historical Time*, trans. Keith Tribe, Cambridge, Mass.: MIT Press.

Lukes, S. 1974. *Power: A Radical View*. London: Macmillan.

Macdonald, M. 1951. 'The Language of Political Theory', in A. Flew, ed., *Logic and Language*, first series. Oxford: Blackwell.

MacIntyre, A. 1966. *A Short History of Ethics*. London: Routledge.

Magee, B., ed. 1978. *Men of Ideas*. New York: Viking Press.

Marcuse, H. 1964. *One-Dimensional Man*. Boston: Beacon Press.

Miller, D. 1983. 'Linguistic Philosophy and Political Theory', in D. Miller and L. Siedentop, eds, *The Nature of Political Theory*. Oxford: Clarendon Press.

Murphy, J. S. 1968. *Political Theory: A Conceptual Analysis*. Homewood, Ill.: Dorsey Press.

Oppenheim, F. 1961. *Dimensions of Freedom: An Analysis*. New York: St Martin's Press.

Perry, C. 1950. 'The Semantics of Social Science', *American Political Science Review*, 44.

Plamenatz, J. 1968. *Consent, Freedom and Political Obligation*, 2nd edn. Oxford: Oxford University Press.

Reichardt, R., and Schmitt, E. 1985. *Handbuch politisch-sozialer Grundbegriffe in Frankreich*. Munich: Oldenbourg Verlag.

Richter, M. 1986. 'Conceptual History [*Begriffsgeschichte*] and Political Theory', *Political Theory*, 14.

Richter, M. 1987. 'The History of Concepts and the History of Ideas', *Journal of the History of Ideas*, 48.

Rorty, R., ed. 1967. *The Linguistic Turn*. Chicago: University of Chicago Press.

Searle, J. R. 1969. *Speech Acts*. Cambridge: Cambridge University Press.

Skinner, Q. 1989a. 'Language and Political Change', in Ball, Farr and Hanson, 1989, ch. 1.

Skinner, Q. 1989b. 'The State', in Ball, Farr and Hanson, ch. 5.

Waismann, F. 1951. 'Verifiability', in A. Flew ed., *Logic and Language*, first series, Oxford: Blackwell.

Wertheimer, A. 1976. 'Is Ordinary Language Analysis Conservative?', *Political Theory*, 4.

White, J. B. 1984. *When Words Lose Their Meaning*. Chicago: University of Chicago Press.

White, J. B. 1987. 'Thinking About Our Language', *Yale Law Journal*, 96.

Wilson, F. G., Wright, B. F., Griffith, E. S., and Voegelin, E. 1944. 'Research in Political Theory: A Symposium', *American Political Science Review*, 38.

CHAPTER 2

Political Theory and the Problem of Anachronism

Conal Condren

Political theory has an uncomfortable relationship with history. Traditionally seen as the principal font of political wisdom, history has long
performed a theoretical function (Nadel 1965: 49ff.). Modern professional historians have been apt to disown political theory, for they now
have other fish to fry; while political theorists, in part the mutating
progeny of the old exemplum history, like to cook up such dishes for
themselves (see Burrow et al. 1983). In the present context, history may
be viewed both as the facts surviving from a hypothetical totality and as a
disciplined study of the residue of human activity. The distinction is
unstable, and what follows is perilously schematic; but it should be
sufficient to make a simple point: that what we accept as political theory
is both partly conditioned and subverted by a dependency on historical
writing. Further, it is unclear whether those calling themselves political
theorists have established sufficiently autonomous and uniform criteria
of judgment to enable them to use history without also importing the
incubus of the historian's own destabilizing priorities. Certainly, as historiography changes, so we can expect it to continue to have a vicarious
impact on political theory. Before discussing such issues, however, a few
words on history as *res gestae* and political theory are in order; for from
this meaning of history arises the primal sense of anachronism, the
consequences of which, I believe, are now at the heart of the troubled
relationship between political theory and history.

Political Theory and History

Political theorists use the past as a quarry; they regard it principally as a
source of useable facts; of entries to, and illustrations of, theoretical
issues.[1] In so far as there is a concomitant emphasis on getting facts right,

45

the historian, even in such a one-dimensional persona as fact-gatherer, may seem to arbitrate over adequate theory; and this, eventually, would threaten the intellectual integrity of the theorist's world. If facts are so important, the theorist may have to bow to the historian, or become one; if not, the theorist and the fact-gathering historian can do little more than pass like strangers in the night. This is no bad outcome if they know they are about quite different business. In practice, of course, there is often no neat delineation of role, and frequently political theorists are given to the sorts of statement that excite historiographical expectations. Jurgen Habermas, for example, has dated the emergence of his much-vaunted 'public sphere' of discourse to 1695, when control of the English press was abandoned, so allowing coffee houses to become free centres of rational discussion. This seems to involve a question of historical fact. If so, it is rather like the assertions of old school textbooks which dated the Renaissance from the fall of Constantinople, so precipitating the flight of manuscript-bearing Greek professors to Italy: crude and question-begging (Habermas 1992, ch. 3).[2] But the Habermasian image of later Stuart England may stand only as a symbolic counterpoint, a projected golden-age ideal for a theoretical argument about the political consequences of modern communications technology. If the theory is really about the eighteenth-century 'bourgeois' public sphere, then historians might well dismiss it; if not, they can only distract attention from an argument about the twentieth century.

None of this is decisive in an academic world altogether more slippery than I am indicating, but with it has come a further form of quasi-subordination of theory to history. Political theory has often been taken to be some form of superstructure uncertainly related to, or generated by, the material facts of history or that rhetorical abstraction, political 'reality'. There may be no convincing theoretical argument for this epiphenomenal status, but it is reinforced institutionally by the manner in which political science departments treat 'theory' as a distinct add-on component in teaching politics. If we posit a simple derivative and rationalizing relationship between theory and practice, or reality, then the intellectual subordination of theory to something, such as a world of historical or social facts, becomes evident. As the historian Namier was alleged to have claimed – tell me what a man believes and I'll tell you his income (or vice versa).[3] Yet even if we retreat to something hermeneutic-ally more nuanced within the terms of this hierarchical image, it is questionable whether we have done more than confuse the clear lines of derivation. We may have replaced an understanding whose only virtue was simplicity, with something that loses even that in the name of plotting more precisely the relationship between theory and practice.

Having barely introduced what will be a ghost in the argument, I want to outline the relationships between political theory and history as discipline. Characterized in the most perfunctory fashion, the historian mediates a past which is always assumed to be partially alien yet potentially intelligible as a past.[4] I shall suggest that, although in a simple form anachronism is only a matter of temporal mislocation, in a necessarily extended sense, it amounts to an illicit – because avoidable – distortion of the mediation process itself; it becomes an undue domestication of the alien.[5] Thus understood, the incubus of anachronism threatens more than the subordination of theory to fact: it raises the spectre of the dissolution either of political theory, or of its relationship with history.

Political Theory and Tradition

In practice, political theory is an accommodating academic mansion, housing a full range of commitments and relationships to political activity itself – a fact which condemns most easy generalizations about theory to the realm of illustratable half-truth. Further, the relationships between what is (somewhat arbitrarily) classified as political theory and history as discipline are quite contingent. In so far as those branches of political theory, such as methodology, game and public choice theory, make no historical claims, they can be put to one side. Qualifications notwithstanding, a large portion of what is called political theory has built into it an historical or quasi-historical dimension.

Like many relatively recent, self-conscious, discursive formations,[6] political theory was quick to project for itself an august tradition, comprising a direct lineage for modern preoccupations and those anticipators who can be seen to belong to our world more ambivalently. The library shelves devoted to political theory hold many a hefty volume on the history of political thought, testimony more to the need to have a history than to write one. They are now commonly joined by snappy anthologized pot-boilers in the Plato to Nato vein, one chapter per great thinker and assuming the tradition the older tomes tried to elucidate. The operation of this sense of tradition is complex: for some, its very existence has been an article of faith (see Gunnell 1979, chs 1–2), and whatever its precise shape, an induction into the doctrines of its major figures is still fundamental to an education in political theory. It provides a stimulus to research, and so its figures characteristically become the means of exploring our own priorities. They succour and repel, acting as sources of edification and indignation. With great economy, the major names can be adjectivally compressed and made to encode whole theories about the modern world. Comprehending much political theory therefore requires the student to understand the deployment of historic emblems, 'Hobbesian', 'Platonic', 'Burkean'. Even if one does not work within the framework of The Tradition, the exploration of texts found within or around that construct remains central to much theory and, more broadly, to a university education in politics. By its own promulgation and transmission, then, political theory is a past-centred activity, yet by habit is only ambivalently historical (see Boucher 1989: 220–37; Gunnell 1979, chs 1–2).

Undoubtedly, the tradition of political theory is no longer the simple linear projection it once was, or can occasionally still seem in its more vulgar cribs. Once, it comprised a handful of major figures largely assumed to be writing on the same level of intellectual coherence as the modern theorist and taken to be addressing invariant issues (obligation, freedom, justice); it is now recognized to embrace differing forms of political writing and a greater diversity of problems (see Pocock 1962a).[7] Figures exclusive to the specialist historian a generation or so ago are now within its compass.[8] Symptomatically, the reasons for this expanding heterogeneity are only partially historiographical. As the institutional structure of contemporary political theory has become more diverse, with more issues becoming problems for the political theorist, so the tradition has been re-cut to fit; its major figures are explored for new insights, oversights and other sundry failings. There is something very traditional in this use of the past. It is an academic analogue of the way self-conscious political groups have habitually maintained a sense of identity, to the extent that only those who have failed to exploit a past's resources have wanted to abandon it, or have seen it as an oppressive plot against them (see Pocock 1962a).

Here we need to distinguish a mere canon of texts from a putative tradition of text-writing. A canon may be only an assemblage of works we have to read for reasons which may not be clear or intrinsic to the works concerned, and so immediately, canonical status may raise questions about aribtrariness of exclusion. To designate something a tradition, however, is to make a putatively historical claim about socialized processes of transmission and communal activity. Traditions should furnish intrinsic grounds for exclusion.[9] Moreover, works may be part of a tradition regardless of their quality. In the study of English literature, the question of canonical status has become contentious; and because the canon is not, overall, a tradition, it has been possible to add works representative of groups previously overlooked.[10] In political theory, however, the issue has been whether what was claimed to be a tradition of theorizing was really any such thing (see Gunnell 1979). Its status is at present uncertain, partly because political theorists have been responsive to critical historiography that has argued for greater contexualization; and this has led to an enhanced awareness that past thinkers were not necessarily trying to write like us, for us and about our problems (see

Skinner 1969). Superficially, there has sometimes seemed to be an easy alliance of interests producing this 'thickish description' of the past. There are good ideological, or canonical, reasons as well as good historical reasons, for including writers such as Mary Wollstonecraft. But for whatever reasons, diversification threatens a subversion of the tradition in any informative sense of the term, and raises serious problems concerning the criteria of selection, judgment and the terms of analysis. The historiographical question now becomes: does augmentation destroy the tradition's character or disclose it as merely canonical? Adding figures, say from China, in the name of representational fairness may create a politically correct canon; but will this render any notion of a tradition historiographically less plausible than it already is? (See Dunn 1996: 13–15.)[11] In so far as there is genuinely a tradition, such reasons for augmenting it will be misguided. As with the simple superstructural relationship between theory and historical fact, the belief in a tradition which at least had simplicity to recommend it may well over-complicate its educational usefulness while continuing to inculcate a range of dubious assumptions about the history of politics. The tradition of political theory then, remains ambivalently between history and a symbolic conspectus of the theoretical and ideological present.[12] The pervasive argot of 'dialogues' with the theorists of the tradition reinforces this interstitial standing. As students know, certainly before they study politics, there is literally no dialogue with the dead. The theorist reads and interprets. To describe this as engaging in a dialogue may sometimes pay more than lip-service to history, but it also encodes the wish to implicate the past in the present. Beguiling as such a fusion of horizons might seem, it is hardly a fiction that encourages a thoroughgoing historicity.

Text and Context

The call for more adequate processes of contextualization for political theory's tradition also marks an important change from previous relationships between theory and history. Context, once construed as war, the smell of social conditions and Namier's determinant of an annual income, has come to mean ideas, arguments, intentions, presuppositions, vocabularies (see Pocock 1962a; Skinner 1969). In a word, it is intellectual history which presses most on political theory and threatens to compromise its tradition, and this too is not static. Before and after World War II, the dominant form of intellectual history was that associated with the historian and philosopher A. O. Lovejoy. This suited the way political theory and its tradition were perceived. Lovejoy's notion of ideas was sufficiently realist for him to envisage as the subject

matter of intellectual history a handful of single concepts, or in stable
unison, 'unit ideas' to be traced across centuries and forms of discourse.
Consequently, his own project was explicitly interdisciplinary and co-
operative (see Lovejoy 1940). As such concepts were largely the
invention of philosophers, intellectual history was apt to become the
history of philosophy. If not, at least a broad sense of philosophy could be
given a wide-ranging explanatory power for intellectual history. Political
theorists also believed in the primacy and continuity of a handful of basic
political conceptions of a fairly philosophic nature, and showed a pro-
clivity to trace them back to Plato and Aristotle; thus, a Lovejoyan wish
for constructive interdisciplinarity looked capable of consummation.
The revisionism of the period after World War II has brought about a
considerable transformation in the sub-discipline and has renegotiated
the relationship with political theory.

The main contours of revisionism, in its Germanic, Anglo-American
and French forms, are sufficiently well known to need no detailed
rehearsal. Despite major differences, they have all questioned the historical reality of over-arching concepts transmigrating between forms of
thinking and widely different writers. This ontological and epistemological scepticism has helped broaden the notion of context. From being
quasi-philosophical, or outrightly philosophical, jigsaws of similarly
abstract ideas, contexts have come to embrace conventions of discourse
as the means by which ideas could be expressed. There has also been
emphasis on integrating a whole range of contexts for any given statement, the main thrust of *Begriffsgeschichte*; and upon more time-bound
intentions (see Koselleck 1985). The upshot has been to make much that
seemed familiar and accessible more alien and rather opaque. Con-
joined with this is found a suspicion of the imposition of contemporary
theories and expectations, which by being familiar have a domesticating,
even theoretically parochializing, effect on alien cultures.[13] These general features of a newer intellectual history were shared with forms of
revisionism in anthropology and political historiography, especially that
which swept to dominance in early modern British history, with their
emphases on detail, locality, contingency and the irrelevance of more
contemporary explanatory theoretical constructs.

The very notion of historical ideas, then, has begun to be transformed;
once-stable concepts shared equably with political theorists have been
particularized. In one fashionable formulation, ideas are answers to
specific questions, and only adequate contextualization – that is, only
good history – can elucidate them (see Collingwood 1939, chs 4–5). In
some moods R. G. Collingwood went so far as to reduce philosophy itself
into a form of history, so reversing realist orthodoxies (see Martin 1995:
204–5). To push the drift of these changes further, it may be that, for the

historian, the ideas of past thinkers are not really tangible subject matter at all; rather, they are the interpretive extrapolations or hypothetical completions of problematic, fragmented evidence.

Certainly, if one looks at the ways in which historians use words like 'idea' and 'concept' when elucidating texts, they appear to be providing interpretive abridgements of obscure or multivalent word use, rather than disclosing a distinct realm of historical (or theoretical) reality reflected in surviving language. If this is so, the way the historian and political theorist complete the evidence by calling it a concept or idea is likely to be very divergent. When a theorist like Kavka writes of Hobbes's theories of obligation, he is refashioning and translating Hobbes's language to bring it into line with what he takes to be theoretically defensible now. The question is what can be rescued for the modern liberal. That desideratum, more or less within the restraints imposed by Hobbes's language, is the main point of reading him. When Glenn Burgess writes of such Hobbesian concepts, a Kavkaesque understanding is exactly what he is trying to avoid (see Kavka 1988: 89ff.; Burgess 1994). What is meant by the concept attributed to Hobbes is a function of the respective worlds in which the political theorist and the intellectual historian operate. One person's 'discovery' of a concept could easily be the other's failure of historical imagination (see Lamont 1979: 20–1). Conversely, the historian's extrapolation of a concept may be a hurdle in the way of the theorist's enterprise of rescuing, rehabilitating, applying or attacking a previous writer. Overall, the difference is between establishing the meaning of, rather than the meaning for; more extremely, between the historian's attempt to establish true or plausible meanings from the philosopher's concern with truths or the truth of meanings (see editors' introduction to Rorty et al. 1984).

Forms of Anachronism

This increasing differentiation of enterprise has arisen largely, I think, because the forms of revisionism to which I have been referring are attempts to work out in practice the implications of the inherited historiographical presupposition that anachronism is to be avoided. And it is within intellectual history that its avoidance is most difficult. In its paradigmatic sense, anachronism refers to the chronological mislocation of an historical happening: simply getting the date or time wrong. There is here an appeal to testable facts, falsifiable claims. Because anachronism in this sense seems straightforward, it has become one of the deadly historiographical sins, involving perhaps the first of the historian's commandments: 'Thou shalt not get things back to front.' The desire to expunge anachronism thus functions as a criterion for disciplinary demarcation. In practice, the isolation of anachronism in this primal sense may be difficult enough; more than historiographical fastidiousness may hang on establishing a factually correct sequence. The question, for example, of whether Wellington gave the order to advance at Waterloo before or after he knew that Blucher was coming through the smoke is of more than historical importance for those promoting British or German national pride. But the difficulty of answering it seems to arise only from lack of conclusive evidence about the timing of two incontestable events. It is from such an understanding of anachronism, predicated on stable identities, that we get the more popular usage of anachronism: designating something which seems archaic because impervious to expected change, or something created and maintained like a museum artefact in a different world.

If anachronism can be restricted to its primal form, it poses no threat either to the practice of history or to the relationships between history and political theory. Theorists can willingly agree that chronological misplacement is erroneous – it is, after all, a form of getting one's facts wrong. There appears nothing in this as such to compromise how theorists talk about texts properly located. That Locke's *Two Treatises* were not written to justify the 1688 Revolution does not in itself foreclose on discussing them as liberal theory.[14]

The problem lies in restricting anachronism to the chronological placement of stable identities. For it is only if one reverts to something like a reified world of Lovejoyan 'Ideas' or hypostatized Platonic forms that the ostensible subject matter of intellectual history and political theory can be given the requisite determinacy to comply easily with caveats about anachronism. Differently expressed, ideas, concepts, theories, are, on most plausible understandings, not like battles and earthquakes. Significant degrees of interpretation, what I have called modes of hypothetical completion, arise at the earliest stages of identification, resulting in an uncertain line between what may be predicated of, and attributed to, such phenomena. If the facts are not hard – that is, if we cannot keep separate attribution from predicate variable – we cannot simply pick them up and put them down elsewhere without altering their identity. By degrees, any such alteration undermines a presupposition enabling the scope of anachronism to be controlled easily. Thus, what apparently offers a simple criterion of demarcation between good and bad history, or even between history and non-history, becomes altogether more extensive in its potential range.

Despite the significance of restricting the range of the concept of anachronism, altogether more attention in the philosophy of history has been devoted to questions of explanation; very little of this has had much discernible impact on how historians write. In fact, problems of historical explanation are second-order ones. As W. B. Gallie argued, historians use explanations to restore narrative coherence. It follows that we have first to establish some sort of narrative before we are in any position to know what might need explaining (1964: 105ff.).[15] To do this, we have to select facts, itself a secondary issue; moreover we have to employ an appropriate vocabulary through which to construct a narrative, in a minimal sense a description. It is with respect to this primary aspect of historical writing – establishing a descriptive sequence, which we may then analyse or explain – that anachronism is so crucial. In specific cases, the descriptive and explanatory aspects of historical writing may be difficult to disengage. In principle, however, it is with respect to the former that anachronism, however understood, is so destructive; it is with respect to the latter that prohibitions upon it are eased.[16] Explanations are frequently fashioned from theories which clearly intrude upon the world described; but what needs explaining is contingent upon how we first describe. We can do this so variously that effectively we can transform the discursive presence of the subject; we can move into and out of recognizable history altogether, creating or evaporating the problems that might require explanation, loading the dice so that only one sort of explanation seems plausible (Veyne 1984: 44–6, 169). In this light, the most important question in the philosophy of history is how to predicate events in time; the attempt to avoid anachronism is the first, if negative, step, which should at least allow us to know if the narrative is history or something else.

If, tautologically, the language of description and predication provides the only means of manifesting an event in historical discourse, it becomes impossible to restrict anachronism to simple chronological mislocation. To reiterate, the difficulty is compounded if we are dealing with altogether 'softer', language-entangled facts, such as theories, of resistance, obligation, marriage, alienation and so on.[17] Consequently, the very notion of anachronism extends away from its paradigmatic form to embrace various types of statement about the past, becoming at once theoretically more interesting and systematically more troublesome. Additional to such piecemeal anachronisms are categorial anachronisms, for the major forms of which I shall provide some rough labels. Taken together, the attempt to avoid them amounts to a constant process of historiographical damage control.

First, there is judgmental anachronism, where the language predicating the event may encourage, or entail, temporally inappropriate judgments. Much of what historians consider to be bias really fits this rubric. It is one thing for me to write a history of Athens highly favourable to the Periclean faction; another to do so because I am assimilating ancient democracy to a modern theory of which I approve, or using the discussion of Athens as a surrogate for advocacy in my own society.

Second, there is what may be called descriptive anachronism. Here, irrespective of issues of approval, an anachronistic description of an event is given, so that it is presented in the narrative as if it belonged to another time. Synoptic descriptions of writers or theories as 'liberal', 'radical', 'conservative', 'totalitarian', where such terms are alien to the language and times of the relevant subjects, bring about an elision between temporally distinct descriptive vocabularies. Similarly, implanting such terms into hypothetical accounts of writers' motivations, intentions or perceptions of their world prepares the ground for an anachronistic reading of their texts (Condren 1994: 15–21, 140ff.; 1989: 525–42). There is in this sense no difference between political theorists who praise or who criticize Locke or Hobbes for being liberals. To describe them so is to establish an identity specifically in terms of the contingent consequences of their subsequent use – for aspects of each thinker have been appropriated to later debates about liberalism. Alternatively, it is simply to impose an identity upon them by virtue of what they inspire in us. It facilitates 'dialogue'.

Given the constant hermeneutic interactions of general and particular, text and context, the identification of such anachronisms is dependent upon an understanding of contexts. As contexts (among which one might place accounts of intention and motivation) are themselves provisional and constructed through descriptions, to facilitate various sorts of explanations and explications, their specification is similarly subject to anachronism. It is precisely a sensitivity to forms of contextual anachronism that led to the historiographical critique of political theory's grand tradition.

The first form of contextual anachronism may simply be called traditional anachronism. A tradition is itself a context for its putative members. It is correct to say that some sense of traditionality will provide illuminating, even necessary, contexts for given texts in political theory. Nevertheless, The Tradition – in which, for example, Machiavelli provided a context for Hobbes, Aquinas for Machiavelli, by virtue of being, for us, the previous thinkers of real note – has proved particularly vulnerable to accusations of anachronism. It has meant mislocating a late-nineteenth- and twentieth-century sense of intellectual tradition, the convenient construction maintained partly for educational purposes, and superimposing it upon the past-awareness of earlier times (see Condren 1985, ch. 3; Pocock, 1962a; Gunnell 1979, chs 1–2; Boucher 1989).

A more general and familiar form of anachronism can be called sequential anachronism. Here a whole series of events is construed teleologically or Whiggishly as leading to some fulfilment;[18] the sequence thus becomes an anachronizing context for anything placed within it, for individual attribute is coloured by a selected outcome. Thus an *oikos* becomes an intimation of a nation. For a generation, the British civil wars were characterized in terms of their supposed place on a trajectory culminating in a mature capitalist empire.

A third form of contextual anachronism is found where the intellectual delineations of the world at one time are ignored for those established at another. This may be called discursive anachronism, and it has proved a major problem for economic historians when dealing with 'economic' discourse in the seventeenth century. There is no shortage of texts seeming to suggest an economic context by virtue of their preoccupation with trade, currency, and so forth, which now make sense to us mainly in the discursive context of economics. It is, however, hard to find a stable contextualizing mode of economic discourse before the eighteenth century. A review of Thomas Mortimer's *The Elements of Commerce* (1772) illustrates this point. For all the attention to trade and money, the whole work is concerned with the notion of the common good: so much so, remarks the reviewer, that it might have been called '*The Elements of Politics*, generally' (Anon. 1773: 363). After the work of Donald Winch (1978), even Adam Smith needs placing in a context of economic theory with a caution irrelevant to the interests of economists.

Finally, it may be that the ways in which familiar forms of discourse have been interrelated are misconstrued. That is, we may reasonably well identify the parts but misread the structural relationship between them. It is particularly difficult to avoid structural anachronism where the relationship between identifiable forms of discourse begins to change to something more familiar. In the seventeenth century the terms 'science' and 'philosophy' were often interchangeable, although there was a clear recognition of the differences between experimental and theoretical philosophy or science. Yet, because we can recognize science becoming distinct from philosophy, we should beware reading back what might be later reasons for maintaining intellectual demarcation, namely the professionalization of both science and philosophy. If Charles Smitt is right, however, the initial bifurcation may have more to do with the practicalities of textbook publishing than with a sense of discipline. The fruits of some philosophy seemed insufficiently reliable to be codified in books for teaching, and so were excluded as science (1988: 792ff.).

More insidious still is the structural anachronism brought about by confusing what might be called horizontal and vertical relationships among forms of discourse which were indeed distinct at the time under discussion. In the Middle Ages there was a clear sense of both theology and logic as disciplines: they were rigidly institutionalized in university study, but they were hierarchically related, logic being a handmaid to theological debate. An account of medieval logic that converts this vertical relation into a horizontal one creates an anachronistic context, no matter how historically sensitive one is to any particular logician. Similarly, the attempt to treat natural law theory in medieval and early modern Europe as if it were quite unrelated to divine law is anachronistic.

The Pervasiveness of Anachronism

In diverse ways then, the processes of historical mediation can result in a bogus familiarity. *Ipso facto*, this may effectively be the mechanism by which some new theory is created. What the historian conventionally regards as a sin may enrich the theoretical world we now inhabit. Viewed either way, anachronism may be consequent upon a failure of historical imagination, or even upon a desire to maintain a mythic, or edifying, significance of the past for the present. Historians often reserve their most severe reproaches for this latter explanation for anachronism, while they constantly renegotiate the limits of the former.[19] Nevertheless, despite their continuing attention to specifics, theoretical confusion on the issue is not unknown. The combined force of these forms of anachronism may even suggest that all historical writing is inherently anachronistic (Lowenthal 1993: 216–17). As Maitland put it, the historian always writes from the outside; it's a little late to be a part of the Middle Ages (Lowenthal 1993: 216–17). However, three things may be noted about such a premature capitulation. First, it is inconsistent with the belief that something of the alien past can be known. Second, the pursuit of an ideal is not invalidated by the failure to achieve it. Third, the ideal appears so utopian only because historians have taken Ranke's rhetorical flourish too literally, that history is establishing things as they really were. So too, it is misleading to think, as R. G. Collingwood (1946) seemed to, that history is a matter of getting inside the minds of historical actors.[20] We lack or eschew the knowledge and priorities of the dead, and we have knowledge and perspectives alien to their times; this all helps to make this access impossible. As Joseph Levinson famously put it, we cannot know the eighteenth-century *Don Giovanni* because we know Mozart is not Wagner (1962, vol. 1, introduction). Anachronism, however, does not lie in *ex post facto* knowledge about the past which provides some of the conditions for being able to write historically. It lies in depictions which are structured by that knowledge. And that in turn is historically fatal, principally in so far as they purport to be descriptions, accounts *of* rather than accountings *for*. Even so, it may seem that anachronism is pervasively awkward. The line between avoidable anachronism and the inescapable presuppositions seemingly entailed in our saying anything about the past is not self-evident. Wherever the line is drawn at any one time, the force of all the above forms of anachronism is usually to diminish the serviceability of a given past. While the determination to avoid them helps create a professional austerity in historical writing, some historians may well find such thoroughness intolerable.

It may be feared that accepting the full consequences of the avoidance of anachronism threatens to reduce history to antiquarianism, or a form of discourse restricted to the cognoscenti. For it is the case that, as history is a form of mediation, audience limitation may provide an educational warrant for some degree of anachronism. This may be so but, like all casuistic doctrines, it serves to underline an ideal by admitting contingent and mitigating circumstances of its breach. It would seem to follow that such teaching anachronisms are acceptable within history only on sufferance, and carry no historiographical authority. Again, it is held that by making the past less serviceable, good causes may suffer. As Lowenthal remarks aptly of *Roots*, it was only because it was anachronistic that it could provide an image of the past which black Americans could grasp as their own (1985: 228): and the last thing they need is for historians to reveal roots to be twigs. In a sense, such fears about the consequences of anti-anachronism may be well founded. They indicate tensions within the established historiographical community between the demands of historicity and general morality; these tensions require some return to a more hallowed exemplum and rhetorical historiography, to philosophy or ideology teaching by examples. In short, the fears serve to manifest the differing priorities that people may have in writing about the past.[21] The work of historians often has the effect of challenging popular, moral-cum-political images of the past, because their professional priorities are apt to diverge from those of the moralist or politician. In any case, concerns about the possible consequences of the rigorous pursuit of historicity are not germane to the present argument. The points are simply that, for good or ill, there is a pronounced drift towards the avoidance of anachronism which helps to define the historian; that fear of the contingent consequences of this does not in itself provide any stable criterion for counteracting this propensity; and that rightly or wrongly, non-anachronistic history carries a considerable, if limited, authority for activities such as political theory.

The problems are most pointed in the history of science, a clarifying model for the problems in political theory. For many years histories of science were dramatically sequentially anachronistic because there was a clearer sense in science than in politics of cumulatively established truth. A historiographical reaction has more recently got dreadfully entangled with the status of truth-claims from which only a clearer sense of intellectual modality can rescue us. One of the most provoking features of Kuhn's work was the ambivalence of its overall argument. It was unclear how far he was making a claim about the nature of scientific truth, which in its Feyerabendian extremity denied a notion of cumulative knowledge; or a claim about how to write non-anachronistic history (Kuhn 1962).[22] Jardine has attempted to specify the formal conditions on which cumulative truth can be accepted without severing all connection with historicity through specifying protocols for the extension of predicates (1980: 107ff.). To abbreviate: where writer A at t1 refers to R through concept a, and writer B at t2 refers to R more correctly through concept b, concept b can be extended to cover a, thus allowing the claim that A attests to the same truth as B. Jardine accepts that, in practice, these conditions are not easily satisfied. But in so far as R is not independent of conceptual elaboration, and thus in so far as the reference function does not operate on a simple shared referent R, then the conditions seem theoretically impossible to fulfil.[23] Moreover, the attempt may be questionable if we are trying to establish A's meaning in using a. Any argument that A really meant b, by virtue of our extending b to replace a, stacks the cards. Jardine's predicate extension will look like descriptive anachronism in aid of the sequential. It may be, in short, that histories of science become the real test case for the implications of anachronism, because of the theoretically strong case for cumulative truth in science.[24] Establishing this may require anachronistic description. In sum, where the philosopher might want to see under what conditions b can be extended to cover a, to establish a shared truth, the historian's task is to make a intelligible without such an extension.[25]

Despite the much weaker atemporal truth-claims that politics can make, this tension still threatens to cramp the style of the theorist. As Margaret Leslie has pointed out, the political theorist needs an anachronistic past unless theory is to be reduced to history; the anachronisms involved in Gramsci's readings of Machiavelli help make him theoretically interesting (Leslie 1970: 443ff., 447).[26] But the pervasiveness of anachronism in political theory has been underestimated;[27] and its fuller consequences return us to the question of the tradition which helps identify political theory itself.

Conclusion

A glance at the development of political theory in early modern Europe, roughly spanning Machiavelli to Locke, can illustrate the point. The very notion of a 'development' of political theory during this, or any, time imposes a sequentially anachronistic trajectory: it selects, streamlines and interconnects the theories of a few according to later standards. Yet the political theorist is unlikely to be happy with the notion that there was no development (Dunn 1996: 22–3). If we do not create a description, via

Jardine's predicate extension, in part governed by what is now theoretically salient, the very notion of the political as we understand it may also be jeopardized. Most political theorists are now historically too sensitive to claim that Machiavelli was the first political scientist, or the initiator of modern political theory, but historical qualifications may not have gone far enough. The term 'politics' re-entered the Latin west through Moerbeke's translation of Aristotle's *Politics*, but its range was variable; according to Nicolai Rubinstein, it became narrowed to mean a republican regime (1987: 45ff.). In fact, Machiavelli rarely uses words with the root *polit*, his writings being organized around a notion of the civic, and *la vita civile* (Whitfield 1989: 169–70). To see him as a political theorist, at least in a literal, minimalist sense, presupposes that 'civic' may be translated as 'political', and this predicate extension allows an assimilating completion, or reconstruction, of his thought to our world. Even if, during the succeeding generations, a vocabulary based on the political became altogether more typical, we still cannot assume that the range of the political was co-extensive with modern usage, and that where there was a distinct notion of political discourse, it was related to other forms of discourse in a suitably modern manner. One common use of 'politics' and its cognates indicated no distinct activity called politics at all, but rather a prudential and calculating dimension to any distinct practice. Such uses are still familiar, if less common. Where we do get a sense of distinctly political activity, involving such staples as government, hierarchy, rule and administration, its study is seen as a branch of something else, typically of theology or of law or rhetoric. What we would classify as political theory was likely to be seen as public law; the expression 'political science' meant jurisprudence; and English common lawyers were able to claim that the language of the common law provided an adequate account of English public life.[28] A notion of a specifically political theory was redundant for some, possibly most, now designated political theorists. Similarly, others could see the Bible as a political text. By this was not meant simply that, in a world of intense religious belief, the way in which the Bible was read would have political consequences. The claim was much stronger: namely, that as politics was a branch of religious knowledge, the Bible provided a necessary grounding which some more secular studies might supplement.[29] Again, since antiquity, rhetoric had been a highly organized theory and practice of discourse, taking the political as its typical subject matter. Yet, until recently, this has notoriously been ignored or transmuted into forms of theory more approachable and neoteric, so creating a most systematic example of discursive anachronism.[30] In short, theories of the autonomy of politics, or even a discrete stable identity called political theory, may well rely on descriptive forms of contextual anachronism. Superficially, the absence or eccentricity of appropriately patterned sets of words around 'politics' and 'political theory' might seem to be just a matter of semantics; but to dismiss it as such is tantamount to discounting evidence from which we have to work. Where we can identify political theory, we are apt to posit a horizontal relationship between it and its neighbours rather than a vertical one: the political is subsumed by more authoritative forms of discourse, providing it with priorities and forms of argument.[31] Indeed, one of the things that might be meant by the ambiguous notion of the secularization of political thought is the gradual process by which the political became related more horizontally to its neighbours.[32]

None of this is to deny that conceptions of politics, or a most general, if unhelpful, sense of political theory existed in early modern Europe. Anyone who reflects on some notion of the political may minimally be styled a political theorist (exactly what is not meant now). Rather, the points are that early-modern political theory is more alien and diverse than we have accepted; and that its apparent familiarity is the result of complementary forms of anachronistic reconstruction. We can maintain this familiarity only by truncating and rearranging the intellectual contexts which thus fix the familiar image of 'political theory'; the theorist's habit of discounting the last two parts of *Leviathan* is an example, now fading. A more vibrant instance is the practice of taking 'absolutism' from its jurisprudential and theological contexts, and opposing it to a gradually victorious 'constitutionalism'.[33] We can also ensure the comforts of domesticity by dint of modernizing translations: we can use 'state' for *polis*, *regnum*, *respublica*, commonwealth, *civitas*. And we can avail ourselves of crudely modernizing descriptors, the terms 'ideological' 'radical' and 'left wing' being among the most obvious.[34] By whatever means, we are furnishing a theoretically useable past, but we may also be propagating myths by sleight of tongue. If this causes concern, we might employ qualifications that at once accept and seek to modify the anachronisms of imposing modern political theory upon early modern Europe. Indeed, most theorists have come to see this whole period as one of a gradual emergence of the modern: a world populated by progenitors and proto-people. While some now place the most dubious of descriptors in scare quotes, they keep them nonetheless. What then, do such cautious sops to Clio's regiment really achieve? The predications still characterize the past in terms of the present, so the tensions between historicity and theory may be acknowledged but are not resolved. For the theorist to remain concerned is to contemplate a historiographical abyss. For the historian to look on indifferently is to gaze with the innocence of the bull on quitting the china-shop.

Notes

1　They are not alone: see Monkkonen 1994. The introduction optimistically surveys some of the issues in the use of historical evidence, but shows an uncertain grasp of the disciplinary difficulties in the face of co-operation between historians, economists, geographers and political scientists.

2　A whole series of obvious questions arise if we are going to take this as a factual claim: what canons of 'rationality' are being presupposed; were contemporaries aware of them; how does one account for the overwhelming ethos of vitriol, unreasonableness and dishonesty characteristic of late Stuart public discourse; how well were people informed; were the coffee houses centres of free debate, or clubs where the congenial and converted chatted to each other; how effective had censorship been; what does one make of periodic concentrations of public debate in the previous century, e.g. 1640–42; 1659–60; what has any of this to do with the development of print and newspapers and their ownership; what of the continuing importance of discussion and rational debate by means other than the printed word; did the Industrial Revolution conveniently start in 1760?

3　The decidedly un-Namierite historian Sir Herbert Butterfield is even more revealing of such attitudes in his private moments. Writing to Betty Behrens, he recommended that, discounting a few academic theorists, it was usually advisable to focus on the political aims of writing and to see the theory as only selected means to their achievement: Churchill Archives, Behrens Papers, Behr/Add 14, 7 May 1941.

4　A fuller account of the nature of historical writing is unnecessary here as I am exploring only one commonly accepted feature. More formal philosophical accounts can be found in Dilthey 1977, Max Weber 1949 and Oakeshott 1983. More informal reflections on the nature of their activity have been provided by historians such as E. H. Carr, Geoffrey Elton, Marc Bloch, Herbert Butterfield, Paul Veyne. Common ground is provided by a caveat against anachronism.

5　This is not to deny the alternative possibility, that of mislocating phenomena too late in a sequence of change. This is what David Wootton has called 'parachronism', something he sees modern historians prone to because of their fear of anachronism, 'prochronism' (see Wootton 1994: 414). In one respect 'parachronism' is simply the other side of the same historiographical counterfeit coin, and thus much of what I have to say applies to such post-dating. It is also less relevant in practice to the relationships between history and political theory.

6　Consider, for example, sociology, which exhibits most of the lineal and pro-motional features of the history of the political theory genre (see Swingefield 1991).

7　Peter Laslett's edition of Locke's *Two Treatises* (1960) made clear in practice what could be done.

8　The Cambridge Texts in the History of Political Thought, series editors Quentin Skinner, Raymond Geuss and Richard Tuck, has been the monument to this expansion (see Dunn 1996: 21).

9　If one is considering the phenomenon of game-playing, there may be a good case for having representative figures from an infinite diversity of games; if one is considering a tradition of chess play it is supremely irrelevant to insist on including a marbles player because as a serious game marbles has been rudely ignored.

10 A canon, in short, may be more an obligatory heap than a system, and so piecemeal additions may not destroy its integrity. There is no obvious reason why in English, Wesleyan hymns and detective stories should not be studied along with Beowulf, Milton, Keats, Austen, Swift and Beerbohm. There is no coherent sense of tradition which embraces them all. If one of sufficient generality can be manufactured, the arbitrariness of exclusion becomes even more evident.

11 C. Northcote Parkinson suggested the admission of Indian and Chinese thinkers in order to overcome parochialism in *The Evolution of Political Thought*.

12 For Dunn, the study of political theory remains intensely, but not completely, historical. He also maintains that within political theory there can be both radical heterogeneity and some cumulative wisdom (1996: 12, 22–3).

13 See, for example, the comments of Paul Veyne, echoing Dilthey and Weber, on the difficulties involved in describing the particular through universals which may be confusingly local projections: 1984: 128–30.

14 One recent and challenging theory is that they have more to do with Charles II's struggle for the control of London and its courts than with James II (see Scott 1991, ch. 14; 1993).

15 The same point holds for more synchronic histories, such as Burckhardt's *The Civilisation of the Renaissance in Italy*, if we take narrative as only a diachronic description. It is with the barest terms of description throughout, or at one time, that I am concerned.

16 The argument effectively brackets a whole range of issues partly contained within the problem of description, most importantly concerning the use of general and particular terms. This issue may help explain the practical entanglements of description and explanation: the general term may sometimes be taken to have predictive power; and when used to describe may be taken to entail an explanation.

17 For an account of how theories of resistance can be fashioned almost entirely through historiographical misdescription, see Condren 1994, ch. 4; and 'Liberty of Office and its Defence in Seventeenth-century Political Argument' (forthcoming).

18 Butterfield's *The Whig Interpretation of History* (1931) made this sort of anachronism notorious, to the extent that 'Whiggish' has become a historian's term of abuse. For the criticism that Behrens imposed a dialectical structure on Whig arguments, see Churchill Archives, Behrens Papers, Behr/Add 14, 7 May 1941, p. 5; cf. 17 December 1940 on its not being historically possible to call Clarendon Whig or Tory.

19 As Veyne (1984: 129) asks rhetorically, '[Is] not the history of historiography partly the history of anachronisms caused by ready-made ideas?'

20 It arises from the more defensible view that understanding the alien is not independent of the operations of the mind.

21 Compare the different sorts of priority in the context of contradictory understandings of anachronism in Lowenthal 1993: 50, 216, 241, 228. See also Butterfield, Churchill Archives, Behrens Papers, Behr/Add 14, 7 May 1941, with letter (undated) 1940, and 13 and 21 November 1940 on being 'fair' as a historian and the historiographical problems inhibiting moral judgment. For a more detailed discussion of the tensions in a rhetorical context, see Condren 1988: 14–18.

22 The preface and introduction make it clear that his disquiet with scientific understanding lay in part with its historiographical implausibility.

23   By a similar logic the historian is rarely if ever able to appeal to what a writer would have accepted as a criterion for avoiding anachronism, for that appeal is likely to be part of the interpretative process and not a neutral independent point of reference.

24   It may also be that the logically limiting case is provided by histories of historical writing which in rejecting sequential anachronism portray the past in terms of a movement towards that rejection.

25   A problematic illustration: A solution has been found to the diaphantine equation, 'Fermat's last theorem', $X^n + Y^n = Z^n$, iff the integer is 2, or trivially 0 (see Hardy and Wright 1968, ch. 13). Despite continuity of language, concepts, notions of proof, from the seventeenth century, Wiles's solution is so dependent upon modern mathematics that it cannot be said to be Fermat's (unknown) solution. We cannot therefore simply extend the Wilesian solution backwards historically speaking, although philosophically we might, claiming that Andrew Wiles and Fermat share the same truth asserted in the equation. Assuming that Fermat was not actually mistaken in believing he had a proof, historically the question is how did he establish it within the terms of seventeenth-century mathematics. His solution may have extended those terms, so what later aspect of mathematics might we legitimately evoke in hypothesizing Fermat's solution and what protocols can we use to control the hypothesis?

26   Or consider the emblematic reduction of Hobbes to stand for a certain sort of empiricist claim through which Talcott Parsons and Jurgen Habermas develop their own social theories. As Habermas (1987: 210ff.) correctly remarks, Hobbes is a 'jumping-off point'.

27   David Wootton seems to underestimate the range of anachronism; his evidence that the Levellers really are more modern than historians might think is provided by isolating paraphrased propositions also found later. This itself seems susceptible to some of the entanglements of anachronism.

28   I am abridging the argument in Condren 1994, ch. 1; but for a fine examination of the imperial scope of legal writing, see Burgess 1992.

29   George Lawson, *Politica sacra et civilis* (1660), Epistle to the reader, makes the point explicitly.

30   In the last twenty years this has begun to change, at least with respect to Hobbes scholarship, and Quentin Skinner's recent work promises a further transformation in what sort of political theorist we might take Hobbes to have been. (See, for example, Skinner 1991; 1994: esp. 280ff.; the arguments of which are elaborated in great detail in Skinner 1996.) Whether the rhetorical theorists with whom Hobbes was engaged are reassigned to political theory, or whether the historical recovery of political rhetoric will further fragment our notion of political theory is yet to be seen.

31   If one looks at early modern publishing and library lists, sometimes there is no classification for politics. The works of what we see as political theory are distributed under other headings (religion, law, history); sometimes we do get *libri politici*, but the content is unreliable, neither necessarily including or excluding the sorts of things we might consider appropriate.

32   Secularization seems potentially to cover at least anticlericalism, a decline in religious faith, and erosion or concentration of religious authority. These all might have distinct histories. Before the eighteenth century, certainly, anticlericalism seems driven by intensity of belief, ignoring which has made much politically significant behaviour and writing inexplicable. For lively and specific discussion, see Scott 1989.

33 For a timely discussion of the discursive, sequential and structural anachronisms involved, see Burgess 1996.
34 Historians and political theorists are becoming more aware of the difficulties in the use of such terms. In the 1940s self-conscious historians worrying about historiographical issues could seem quite unaware that 'left' or 'right wing' could be anachronistic. Butterfield, in trying to explain why Tories generally wrote poor pamphlets, simply wrote to Betty Behrens that it is left-wingers who tend to be doctrinaire, a propensity which aids good pamphlet writing; so the Whigs were good, the Tories likely to be bad. Whatever Behrens replied, her essay arising from their discussions writes blithely of the 'Country . . . left' providing most of 'the ideology and personnel of the Whig party'. Cf. Butterfield, Churchill Archives, Behrens Papers, Behr/Add 14, 11 November 1940; Behrens 1941: 42. Fifty years later, hardly any professional historian would be so nescient as Butterfield. The situation is less clear among political theorists and literary scholars.

References

Anon. 1773. *The Monthly Review*, vol. 48.
Behrens, B. 1941. 'The Whig Theory of the Constitution in the Reign of Charles II', *Cambridge Historical Journal*, 7, no. 1.
Boucher, David. 1989. 'Philosophy, History and Practical Life: the Emergence of the History of Political Thought in England', *Australian Journal of Politics and History*, 35.
Burgess, Glenn. 1992. *The Politics of the Ancient Constitution: An Introduction to English Political Thought, 1603–1642*. London: Macmillan.
Burgess, Glenn. 1994. 'On Hobbesian Resistance Theory', *Political Studies*, 42.
Burgess, Glenn. 1996. *Absolute Monarchy and the Stuart Constitution*. New Haven: Yale University Press.
Burrow, J., Collini, S., and Winch, D. 1983. *That Noble Science of Politics*. Cambridge: Cambridge University Press.
Butterfield. H. 1931. *The Whig Interpretation of History*. London: G. Bell.
Churchill Archives, Behrens Papers.
Collingwood, R. G. 1939. *An Autobiography*. Oxford: Clarendon Press.
Collingwood, R. G. 1946. *The Idea of History*. Oxford: Clarendon Press.
Condren, C. 1985. *The Status and Appraisal of Classic Texts*. Princeton: Princeton University Press.
Condren, C. 1988. 'From Premise to Conclusion: Some Comments on Professional History and the Incubus of Rhetorical Historiography', *Parergon* n.s., 6.
Condren, C. 1989. 'Radicals Moderates and Conservatives in Early Modern Political Thought: A Case of Sandwich Islands Syndrome?', *History of Political Thought*, 10.
Condren, C. 1994. *The Language of Politics*. London: Macmillan.
Condren, C. Forthcoming. 'Liberty of Office and its Defence in Seventeenth-Century Political Argument' *History of Political Thought*.
Dilthey, W. 1977. *Understanding Other Persons and Their Forms of Life*, trans. R. M. Zaner. The Hague: Martinus Nijhof.

Dunn, J. 1966. *The History of Political Theory and Other Essays*. Cambridge: Cambridge University Press.

Gallie, W. B. 1964. *Philosophy and the Historical Understanding*. London: Chatto and Windus.

Gunnell, John. 1978. 'The Myth of the Tradition', *American Political Science Review*, 72.

Gunnell, John. 1979. *Political Theory: Tradition and Interpretation*. Cambridge Mass.: Winthrop Publishers.

Habermas, Jurgen. 1987. *The Theory of Communicative Action: Life World and System: A Critique of Functionalist Reason*, trans. Thomas McCarthy. Cambridge: Polity Press.

Habermas, Jurgen. 1992. *The Structural Transformation of the Public Sphere*, trans. Thomas Burger assisted by Frederick Lawrence. London: Polity Press.

Hardy G. H., and Wright, E. M. 1968. *An Introduction to the Theory of Numbers*. Oxford: Clarendon Press.

Jardine, N. 1980. ' "Realistic" Realism and the Progress of Science', in Christopher Hookway and Philip Pettit, eds, *Action and Interpretation*. Cambridge: Cambridge University Press.

Kavka, Gregory S. 1988. 'Some Neglected Liberal Aspects of Hobbes's Philosophy', *Hobbes Studies*, 1.

Koselleck, R. 1985. *Futures Past: On the Semantics of Historical Time*, trans. K. Tribe. Cambridge, Mass.: MIT Press.

Kuhn, Thomas S. 1962. *The Structure of Scientific Revolutions*. Chicago: Chicago University Press.

Lamont, W. 1979. *Richard Baxter and the Millennium*. London: Croom Helm.

Locke, John. 1960. *Two Treatises of Government*, ed. P. Laslett. Cambridge: Cambridge University Press.

Leslie, M. 1970. 'In Defence of Anachronism', *Political Studies*, 18.

Levinson, J. 1962. *Confucian China and its Modern Fate*. London: Routledge, Kegan Paul.

Lovejoy, A. O. 1940. 'Reflections on the History of Ideas', *Journal of the History of Ideas*, 1.

Lowenthal, D. 1985 edn. *The Past is Foreign Country*. Cambridge: Cambridge University Press.

Martin, Rex. 1995. 'Collingwood's Claim that Metaphysics is an Historical Discipline', in David Boucher, James Connelly and Tariq Modood, eds, *Philosophy, History and Civilisation*. Cardiff: University of Wales Press.

Monkkonen, E. H., ed. 1994. *Engaging the Past: The Uses of History across the Social Sciences*. Durham, NC: Duke University Press.

Nadel, George. 1965. 'The Philosophy of History before Historicism', in Nadel, ed., *Studies in the Philosophy of History*. New York: Harper.

Oakeshott, M. 1983. *On History and Other Essays*. Oxford: Blackwell.

Pocock, J. G. A. 1957. *The Ancient Constitution and the Feudal Law*. Cambridge: Cambridge University Press.

Pocock, J. G. A. 1962a. 'The History of Political Thought: A Methodological Enquiry', in Peter Laslett and W. G. Runciman, eds, *Philosophy, Politics and Society*. Oxford: Blackwell.

Pocock, J. G. A. 1962b. 'The Origins of the Study of the Past: A Comparative Approach', *Comparative Studies in Society and History*.

Rorty, R., Schneewind, J. B., and Skinner, Q., eds., 1984. *Philosophy in History*. Cambridge: Cambridge University Press.

Rubinstein, N. 1987. 'The History of the Word *Politicus*', in A. Pagden, ed., *The Languages of Political Theory in Early Modern Europe*. Cambridge: Cambridge University Press.

Scott, J. 1989. 'England's Troubles: Exhuming the Popish Plot', in T. Harris, M. Goldie and P. Seaward, eds, *The Politics of Religion in Restoration England*. Oxford: Blackwell.

Scott, J. 1991. *Algernon Sidney and the Restoration Crisis, 1677–83*. Cambridge: Cambridge University Press.

Scott, J. 1993. 'The Law of War: Grotius, Sidney, Locke and the Political Theory of Rebellion', *History of Political Thought*, 14.

Skinner, Q. 1969. 'Meaning and Understanding in the History of Ideas', *History and Theory*, 8.

Skinner, Q. 1991. 'Thomas Hobbes: Rhetoric and the Construction of Morality', *Proceedings of the British Academy*, 76.

Skinner, Q. 1994. 'Moral Ambiguity and the Renaissance Art of Eloquence', *Essays in Criticism*, 44.

Skinner, Q. 1996. *Reason and Rhetoric in the Philosophy of Thomas Hobbes*. Cambridge: Cambridge University Press.

Smitt, Charles. 1988. 'The Rise of the Philosophical Textbook,' in Quentin Skinner and Eckhard Kessler, eds, *The Cambridge History of Renaissance Philosophy*. Cambridge: Cambridge University Press.

Swingefield, Alan. 1991 [1984]. *A Short History of Sociological Thought*. London: Macmillan.

Veyne, Paul. 1984. *Writing History: Essay on Epistemology*, trans. M. Moore-Rinvolucri. Manchester: Manchester University Press.

Weber, Max. 1949. *The Methodology of the Social Sciences*, trans. E. A. Shils and H. A. Finch. Glencoe, Ill.

Whitfield, W. H. 1989. *Discourses on Machiavelli*. Cambridge: Heffer.

Winch, Donald. 1978. *Adam Smith's Politics: An Essay in Historiographical Revision*. Cambridge: Cambridge University Press.

Wootton, David. 1994. 'Leveller Democracy and the Puritan Revolution', in J. H. Burns, ed., *The Cambridge History of Political Thought, 1450–1700*. Cambridge: Cambridge University Press.

CHAPTER 3

Utilitarianism as a Public Philosophy

Robert E. Goodin

Utilitarianism is a doctrine which, in its standard nineteenth-century formulation, directs us to produce 'the greatest happiness'.[1] In its most useful modern reformulation, it is 'the moral theory that judges the goodness of outcomes – and therefore the rightness of actions insofar as they affect outcomes – by the degree to which they secure the greatest benefit to all concerned' (Hardin 1988: xv).

Utilitarianism is an ethical theory with political consequences. It is an ethical theory in the sense that it tells us what is right and wrong, good and bad. It is political in that some of its most central pronouncements touch upon the conduct of public life. Indeed, it purports to provide a complete political theory, a complete normative guide for the conduct of public affairs.

An 'ethic' is, strictly speaking, a theory of the good and bad, right and wrong. The term, however, has come to connote more narrowly a theory of right conduct at the level of personal conduct. Ethics has come to be seen, quintessentially, as an answer to the question of 'What should I do?' What is central to ethics thus understood is our intimate, individual affairs. What it is that is right for us to do jointly, in the conduct of our public lives, is seen to derive from that.

Of course, this line of thought is quite right, in one sense. From most modern perspectives, if not from certain more ancient ones, The Politics always has to be parasitic upon The Ethics. Any political theory that purports to tell us what we should do (in more than a crassly prudential or pragmatic sense of 'should') needs an ethical theory of some sort or another to provide its normative bite. Here I shall be disputing whether that normative theory necessarily has to be parasitic upon – to be rooted in, to have its primary application to, to be tested first and foremost against its implications for – personal conduct.

My thesis is that at least one normative theory, utilitarianism, can be a good normative guide to public affairs without its necessarily being the best practical guide to personal conduct. It is right there, too, after a fashion. But special circumstances confound the direct application of utilitarianism to personal affairs. In such circumstances, utilitarianism recommends that people's conduct be guided by more indirectly utilitarian mechanisms – obeying rules of conduct or developing traits of character, themselves chosen on utilitarian bases, rather than trying to apply the utilitarian calculus directly in each instance.

There are special circumstances governing public life, too, however. Just as the special circumstances of private life are such as to drive us away from utilitarianism in any direct form, so the special circumstances of public life are such as to drive us toward it. Those special circumstances make public life particularly conducive to the forthright application of utilitarian doctrine. Indeed, in my view, they make it almost indecent to apply any other.

Rejecting Reductios

My larger argument is that there are strong interrelationships between political theory and public policy, each having much to teach the other. Most of the cross-fertilization to be discussed will be substantial in character. At the outset, however, let us look to a more methodological plane.

One of the more interesting phenomena in public policy, with clear counterparts in political theory, is the phenomenon of 'a solution in search of a problem' (Olsen 1972; March and Olsen 1976). This reverses the ordinary order of rational decision-making, which (according to certain narrow-minded canons of rationality) ought to start with a problem and proceed linearly toward a solution. In another way, though, it makes perfectly good sense to start the other way around. Often we discover nifty tricks or techniques, having no immediate use for them, or having initially developed them for one purpose to which we now find them ill-suited; we simply store them away in our tool kit for use later. Like any good artisan, when presented with problems we look first to our existing tool kit to see if we have something readily to hand that is suited to the task, rather than fashioning a wholly new instrument for every task.

In the realm of public policy-making, the clearest cases of this phenomenon, as so many others, come in connection with weapons acquisition. Take the case of the cruise missile, for example. It was first seriously mooted within the United States military establishment as an unarmed decoy to draw Soviet fire away from B-52 bombers. Later proposals offered it, in armed form, as the essential weaponry for a 'stand-off bomber' that could destroy targets without penetrating enemy airspace.

Later still, it was offered in land- and sea-based forms as a ground-hugging missile that could evade enemy radar (Levine 1977). Across its various incarnations, the problems differ but the solution – the cruise missile – remains the same.

Within the realm of political theory, the fate of utilitarianism is not very different. In the megalomaniacal phrases of its founder and early advocates, of course, utilitarianism was touted as a universal panacea – for ethical problems large and small, simple and complex, personal and impersonal, public and private, individual and collective.[2]

In a way, the founders were right to present their theory in this fashion. The value theory underlying utilitarianism is such that it should apply equally to all those realms. There are no grounds, within utilitarianism, for restricting the scope of its own application. Should utilitarianism turn out to constitute a credible theory only within some more restricted realm, that would prove to be a serious flaw, for utilitarianism provides no internal grounds for circumscribing its own scope in such ways.

Theories with such universal pretensions inevitably present their opponents with easy targets. A single counter-example defeats a universal claim, and anti-utilitarians have been ingenious in concocting painfully cute counter-examples. These counter-examples have depicted merely (often barely) possible worlds, more often than probable ones; they have been contrived, more often than commonplace. But no matter. Its universalist pretensions make utilitarianism absolutely fair game for purveyors of such fantasies.

One perfectly viable alternative for utilitarians confronted with such fantastic scenarios is for them simply to wear such embarrassment. What those counter-examples do – all that they do – is to conjure up a situation in which doing the utility-maximizing thing would lead to intuitively unappealing results. The circumstances they depict, however, are far from those to which our standard intuitions are shaped. (They involve things like promises to dying friends on otherwise unpopulated desert islands, 'super-efficient pleasure machines', and such like.) Precisely because of that, we may well decide that it is our intuitions rather than the utilitarian prescriptions that ought to be readjusted in such unusual circumstances. The right way to treat anti-utilitarians who offer such contrived counter-examples might well be to out-smart them, embracing what they offer as a reductio as being actually the correct (however counter-intuitive) solution to such (decidedly non-standard) situations.[3]

Patently crazy counter-examples, however, only ever formed part of the critics' case against utilitarianism. Another important strand has to do with the inappropriateness of utilitarianism as a code of personal conduct. These criticisms, too, are licensed by utilitarianism's universalist

pretensions. It has – given its universalistic pretensions – direct implications for personal conduct. So to some extent utilitarianism was always
going to have to lay itself open to this line of attack.

Friends of utilitarianism have tended to lead with their chins in this
regard. There was an important shift among utilitarian writers that came
somewhere between Sidgwick's 1874 *Methods of Ethics* (where public
affairs loomed large) and G. E. Moore's 1903 *Principia Ethics* (where the
greatest good is defined in terms of more private ideals, such as friendship and aesthetic appreciation). Whatever the cause of that shift, its
consequences could not have been more deleterious to the proper
defence of the utilitarian cause.

Throughout the twentieth century, defenders of utilitarianism have
been primarily concerned to defend it in its least plausible form, as a
code of personal conduct. They have retained that focus even when, of
late, reapplying it to public affairs (see Singer 1979; Brandt 1979; 1992,
esp. chs 12–19). To them, the question of war is whether we individually
should kill enemy soldiers or defenceless civilians, rather than whether
we collectively should wage pointless wars. The question of famine is seen
as whether we individually should send food to the starving, rather than
as whether we collectively should work to reform social structures and
consequent exchange entitlements (contrast Singer 1972 with Drèze and
Sen 1989).

Attacks upon utilitarianism as a personal code are on powerful
grounds. No one wants to run one's life like Gradgrind, the Dickensian
parody of a good utilitarian. Furthermore, no one can: the calculative
load imposed by utilitarian maximization would absorb all one's time
and attention, leaving none for acting on the conclusions of the calculations. In personal life, most dramatically, there simply has to be more
scope for considerations of uncalculating affection, standing rules of
conduct and qualities of character.

With enough twisting and turning, of course, you can get from anywhere to anywhere. But that is no defence: the sheer fact that twisting
and turning is required in itself constitutes a telling criticism (Barry
1989: 341). If that is where you want to end up – if what centrally matters,
in an assessment of an ethical theory, is its ability to give a clear and
coherent account of ordinary intuitions about how we ought conduct
our personal affairs – then it seems that utilitarianism is not a good place
to start.

Of course, utilitarianism does purport to give an account of how to
lead our personal and public lives. Furthermore, early, straightforward
and frankly simple-minded applications of the utilitarian maxim to
personal ethical dilemmas have, of late, given way to more sophisticated
accounts that take due notice of the 'limits of reason' facing isolated

individual choosers in their own daily lives. The upshot is a utilitarian theory of personal morality much nearer to ordinary intuitions.

But that is a defence of utilitarianism at it weakest. If well-defended on that front, utilitarianism might avoid being dismissed on those grounds alone. However good that defence, though, it is in the nature of defensive manoeuvres that they only ever avert defeat: they never actually secure victory. The most we might hope is that those defences of utilitarianism as a personal ethical code might prevent people from dismissing it. No one is going to embrace utilitarianism for the brilliance of its answer to those conundrums alone.

Public versus Private Moralities

The strength of utilitarianism, the problem to which it is a truly compelling solution, is as a guide to public rather than private conduct. There, virtually all its vices – all the things that make us wince in recommending it as a code of personal morality – loom instead as considerable virtues.

Consider first the raft of criticisms couched in terms of the *impersonality* of utilitarianism. Like all universalist philosophies, utilitarianism asks us to take 'the view from nowhere'. There is no obvious place within utilitarian theories for people's idiosyncratic perspectives, histories, attachments, loyalties or personal commitments.

The essence of the communitarian challenge is that everyone comes from somewhere. There are no free-floating individuals, of the sort with which liberals generally, and utilitarians paradigmatically, populate their moral theories (Sandel 1982; 1984; Kymlicka 1989; Avineri and de-Shalit 1992). People have, and upon reflection we think they should have, principled commitments and personal attachments of various sorts.

As an account of the peculiar role responsibilities of public officials (and, by extension, of ordinary individuals in their public capacities as citizens) that vice becomes a virtue, though. Those agents, too, have to come from somewhere, bringing with them a whole raft of baggage of personal attachments, commitments, principles and prejudices. In their public capacities, however, we think it only right and proper that they should stow that baggage as best they can.

Complete neutrality might be an impossible ideal, but it seems indisputable that it is an ideal which people in their public capacities should strive to realize. That is a central part of what it is to be a public official. Public servants should serve the public at large and not play favourites.

Or consider, again, criticisms revolving around the theme that utilitarianism is a coldly *calculating* doctrine.[4] In personal affairs that is an unattractive feature. There, we would like to suppose that certain sorts of actions proceed immediately from the heart, without much reflection, much less any real calculation of consequences. Among intimates it would be extremely hurtful to think of every kind gesture as being contrived to produce some particular effect.

The case of public officials is, once again, precisely the opposite. There, it is the height of irresponsibility to proceed careless of the consequences. Public officials are, above all else, obliged to take care: not to go off half-cocked, not to let their hearts rule their heads. In Hare's telling example, the worst thing that might be said of the Suez misadventure was not that the British and French did some perfectly awful things (which is true, too) but that they did them so utterly unthinkingly (Hare 1957).

Related to the critique of utilitarianism as a calculating doctrine is the critique of utilitarianism as a *consequentialist* doctrine. According to utilitarianism, the effects of an action are everything. There are no actions which are, in and of themselves, morally right or wrong, good or bad. The only things that are good or bad are the effects that actions produce.

That proposition runs counter to certain ethical intuitions which, at least in certain quarters, are rooted deeply. Those who harbour a Ten-Commandment view of the nature of morality see a moral code as being essentially as a list of 'thou shalts' and 'thou shalt nots' – a list of things that are right or wrong in and of themselves, quite regardless of any consequences that might come from doing them (Anscombe 1958; Williams 1973; Fried 1978).

That may or may not be a good way to run one's private affairs. Even those who think it is, however, tend to concede that it is no way to run public affairs. It is in the nature of the role responsibilities of public officials that they are morally obliged to 'dirty their hands' – make hard choices, do things that are wrong (or would ordinarily be wrong, or would be wrong for ordinary private individuals) in the service of some greater public good. It would be irresponsible of public officials (in any broadly secular society, at least) to adhere mindlessly to moral precepts read off some sacred list, literally 'whatever the consequences'.[5] Doing right though the heavens fall is not a particularly attractive posture for public officials to adopt.

Yet other critics berate utilitarianism not so much because it dictates maximization and thus engenders a coldly calculating, consequentialistic attitude, but rather because of what it would have us maximize. There is, such critics say, something necessarily *crass* about whatever utilitarians take as their maximand. That maximand has subtly shifted over the years. Modern utilitarians now go well beyond Bentham's calculus of pains and pleasures, so it is no longer true to say that utilitarianism is necessarily a crassly 'hedonic' philosophy. But dress up their maximand as they will, modern utilitarians must necessarily be involved in maximizing satisfactions. Genuinely 'higher' concerns are genuinely hard to accommodate within utilitarianism. The higher they are, the less of a place such higher ideals have within any genuinely utilitarian framework.

Aesthetes bemoan the poverty of a life lived according to such purely utilitarian precepts. If beauty lies only in the eye of the beholder, then it amounts to no more than an illusion which we create for ourselves; and beauty is emptied of any independent value. If there is nothing that is good in and of itself, then there is no external standard by which to validate our subjective valuations. There is nothing to live for, nothing to die for. We are ourselves the only ultimate source of value in the universe. The external world of values is thus demystified, but at the same time diminished for us. For aesthetes, no one would want to live their lives in a utilitarian universe so empty of external meanings and values.

Here again, what would diminish private life is perfectly suitable for circumscribing public life. The classically utilitarian habit of asking 'Of what use is it to me?' (or in more public-spirited fashion, 'Of what use is it to us?') may be a crass way of judging what to do in one's personal affairs. There may well be some things that are good or bad, right or wrong, for private individuals to be or to represent or to do, whether or not they would be of any use to anyone. Whatever we might say of the merits of that as a personal code, it has distinctly limited appeal as a guide for public officials.

Even if it would be right for private individuals to adopt a code of pointless self-sacrifice, it seems transparently wrong for public officials to impose such sacrifices upon any who refuse to undertake them voluntarily. The root intuition here is perhaps best captured by saying that rulers have no right to wage holy wars – anyway, not ones waged on behalf of gods in whom their subjects no longer have any faith.

Forms of Utilitarianism

Perhaps it is now novel to look at utilitarianism as a public philosophy. In earlier times, it was more of a commonplace to suggest that utilitarianism constitutes a solution to public, rather than personal, moral problems; to defend it as a public philosophy, rather than as a personal moral code.

That much is clearly suggested by reflection upon the corpus and the personal history of the founders of the utilitarian tradition (Halévy 1928; Plamenatz 1958). Jeremy Bentham was famous in his own day primarily as a reformer of legal systems; James Mill as an essayist on government; John Stuart Mill as an essayist, social reformer and parliamentarian; John Austin as a jurisprude. The bulk of Bentham's large corpus is given over to constitutional codes, systems for penal reform, and such like. The two Mills fixed their focus equally firmly on public affairs ranging from histories of British India to political economy and women's suffrage.[6]

Over the years, there have grown up a great many diverse forms of utilitarianism. To some extent, this amounts to distinction-mongering for the sheer sake of it. The distinctions do matter – but mainly for the fine-grained forms of utilitarianism which might properly characterize personal moral codes but which cannot characterize public ones. If my survey of a hundred years' worth of analytic work in this area seems cavalier, riding roughshod over distinctions which have been honed by many hands with loving care, that is only because those fine distinctions are irrelevant or worse for the rough-and-ready form of utilitarianism which is the only form that public officials can deploy.

One dimension, already alluded to, along which these various utilitarianisms differ concerns the *content* of the utilitarian maximand. In its Benthamite formulation, it was some state of mind ('happiness'; 'the balance of pleasure over pain') that was supposed to be maximized. That variant can be called 'hedonic (or hedonistic) utilitarianism'. Subsequent utilitarians, whilst preserving the basic spirit, watered down its hedonism. First came the recognition that people sometimes derive satisfaction from things that do not literally give them a pleasurable buzz: that recognition gave rise to a revised utilitarianism that would have us maximize 'preference satisfaction' (call this 'preference utilitarianism'). Next came the recognition that people sometimes would derive satisfaction from something in a way that they do not presently recognize: that gave rise to a further revised utilitarianism that would have us maximize people's 'interests' or 'welfare' (call this 'welfare utilitarianism').[7]

The last is the form of utilitarianism that I shall be advocating. That choice is an easy one. In this list, each successive refinement subsumes the former. Preference utilitarianism subsumes hedonic utilitarianism, assuming that people ordinarily actually prefer (among other things) to experience pleasure and avoid pain. Welfare utilitarianism subsumes preference utilitarianism, assuming that promoting people's welfare interests will ordinarily lead to higher levels of preference satisfaction in the future. What is added with each refinement in the list is something which anyone working within the spirit of utilitarianism should surely want to incorporate among sources of utility.

While that choice of welfare utilitarianism is driven primarily by philosophical considerations, it is also ratified by pragmatic considerations concerning the peculiar circumstances of policy choice in the public sphere. People's pleasures vary, their preferences are idiosyncratic. Basic interests, in contrast, are pretty standard across all individuals. Policymakers, of necessity, make choices that affect a wide range of people.

They might well be overwhelmed by the diversity of pleasures and preferences; if that were the focus dictated by the most philosophically credible form of utilitarianism, they might be forced to abandon utilitarianism as a public philosophy. Their task is rendered far more manageable by the relative commonality of people's basic welfare interests.

Utilitarianisms also differ in the *modal status*, as well as in the content, of the maximand. The crux is whether we should be concerned only with what is actually there – only with real people, their preferences, their pleasures and pains, their welfare – or whether we should allow our maximizing to range across all possible people (and their preferences, pleasures or pains, welfare). While 'welfare utilitarianism' is my own favoured variety, the differences here in view come out most clearly with reference to 'preference utilitarianism'.

One strand of utilitarianism would have us maximize preference satisfaction across all possible preferences and people. That, arguably, is the classically Benthamite approach. But it leads to 'repugnant conclusions' for population policy: maximizing utility in that way would lead to a population explosion, as we bring more people into the world up to the point where any new person's utility from being born is outweighed by the disutility that that extra person's existence causes to everyone already there (Parfit 1984: 381–91). That is what is wrong with maximizing preference satisfaction across all possible people. What is wrong with maximizing preference satisfaction across all possible preferences is that it leads to absurdly 'adaptive preferences': if you cannot get what you want, you should simply revise your preferences so you want what you can easily get. The ancient Stoics thought that a good idea, but surely few of us would find the satisfaction of preferences chosen on that basis alone all that satisfying.

Another form of utilitarianism focuses on satisfying actual preferences of actual people. That would certainly avoid each of those problems posed above. But it would also debar utilitarians from doing one of the things that utilitarians have always wanted to do. That is to use utilitarian criteria to guide policy-makers in choosing among a whole range of alternative devices (ranging from legal institutions to educational curricula) by which people are socialized in one way rather than another and, in so doing, by which their preferences are shaped. Perhaps it is that aspiration itself that utilitarians ought abandon. But upon reflection, perhaps there is no need for them to do so.

The example deployed above against letting utilitarianism range over all possible preferences is an argument couched in terms of what might be called 'directly' adaptive preferences. Perhaps the satisfaction of easily satisfied preferences is not really satisfying when you have chosen those preferences precisely because they will be easy to satisfy. But perhaps the satisfaction of such preferences would be not at all unsatisfying if those preferences had been inculcated in you by some external agency, some socialization device, which was itself intentionally chosen for just those attributes by some utilitarian social planner. Arm's-length, indirectly adaptive preference formation – which is, after all, the principal form that public policy-makers practise – might well be able to serve utility-maximizing ends, even if directly adaptive preferences cannot.

I am inclined to commend a form of utilitarianism which takes actual people as given, but which maximizes across all their possible preferences. Perhaps the easiest way of making that case is merely to recall that people's preferences are bound to undergo changes between the time their choices are made and the time the consequences of those choices are felt. Clearly, anyone moved by the spirit underlying utilitarianism should say that we ought to look at the preferences which those people will actually have by the time the consequences are felt, rather than upon the preferences which they had when the choice was made but which have long since disappeared.

That form of utilitarianism has further virtues: it is consistent with our utilitarian desire to employ our principles to shape socialization, and with the form of welfare-utilitarianism that we have other reasons for favouring. The most plausible way to construe 'welfare interests' is, after all, as a form of 'possible preferences' – as those things which people counterfactually would favour, under certain privileged circumstances which do not necessarily prevail.

Finally, to complete this short survey, various utilitarianisms differ according to what they regard as the appropriate *object* of the utility calculus. What is it that the utility calculus is to be used to choose? 'Act utilitarianism' says that each of our actions, one-by-one, should be chosen so as to maximize overall utility. 'Rule utilitarianism,' in contrast, says that we should employ the utility calculus to choose among rules (habits, norms, patterns of behaviour) in such a way as to maximize over-all utility. That pretty well exhausts the traditional catalogue of options (Lyons 1965; Smart 1967; 1973; Hare 1981; Hardin 1988). To that tradi-tional catalogue have recently been added proposals for using the utility calculus to choose motivational structures, or character traits, which will in turn maximize overall utility (Adams 1976; Brandt 1988; 1992: 263–89).

The crucial argument usually offered in favour of act utilitarianism goes as follows. In any given instance, either act utilitarianism and rule or motive utilitarianism recommend we do the same thing; or else act utilitarianism recommends that we do one thing, whereas following rules or motives chosen on utilitarian grounds would have us doing some-thing else. In the former case, the other forms of utilitarianism are extensionally equivalent to act utilitarianism. Wherever they differ in their recommendations, they are inferior to act utilitarianism on straightforwardly utilitarian grounds: slavishly following a rule or disposition chosen on utilitarian grounds, when more utility could be achieved by doing something else, cannot be the utilitarian thing to do.

That argument is compelling in its own terms. But its terms are not of this world, for individual moral agents or (more especially) for social policy-makers, either. The argument presupposes that we are able to perform utility calculations that typically range across an enormous number of individuals and options – and that we are able to do so reliably, instantaneously and without cost. This is to assume away the 'limits of reason' that characterize the real world for individual agents and, all the more so, for social policy-makers.

The arguments in favour of some form of rule utilitarianism at the social level (and, correlatively, some form of motive utilitarianism at the individual level) are built in large part out of those limits of reason. At the individual level, rules serve to maximize utility in the real world, in a way that act-by-act calculations of utility cannot, by being easier to communicate, easier to inculcate, easier to remember, and easier to apply (Hare 1981; Hardin 1988).

Crucially, at the social level, rules are publicly accessible in a way that private utility calculations are not. In an ideal world in which everyone had perfect information, anyone could replicate anyone else's utility calculations. But in the real world, no one has perfect information; and, furthermore, each of us is privy to different bits of the overall picture. Thus, what I think, given what I know, is the best act-utilitarian action for you to perform may not be (typically is not) the action that you think, given what you know, is the one that act-utilitarianism would most highly recommend to you.

That matters because much of the utility that utilitarians would have us maximize comes from co-ordinating the actions of a great many individual agents. Often the only way to maximize the utility that arises from my act is by knowing (or guessing) what others are likely to do. But knowing that with any certainty is, for the reasons just given, impossible in a world populated by act-utilitarian agents. The best way to co-ordinate our actions with others, and thereby maximize the utility from each of our actions as individuals, as well as from all of our actions collectively, is to promulgate rules (themselves chosen with an eye to maximizing utility, of course) and to adhere to them.[8]

If adherence to rules is justified in these terms, then there is no risk of the sort of 'rule fetishism' of which act utilitarians complain in their critiques of rule utilitarianism. We choose the rule because it is the one which would yield more utility overall than would general adherence to any other rule. We follow that rule, in its various edicts, because we think that the effects will maximize utility, either directly or indirectly. We follow that rule even where we are pretty confident that doing so will not maximize utility in that instance, because of the larger general benefits to be had by society at large (and, incidentally, by us individually) from our being known by others to be rule-followers. But when, just occasionally, following a rule would have truly grievous utility consequences, we would be perfectly licensed to abandon the rule by the self-same logic that led us to adopt rules and generally to follow them. Rule utilitarians can, thus, lie to Nazis about the Jews hidden in their attic, in a way that Kantian rule-followers might find hard.

Replies to Some Standard Objections

In like fashion, the public rather than private application of utilitarian precepts helps us evade some of the most standard practical objections to the doctrine. Primary among them is the objection that utilitarianism can never be implemented in practice, because it requires us to engage in impossible 'interpersonal utility comparisons'.[9]

Whatever course of conduct we pursue, there are likely to be some people who gain and others who lose. If we are supposed to be maximizing utility across all those people, we obviously need some standard for comparing the gains of the one group with the losses of the other. Critics, however, have complained that we have no way of getting inside another's head, experiencing their pleasures and pains as they do themselves. In Jevons's famous phrase, 'Every mind is inscrutable to every other mind . . . [so] no common denominator of feeling is possible.' That is said to render utilitarian maximization impossible, for all practical purposes (Jevons 1911: 14. Robbins 1932: 122–5; 1938).

In the absence of interpersonal comparisons, the most we can have are the weak Pareto-style comparisons upon which so much of modern welfare economics rests. We can say a state of affairs is indisputably superior to another if someone is better off and no one worse off. But that Pareto principle suffers from various defects: it is indecisive, leaving altogether too many alternatives unranked (in any large-scale application, most options will make at least a few people worse off); and it is essentially conservative (redistribution of resources can never be justified on utility-maximizing grounds if we have no way to say that gainers would gain more than losers would lose). Such problems have driven welfare economists to a variety of ruses to reinstate something akin to interpersonal comparisons, whether through the 'hypothetical compensation test' of Kaldor and Hicks, or through the focus upon 'primary goods' in Rawls or 'capabilities' in Sen (Hicks 1939; Kaldor 1939; 1946–47; Rawls 1971: 90–5; Sen 1982a: 203–4; 1985a).

That latter strategy of making interpersonal comparisons via something akin to welfare interests is particularly apt.[10] The objection to interpersonal comparisons was only ever compelling against now-abandoned forms of crude hedonistic utilitarianism, anyway. To compare pleasures and pains across individuals, we may well need to get inside one another's heads. But that is unnecessary, once we have shifted to talking of what counter-factually *would* give them pleasure or pain. To answer such questions, we necessarily abstract from what actually does give them pleasure to what would (more food, healthier lives and so on). Having abstracted from actual preferences to hypothetical preferences, there ceases to be any barrier of a strictly metaphysical sort to comparing those abstractions across individuals. We are working well outside their heads already.

Practical people engaged in the real business of the world have always found it hard to take seriously such worries about interpersonal utility comparisons. Typical of their reaction is that of Pigou, who scoffs, 'Nobody can prove that anybody besides himself exists, but, nevertheless, everybody is quite sure of it' (Pigou 1951: 292; cf. Little 1957, ch. 4; Barry 1965: 44–7).

There are ways of making these worries look more than a little silly. Public debate, deliberation and even conversation would, on the selfsame grounds, prove impossible. If the problem with interpersonal comparisons of utility is that we cannot look into other minds, then there is a parallel problem with looking into their minds to see what they mean when uttering a statement. That does not stop us from talking – or even, after a fashion, conversing. We simply employ a 'principle of charity': we assume that they, like us, try to talk sense, and we ascribe meaning to their utterances accordingly. In trying to make sense of interpersonal utility comparisons, we need do no more than that. We need simply assume that others are much like ourselves, and act accordingly. Interpersonal interactions could not proceed otherwise – neither could politics.

Such procedures, inevitably, give rise to comparisons of utility that are only rough and ready. But perhaps it would amount to spurious precision to strive for more, given the various other uncertainties and ambiguities that characterize the context in which public policies are made. It would be folly to strive for accuracy to the fourth decimal place in one element of our utility sums, when other elements of it are reliable only to the first. That concession, if true, means that there will inevitably be some imprecision in our public utility calculations. It follows that utilitarian policy recommendations will still be indeterminate. That is not necessarily a telling criticism of utilitarianism, though. It merely amounts to saying that utilitarianism leaves some room for public debate and deliberation – in other words, for politics as ordinarily conceived. We would, I think, worry about any political theory that did not do that.[11]

Furthermore, even where utilitarianism proves indeterminate, it sets the terms of that public debate. It tells us what sorts of considerations ought to weigh with us, while often allowing that how heavily each of them actually weighs is legitimately open to dispute. Even where utilitarianism is indeterminate, it is not silent. To fill in those lacunae, we do not need to turn to other principles. Rather, in such cases utilitarianism speaks with many voices, and political argument can consist simply in a debate among them.

Once we have at least rough-and-ready interpersonal comparisons on the table, we can resume discussing the utilitarian merits of alternative distributions of the national dividend. Of course, which distribution utilitarianism recommends depends upon certain empirical facts. That in itself has long been taken to be a criticism of utilitarianism. If the facts turn out one particular way, utilitarianism might find itself recommending distributional policies that are intuitively outrageous.

Utilitarianism might recommend feeding Christians to the lions, if it so happens that the utilities of the spectators enjoying the show (plus that of the lions enjoying the meal) exceed the disutilities of the Christians being sacrificed. Or utilitarianism might recommend dissecting one person and distributing her body parts to various others in need of transplants, if it so happens that the utilities of the recipients exceed the disutility of the 'donor'. Or utilitarianism might recommend the hanging of an innocent person to assuage an angry mob, if it so happens that the utilities of those spared the mob's wrath exceed the disutility of the hanging victim. Or utilitarianism might recommend giving all resources to a handful of people, if it so happens that those people are 'super-efficient pleasure machines' capable of translating resources into satisfaction at a fantastic rate; or it might recommend giving no resources to the handicapped, if it so happens that those people are particularly inept at translating resources into satisfaction.

There is no denying that utilitarian prescriptions might turn out that way. There is no telling how the numbers will come up in each and every case. But, again, advocating utilitarianism as a public philosophy spares us the burdens associated with maximizing at the margins in each and every case. It involves instead adopting institutions and policies, on a utilitarian basis; and those must be publicly accessible and relatively long-lasting. That means that in choosing institutions and practices and policies we cannot maximize at the margins, adapting our choices to peculiarities of utility mixes in particular cases. We must instead adapt our choices to standard situations recurring across protracted periods, and do so in full knowledge that the nature of our choices will sooner or later become common knowledge.

That fact ensures, in part, that utilitarianism, as a public philosophy, will have few grievous distributional consequences. Many of the cases involving sacrificing the interests of the few to the many generate the purported utilitarian payoffs only if they never become public knowledge. Once it is known that, as a matter of policy, we are willing to hang innocent people to assuage a baying mob or to carve up one person to generate spare parts for others, then everyone starts worrying, 'Who will be next?' The anxieties associated with such thoughts occurring among the whole population more than suffice to cancel the utility advantages of carving up one person or throwing one prisoner to the mob on any given occasion.

Utilitarianism, as a public philosophy, must adopt institutions, practices and policies suited to recurring standard situations and individuals. There may be a very few people who are vastly better and a very few who are vastly worse than others at translating resources into utility. But assuming, with Bentham and his followers, that most people are pretty much alike in this respect – and assuming, further, that most goods display 'diminishing marginal utility' – then the utility-maximizing distribution of resources will inevitably be a broadly egalitarian one.

Anti-utilitarians complain loudly that utilitarianism disregards the morally crucial fact of the 'separateness' of persons.[12] That complaint is, however, untrue in two crucial respects. First, utilitarians regard each person as a distinct locus of value: in generating the utilities that end up being aggregated, 'each counts for one and no one counts for more than one', in Bentham's famous phrase. Of course, in the process of aggregating, the boundaries between you and me, your utilities and mine, get lost. But, second, empirical assumptions of broad similarity among people and generally diminishing marginal utility across all resources lead utilitarians to embrace policies and practices and institutions that are broadly egalitarian in form. That ensures that there will be a strong utilitarian presumption against exploiting some people for the benefit of others.

Conclusion

One of the great advantages of utilitarianism has always been that it promises to yield determinate, no-nonsense advice on practical matters. One of its great disadvantages has always been that it has a tendency to do so in a singularly formulistic way. List the alternatives, list the consequences, attach utility numbers to each and crank the adding machine's handle. But, critics say, nothing quite so easy could possibly be right.[13] There is no denying that many of the applications of utilitarianism to problems of public policy are just as rote as that. In a way, though, it is a virtue of utilitarianism that it is an ethic which admits of rote learning. Better that an ethic be applied by rote than not at all, if those are the only options – as often they are, given the limits to policy-makers' time, attention and talents.

In any case, utilitarianism of the most formulistic sort is sometimes transparently the right way to approach a policy problem. Suppose we are trying to assess the economic effects of income-transfer programs, for example. Then balance-sheet thinking is precisely what we need. The traditional complaint against generous income-support programs is that, if people can get something for nothing, they will not bother working for a living in the present or saving for the future. But the magnitudes here clearly matter. American evidence suggests, for example, that in exchange for a 4.8-per-cent reduction of labour supply (and a reduction in private savings of between zero and 20 per cent) we get a 75-per-cent reduction in poverty and a 19-per-cent increase in equality (measured by the Gini coefficient) (Danzinger et al. 1981: 1019). Whether we think on balance that the gains are worth the costs is an open question: that depends on the relative weights we attach to each of those factors. But whichever way we go on that concrete case, listing the various effects and weighing them against one another surely is the right way to go about making an economic assessment of that sort.

Transparently right though such formulistic approaches to policy puzzles sometimes are, however, it would be wrong to judge utilitarianism wholly in light of them. In coming to an overall assessment of utilitarianism as a public philosophy, it would be wrong to fixate upon the most formulistic derivations of its least imaginative practitioners. We should attend as much to the more creative uses that can be made of the tools with which utilitarianism provides us, to possibilities that arise from working 'in the shadows of utilitarianism', in Hart's phrase (1979; 1983: 222). In a range of policy applications, I have attempted time and again to show how utilitarianism's central concepts might, given certain features of the problem at hand, yield determinate policy advice – without resorting to a simple-minded, and often simply impossible, process of cranking through the formula to reach a direct determination of what is likely to maximize sum-total utility.

Thus, for example, it is possible to say that unilateral nuclear disarmament would have been a good policy in an essentially bipolar world – not because that would maximize utility (absent probability numbers, that is a sum that cannot be done), but rather because it would make a modal change in the possibility of truly awful outcomes (see Goodin 1995, ch. 17). It is possible to say that an unconditional income guarantee (negative income tax, basic income, call it what you will) is a good thing – not because that policy would necessarily maximize overall social utility in the presently prevailing circumstances, but rather because it would be minimally sensitive to shifts in prevailing social circumstances, which always change far more rapidly than social policy. For that reason, unconditional income guarantees would be more likely to maximize utility across that wide range of changing circumstances (see Goodin 1995, ch. 14). Or, again, policies to buffer people against radical changes to the course of their lives would be a good thing – not because those are the most satisfying lives that people might live, but rather because the chopping and changing required to get to something else would be profoundly disruptive of what people find ultimately satisfying in their lives (see Goodin 1995, chs 10–13).

Of course, the bottom line in all those cases is that the policies are justified because ultimately they maximize utility in some sense or another. Mine would hardly be a utilitarian theory at all, were it otherwise. Invariably, though, those are judgments made employing the apparatus of utilitarianism but without having recourse to fine-grained calculations of sums. The considerations that are deemed decisive there for policy questions are indisputably utilitarian-style considerations, bearing directly upon the preference satisfaction of people. The point just is that those considerations can indeed prove determinative as regards utilitarians' policy recommendations, well ahead of doing a full-dress utility count.

My concern, then, is with utilitarianism as a public philosophy, with the ways in which utilitarianism can be a good guide to public policies without necessarily being a good guide to private conduct. Nonetheless, in adducing many of its most important implications for public policy, it is important to see at least in broad outline how it would set about shaping private conduct.

Utilitarians, and consequentialists, are outcome-oriented. In sharp contrast to deontological approaches in the style of the Ten Commandments, which specify certain actions to be done as a matter of duty, utilitarian theories assign people responsibility for producing certain results, leaving the individuals concerned discretion in how to achieve those results. The same basic difference in the two theories' approaches to assigning moral jobs reappears across all levels of moral agency, from private individuals to collective actors. The utilitarian approach to international protection of the ozone layer is to assign states responsibilities for producing certain effects, leaving them broad discretion in execution (see Goodin 1995, ch. 18). The utilitarian approach to the ethical defence of nationalism is couched in terms of delimiting state boundaries so as to assign particular responsibility for every person to some particular organization (see Goodin 1995, ch. 16). And, at a more domestic level, the distinctively utilitarian approach to the allocation of legal liabilities is to assign them to whomsoever can best discharge them (see Goodin 1995, chs 5–7).

The advantage of utilitarianism as a guide to public conduct is that it avoids gratuitous sacrifices and ensures that policies are sensitive to people's interests, desires or preferences. The failing of deontological theories, applied to those realms, is that they fixate upon duties done for the sake of duty rather than for the sake of any good that is done by doing one's duty. Perhaps it is permissible for private individuals in the course of their personal affairs to fetishize duties done for their own sake. It would be a mistake for public officials to do likewise, not least because it is impossible: the fixation upon motives makes no sense in the public realm, and might make precious little sense in the private one (see Goodin 1995, ch. 3).

The reason public action is required arises from the inability of uncoordinated individual action to achieve certain morally desirable ends. Individuals are rightly excused from pursuing those ends: the inability is real, the excuses perfectly valid. But libertarians are right in their diagnosis, wrong in their prescription (see Goodin 1995, ch. 2). The same thing that makes those excuses valid at the individual level – the same thing that relieves individuals of responsibility – makes it morally incumbent upon individuals to organize themselves into collective units that are capable of acting where they as isolated individuals are not.

When they organize themselves into collective units, collective deliberations inevitably take place under very different circumstances, and their conclusions inevitably take different forms. Individuals are morally required to operate in that collective manner, in certain crucial respects. But they are practically circumscribed in how they can operate, in their collective mode. And those special constraints, characterizing the public sphere of decision-making, give rise to the special circumstances that make utilitarianism peculiarly apt for public policy-making (see Goodin 1995, ch. 4). Government House utilitarianism, thus understood, I would argue, is a uniquely defensible public philosophy.

Notes

Adapted from Goodin 1995: 3–27, by permission of the author and copyright holders, Cambridge University Press. I am grateful for comments on earlier drafts of this chapter from Peter McCarthy, Doug MacLean and Jeremy Waldron.

1 This is the phrase favoured by Bentham (1789, ch. 1, sec. 1), and his nineteenth-century friends and foes alike (see Lively and Rees 1978). It supplanted the earlier, careless phrase of Bentham (1776: 3) – 'the greatest happiness of the greatest number' – which critics always delight in describing as a mathematical impossibility (see Hardin 1988: 21–2).
2 Bentham (1776; 1789) and the elder Mill (1823) were bad enough, but worse still in this respect were the lesser lights among their circle, so ably satirized by Dickens in *Hard Times* (1854).
3 The technique, described in Dennet's *Philosophical Lexicon*, is named after the distinguished utilitarian, J. J. C. Smart.

4   In the distopia called Utilitaria created by Lukes (1993: 428) 'Calculating is the national obsession.' This goes far toward explaining what he finds so awful about the place.

5   Various writers try to find a halfway house in notions of the 'unthinkable' (Williams 1973: 90–3) or the 'morally impossible' (Hampshire 1972/1978: 9 ff.) or the intolerably 'cruel' (Shklar 1984, ch. 1) or 'human rights', marking the limits of what politicians should even consider doing. But of course refusing to think about grossly evil outcomes is not, in general, a good way of guaranteeing that they, or something worse, do not happen.

6   Lest all that seem to amount to a *post hoc* reconstruction of what the nineteenth-century utilitarians were up to, consider the younger Mill's self-conscious reflection upon the utilitarian tradition which he inherited. In his memorial essay on Bentham, John Stuart Mill writes: 'It is fortunate for the world that Bentham's taste lay rather in the direction of jurisprudential than of properly ethical inquiry. Nothing expressly of the latter kind has been published under his name, except the "Deontology" – a book scarcely ever . . . alluded to by any admirer of Bentham without deep regret that it ever saw the light.'

   Turning from what Bentham did badly to what he did well, Mill continues, 'If Bentham's theory of life can do so little for the individual, what can it do for society? It will enable a society . . . to prescribe the rules by which it may protect its material interests. It will do nothing . . . for the spiritual interests of society . . . What a philosophy like Bentham's can do [is to] . . . teach the means of organizing and regulating the merely business part of the social arrangements' (Mill 1838: 104–6). That is a fair assessment of Bentham, and of the tradition to which he gave rise. And whilst John Stuart Mill himself aspired to do better, it is in the end fair reflection, too, of his utilitarian accomplishments.

7   'Interests' or 'welfare,' in so far as they are (as here) to be distinguished from preference satisfaction, are best analysed as references to resources or basic capabilities which will prove useful to people whatever their ultimate ends (Barry 1964; Sen 1985a). There is sometimes discussion of a fourth class of 'ideal utilitarianism', the central claim of which is that certain ideals (things, attributes) are good independently of people's desire for them: that counts as a form of utilitarianism at all, I would argue, only if it can be assimilated under this last category. The 'higher pleasures' of Mill (1863) are arguably higher in precisely the sense of having a higher utility yield, if achieved: arguably it is precisely that to which people are testifying when Mill would have us ask anyone who has experienced both higher and lower which they would prefer.

8   All the standard arguments for rule utilitarianism seem to turn, at crucial points, on some such proposition (see Hodgson 1967; Regan 1980; Hare 1981; Hardin 1988; Honoré 1993).

9   The following paragraphs draw loosely upon my previous discussion of this topic (Goodin 1975; 1982b: 16–8).

10 Indeed, it represents a return to the older 'material welfare' school of Marshall and Pigou, wherein 'the comparison of needs, not the comparison of subjective desires, was what they usually meant by comparing utilities of different people'; their focus was accordingly upon observable indicators of 'industrial efficiency', such as inadequacy of people's diets and measures of mortality and morbidity (Cooter and Rappoport 1984: 516).

11 That is a more straightforward way of saying what is wrong with Sidgwick's (1874/1907, bk 4, ch. 5, sec. 3) behind-the-back version of 'government house utilitarianism': the problem is not that it violates some high-minded

Kantian publicity principle but that it is a political theory that curiously cuts out politics altogether (cf. Williams 1973: 138–40; Sen and Williams 1982: 16).

12   This theme – recurring throughout Rawls (1971), Williams (1973), Nozick (1974) and Dworkin (1977) – is most effectively summarized in Hart (1979).

13   The comment of Hampshire (1972: 1) that utilitarianism has 'now become an obstruction' to enlightened policy seems primarily a reference to the fact that the same utilitarian cost–benefit logic that served the Kennedy Administration so well in reforming the Defense Department (Hitch and McKean 1960) led to such disastrous consequences in Vietnam (Halberstam 1969).

References

Adams, Robert Merrihew. 1976. 'Motive Utilitarianism', *Journal of Philosophy*, 73.

Anscombe, G. E. M. 1958. 'Modern Moral Philosophy', *Philosophy*, 33.

Avineri, Shlomo, and de-Shalit, Avner, eds. 1992. *Communitarianism and Individualism*. Oxford: Oxford University Press.

Barry, Brian. 1964. 'The Public Interest', *Proceedings of the Aristotelian Society (Supplement)*, 38.

Barry, Brian. 1965. *Political Argument*. London: Routledge & Kegan Paul.

Barry, Brian. 1989. *Democracy, Power and Justice*. Oxford: Clarendon Press.

Bentham, Jeremy. 1776. *A Fragment on Government*, ed. J. H. Burns and H. L. A. Hart. Cambridge: Cambridge University Press, 1988.

Bentham, Jeremy. 1789. *An Introduction to the Principles of Morals and Legislation*, ed. J. H. Burns and H. L. A. Hart. London: Athlone Press, 1970.

Brandt, Richard B. 1979. *A Theory of the Good and the Right*. Oxford: Clarendon Press.

Brandt, Richard B. 1988. 'Fairness to Indirect Optimistic Theories in Ethics', *Ethics*, 98.

Brandt, Richard B. 1992. *Morality, Utilitarianism and Rights*. Cambridge: Cambridge University Press.

Cooter, Robert, and Rappoport, Peter. 1984. 'Were the Ordinalists Wrong about Welfare Economics?', *Journal of Economic Literature*, 22.

Danziger, Sheldon, Haveman, Robert, and Plotnick, Robert. 1981. 'How Income Transfer Programs Affect Work, Savings and Income Distribution', *Journal of Economic Literature*, 19.

Davidson, D. 1986. 'Judging Interpersonal Interests', in J. Elster and A. Hyland, eds, *Foundations of Social Choice Theory*. Cambridge: Cambridge University Press.

Dickens, Charles. 1854. *Hard Times*. Harmondsworth, Mddx: Penguin, 1969.

Drèze, Jean, and Sen, Amartya. 1989. *Hunger and Public Action*. Oxford: Clarendon Press.

Dworkin, Ronald M. 1977. *Taking Rights Seriously*. London: Duckworth.

Fried, Charles. 1978. *Right and Wrong*. Cambridge, Mass.: Harvard University Press.

Fried, Charles. 1981. *Contract as Promise*. Cambridge, Mass.: Harvard University Press.

Goodin, Robert E. 1975. 'Cross-cutting Cleavages and Social Conflict', *British Journal of Political Science*, 5.

Goodin, Robert E. 1982a. 'Discounting Discounting', *Journal of Public Policy*, 2.
Goodin, Robert E. 1982b. *Political Theory and Public Policy*. Chicago: University of Chicago Press.
Goodin, Robert E. 1995. *Utilitarianism as a Public Philosophy*. Cambridge: Cambridge University Press,
Halberstam, David. 1969. *The Best and the Brightest*. New York: Random House.
Halévy, Elie. 1928. *The Growth of Philosophic Radicalism*, trans. Mary Morris. London: Faber & Faber.
Hampshire, Stuart. 1972. 'Morality and Pessimism: Leslie Stephen Lecture, University of Cambridge', reprinted in Hampshire, ed., *Public and Private Morality*. Cambridge: Cambridge University Press, 1978.
Hardin, Russell. 1988. *Morality within the Limits of Reason*. Chicago: University of Chicago Press.
Hare, R. M. 1957. 'Reasons of State', in Hare, *Applications of Moral Philosophy*. London: Macmillan, 1972.
Hare, R. M. 1981. *Moral Thinking*. Oxford: Clarendon Press.
Hart, H. L. A. 1979. 'Between Utility and Rights', in Alan Ryan, ed., *The Idea of Freedom*. Oxford: Clarendon Press.
Hart, H. L. A. 1983. *Essays in Jurisprudence and Philosophy*. Oxford: Clarendon Press.
Hicks, John R. 1939. 'The Foundations of Welfare Economics', *Economic Journal*, 49.
Hitch, Charles J., and McKean, Roland N. 1960. *The Economics of Defense in the Nuclear Age*. Cambridge, Mass.: Harvard University Press.
Hodgson, D. H. 1967. *The Consequences of Utilitarianism*. Oxford: Clarendon Press.
Honoré, Tony. 1993. 'The Dependence of Morality on Law', *Oxford Journal of Legal Studies*, 13.
Jevons, Stanley. 1911. *The Theory of Political Economy*, 4th edn. London: Macmillan.
Kaldor, Nicholas. 1939. 'Welfare Propositions of Economics and Interpersonal Comparisons of Utility', *Economic Journal*, 49.
Kaldor, Nicholas. 1946–7. 'Community Indifference: A Comment', *Review of Economic Studies*, 14.
Kymlicka, Will. 1989. *Liberalism, Community and Culture*. Oxford: Clarendon Press.
Levine, Henry D. 1977. 'Some Things to All Men: The Politics of Cruise Missile Development', *Public Policy*, 25.
Little, I. M. D. 1957. *A Critique of Welfare Economics*, 2nd edn. Oxford: Clarendon Press.
Lively, Jack, and Rees, John, eds. 1978. *Utilitarian Logic and Politics*. Oxford: Clarendon Press.
Lukes, Steven. 1993. 'Five Fables about Human Rights: What Would It Be Like If', *Dissent*, Fall.
Lyons, David. 1965. *The Forms and Limits of Utilitarianism*. Oxford: Clarendon Press.
March, James G., and Olsen, Johan P. 1976. *Ambiguity and Choice in Organizations*. Bergen: Universitetsforlaget.
Mill, James. 1823. *Essays on Government, Jurisprudence, [etc.]* Reprinted as *James Mill: Political Writings*, ed. Terence Ball. Cambridge: Cambridge University Press, 1992.
Mill, John Stuart. 1838. 'Essay on Bentham', *London and Westminster Review*, August. Reprinted 1962: *Utilitarianism: On Liberty; Essay on Bentham*, ed. M. Warnock, Cleveland: Meridian.
Mill, John Stuart. 1863. *Utilitarianism*. London: Parker & Son. Reprinted 1962: *Utilitarianism: On Liberty; Essay on Bentham*, ed. M. Warnock, Cleveland: Meridian.

Nozick, Robert. 1974. *Anarchy, State and Utopia.* Oxford: Blackwell.

Olsen, Johan P. 1972. 'Public Policy-making and Theories of Organizational Choice', *Scandinavian Political Studies,* 7.

Parfit, Derek. 1984. *Reasons and Persons.* Oxford: Clarendon Press.

Pigou, A. C. 1951. 'Some Aspects of Economic Welfare', *American Economic Review,* 41.

Plamenatz, John. 1958. *The English Utilitarians.* Oxford: Blackwell.

Rawls, John. 1971. *A Theory of Justice.* Cambridge, Mass.: Harvard University Press.

Regan, Donald H. 1980. *Utilitarianism and Co-operation.* Oxford: Clarendon Press.

Robbins, Lionel. 1932. *Essay on the Nature and Significance of Economic Science.* London: Macmillan.

Robbins, Lionel. 1938. ' Interpersonal Utility Comparisons', *Economic Journal,* 48.

Sandel, Michael J. 1982. *Liberalism and the Limits of Justice.* Cambridge: Cambridge University Press.

Sandel, Michael J., ed. 1984. *Liberalism and Its Critics.* Oxford: Blackwell.

Sen, Amartya. 1982a. *Choice, Welfare and Measurement.* Oxford: Blackwell.

Sen, Amartya. 1982b. 'Rights and Agency', *Philosophy and Public Affairs,* 11.

Sen, Amartya. 1985a. *Commodities and Capabilities.* Amsterdam: North-Holland.

Sen, Amartya. 1985b. 'Well-being, Agency and Freedom', *Journal of Philosophy,* 82.

Sen, Amartya, and Williams, Bernard, eds. 1982. *Utilitarianism and Beyond.* Cambridge: Cambridge University Press.

Shklar, Judith N. 1984. *Ordinary Vices.* Cambridge, Mass.: Harvard University Press.

Sidgwick, Henry. 1907. *The Methods of Ethics,* 7th edn. London: Macmillan; originally published 1874.

Singer, Peter. 1972. 'Famine, Affluence and Morality', *Philosophy and Public Affairs,* 1.

Singer, Peter. 1979. *Practical Ethics.* Cambridge: Cambridge University Press.

Smart, J. J. C. 1967. 'Utilitarianism', in Paul Edwards, ed., *Encyclopedia of Philosophy,* vol. 8. New York: Macmillan.

Smart, J. J. C. 1973. 'An Outline of a System of Utilitarian Ethics', in Smart and Williams, 1973.

Smart J. J. C., and Williams, Bernard. 1973, *Utilitarianism, For and Against.* Cambridge: Cambridge University Press.

Van Parijs, Philippe, ed. 1992. *Arguing for Basic Income.* London: Verso.

Williams, Bernard. 1973. *Problems of the Self.* Cambridge: Cambridge University Press.

CHAPTER 4

Rational Choice Political Theory

Geoffrey Brennan

Rational choice political theory, RCPT henceforth, is the application of the analytic methods and techniques of modern economics to the study of political processes. Its ambitions are twofold. First, it aims to render political science as one aspect of a single over-arching social theory; economics (conceived as the study of markets), politics (conceived as the study of political processes) and rational choice sociology (as, say, represented in the work of James Coleman or the journal *Rationality and Society*) are all different applications of this theory. Second, it aims to provide a rational basis for the normative assessment of political arrangements in the context of the economist's theory of the state.

These two ambitions correspond to two emergent strands in RCPT. One, from the political science end, is represented by theorists like Ken Shepsle, James Alt, and, rather earlier, Bill Riker (see Alt and Shepsle 1990; Riker 1982). The other strand, from the welfare economics end, is represented by James Buchanan and his 'constitutional political economy' group and, to a lesser extent, by theorists like George Stigler and the 'private interest regulation' theorists associated with the Chicago School of economics (see Stigler 1982). These two strands have slightly different emphases. The political scientists are, for example, typically more insistent on the 'positive' character of their enterprise; they sometimes appear anxious to distance themselves from what is often identified as an ideological cast to the Virginia (Buchanan) and Chicago (Stigler) Schools of 'public choice theory' or 'political economy'. The term 'rational choice political theory', is itself a reflection of that attempted distancing. I use that term here in preference to 'public choice theory' or 'modern political economy' for two reasons. It is more descriptive (I believe, for example, that the notion of public *choice* is somewhat misleading); and I too want to avoid ideological connotations. For reasons that I will elaborate below, I prefer the term 'rational *choice* political theory' to 'rational *actor* political theory', despite the fact that the natural acronym for the latter (RAPT) has ravishing connotations.

On any reckoning, RCPT is one of the fastest-growing, and in that sense influential, developments in theoretical political science. Within economics, RCPT is still regarded as a rather quaint specialization: although 'public choice' articles appear occasionally in the most prestigious economics journals, they are much less common than RCPT pieces in the top political science journals (the *American Political Science Review* most notably). My political science confreres who are expert in these things tell me that the demand for the graduates of the departments that favour RCPT (Stanford, Harvard, and particularly Rochester) remains vigorous in an otherwise fairly stagnant market (a fact which the economist in me is inclined to see as one test of RCPT's significance).

Of course, not everyone believes that the rapid rise of RCPT is a good thing. Scholars committed to a more traditional form of political analysis are inclined to see rational choice theory as a method that has failed spectacularly in one arena of enquiry, now being applied to another area where no help is required – rather as a government with troubles at home may seek to suppress them through an assault on some neighbouring territory. In the Australian context, for example, RCPT is more conspicuous as something to react against than as an area to be developed or studied. As far as I know, there is no one in an Australian political science department who could reasonably be described as a RCPT-specialist: there are a few economists (perhaps three, myself included) who could be so described. At the same time, RCPT can hardly be said to have gone unnoticed by critics.

In this chapter, I do not intend at all to respond to the critics. Nor do I aim to survey the main results in the RCPT literature: that would be a huge task and has in any case been well-handled by Dennis Mueller in his second edition of *Public Choice* (1989) (though RCPT is an expanding field, and the Mueller book is now over five years old). Rather, what I attempt here is to provide a fairly austere abstract characterisation of the 'economic method' (the 'rational choice' method more generally), focusing in particular on what I see as its basic ingredients. I shall then say a little about how I see this method translating to political analysis – what central questions RCPT engages, and what might be the primary difficulties and distinctive features of the political application of rational choice theory.

It occurs to me that the exercise I am engaged in here is itself an illustration of some aspects of the method I seek to describe. That is, I shall endeavour to specify the theory by reference to its basic axioms: the style of the chapter is axiomatic and abstract. And I shall attempt to divide that axiomatic base into its several independent elements: the exercise is to that extent reductionist. Perhaps the instinct towards abstraction and towards the identification and disentangling of the more basic elements in the theory reflects my disciplinary origins, but I confess that this is the only way I can see it as being useful to proceed.

A Map

Let me briefly list what I see as RCPT's core properties. These are:
1. a predilection for formal deductive method, deriving 'interesting' (i.e. non-obvious, often counter-intuitive) propositions via sometimes long and complex chains of logical reasoning from a minimal set of plausible axioms;
2. a concern with 'equilibrium' analysis;
3. methodological individualism;
4. the assumption of individual rationality;
5. the self-interest assumption.

These properties together suggest features of the social order that are of particular relevance to RCPT analysis – in particular, the role of relative prices and changes in them as basic elements in social explanation; and somewhat analogously, the role of incentives in explaining the workings of alternative institutional arrangements.

I shall, in the later part of the chapter, indicate what these core properties imply for perceptions of the central problems of politics, and what they seem to background or omit that may be of relevance in political analysis. However, my first task is to describe what I see to be at stake in each of the core properties I have listed, and what work each does in the RCPT scheme. Where my own views differ significantly from what I take to be the mainstream view, I shall indicate the divergence.

The Axiomatic Method

In constructing the foregoing list, I have attempted to move from the general to the specific. I believe it to be perfectly possible, for example, to have a formal axiomatic theory of politics that does not depend on rational choice assumptions, does not use an individualist methodology, relies on a kind of dis-equilibrium analysis, and so on. On the other hand, it is difficult to conceive of any form of rational choice theory that is not committed to explicit theorizing, the development of formal models, and a strong predilection for parsimony in assumptions, and that does not exhibit considerable scepticism towards intuitionism as a research method. Indeed, I suspect that, for many RCP theorists, commitment to the axiomatic method is the most basic of their commitments.

It seems likely that they would modify much in the basic scheme, treating aggregations of one kind or another (e.g. firms or political parties) as units and adopting models of nonrational behaviour (such as behaviour based on habit), provided the axiomatic method is retained. After all, if the theory fails to produce explanations of political phenomena that are acceptably close to reality (within the boundaries of empirical fit that the level of abstraction permits), then the behavioural axioms have to be varied in some fashion. For RCP theorists, theoretical coherence is interpreted as logical consistency: conventional logic, perhaps aided by mathematical technique, is the main work-horse of analysis.

Although economics is usually identified as having its origins in Adam Smith, the most natural intellectual forebear of RCPT is Thomas Hobbes – not so much for his individualist method but for the stark lines of his intellectual scheme. It is said of Hobbes that his intellectual icon was Euclid, and that he sought in his political theory to exemplify the same logical purity and theoretical elegance that Euclid brought to geometry. That is also an aspiration central to RCP theorists – perhaps the most central aspiration of all.

Equilibrium Analysis

RCPT is most naturally identified as a creature of the Enlightenment. Enlightenment social theorists had as an explicit object the application of the (then) new physics to the social context. Again, Hobbes is probably the clearest example of this: his contact with Galileo and the self-conscious framing of his thought along Galilean lines are legendary. The legacy (in modern economics and RCPT equally) of that association is twofold: first, the concept of social equilibrium is a core part of the analytic repertoire; and second, such social equilibrium is conceived as a balancing of oppositional forces. Within economics, most analysis is of the 'comparative static' kind: the equilibrium resulting from one set of underlying parameters is compared with the equilibrium resulting when some member of that set is changed. The change in the equilibrium is the outcome caused by the changed parameter. Often (routinely, I would say), little attention is directed at the process by which the shift from one equilibrium to another is secured, although RCP theorists are aware that (at least in principle) not all 'equilibrating' processes are convergent. Some economists have attempted to develop a genuinely dynamic analysis, in which issues like the time path to equilibrium and path dependence have been central. Others (the so-called Austrian School most notably) have been concerned with a kind of 'disequilibrium' analysis, one in which the economy is always in transition from one notional equilibrium to some other, and is continually being shocked by further changes in relevant underlying conditions. The Austrians (Menger, von Mises, Hayek for example) have always been the most determinedly anti-Newtonian of economists, the most radically subjectivist about preferences, and the most aggressively anti-scientistic. There are few Austrians among the RCPT community, though several of Buchanan's works reveal distinct Austrian sympathies (especially *Cost and Choice*). More generally, however, RCPT has been relatively unconcerned with dynamic equilibrating processes (and they have not been a success story in economics either). In fact, RCPT has been not much concerned with comparative statics. There has been much more concern about the *structure* of political equilibrium: the way in which various component forces balance, and how, under particular institutional arrangements, the equilibrium corresponds to the preferences of citizens. There is something of an analogy here with game theory in ordinary economics. Game theory helps to uncover the structure of the relations between actors, and the nature of the interdependence between them, and perhaps the connection between any emergent equilibrium and the underlying preferences of players (most notable perhaps in the familiar 'prisoners' dilemma'). Game theory is not especially useful in tracing the effect of changes in some exogenous parameter (the weather, say) on the social and economic equilibrium (which is the task of comparative static analysis).

There is, however, one kind of comparative static analysis that is extensively used in the political applications of the economic method, namely, comparative institutional analysis. This method compares equilibria under different institutional arrangements (e.g. direct v. representative democracy; unicameral v. bicameral legislatures; divided v. unified powers; simple majority v. more restrictive voting rules; and, especially, the provision of a particular good in the competitive market v. the level of provision that would emerge under democratic politics). In terms of the political application, there has been much attention to 'institutional design', to the question of what institutional order it might be best to impose *ab initio* (or at least the working properties of alternative orders so imposed) rather than the issue of institutional reform or reshaping, in which issues like the trans-equilibrium path and the possibility of path dependence are more critical.

One particular preoccupation of RCP theorists that merits explicit attention here is the question of whether any political equilibrium actually exists. The problem of cyclical majorities – the idea, that is, that there may in general exist no political outcome that cannot be defeated by *some* majority – has been a major concern for RCPT scholars since the time of Condorcet (see Sommerlad and McLean 1989). Concern arises partly because the absence of any stable equilibrium seems to undermine the possibility of general political analysis; and partly because of the normative implication that *no* point in policy space can be ruled out of contention as a stopping point in some otherwise inconclusive sequence of majority-approved moves. A brief clarification might be in order here. The issue is *not* the point made in Arrow's famous impossibility theorem (which reveals a concern about whether any political equilibrium can be normatively defended).[1] Arrow's theorem applies, for example, no less to competitive markets, where there is a stable equilibrium, than to majoritarian politics. The problem of cyclical majorities is that majority rule as such is not sufficient to ensure a stable equilibrium. Accordingly, the picture of democratic politics that RCPT offers is one of a process always ready to erupt into cyclical chaos. Institutional arrangements – party systems or committee systems or bicameralism or presidential veto or whatever – all tend to be viewed, at least initially, in terms of their capacity to suppress that underlying instability. Sometimes (more often than appears to be justified), RCP theorists appeal to the special uni-dimensional case where the familiar median voter theorem applies and a stable equilibrium does emerge.[2] However, the uni-dimensional case is special. The expedient of assuming uni-dimensionality does enable systematic analysis to proceed: changes in the prevailing tax regime can, for example, be traced to changes in the equilibrium level of public spending, other things being equal; a shift from pollution taxes to direct regulation can be shown to affect the equilibrium level of government intervention and hence the equilibrium level of pollution (in the presence of government anti-pollution policies); and so on. However, the possibility of such analysis is bought only at the price of introducing the very kind of ad hocery that RCP theorists find objectionable in political science of a more traditional style. To impose the assumption of stability on political processes simply because it is analytically convenient, when we know that stability is a major analytic puzzle, seems deeply unsatisfactory theoretically (it is in the 'assume a can-opener' class of solutions). As I shall argue below, the issue of majority cycling may well be less of a problem than RCP theorists have been inclined to think, because interests are not as central a determinant of electoral preference as the standard RCPT account assumes. But more of this under 'Rational Actor Theory in Politics', below.

Methodological Individualism

Economists are, or claim to be in their methodologically more self-aware moments, committed to methodological individualism. To many social theorists (most sociologists in particular), methodological individualism is anathema, the central heresy; and it is perhaps this fact more than any other that makes communication between economists and sociologists so difficult. My suspicion is that, when conscientious social theorists disagree about so fundamental a matter, they are likely to be talking at cross-purposes.

As I see it, methodological individualism is the requirement that any fully satisfactory social explanation must be consistent with a credible account of the behaviour of the individuals who compose that society. There must, at base, be a satisfactory psychology. This does not invalidate (as Nozick 1977 and Jackson and Pettit 1992 rightly point out) social explanations that run in terms of groups (say firms or political parties) or other social aggregations (age distribution, population level, aggregate consumption, GDP, interest rates). But such explanations are only partial, and one important dimension of this partiality lies in the direction of a finer level of disaggregation. For example, much ordinary micro-economics treats firms as if they were primary actors in markets – the 'producers' in producer–consumer interactions. Downs's important early work in RCPT treats political parties in much the same way. Neither move seems to create much anxiety among its exponents. Yet in both cases it is implicitly recognized that the use of such aggregations invites enquiry along more reductionist lines (even if that enquiry is going to be set aside for the time being.) No one after all (the economist perhaps least of all) is going to be deeply concerned about *partial* explanation: in a world of finite brains, all explanation is partial at some level. There would be little point to the abstraction, assumptional austerity, and explanatory elegance on which economists place such weight if 'total' explanation were feasible. But economists accept, at least in principle, that firms represent something to be explained in terms of more basic elements, as well as something that can be used to explain. Although the literature on why firms exist at all, for example, is not large, it is readily reckoned to be extremely important. And the connected literature on the internal structure of firms and why firms can be plausibly modelled to act as the micro-economic textbooks claim they do is recognized as being significant even by economists who are not engaged in it. Similarly, macro-economists have long accepted in principle that they need to find proper 'micro-foundations' for the aggregative relations they proffer between consumption, investment, income, debt-financing, and so on. They recognize that the 'microfoundational' quest may challenge both the understanding of the macro-relationships and the formulation of basic micro-postulates. And even if that quest still lies in the too-hard basket, there is a recognition that something important is awaited.

Similarly, RCP theorists who are content to treat political parties as causal agents in, say, their account of electoral competition will also acknowledge the importance of disaggregation of parties into the various component players (parliamentary members, general members, aspiring candidates) and within the set of parliamentary members, into leader, aspiring leader(s), etc. For the RCPT exponent, the conduct of the party must ultimately be understood as the aggregation of the actions of the individuals who make it up.

There is, I think, little doubt that methodological individualism is connected to the *normative* individualism that is common among economists and RCP theorists more generally. The idea that persons matter *morally* is often connected to ideas of human agency, to conceptions of persons as (relatively) independent actors with their own personal projects, the pursuit of which is important both as an ideal and as a partially fulfilled fact. But I am uncertain whether there is any purely logical connection here – and I am inclined to think not. One could, in other words, coherently occupy both positions: have an essentially collectivized view of 'the good', and still believe that the best way of analysing social phenomena (and the promotion of that good) was via an individualist methodology. Alternatively, one could believe that groups of one kind or another (classes, say) were the primary actors in social life, and yet that the well-being of individual persons was the primary good. Neither of these possibilities strikes me as either implausible or entirely unfamiliar.

The most common criticism of methodological individualism is that it implies a form of atomism – that it postulates a total independence of persons, a total detachment from the social structure of which those persons are a part. At one level, this charge is clearly misplaced. Economics is precisely about the relations between individual agents: its object is to explain the nature and extent of agent interdependence. No account of social phenomena that relies on an account of Crusoe on his island can be satisfactory until and unless Friday is admitted. To think otherwise – to think, for example, that economics is exhausted by rational decision theory – is simply a mistake, and remains a mistake even though a proportion of the economics profession commit it.

In fact, the issue between methodological individualists and their critics is not that the former assume independence and the latter interdependence: the issue is, rather, the nature of the interdependencies under examination and the mechanism through which they operate. Economics focuses on those interdependencies that arise because of possible gains for co-operation in the pursuit of the conceptually distinct purposes that individual agents are presumed to possess. Economics tends to background social psychological influences that may affect the purposes themselves: preferences are, in other words, treated as exogenous. The assumption that preferences are external matches naturally with a simple view of interest-based egoism – a picture of people motivated primarily by a concern for food, clothing, shelter and personal survival (Hobbes) – though other motivational pictures could well be admitted. For example, in the work that Pettit and I have done and plan to do on 'regard' (fame and shame and their role in the working of social institutions), we accept the desire for social acceptance as a primary motivating force: we see in this no assault on the principles of RCPT. Indeed, we are inclined to describe our domain of enquiry as 'the economy of regard' in order to identify the enterprise with the RCPT tradition.

Sociologists, by contrast, are generally much more concerned with interdependencies that result from the impact of direct psychological factors. Some social psychologists, for example, regard an individual's ends as essentially derivative from the social group with which the individual identifies. In this sense, the social group becomes the primary actor. Questions still arise as to why individuals come to identify with the particular groups they do identify with; and how new social groups might form and old ones change. Most of those questions are, it seems to me, amenable to methodological individualism. However, at any point in time, such questions are probably of second-order significance. That is, at any particular time and place, the landscape of relevant groups may be largely fixed, and that landscape constitutes the terrain on which any task of social explanation is to be engaged. This possibility is more relevant for politics than for economics if, as I believe and shall argue briefly below, self-identification plays a more critical role in electoral choice than in market choice.

At this point, however, I want to finish my discussion of methodological individualism with a more general observation about psychology. As I see it, one of the claims that might be made for methodological individualism is precisely that it provides a role for psychology, and hence access to that element of truth in the 'human sciences' that is accessible to introspection. I mean by this that there is a special kind of truth recognition, accessible to social scientists by virtue of the fact that scientists are of the same kind as the object of their study: whatever else, an individualist methodology provides scope for that possibility in a way that more aggregative analysis does not. Yet recent economics on the whole (the Austrians perhaps apart) has been inclined to treat human behaviour as if it were totally inscrutable, beyond the observable regularities that arise through predictable responses to changes in relative prices. The behaviourist tradition, particularly in its 'revealed preference' variant, has attempted to finesse all psychological questions and to mistrust as 'unscientific' anything that people say or anything that is accessible through introspection. This practice puzzles me because it ignores sources of knowledge that the individualist method makes accessible. Its application of 'rational actor' ideas to the political arena is as puzzling as the traditional application of them to the market.

Rationality

If titles were any guide, the concept of rational action would be the *sine qua non* of RCPT. The picture is, however, more complicated. For one thing, the axiomatic method and the appeal to methodological individualism are no less fundamental and may be more so. For another, and more importantly in my view, one of the ironies of applying rational actor theory to the political context is that, for a critical set of players in the electoral context – namely voters – the idea of rational *action* is particularly strained. (This applies particularly to the study of electoral competition, the focus of much of RCPT – see under 'Rational Actor Theory in Politics', below.) I shall later explain what I mean by this claim and attempt to justify it. At this point, let me just assert that the concept of 'rational irrationality' is one that has particular relevance to electoral behaviour; thus, the issue of whether rational *agents* would choose what RCPT has standardly identified as the 'rational action' (the *action* that best promotes the purposes of the actor) is highly problematic.

It may be useful here to lay out briefly what is entailed in the 'rationality' assumptions that I see the RCP theorist as being committed to, before taking up the issue of what that implies for political behaviour. In economics and the decision theoretic structure that it adopts, rationality is understood as a structural feature of agent choice that connects the chosen option to agent belief and agent purposes in a direct way: agents are rational if they choose that option which they believe best fulfils their purposes, all things considered. Logically there is no implication that rational agents so defined are 'single-minded' in the sense that they can weigh all their distinct and potentially competing purposes into a single-valued 'purpose function'; they may, for example, order the world by vector-dominance, in the way the Pareto criterion orders the utilities of different agents. Nevertheless, the agent's single-mindedness in this sense is usually assumed. Agents are also taken to be single-minded in another sense: their purposes and the relative values of those purposes are taken to be relatively stable over time. Again, this assumption is not strictly entailed by rationality: it would be possible for agents to choose according to their purposes at any point, and still reveal chaotic action over time if those purposes were sufficiently febrile. Accordingly, although (occasional) preference change is not ruled out, the working assumption is that preferences are stable.

It is important to note that the assumption of rationality so understood says nothing (or next to nothing) about the *content* of preferences. Apart from self-contradictory purposes – say, the purpose of imposing maximal harm on oneself – almost anything goes. Rationality does not, specifically, entail egoism. The proposition that agents are rational egoists embodies *two* independent assumptions: that agents are rational; and that they are egoistic. A clear distinction, therefore, has to be drawn between rationality on the one hand, and the particular behavioural model of persons as wealth-maximizers on the other. The former does not entail the latter. It is also worth nothing that rationality is not a theory of calculation: there is no necessary implication that agents weigh up the costs and benefits of various actions in terms of their various purposes achieved and forgone. It may be that this form of calculation is the best route to rational action – or it may not be. If an agent's calculative abilities are limited (whose are not?), various rules of thumb and/or non-calculative dispositions may select the relevant action more reliably than ratiocination. Within the RCPT world, the unexamined life may well go better for one than the examined, a long-standing philosophers' prejudice to the contrary notwithstanding. The point at issue here generalizes. I have been careful to speak of rational *choice* theory rather than rational actor theory, and to speak of the requirements of rationality in terms of *options* rather than *actions*. I have explicitly allowed for the possibility that the options available for choice may be dispositions rather than particular actions. As Parfitt (1984), Elster (1979) and many others have argued, it may well be that life will go better overall for agents if, instead of choosing each action according to rationality requirements, they choose their *dispositions* on that basis. For example, a disposition to keep promises may be personally profitable, because others will trust you in mutually beneficial arrangements when they could not (rationally) trust those who always choose actions according to their interests. Individuals who (rationally) place themselves in thrall to a disposition of this kind do not choose every *action* rationally, and in that sense are not rational actors even though they have made a rational *choice* (among dispositions, one of which is to choose each action rationally). Such complications are not beyond the reach of rational choice theory.

It is sometimes argued that the assumption of rationality without any specification of agent purposes or the *content* of agent 'preferences' (the weighted sum of purpose-achievement) is entirely formal and has no empirical content at all. That is not so. Rationality does enable prediction of agent response to changes in relative prices: if a purpose becomes more expensive in terms of other purposes forgone, the rational agent will (except under extremely special conditions) achieve less of it, *ceteris paribus*. In other words, demand curves are (virtually always) downward-sloping, whatever the object demanded actually is. This fact is the basis for all comparative static propositions in economics, and of all incentive-based propositions in comparative institutional analysis, the empirical content of which is considerable. Of course, it is always available to the economist to claim, when such propositions are empirically falsified, that the relevant demand curve has shifted – that *ceteris* are not *paribus*. But beyond a certain point, this is merely a concession that relative price change is not where the action is – or perhaps that agent purposes/ preferences are too unstable for the idea of rationality to have much value. In this sense, the consistent failure of comparative static propositions and their comparative institutional analogues would be grounds for rejecting RCPT as a useful approach. (Which is not to say that other approaches are better: politics may simply not admit of coherent analysis of the kind to which RCPT aspires.)

One aspect of the rationality apparatus that economists have not much attended to is the role of agent beliefs. In general, the rational choice will be a function of the beliefs the agent holds. There is then an issue as to the status of those beliefs – whether rationality assumptions require that those beliefs must reflect (only?) available information, and/or that beliefs must respond to new information in particular ways. An agent who acts in accordance with irrational beliefs cannot, presumably, be rational – though what would count as an 'irrational belief' is perhaps not entirely clear. At the very least, rational belief seems to require that beliefs should respond to new evidence, in the direction that evidence indicates. A stronger requirement would be that beliefs respond to the 'appropriate' extent, with 'appropriateness' here depending on the confidence with which initial beliefs are held. Both these requirements would be consistent with initial beliefs being 'wrong', or unsupported by the evidence available. Focusing on the role of beliefs in the rational actor story raises important questions about where beliefs come from and, more particularly, how those beliefs are influenced by social considerations. Presumably 'common knowledge', the beliefs of relevant authorities, agents' beliefs about others' beliefs, and so on are all to some extent socially constructed. In this sense, RCPT can be hospitable to some kinds of quasi-postmodern gestures, though of course its basic epistemological stance is thoroughly realist.

Self-interest

Economists are notoriously slippery on the question of self-interest. We often seem to oscillate between two understandings of self-interest: as a substantive empirical claim, and as a kind of analytic *a priori*. In part, this is because the assumption does double duty in RCPT. To put that better: RCPT itself does double duty, both as a 'science of politics' and as a 'logic of politics'. For the former purpose – that is, for deriving predictions about patterns of electoral support for particular policies, or for the conduct of various agents in the political process – one needs a tolerably clear specification of agent preferences. *Homo economicus*, the venal egoist, is one such specification. As such, *Homo economicus* is a caricature ('abstraction' might be a more generous term) that has its uses in market settings, and RCP theorists have been insistent on assuming behavioural symmetry across institutional forms. Whether the objective of RCPT is to develop a single over-arching theory of social interaction or to compare the working properties of markets and democratic politics for normative purposes, the RCPT enterprise seems to require that agents bring to those institutional forms the same basic motivational structure. As Buchanan (1989) has put it, the onus of proof would seem to lie with those who would violate this 'nonschizophrenia' assumption. In other words, the only admissible propositions about interactions between motivation and institutional form would be those consistent with rationality axioms themselves. Simply to assume some form of 'multiple hats' model of human behaviour, so that the same agents are motivated quite differently in their market and political roles, seems totally arbitrary and represents a position to which RCPT is opposed on principle. Of course, abstractions that are acceptable in one context may not be acceptable in another – though why this should be so would itself be a matter to be explained. Supposing, however, that some such explanation could be given, then RCPT may demand a more general model of human motivation than economics uses, precisely because of the wider range of issues at stake: some sacrifice in motivational 'abstraction' might well be required to secure the wider compass of institutional contexts. I shall argue later that the political application of rational choice theory does require a more elaborate model of human motivation than the theory of market choice requires. But I shall also argue that, even with this broader model, a self-interested conception of political behaviour is inappropriate.

It may be useful at this point to offer a brief taxonomy of 'self-interest' possibilities. One relevant aspect of self-interest is the question of the content of agents' preferences. To formulate the issue here in terms of utility functions, one can distinguish between the case where the arguments in agent i's utility function are parameters that have agent i's own designation. Take aggregate own-consumption, C_i, as a typical contender here. We can distinguish analytically between the following three possible utility functions:

1. $Ui = f(Ci)$
2. $Ui = g(Ci, Cj)$
3. $Ui = h(\Sigma Ci)$

where Ui is the individual i's utility; Ci, Cj are the total consumption levels of individuals i and j respectively; and ΣCi is the aggregate consumption of all members of the relevant society.

The first of these equations is what we normally think of as economic egoism. The second admits some altruism towards j (assuming Cj is positively valued): how much depends on the precise form of the function g. The third illustrates a form of public interest: i cares only about total consumption for the group, and not at all about their own share. We might think of equation 3 as a denial of self-interest.

Yet one important aspect of the self-interest assumption can accommodate equation 3. For example, consider two agents, i and j; both of them are concerned only about the community as a whole, but each has different views about how the various aspects of community parameters should be weighed. For example, let $\cancel{E}$ be a general measure of the distribution of consumption (the variance, say) across the group.

4. $\begin{cases} Ui = h(\Sigma Ci, \cancel{E}) \\ Uj = k(\Sigma Ci, \cancel{E}) \end{cases}$

Note that there is no sacrifice of methodological individualism in these equations: both i and j have their own identifiable individual preferences, their own behavioural postures; there is no 'joint utility' as such at stake here at all. Note too that both are loosely 'selfless', in that they care only about aggregate consumption and the (anonymous) characterisation of its distribution. But because h and k are different functions, there is a dimension of conflict, which may be larger or smaller depending on how alike h and k are. This property of 'conflict at the margin' (what Jim Buchanan and I have referred to rather misleadingly as 'non-tuism') is critical for the logic of interaction that is one important aspect of the RCPT enterprise. This marginal conflict is clearly very much weaker than the simplified formulation of self-interest in equation 1 above, since it obtains not only for equation 4, but also for 2 and 1 as well.

Moreover, it is one thing to say that 'ultimately' all agents are 'really' only concerned with their aggregate own-consumption (I have put the typical weasel words in quotation marks); it is another entirely to say that most agents are somewhat concerned with their own-consumption some of the time. Yet it is only the latter assumption that is required for standard comparative static propositions: only the latter assumption that is required for incentive effects to be relevant in institutional design/reform.

Of course, the *Homo economicus* assumption is extremely powerful in political analysis: it predicts, as a first-order matter, that patterns of electoral support for particular policies will follow the redistributive effects of those policies. Of course, preferences will also reflect different voter-citizen 'tastes' for particular public goods – defence, law and order, education, public health, etc. But considerations of tastes are arguably second-order for most voters in the neighbourhood of equilibrium, and difficult to predict; whereas the income-redistributive effects of policies are usually relatively transparent. Accordingly, under *Homo economicus* assumptions, we can reasonably reliably predict how particular voters will vote according to whether particular policies serve to increase or decrease their individual incomes. On the supply side of politics, the *Homo economicus* assumption predicts how any genuine discretion assigned to political 'agents' (politicians and bureaucrats) will be used: to promote, at citizens' expense, activities that political agents desire (the non-tuism dimension). We can also predict the form that such exploitation will take: to increase the long-term expected incomes of the political agents themselves. It is this strong form of 'self-interest' that has proven such a contentious feature of (much) RCPT analysis. Critics have insisted that there *is* a substantial portion of public-interest motivation in politics, both on the part of voters and on the part of politicians and bureaucrats; and that the failure to recognize this fact leads not only to an erroneous analysis of political process, but also to inappropriate recommendations about institutional arrangements. On the latter front, the institutional recommendations have been inappropriate not just because they have ignored the presence of a resource (public-interest motivations) that might be allowed freer rein, but also because the institutional forms introduced may have served to undermine the public-spiritedness that would otherwise be around. In this sense, so the critics have it, the political theory of *Homo economicus* may become self-fulfilling.

Many traditional political theorists have, of course, wanted to allow for the self-interest of politicians and bureaucrats without wanting to specify that self-interest in such narrowly venal terms. Politicians may be interested in fame and/or the exercise of power for its own sake. Bureaucrats may be interested in security, or in the size of their particular empire (independently of the additional income, if any, that may bring). Such modifications of the model involve a reflection of narrow interpretations of *Homo economicus*, but they clearly do not represent any kind of attack on the rational choice logic, and hence no fundamental critique of RCPT.

Of course, there remains an issue about the relevance of *Homo economicus* within politics. Are political actors as public-spirited as the critics of *Homo economicus* modelling claim? If not, if *Homo economicus* is to be justified as a useful simplification in market contexts, does it remain as useful a simplification in the political setting as in the market setting? Does the assumption that people will behave as *Homo economicus* establish (or encourage) the behaviour it describes? If we can make people more public-spirited by assuming that they are so, by what process is this moral alchemy wrought?

All these are interesting and important questions, but as I have indicated I do not see them as involving any kind of fundamental attack on RCPT. RCPT is *not* committed to *Homo economicus* as a behavioural model: it can (and in my view should) work with a more general motivational model which can retain significant elements of a generalized self-interest orientation. The assumption that own-consumption, narrowly conceived, plays some reasonably significant role in human motivation strikes me as thoroughly plausible. There is no need to embrace false dichotomies between extreme positions on either side. The choice is not between *Homo economicus* and *Homo heroicus*; even if it were, the precise content of heroic motivations would have to be subject to wide consensus before we could ignore the conflictual possibilities with which RCPT deals.

Rational Actor Theory in Politics

So far, I have focused on rational choice theory as a means of doing social science. I want now to direct attention to the political applications specifically. The first general point to be made is that self-interest, even weakly interpreted, lends a sceptical cast to all questions of social organization. We cannot rely entirely on the public-interestedness of other persons to pursue our goals: civic virtue is scarce. This means that institutional arrangements that bend interests to the service of duty are desirable, other things being equal, in all arenas in which we rely on others' sense of duty. We are always vulnerable in social life to the possibility that others will pursue their own distinct goals at our expense, and we naturally seek institutions that maximally exploit the possibilities for universally agreeable co-operation. The market, at least in its idealized competitive version in the provision of 'private goods', is widely acknowledged to be one such institution: the incentive structure of the market, in this case, is such as to bend interests to the service of duty *perfectly*. An obvious question is whether the incentive structure embodied in democratic politics is analogously successful. In order to answer this question, RCPT analysts naturally look to those aspects of democratic politics that seem most likely to create incentives for political agents to act in the public interest: RCPT is thus led to focus on electoral processes, and on electoral competition specifically. The central question at issue has been whether, and to what extent, competition between candidates or parties encourages them to offer policies that promote the citizens' interests (as those citizens perceive them). This concern represents the context for the large literature on 'spatial competition', both in the simplified and obligingly tractable uni-dimensional case, and also in the multi-dimensional case where all the problems of instability of equilibrium arise.

Such instability is, as I noted under 'The Axiomatic Method' above, perceived as a 'problem' for two reasons. First, instability provides scope for exploitation by political agents: such scope is the thrust of McKelvey's famous theorem to the effect that strategic agenda-setters can *always* achieve their ideal (see McKelvey 1976). Second, instability makes it virtually impossible to do any substantial analysis at all: if there is no equilibrium, there can be no comparative statics. But instability results represent a 'problem' for yet another reason: namely, that we do not seem to observe the kinds of wild fluctuations in policy outcomes that the majoritarian logic suggests we should. As Tullock (1981) puts it in the title of a relevant article, 'Why So Much Stability?' There are several kinds of answer to this question, but one important line is that the various institutions in place operate to limit choices in such a way that stability prevails. Parliamentary institutions (such things as parties, committee systems, bicameralism, etc.) are then perceived through an analytic lens that identifies the suppression of instability as a major role (perhaps the most important role) that such institutions might perform. This is a perception that is distinctive, I think, to RCPT.

Thus, rational choice theory has a problem in its application to politics by virtue of outcome instability; it also has a problem in relation to rationality. It has long been recognized that voters will be 'rationally ignorant' about political outcomes. In other words, it does not pay rational voters to acquire the kind of information necessary to assess the details of public policies because rational voters cannot reasonably expect to be causally efficacious in bringing about their preferred outcomes. It has also been recognized that instrumental considerations cannot explain why people vote. But the same logic means that instrumental considerations cannot explain *how* people vote either. If the act of voting cannot be explained as a means to bring about a desired electoral outcome, then both the fact of voting and the content of voting must be explained in other ways. In another setting (Brennan and Lomasky 1993), I attempted to advance an account of voting behaviour that is consistent with the axioms of rationality. That account depends, as any rational account must, on the voter deriving benefits from the act of voting independently of the outcome the vote 'brings about'. In our account, we term such benefits 'expressive'. We argue that a 'veil of insignificance' lies between individual vote and electoral outcome; this causes predictable changes in the considerations that will secure (rational) votes, compared with the situation in which the 'chooser' is decisive (as in ordinary market choice). In particular, symbolic considerations (including for example the desire to perform moral action for its own sake) play a predictably greater role in politics than they do in markets. Whether that account of electoral behaviour is descriptively more accurate than the RCPT orthodoxy is still contested. It is incontestable, though, that the revealed preference logic of market analysis fails in the electoral setting: the logic of rationality provides no grounds for believing that voters will vote for the electoral outcomes they prefer. There is, therefore, no reason to believe that voters will vote their

interests, and no reason to think that considerations of interests will play
the role in politics that RCP theorists have traditionally claimed. Large-
number electoral politics generates a demonstrable kind of 'rational
irrationality' – something which is distinctive to large-number collective
activities and specifically is not present in decentralized idealized market
settings. RCPT's ambitions to provide a synthetic social theory based on a
single unifying account of human behaviour are, on this account, at risk:
what rationality implies behaviourally in electoral politics is likely to be
very different from what it implies in markets. The 'sciences' of
democratic politics and market economics are related, but they are
distinct and somewhat less integrated than a simple 'economic theory of
politics' might lead one to believe.

One implication of the 'rational irrationality' of electoral politics
that is worth noting deals with majority cycling. Although the *logic* of
majoritarian instability is not affected by the 'veil of insignificance', both
the capacity for strategic manipulation of that instability and the empirical likelihood of the instability itself seem to be significantly moderated
once interest-based voting is called into question. The standard examples
of strategic redistribution among voters to secure ever new coalitions
of majority support become extremely strained when voters do not
routinely vote their interests. Voter 'rationality' may disappear, but electoral equilibrium may reappear. Perhaps not everything is lost.

A Response to Four Particular Critiques

By way of clarifying the ambitions and the nature of RCPT, I wish to
respond briefly here to four criticisms of RCPT that have arisen in verbal
presentations of earlier versions of this chapter. I shall label these
critiques the 'universalist', the 'imperialist', the 'exclusivist' and the
'heterogeneous'.

The charge that RCPT is universalist takes the form of the challenge
that politics in, say, imperial Rome or imperial China or nineteenth-
century Japan is simply not amenable to RCPT analysis – that RCPT is a late-
eighteenth-century construction oriented around nineteenth- and
twentieth-century Western (maybe English-speaking) political practice,
and should identify itself explicitly as so constrained. There is, it seems,
more to this critique than meets the eye. The effect is not only to limit
the scope of application of rational choice methods, but also to suggest
grounds for such limitation that lie outside the considerations that RCPT
readily admits. In particular, if ideas about politics are themselves an
independent force in the practice of politics, a theory of political process
must include explicitly or implicitly a theory of ideas.

Of course, a rational choice account of the politics of imperial Rome
would look rather different from a rational choice account of contem-

porary US politics, for reasons that RCPT would readily admit. Institutional arrangements are very different. So perhaps might be the detailed motivations of relevant actors, and specific beliefs about other actors' response to particular courses of action. I see no reason why RCPT cannot accommodate these factors. But I do not think that RCPT analysts would think that actors' own theories about the nature of what they were doing in participating in politics (that is, what *we* identify as politics) would be of fundamental explanatory power – any more than conventional economic history would hold that medieval banking institutions' lack of access to economic theory much affected the actual working of usury laws. RCPT may be wrong in this: that is, beliefs about the economic effects of particular regulations seem likely to play a rather larger role in political decisions to impose such regulations than in coherent explanations of what the economic effects actually are. Nevertheless, with such beliefs taken as given, there is still an RCPT account of medieval usury laws or politics in imperial Rome to be offered, and that account may well be full of insights. It is certainly not obvious to me that any such account is *a priori* useless. It is, after all, a standard feature of RCPT analysis, as of most economics, that 'preferences' are taken as exogenous and beyond explanation within the RCPT scheme. RCPT is clearly *not* universalist in the sense that it attempts to explain *everything*: no theory can.

The 'imperialist' critique I take to be the charge that RCPT identifies political process excessively through an economic lens, and with excessive appeal to market analogies. I have some sympathy with this view. There is always a danger that RCPT analysts extrapolate too casually from established economic analogues. The voting case is one example. But here, it seems to me, the strength of the rational choice method is most evident. The logic is capable of showing why particular extrapolations are inappropriate (as I believe it does in the voting case). As I have indicated, there are several ways (important ones, in my view) in which rational choice models of markets must be modified in order to apply to politics.

The 'exclusivist' critique is often bracketed with the 'imperialist' – perhaps because both are seen as evidence of intellectual arrogance – though, as I understand them, the two are quite different. The exclusivist critique centres on the perception that RCPT distinctively claims that the only proper way of doing political analysis is the rational choice theory way. The contrast here might be with the Nietzschean notion of looking at the world through multiple windows: RCPT does not accommodate, it is argued, more than one eye. In one sense, that charge is absolutely correct. If there are rival explanations of some social phenomenon which offer logically inconsistent accounts of causation, RCPT is committed to the proposition that both cannot be right, and this is so whether RCPT happens itself to constitute one of the 'explanatory accounts' or not. On the other hand, if there are two accounts that are merely different, RCPT attempts to accommodate both; if doing so violates perceptions of what theory simplicity will accommodate, it attempts to accommodate the account with the greater explanatory power. RCPT should not be under-estimated in its capacity to do this – it can, in sensitive hands, be extraordinarily hospitable. That 'hospitality' may, of course, be seen as making the point: RCPT swallows what it can coherently swallow, and spits everything else out; in that lies its exclusivist ambitions. If RCPT's hos-pitality is so identified, then I plead guilty as charged. Eclecticism is acceptable as long as it is seen as a means of dealing sequentially with different aspects of a (directly unmanageable) larger theory: but eclec-ticism as logical incoherence is, in my view, simply muddled thinking.

The final critique I have labelled the 'heterogenous' critique, for want of a better term. It arises from an observation by John Braithwaite (1989) that sometimes (often perhaps) in social contexts, agents respond to the same apparent stimulus in directly opposite ways. The example cited relates to the pattern of responses to increased police presence on streets: in some cases the level of criminal activity increases, and in some cases it decreases. A similar example emerges from the effects of increased surveillance in the enforcement of nursing home regulations (see Braithwaite 1997) where some regulations increase and some decrease their compliance. In fact, Braithwaite's own explanation of these divergencies in behavioural response seems to me to be fully consistent with rational choice analysis. What is at stake is the trade-off between two desires: to avoid the 'direct' cost (being picked up by the police, or non-compliance with the standards of regulation in the nursing-home case); and to avoid the shame (being shown to be afraid of the police, or being unprofessional in complying only when compelled to).

Such cases do not, I think, reveal a basic flaw in the RCPT framework; rather, they show that detailed knowledge about actors' motivations is required in order to make RCPT operational. I do not, as I have indicated, see the introduction of shame/fame/social approval as in any way undermining the rational choice method or, for that matter, basic egoism. The message rather is that allowance ought to be made in rational choice analysis for a tolerably rich motivational structure and, within that structure, for some motivational heterogeneity.

Conclusion

In this chapter I have approached the application of rational actor theory to politics in a characteristically RCPT way. I have tried to lay out the basic axioms of the theory, and then enquire how well they suit the application to the political context. At one level, the answer seems to be 'not too well'. Two problems in particular arise. One is the difficulty, in general, of securing (stable) equilibrium under majority rule. Given the importance of equilibrium as an analytic device in all rational choice analysis, this difficulty is not negligible. The second issue is the behaviour of voters in democratic elections. If, as I have argued, voters do not, as a matter of the logic of electoral choice, vote for the electoral outcomes that they *prefer*, then electoral processes do not elicit 'rational' behaviour in the normal sense; no RCPT account of democratic politics that depends on the claim that electoral processes are rational in this sense can be totally adequate. This is not merely a question of whether, and to what extent, individual (self-)interest plays a major role in electoral politics – though that is surely one aspect. The problem is a logical one, and substantially independent of the content of voters' preferences over electoral outcomes. For this reason, any truly rational actor theory of politics will look rather different from a rational actor theory of markets: if a synthesis of the analysis of economics and politics is possible, it is a more complex, subtle and abstracted synthesis than most RCPT exponents seem to believe.

Is it then the case that RCPT is a bankrupt enterprise – a blind alley in the history of social science? Should we, as some critics have argued, abandon the whole RCPT endeavour and return to the 'historical' eclectic inductive methods of traditional political science? I do not myself draw that conclusion. To say that RCPT has the resources for self-criticism is not to say that RCPT is self-destructive. The careful spelling out of what the basic axioms of the theory tell us about political processes seems to me to be a worthwhile enterprise, no less interesting by virtue of its being more than a direct application of simple micro-economics. The RCPT tradition is too rich with genuine insights, too suggestive of questions for exploration, to be abandoned after a mere decade or two of its life.

On the other hand, it does seem to me that RCPT as it is commonly practised needs amendment and modification in a number of directions. First, RCPT needs to present a coherent theory of voter behaviour. (Enough has been said about this here to indicate what I think such a theory would look like.) Second, RCPT needs to allow more explicitly for the possibility of public-interest motivations and for greater motivational heterogeneity across individuals. One aspect of this motivational array is the need to allow for regard (fame and shame) as important motivators alongside 'interests' as conventionally conceived. There is, as I see it, an important research program in rational choice analysis at stake in this extension of motivational structure (which Philip Pettit and I hope to engage in future work). Third, and relatedly, RCPT needs to pay more attention to selection devices (screens) in political contexts: incentive devices (sanctions) are not unimportant, but they are not the only institutional mechanism in place and are not always the most important. Fourth, to introduce a slightly parochial element, RCPT ought to be generalized to deal with systems beyond the United States system. RCPT is largely an American invention and represents a larger part of political science in America than elsewhere: it is not suprising that, implicitly or explicitly, it draws heavily on American institutions and the American experience. But RCPT has, by its nature, broader aspirations. It deserves a more general application: to the British system; to the Australian system (which as a UK–US hybrid with its own distinctive institutional features makes an interesting case study); and to the various European systems.

In other words, there is a lot of life still left in the RCPT enterprise. Perhaps pursuing that life will serve only to reveal further limitations in the theory itself and in the kind of approach it offers. Perhaps. But, in my judgment, RCPT still represents the most systematic approach to the study of political processes and the most promising source of genuine understanding currently available.

Notes

1 Arrow's theorem states that no collective ordering can in general be derived from a set of individual orderings without violating certain apparently reasonable ethical requirements (see Arrow 1963).
2 The median voter theorem states that electoral competition between two parties, or candidates, generates an equilibrium outcome at the ideal point of the median voter, given reasonable assumptions about voter preferences. The median voter is therefore that voter whose ideal point is such that there are an equal number of voters' ideal points to either side of the median voter's.

References

Alt, James, and Shepsle, Kenneth, eds. 1990. *Perspectives on Positive Political Economy*. Cambridge: Cambridge University Press.
Arrow, K. 1963. *Social Choice and Individual Values*. New Haven: Yale University Press.
Braithwaite, John. 1989. *Crime, Shame and Reintegration*. Cambridge: Cambridge University Press.
Braithwaite, V. 1997. 'Games of Engagement', *Law and Policy*, forthcoming.
Brennan, G., and Lomasky, L. 1993. *Democracy and Decision*. Cambridge: Cambridge University Press.
Buchanan, J. M. 1969. *Cost and Choice*. Chicago: Markham Publishing Company.
Buchanan, James. 1989. 'Constitutional Economics', in J. Eatwell and P. Newman, eds, *The New Palgrave: A Dictionary of Economics*. London: Macmillan.

Elster, J. 1979. *Ulysees and the Sirens*. Cambridge: Cambridge University Press.

Jackson, F., and Pettit, P. 1992. 'Explanatory Ecumenism', *Economics and Philosophy*, 8, February.

McKelvey, R. 1976. 'Intransitivities in Multi-dimensional Voting Models and Some Implications for Agenda Control', *Journal of Economic Theory*, 12.

Mueller, Dennis. 1989. *Public Choice II*. Cambridge: Cambridge University Press.

Nozick, R. 1977. 'On Austinian Methodology', *Synthese*, 36.

Parfitt, D. 1984. *Reasons and Persons*. Oxford: Oxford University Press.

Riker, William. 1982. *Liberalism against Popularism*. San Francisco: W. H. Freeman.

Self, P. 1993. *Government by the Market*. Basingstoke: Macmillan.

Sommerlad, F., and McLean, I., eds. 1989. *The Political Theory of Condorcet*. Oxford: Oxford University Faculty of Social Studies, Working Paper 1/89.

Stigler, George, 1982. 'Economists and Public Policy', *Regulation*, May–June.

Stretton, H., and Orchard, L. 1994. *Public Goods, Public Enterprise, Public Choice: Theoretical Foundations of the Contemporary Attack on Government*. New York: St Martins Press, and Basingstoke: Macmillan.

Tullock, G. 1981. 'Why So Much Stability?', *Public Choice*, 37.

CHAPTER 5

Republican Political Theory

Philip Pettit

Republican political theory takes its starting point from a long-established tradition of thinking about politics (Pocock 1975). The republican tradition is associated with Cicero at the time of the Roman republic; with a number of writers, pre-eminently Machiavelli – 'the divine Machiavel' of the *Discourses* – in the Renaissance Italian republics; with James Harrington, Algernon Sydney and a host of lesser figures in and after the period of the English Civil War and commonwealth; and with the many theorists of republic or commonwealth in eighteenth-century England, the United States and France. These theorists – the commonwealthmen (Robbins 1959) – were greatly influenced by John Locke and, later, the Baron de Montesquieu; indeed they claimed Locke and Montesquieu, with good reason, as their own. They are well represented in documents like *Cato's Letters* (Trenchard and Gordon 1971) and, on the American side of the Atlantic, the *Federalist Papers* (Madison et al. 1987).

The commonwealthmen helped to shape habits of political reflex and thought that still survive today. Their distinctive refrain had two parts: the cause of freedom rests squarely with the law and the state – it is mainly thanks to the constitution under which they live that people enjoy freedom; but the authorities are also an inherent threat and people have to strive to 'keep the bastards honest'. The price of liberty is civic virtue, then, where that includes both a willingness to participate in government and a determination to exercise eternal vigilance in regard to the governors. The commonwealthmen tended to advocate the removal of the monarchy in America, but in England most were content to see the king constitutionally fettered. England was 'a nation', in Montesquieu's (1989: 70) unmistakeable reference, 'where the republic hides under the form of monarchy' (Rahe 1992: 524).

I find the republican tradition of thought a wonderful source of ideas and ideals, and in this chapter I hope to communicate why (see Pettit 1997). But I should mention that I am not alone in finding the tradition inspirational. Historians like John Pocock (1975) and Quentin Skinner (1978; 1983; 1984) have not only made the republican way of thinking visible to us in the past couple of decades; they have also shown how it can give us a new perspective on contemporary politics. Skinner in particular has argued that it can give us a new understanding of freedom, and my own argument builds on this. Legal thinkers like Cass Sunstein (1990; 1993a; 1993b), on the other hand, have gone back to the republican tradition in its distinctively American incarnation in the late 1800s and have made a strong case for the claim that the tradition suggests a distinctive way of interpreting the US Constitution and, more generally, that it gives us an insightful overview of the role of government. Criminologists and regulatory theorists like John Braithwaite, with whom I have actively collaborated (Braithwaite and Pettit 1990), find in the republican tradition a set of compelling ideas; it enables us to articulate both the demands that we should place on a regulatory system – say, the criminal justice system – and the expectations that we should hold out for how those demands can be best met (Ayres and Braithwaite 1992). And these are just a few thinkers among many commentators who have begun to chart republican connections, and sometimes to draw actively on republican ideas, in recent years.[1]

My own approach to republican political theory is to give centre place to the notion of freedom that was shared among republican thinkers generally, and to derive other republican claims from the commitment to this ideal. In this chapter I will present the republican ideal of freedom in the first section and then try to illustrate, in the second, the way in which that ideal has significance for contemporary political thought.

The Republican Ideal of Freedom

The Constant Connection

Early in the nineteenth century Benjamin Constant (1988) delivered a famous lecture entitled 'The Liberty of the Ancients and the Liberty of the Moderns'. He depicted the liberty of the moderns, in the familiar negative or liberal fashion, as the absence of interference. I am free in this sense 'to the degree to which no human being interferes with my activity' (Berlin 1958: 7). Constant depicted the liberty of the ancients, on the other hand, as the liberty associated, ideally, with being a direct participant in a self-governing democracy. I am free in this sense, not through being uncontrolled by others, but through sharing with others the power to control all. The liberty of the ancients is the most prominent form of what Isaiah Berlin (1958) later called positive freedom.

The most important observation in introducing the republican conception of freedom is to recognize Constant's image of the liberty of the ancients as a caricature that served to hide the true republican way of thinking, only recently so prominent, from his contemporaries' eyes. Constant may not have been consciously propagandizing, but what he achieved was to mesmerize later generations into thinking that the only feasible, perhaps the only sensible, notion of freedom was the liberal idea of freedom as non-interference. The liberty of the ancients is no match for freedom as non-interference – even if it is thought desirable, it must be judged to be unattainable. The effect of setting up the two as the only relevant alternatives was to give victory, inevitably, to the liberal ideal.

The republican way of thinking about freedom, effectively suppressed by Constant, represents it as non-domination, not as direct democratic standing. And the difference between freedom as non-interference and freedom as non-domination is easily explained. Assume that one person dominates another to the extent that they have the capacity to interfere arbitrarily – to interfere on an arbitrary basis – in some or all of the other's choices (Pettit 1996; 1997). Freedom as non-interference makes the absence of interference sufficient for freedom; in contrast, freedom as non-domination requires the absence of a capacity on the part of anyone else – any individual or corporate agent – to interfere arbitrarily in their life or affairs. The difference between the two ways of conceiving of liberty may seem slight, but a little reflection will reveal hidden dimensions to the contrast.

Interference and Arbitrary Interference

The two conceptions of freedom both invoke the notion of interference, and we may begin our exploration of the contrast between the two ways of conceiving liberty with a comment on this. The first thing to note is that, on almost all accounts, the intrusions that count as interference have to be intentional acts, or at least acts for which the agent can be held responsible (Miller 1990: 35): they have to be intentional or quasi-intentional. The reason for this stipulation is that freedom under most accounts is a condition defined in relation to other intentional agents, not a condition defined by reference to favours bestowed by nature: not a condition defined by how far a person escapes various brute, non-intentionally imposed limitations (see Spitz 1995: 382–3).

The intrusions that constitute interference may be restricted to acts that make certain options impossible for the agent; or they may be extended to include acts that coerce or manipulate the agent in choosing between options. I shall assume that, for both conceptions of freedom, interference is to be understood in the broader fashion. Under this way of taking them, acts of interference include any acts that worsen the agent's situation – or least worsen it significantly – either by reducing the alternatives available in choice, or by raising the actual or expected costs associated with some of the alternatives. Thus the agent may be stopped from doing something; the agent may be threatened with some extra cost, say some penalty, in the event of doing it; or the agent may simply be penalized for having done the act in question.

Freedom as non-interference invokes the notion of interference; freedom as non-domination goes further and invokes arbitrary interference: interference on an arbitrary basis. What makes an act of interference arbitrary, then, in the sense of being perpetrated on an arbitrary basis? An act is perpetrated on an arbitrary basis, we can say, if it is subject only to the *arbitrium*, the decision or judgment, of the agent; the agent was in a position to choose it or not choose it, at their pleasure. When we say that an act of interference is perpetrated on an arbitrary basis, then, we imply that like any arbitrary act it is chosen or not chosen at the agent's pleasure. And in particular, since interference with others is involved, we imply that it is chosen or rejected without reference to the interests, or the opinions, of those affected. The choice is not forced to track what the interests of those others require according to their own judgments.[2]

Under this conception of arbitrariness, then, an act of interference is non-arbitrary to the extent that it is forced to track the interests and ideas of the person suffering the interference. Since the interests and ideas of the person involved may make inconsistent demands, non-arbitrariness consists in recognition of the relevant ones. I may have an interest in the state imposing certain taxes or in punishing certain offenders, for example, and the state may pursue these ends according to procedures that conform to my ideas about appropriate means. But I may still not want the state to impose taxes on me – I may want to be an exception – or I may think that I ought not to be punished in the appropriate manner, even though I have been convicted of an offence. In such a case, my relevant interests and ideas are those that are shared in common with others, not those that treat me as exceptional, since the state is meant to serve others as well as me. And so, in these cases, the interference of the state in taxing or punishing me is not conducted on an arbitrary basis and does not represent domination.

The republican tradition of thinking took a distinctive view of what is required for an act of interference – in particular, an act of legal or government interference – to be non-arbitrary, and I follow that tradition in giving this account. Consider the complaint of Tom Paine

(1989: 168) against monarchy: 'It means arbitrary power in an individual person; in the exercise of which, *himself*, and not the *res-publica*, is the object'(cf. Sydney 1996: 199–200). What is required for non-arbitrary state power, as this comment makes clear, is that the power be exercised in a way that tracks, not the power-holder's personal welfare or world-view, but rather the welfare and world-view of the public. The acts of interference perpetrated by the state must be triggered by the shared interests of those affected; and the interpretation of what those interests require must be shared, at least at the procedural level, by those affected.

Thus there are two antonyms for freedom: one opposes freedom directly to interference, but the second varies this opposition in two ways. The second antonym of freedom involves not interference as such, only interference on an arbitrary basis. Moreover, this second antonym of freedom does not require actual arbitrary interference, only vulnerability to someone with the capacity for such interference.

The second antonym has the effect of making it harder for someone to lose their freedom or to have their freedom reduced. For if an agent interferes non-arbitrarily in their choices, that does not offend as such against their freedom; whatever damage is done by the interference, the non-arbitrariness is enough to ensure that their freedom is not compromised. But the second antonym also has the contrary effect of making it easier, not harder, for someone to suffer a loss of freedom. For if an agent has the capacity to interfere arbitrarily in any of their choices, then that in itself compromises their freedom; they suffer a loss of freedom even if the other person does not actually exercise the capacity for interference.

The Harder-to-lose-freedom Effect

The harder-to-lose-freedom effect makes for a difference in the law's impact on liberty under the two conceptions. Under freedom as non-interference, a regime of law, being necessarily coercive, systematically compromises people's freedom, even if the consequence of putting the regime into operation is that less interference takes place overall. Subjection to the law, in and of itself, represents a loss of liberty. Under the second conception, however, subjection to the law need not represent a loss of liberty for anyone who lives under it, provided – and of course it is a big proviso – that the making, interpretation and implementation of the law are not arbitrary: provided that the legal coercion involved is constrained to track the interests and ideas of those affected. The proviso, intuitively expressed, is that the legal regime represents a fair rule of law.

A regime of legal coercion and restraint, while not itself constituting a compromise of liberty, may have the same effect as a natural obstacle in limiting the choices available to people or in making them more costly: in defining the range over which people enjoy undominated choice. Proponents of freedom as non-interference do not count natural obstacles as factors that compromise liberty – because they are in no way intentional – but they do admit that such obstacles affect the range of choice over which freedom as non-interference may be exercised; the obstacles condition freedom, as we might put the distinction, but they do not compromise it.[3] Proponents of freedom as non-domination move the locus of this boundary between compromising and conditioning factors. For them, the interference associated with a fair rule of law, like the natural obstacle, conditions people's liberty but does not in itself compromise it: the law does not in itself count as infringing or violating or reducing or offending against people's liberty.[4]

Hobbes and Bentham are the great advocates of the idea that law in itself represents a compromise of liberty. 'As against the coercion applicable by individual to individual, no liberty can be given to one man but in proportion as it is taken away from another. All coercive laws, therefore, and in particular all laws creative of liberty, are as far as they go abrogative of liberty' (Bentham 1843). Or as Hobbes had put it: 'The Liberty of a Subject, lyeth therefore only in those things, which in regulating their actions, the Soveraign hath praetermitted' (Hobbes 1968: 264).

But Hobbes and Bentham were consciously breaking with a longer tradition of thought – the republican or commonwealthman tradition – in taking this line (Skinner 1983). That tradition was defended in the first instance by James Harrington (1992: 20), who argued that Hobbes was confusing freedom from the law with freedom proper: freedom by the law. John Locke took Harrington's side, embracing 'freedom from Absolute, Arbitrary Power' as the essential thing and presenting law as essentially on liberty's side: 'that ill deserves the Name of Confinement which serves to hedge us in only from Bogs and Precipices . . . the end of Law is not to abolish or restrain, but to preserve and enlarge Freedom' (1965: 325, 348). William Blackstone (1978: 126) represents the eighteenth-century orthodoxy when he follows the same line: 'laws, when prudently framed, are by no means subversive but rather introductive of liberty; for (as Mr Locke has well observed) where there is no law there is no freedom'.

The difference between the two conceptions of liberty in their attitude to the law was of great significance from the point of view of Hobbes and Bentham. The view that all law compromises people's liberty enabled Hobbes to withstand the criticism that he anticipated from republicans, that his Leviathan was utterly inimical to freedom, constituting an arbitrary rule as distinct from a rule of law: an arbitrary rule as distinct from the republican vision of an 'empire of laws, and not of men'

(Harrington 1992: 8). And the same view enabled Bentham and those friends of his who opposed the American cause in the 1770s to argue against the colonists' main complaint. This was that, since the British parliament was not constrained in the laws that it passed for the governance of the American colonies – since it was not constrained in the same way that it was constrained in Britain itself – those laws represented an arbitrary interference with Americans and compromised their liberty (Lind 1776). Hobbes could argue that Leviathan did no worse than commonwealths in respect of the liberty of its subjects, since all law compromises liberty. And Bentham and his friends could argue on the same grounds that, in regard to liberty, Americans fared no worse under the law imposed by the British parliament than those in Britain itself.

So much for the harder-to-lose-freedom effect of opposing freedom to non-domination, not non-interference. But what of the easier-to-lose-freedom effect of shifting the antonym?

The Easier-to-lose-freedom Effect

This effect comes of the fact that someone loses freedom, not just to the extent that another person interferes on an arbitrary basis in their choices, but to the extent that another agent has the capacity to do this. With freedom as non-domination, a person loses freedom to the extent that they live under the thumb of another, even if that thumb is never used against them. Suppose that, under the existing laws and mores, a wife may be abused on an arbitrary basis by her husband, at least in certain areas and in a certain measure. Even if her husband is a loving and caring individual, such a wife cannot count as fully free under the construal of freedom as non-domination. And neither can the employee who lives under the thumb of an employer, nor the member of a minority who lives under the thumb of a majority coalition, nor the debtor who lives under the thumb of a creditor, nor anyone in such a subservient position.

Where the first effect of shifting the antonym shows up particularly in the assessment of law and liberty, the second relates to the association between law and slavery. As it became a matter of common assumption after Bentham that law represents a compromise of liberty, albeit a compromise that may be for the good overall, so it became impossible to maintain that to be unfree is always, in some measure, to be enslaved (Patterson 1991); no one was prepared to say that the law makes slaves of those who live under it. But before Bentham, when freedom was opposed first and foremost to domination, the association between unfreedom and slavery was complete. To be unfree was to live at the mercy of another; and that was, to live under a condition of enslavement to them.

Thus, Algernon Sydney (1990: 17) could write in the 1680s: 'liberty solely consists in an independency upon the will of another, and by the name of slave we understand a man, who can neither dispose of his person nor goods, but enjoys all at the will of his master'. And in the following century, the authors of *Cato's Letters* could give a characteristically forceful statement to the theme. 'Liberty is, to live upon one's own Terms; Slavery is, to live at the mere Mercy of another; and a Life of Slavery is, to those who can bear it, a continual State of Uncertainty and Wretchedness, often an Apprehension of Violence, often the lingering Dread of a violent Death' (Trenchard and Gordon 1971, vol 2: 249–50).

The easier-to-lose-freedom effect of opposing liberty to domination connects with the slavery theme, because one of the striking things about a slave is that they remain a slave even if their master is entirely benign and never interferes with them. As Algernon Sydney (1990: 441) put it, 'he is a slave who serves the best and gentlest man in the world, as well as he who serves the worst'. Or as it was put by Richard Price (1991: 77–8) in the eighteenth century: 'Individuals in private life, while held under the power of masters, cannot be denominated free, however equitably and kindly they may be treated. This is strictly true of communities as well as of individuals.' There is domination, and there is unfreedom, even if no actual interference occurs.

I mentioned that the first effect of opposing freedom to domination provided an argument for the defenders of the American cause: while those in Britain were not made unfree by the law, given that the law could not be arbitrarily imposed there, those in America did not enjoy a similar status under the law. I should add that the second effect enabled them to sheet this argument home. They were in a position to argue that, even though the British parliament did not interfere much in American affairs – even though it levied only a small tax – still, because it could levy whatever tax it wished, without any serious restraint on its will, it related to the American colonists as master to slave.

Joseph Priestley (1993: 140) offers a nice example of this line of argument.

Q. What is the great grievance that those people complain of? A. It is their being taxed by the parliament of Great Britain, the members of which are so far from taxing themselves, that they ease themselves at the same time. If this measure takes place, the colonists will be reduced to a state of as complete servitude, as any people of which there is an account in history. For by the same power, by which the people of England can compel them to pay *one penny*, they may compel them to pay the *last penny* they have. There will be nothing but arbitrary imposition on the one side, and humble petition on the other.

Three Further Remarks

My comments on the two main differences associated with opposing freedom to domination rather than to interference should serve to make the notion intelligible. I want to add three further remarks, however, in order to underline some points that are important for understanding it fully.

First, although domination is constituted by one agent's having the capacity to interfere on an arbitrary basis in the affairs of another, some plausible empirical assumptions link it with a shared awareness on the part of the individuals or groups involved that this capacity exists. The question of whether you are undominated is bound to be of interest to anyone. The facts that make you undominated, if indeed you are such – the facts about your comparative resources, for example, and about the degree to which you are protected by legal and other means – are bound to be salient to all involved. Under standard assumptions as to people's inductive and inferential abilities, it follows that the fact of non-domination will be a matter of common recognition among the individuals in question (Lewis 1969: 56). And that is something of the greatest significance. For it means that under standard ways of achieving it, freedom as non-domination is intimately linked with the ability to look others in the eye, without having to defer to them or fear them. Montesquieu (1989: 157) emphasizes this theme when he writes: 'Political liberty in a citizen is that tranquillity of spirit which comes from the opinion each one has of his security, and in order for him to have this liberty the government must be such that one citizen cannot fear another citizen.'

The second remark that I want to make is also about domination. If someone is to enjoy freedom as non-domination, it is not enough that the other people are unlikely to exercise arbitrary interference; those other people must lack the capacity to interfere arbitrarily in that person's life, not just be unlikely to interfere. Suppose that you are subject to interference on an arbitrary basis from someone who, as it happens, really likes you and is extremely unlikely to interfere. If it still remains the case that, by the ordinary standards of free-will attribution, they have a capacity to interfere or not to interfere, and this on a more or less arbitrary basis, then you are dominated in some measure by them and are thus far unfree. This is not a hard line to take, since you clearly suffer to the extent that the person has the capacity to interfere arbitrarily with you: you suffer to the extent that such interference is accessible to them as an agent, however improbable it is that they will exercise it. Their capacity for arbitrary interference means, for example, that you lack grounds for the subjective state of mind that goes with freedom as non-domination; you have reason to defer to the person in question and to look for their continued favour.

The third and last point is the most important. When Bentham and his associates came to reject the notion of freedom as non-domination, freedom as non-slavery, one theme in their reflections was that this sort of freedom did not come in degrees and so, unlike the rival conception, lent itself to 'panegyric and careless declamation' (Paley 1825: 359–60; Long 1977: ch. 4). John Lind (1776: 25) expressed the criticism strongly in his attack on Richard Price's talk of the American colonists as slaves. 'Things must be always at the maximum or minimum; there are no intermediate gradations: what is not white must be black.' The third point I want to make is that this perception is mistaken. Freedom as non-domination is not an all-or-nothing matter.

The point should be obvious on a little reflection. Agents may have a more or less ready capacity to interfere. And the interference for which they have a capacity may be more or less serious, and may be available more or less without cost: say, without risk of retaliation. Thus the freedom as non-domination of those they are in a position to affect may be more or less intense; the weaker the agents, the greater the freedom of those they may affect.

Intensity, I should add, is only one dimension in which freedom as non-domination may vary. As it is more or less intense, so freedom as non-domination may also be of one or another extent: it may be available for a smaller or larger number of choices, for choices that are more or less costly, and for choices of intuitively lesser or greater significance. Even if we have attained the highest possible intensity of non-domination for people in a society, there may be room for improving the range of undominated choice that is available to them: we may make the range of choice larger, or less costly, or intuitively more significant. Even if we remove all compromising influences on freedom as non-domination, it may still be possible to remove conditioning influences as well.

Thus, freedom as non-domination may be increased in either of two broad dimensions, intensity or extent; and we must decide how those dimensions are to be weighed against one another (Pettit 1997: ch. 3). Indeed, a similar problem arises with freedom as non-interference: it increases in intensity so far as interference is blocked, and increases in extent so far as the range of unobstructed choice is expanded, say, by providing people with extra resources. But I can overlook such problems of weighting here, as I shall be concerned with the promotion of these values only in the dimension of intensity. The question I address in the next section bears only on what is required for maximizing equal non-domination in the dimension of intensity.

The Significance of the Republican Ideal

The Paley Connection

Perhaps the most important figure in the demise of the republican ideal – someone more important even than Constant – is William Paley. Paley may have been the only writer in his time to recognize clearly the shift that was taking place – indeed, he argued for it. This was the shift from the received notion of freedom as non-domination, freedom as security against interference on an arbitrary basis, to freedom as non-interference. He sets out his view with admirable clarity in *The Principles of Moral and Political Philosophy*, which was first published in 1785 and was continually reprinted throughout the nineteenth century (Paley 1825).

Paley recognizes in this work that the usual notion of civil liberty, the one that agrees with 'the usage of common discourse, as well as the example of many respectable writers' (357), is that of freedom as non-domination. 'This idea places liberty in security; making it to consist not merely in an actual exemption from the constraint of useless and noxious laws and acts of dominion, but in being free from the *danger* of having such hereafter imposed or exercised' (357; original emphasis). But Paley argues against this received notion, and in favour of a Benthamite version of freedom as non-interference, on an extraordinary basis. He argues that the ideal in question, however well-established, is excessively demanding on the state: 'those definitions of liberty ought to be rejected, which, by making that essential to civil freedom which is unattainable in experience, inflame expectations that can never be gratified, and disturb the public content with complaints, which no wisdom or benevolence of government can remove' (Paley 1825: 359).

How could Paley have thought that freedom as non-domination was the received ideal of freedom and yet that it was too demanding on the state? My hunch is that for Paley, as for most progressive thinkers of the late eighteenth century, it was no longer possible to think that political citizenship and consideration could be restricted, as traditional republicans had taken it to be restricted, to propertied males: women and servants could not be systematically and permanently excluded from concern. 'Everybody to count for one, nobody for more than one', in the slogan ascribed to Bentham by John Stuart Mill (1969: 257). Thus, whereas traditional republicans could think that everyone relevant to the state's concern – every propertied male – might aspire to be free in the sense of not being subject to anyone's domination, egalitarians like Paley could not say this without seeming to embrace a wholly revolutionary doctrine: a doctrine that would require the upturning of relations between men and women, masters and servants. Their response was to deflate the ideal of freedom – to reduce it from non-domination to non-interference – at the same time that they argued that the constituency of political concern should be expanded. What they gave with the one hand, they took away with the other.

Why is the republican conception of liberty politically significant for the modern state? In a word, because it would recall the state to performing, in relation to citizens generally, the service that a republic – even a republic hidden under the form of a monarchy – was expected to perform for traditional elites. It may indeed have been impossible for someone like Paley or Bentham or Constant to envisage a state that would liberate servants as well as masters, women as well as men. But this is no longer an obviously infeasible ideal, even if it is obviously unattained. The limits on what we can envisage the state doing, and the limits on what we can imagine civil society allowing the state to do, have shifted dramatically over the last couple of centuries or so. Republicanism went underground at the time when the state began to become inclusivist, thereby permitting the state to become simultaneously more or less minimalist.[5] It is high time that the doctrine was restored to prominence, allowing us to consider the direction that an inclusive republic – a republic dedicated to the general promotion of freedom as non-domination – would have to take.

I have tried to display the significance of the republican perspective elsewhere, examining the impact of the republican ideal on our notions of equality and community; on the policy-commitments that we prescribe for the modern state; on the way we conceive of constitutional and democratic values and institutions; on the approach that we take to issues of regulation and control; and on the image we have of how the state should relate to civil society (Pettit 1997). In order to illustrate the way in which the republican perspective can affect our thinking, I will concentrate here on its significance for issues of redistribution. This theme is particularly relevant, because it is at the centre of contemporary political discussions, and it also connects with the hostile reaction of Paley and others like him to the republican ideal.

Freedom as Non-interference, and Redistribution

How far is the maximal equal distribution of freedom as non-interference consistent with inequalities in other dimensions? How far is it consistent, for example, with different levels of provision in basic goods like food and shelter, modes of transport and media of reliable information; in basic services like medical care, legal counsel and accident insurance; in human capital of the kind associated with training and education; in social capital of the sort that consists in being able to call with confidence on others; in political capital such as office and authority confer; and in the material capital that is necessary for production? How far is it likely to require putting inequalities in these matters right or at least alleviating their effects: in particular, coercively putting them right, or coercively alleviating their effects, under state initiatives? How far is it likely to require what I shall describe, in a word, as redistribution?

The common wisdom on this question is that the maximal equal distribution of freedom as non-interference would leave a lot to be desired in regard to redistribution: it would fall short, under most conceptions, of achieving distributive justice (Rawls 1971). I think that wisdom is well placed and I wish to argue that, in this respect, freedom as non-domination represents a sharply contrasted ideal: the maximal equal distribution of such freedom requires a much more substantial commitment to redistribution.

Before coming to that argument, however, it will be useful to see why the connection between freedom as non-interference and distributive justice is so loose. Two questions arise from the viewpoint of freedom as non-interference, when any such issue of redistribution is considered. First, how far will redistribution entail interference in people's lives by the state? And second, how far will redistribution lower the probability of interference by other agents?

The answer to the first question is that redistribution always entails a degree of interference by the state. For even the most basic form of redistribution involves taxing some to give to others, and that in itself constitutes interference; it deprives those who are taxed of a choice in how to use their money. Besides tax, most forms of redistribution also require inspectors and other officials to oversee the operation. Thus the redistributive measures involve the creation of new possibilities of interference in people's lives.

The answer to the first question means that the onus of proof always lies, from the perspective of freedom as non-interference, with those who counsel redistribution. Whether redistribution in any area is to be supported, then, depends on whether the answer to the second question shows clearly that the margin whereby redistribution will reduce interference in a society is greater than the margin whereby it introduces interference itself. The margin of projected improvement will have to be large enough to ensure that even when we discount for the less-than-certain nature of the projection, the argument squarely favours redistribution.

Nevertheless, it is not easy to find grounds to defend the required answer to the second question. It is always possible for the opponent to argue that, so long as we do not think of the relatively advantaged as downright malicious, we must expect them not to be generally disposed to harm the disadvantaged, and not to be generally in need of curtailment by the redistributive state. Perhaps employers are in a position under the status quo to interfere in various ways with their employees. But why expect them to interfere rather than striving for good and productive relationships? Perhaps husbands are able, given their greater strength and greater cultural backing, to abuse their wives. But why expect them to practise such abuse rather than remaining faithful to their affections and commitments? Perhaps those who lack medical care and legal counsel are prey to the unscrupulous. But why expect doctors and lawyers to be unwilling to provide essential services *pro bono*, especially when they can make good publicity of providing such services?

I sympathize with the drift of these rhetorical questions, believing that it is a mistake to demonize the relatively advantaged and see them always as potential offenders (Pettit 1995). But the effect of the questions in the context of endorsing an ideal of freedom as non-interference is what concerns me now, not the propriety of raising them. The effect is to lead those who take the ideal as the only relevant yardstick of social performance not to require much in the way of redistribution: not to require much in the way of what we intuitively describe as distributive justice. It is quite possible to believe that the regime under which freedom as non-interference is equally distributed at maximal levels is a regime that allows great inequalities in other regards.

Freedom as Non-domination, and Redistribution

We can begin to recognize the significance of the republican ideal of freedom when we notice that its connection with redistribution is different from that of freedom as non-interference. We have seen that the project of equalizing freedom as non-interference at the maximal possible level is hostile to redistribution in two ways. First, it introduces a presumption against redistribution; it casts the onus on the side of anyone who wants to argue for redistribution. And second, it ensures that any argument for redistribution must be probabilistic in a manner that is bound to make it easy to resist. I wish to argue that the ideal of maximizing freedom as non-domination at the maximal level possible differs from the associated ideal of freedom as non-interference in both these respects.

Freedom as non-interference introduces a presumption against redistribution, because redistribution is itself a species of the evil of interference. But no corresponding argument is available with freedom as non-domination. For if the redistributive measures adopted can be pursued under a fair rule of law, and are so pursued, then they do not themselves introduce any form of domination. I assume that many of the redistributive measures contemplated in discussions of distributive justice can be pursued under a fair rule of law. Freedom as non-domination, then, does not introduce any presumption against re-distribution of the kind associated with freedom as non-interference. If redistributive measures are used in the promotion of non-domination, the good at which they are directed does not have to be balanced against a violation of that very good in the process of production; the process of production need not itself represent a form of domination.

The process is not entirely innocent, of course. As we mentioned, any rule of law, and certainly any redistributive rule of law, is going to remove certain choices or raise the costs of pursuing them. But this way of restricting choice, this way of conditioning people's freedom as non-domination, falls far short of compromising such freedom on their part. If it succeeds in reducing the extent to which the poor or the sick or the needy have their freedom compromised, then this cost in the con-ditioning of the freedom of people generally is well worth paying.

Here is another way of thinking about the point. Redistribution under a fair rule of law counts in the republican ledger-book as a form of conditioning of liberty on a par with the conditioning effected by factors like poverty or disability or illness or whatever. Redistribution involves moving around the factors that serve as conditioning influences on freedom: and this, without itself dominating anyone; without itself com-promising anyone's freedom as non-domination. If that reshuffling of freedom-relevant factors can itself increase the degree of equal freedom in the society, then there is little or no question to raise about it. There is no reason to have a presumption against it.

This argument, I hasten to emphasize, is advanced under the assumption that the redistribution effected is achieved under a fair rule of law. And that assumption remains plausible only up to a certain level, and only under a certain kind, of redistribution by a state. Suppose that the redistribution allowed involves the exercise of unconstrained discretion by individual agents of the state; the discretion may arise in the way goods are taken from some, for example, or in the way goods are given to others. Or suppose that the redistribution is so extensive, or subject to such frequent adjustments, that people hardly know where they stand relative to the state. Under any such suppositions, the prospect of redistribution looks very unattractive from a republican point of view.

The republican tradition of thinking has always put the state under severe scrutiny, for fear that state authorities will ever become, or ever support, relatively arbitrary powers. In arguing that the ideal of freedom as non-domination is not hostile to redistribution, in particular not hostile in the manner of freedom as non-interference, I do not mean to reject that tradition. I think that, if we treasure freedom as non-domination, then we have to be vigilant about not allowing the state certain sorts of power; we have to be careful to see that it is subject to all sorts of constitutional and other constraints. My point has been only that, provided a state can be sufficiently constrained – and that may be a very big proviso – there is nothing inherently objectionable about allowing it to use redistributive means for promoting antipower.[6]

The second point that we noticed about the redistributive significance of equalizing non-interference was that the question of whether any redistributive measure increased people's freedom as non-interference remained inevitably a probabilistic matter. Perhaps we can interfere with employers to ensure that they do not interfere in certain ways with their employees. Perhaps we can interfere with husbands to ensure that they do not interfere in certain ways with their wives. But before we think of practising interference, we have to convince ourselves that some shaky arithmetic comes out right. We have to convince ourselves that there is a suitably high probability of a suitably large reduction in the practice of interference by employers and husbands. That thought may well give pause to any projects of redistribution that the ideal of freedom as non-interference is otherwise likely to sponsor.

Like the matter of the presumption against redistribution, however, the ideal of freedom as antipower, freedom as non-domination, has quite a different impact here. Suppose that an employer has the capacity in some measure to interfere arbitrarily in the affairs of an employee. Employment is so scarce and the prospect of unemployment so repellent, that the employer can alter agreed conditions of work, make life much tougher for employees, or even practise some illegal interference in their affairs, with relative ease. And suppose now that we contemplate introducing a system of unemployment benefits, or a set of health and safety regulations, or an arrangement for arbitrating workplace disputes, that would improve the lot of employees. Do we have to do a range of probabilistic sums before we can be sure of the benefits of such a redistributive regime?

Assuming that the regime is consistent with a fair rule of law, and does not itself introduce an independent source of domination – provided it does not have any dominational side-effects – it should be clear that no such sums are necessary. Just the existence of reasonable unemployment benefits is bound to reduce the extent to which an employee is willing to tolerate arbitrary interference by an employer, and by the same token reduces the capacity of the employer to interfere at will and with impunity in the lives of employees. There is no uncertainty plaguing the connection. Or at least there is no uncertainty of the kind that makes the connection with freedom as non-interference so problematic.

Similar points go through on a number of fronts. The fact that people are poor or illiterate or ignorant or unable to get legal counsel or uninsured against illness or incapable of getting around – the fact that they lack basic capabilities in any of these regards (Sen 1985) – makes them subject to a certain sort of exploitation and manipulation. Other things being equal, then, any improvement in their lot is bound to reduce the capacity of others to interfere more or less arbitrarily in their lives. And that means that, other things being equal – dominational side-effects being absent – any such improvement is bound to increase their freedom as non-domination.

The crucial difference in this second respect between the ideals of freedom as non-interference and freedom as non-domination comes of the fact that the first ideal is compromised only by actual interference, the second by the capacity for interference, in particular the capacity for arbitrary interference. It may be unclear whether a given measure will actually reduce the overall level of interference practised by the more advantaged, while it is absolutely certain that the measure will reduce their capacity for interference.

Suppose that the employer in our earlier example is actually benign, or actually committed to a smooth and productive workplace, and thus is unlikely ever to interfere in the affairs of employees. The introduction of employment benefits, or health and safety regulations, or arbitration procedures, will not significantly reduce the probability of interference in such a scenario; that probability is already negligible. But still, the introduction of any such scheme will certainly reduce the employer's capacity for arbitrary interference. For whether the employer interferes or not will no longer be dependent on their good grace; it will be substantially determined by factors outside the employer's will.

Some will retort at this point that there is no reason why we should want to reduce the capacity of an employer to interfere with employees, especially given the cost of doing so, when it is certain that no interference will actually occur. But that is to shift the issue from the matter of what the ideal of freedom as non-domination would require – and, in particular, from the observation that it would require, other things being equal, that the employer is constrained – to the issue of whether it is an attractive ideal. My aim here is not to argue that it is an attractive ideal (on this issue see Pettit 1997), only that it is a redistributively demanding one.

We saw earlier that freedom as non-interference may be maximized, and maximized under the constraint of more or less equal distribution, without any significant redistribution of resources being required. What we have now seen is that, in this respect, as in so many others, freedom as non-domination is quite different. The republican ideal, just in itself, may be capable of encoding the redistributive measures that many of us would think it reasonable to require of the modern state. While remaining an ideal of liberty, it may give adequate expression to the more demanding aspirations that the non-libertarians amongst us find compelling.

Notes

I am most grateful to Geoffrey Brennan and Michael Smith for helpful discussions of the material. I was enormously helped by comments received when the paper was presented to a meeting in New Orleans organised by the Murphy Institute of Political Economy, Tulane University, and the International Society for Economics and Philosophy.

1 For example, Michelman 1986, Elkin 1987, Pagden 1987, Taylor 1989, Oldfield 1990, Fontana 1994, Hutton 1995, Blom 1995, Spitz 1995, Viroli 1995.

2 Notice that an act of interference can be arbitrary in the procedural sense intended here – it may occur on an arbitrary basis – without being arbitrary in the substantial sense of actually going against the interests or judgments of the persons affected. An act is arbitrary, in this usage, by virtue of the controls – specifically, the lack of controls – under which it materializes, not by virtue of the particular consequences to which it gives rise. The usage I follow means that there is no equivocation involved in speaking, as I do, either of a power of arbitrary interference or of an arbitrary power of interference. What is in question in each case is a power of interfering on an arbitrary, unchecked basis.

3 When proponents of this ideal speak of making freedom as non-interference effective, not just leaving it as a formal freedom, I assume that they often have in mind removing or reducing the obstacles that condition the exercise of freedom as non-domination: extending the range of choice available to people. See Van Parijs 1995.

4 The extreme case of legal interference is punishment for an offence. Such punishment will always condition people's freedom as non-domination: removing the capacity for undominated choice (capital punishment); restricting the range over which such choice may be exercised (prison); or raising the costs of making certain undominated choices (fines). But it need not result in the person punished having their liberty compromised through subjection to the arbitrary will of another. This remark is not meant to make legal punishment seem any more tolerable, only to articulate a perhaps surprising corollary of the conception of freedom as non-domination.

5 Liberalism can be identified as the movement that took freedom as the primary ideal and that construed it as non-interference. In this case, then short of taking on a secondary ideal – something like the second principle of justice proposed by Rawl (1971) – or of insisting on making freedom more and more effective – see Van Parijs (1995) – it will tend to support a minimal state. Left-leaning liberals, of course, generally want to follow the sorts of lines represented by Rawls and Van Parijs. For more, see Pettit (1997, Introduction).

6 Libertarians often say that they are against big government. Republicans are also against big government, but in a different sense. They object, not necessarily to government's having redistributive rights and responsibilities, but rather to the government's having power to act arbitrarily in the pursuit of redistributive ends; the pursuit must always be governed by a fair rule of law.

References

Ayres, Ian, and Braithwaite, John. 1992. *Responsive Regulation*. New York: Oxford University Press.

Bentham, Jeremy. 1843. 'Anarchical Fallacies', in *The Works of Jeremy Bentham*, ed. J. Bowring, vol. 2. Edinburgh.

Berlin, Isaiah. 1958. *Four Essays on Liberty*. Oxford: Oxford University Press.

Blackstone, William. 1978 [1783]. *Commentaries on the Laws of England*, 9th edn. New York: Garland (facsimile).

Blom, Hans W. 1995. *Causality and Morality in Politics: The Rise of Naturalism in Dutch Seventeenth-Century Political Thought*. The Hague: CIP-Gegevens Koninklijke Bibliotheek.

Braithwaite, John, and Pettit, Philip. 1990. *Not Just Deserts: A Republican Theory of Criminal Justice*. Oxford: Oxford University Press.

Constant, Benjamin. 1988. *Constant: Political Writings*, ed. B. Fontana. Cambridge: Cambridge University Press.

Dworkin, Ronald. 1978. *Taking Rights Seriously*. London: Duckworth.

Elkin, Stephen L. 1987. *City and Regime in the American Republic*. Chicago: Chicago University Press.

Fontana, Biancamaria, ed. 1994. *The Invention of the Modern Republic*. Cambridge: Cambridge University Press.

Harrington, James. 1992. *The Commonwealth of Oceana, and A System of Politics*, ed. J. G. A. Pocock. Cambridge: Cambridge University Press.

Hobbes, Thomas. 1968. *Leviathan*, ed. C. B. MacPherson. Harmondsworth, Mddx: Penguin.

Hutton, Will. 1995. *The State We're In*. London: Cape 1995.

Lewis, David. 1969. *Convention*. Cambridge, Mass.: Harvard University Press.

Lind, John. 1776. *Three Letters to Dr Price*. London: T. Payne.

Locke, John. 1965. *Two Treatises of Government*, ed. Peter Laslett. New York: Mentor.

Long, Douglas C. 1977. *Bentham on Liberty*. Toronto: University of Toronto Press.

Madison, James, Hamilton, Alexander, and Jay, John. 1987. *The Federalist Papers*, ed. Isaac Kramnik. Harmondsworth, Mddx: Penguin.

Michelman, Frank. 1986. 'The Supreme Court 1985 Term', *Harvard Law Review*, 100.

Mill, J. S 1969. *Essays on Ethics, Religion and Society* (*Collected Works*, vol. 10). London: Routledge.

Miller, David. 1990. *Market, State and Community*. Oxford: Oxford University Press.

Montesquieu, Charles de Secondat. 1989. *The Spirit of the Laws*, trans. and ed. A. M. Cohler, B. C. Miller and H. S. Stone. Cambridge: Cambridge University Press.

Oldfield, Adrian. 1990. *Citizenship and Community: Civic Republicanism and the Modern World*. London: Routledge.

Pagden, Anthony, ed. 1987. *The Languages of Political Theory in Early Modern Europe*. Cambridge: Cambridge University Press.

Paine, Tom. 1989. *Political Writings*, ed. Bruce Kuklick. Cambridge: Cambridge University Press.

Paley, William. 1825. *The Principles of Moral and Political Philosophy* (*Collected Works*, vol. 4). London: C. and J. Rivington.

Patterson, Orlando. 1991. *Freedom in the Making of Western Culture*. New York: Basic Books.

Pettit, Philip. 1995. 'Institutional Design and Rational Choice', in R. E. Goodin, ed., *The Theory of Institutional Design*. Cambridge: Cambridge University Press.

Pettit, Philip. 1996. 'Freedom as Antipower', *Ethics*, 106.

Pettit, Philip. 1997. *Republicanism: A Theory of Freedom and Government*. Oxford: Oxford University Press.

Pocock, J. G. A. 1975. *The Machiavellian Moment: Florentine Political Theory and the Atlantic Republican Tradition*. Princeton, NJ: Princeton University Press.

Price, Richard. 1991. *Political Writings*, ed. D. O. Thomas. Cambridge: Cambridge University Press.

Priestley, Joseph. 1993. *Political Writings*, ed. P. N. Miller. Cambridge: Cambridge University Press.

Rahe, Paul Anthony. 1992. *Republics, Ancient and Modern: Classical Republicanism and the American Revolution*. Chicago: University of Chicago Press.

Rawls, John. 1971. *A Theory of Justice*. Oxford: Oxford University Press.

Robbins, Caroline. 1959. *The Eighteenth Century Commonwealthman*. Cambridge, Mass.: Harvard University Press.

Sen, Amartya. 1985. *Commodities and Capabilities*. Amsterdam: North-Holland.

Skinner, Quentin. 1978. *The Foundations of Modern Political Thought*, 2 vols. Cambridge: Cambridge University Press.

Skinner, Quentin. 1983. 'Machiavelli on the Maintenance of Liberty', *Politics*, 18.

Skinner, Quentin. 1984. 'The Idea of Negative Liberty' in R. Rorty, J. B. Schneewind and Q. Skinner, eds, *Philosophy in History*. Cambridge: Cambridge University Press.

Spitz, Jean-Fabien. 1995. *La Liberté Politique*. Paris: Presses Universitaires de France.

Sunstein, Cass R. 1990. *After the Rights Revolution: Reconceiving the Regulatory State*. Cambridge, Mass.: Harvard University Press.

Sunstein, Cass R. 1993a. *The Partial Constitution*. Cambridge, Mass.: Harvard University Press.

Sunstein, Cass R. 1993b. *Democracy and the Problem of Free Speech*. New York: Free Press.

Sydney, Algernon. 1990. *Discourses Concerning Government*, ed. T. G. West. Indianapolis: Liberty Classics.

Sydney, Algernon. 1996. *Court Maxims*, ed. H. W. Blom, E. H. Muller and Ronald Janse. Cambridge: Cambridge University Press.

Taylor, Charles. 1989. 'Cross-Purposes: The Liberal-Communitarian Debate', in N. L. Rosenblum, ed., *Liberalism and the Moral Life*. Cambridge, Mass.: Harvard University Press.

Trenchard, John, and Gordon, Thomas. 1971. *Cato's Letters*. 6th (1755) edn. New York: Da Capo.

Van Parijs, Philippe. 1995. *Real Freedom for All*. Oxford: Oxford University Press.

Viroli, Maurizio. 1995. *For Love of Country*. Oxford: Oxford University Press.

CHAPTER 6

Liberalism, Multiculturalism and Oppression

Chandran Kukathas

Indeed, Hobbes, without being himself a liberal, had in him more of the philosophy of liberalism than most of its professed defenders. . . . It was Richard Cumberland with his 'social instinct' and later Adam Smith with his 'social passions' who bewitched liberalism by appearing to solve the problem of individualism when they had really only avoided it. [Oakeshott n.d.: lvii and n.]

So that in the nature of man, we find three principal causes of quarrel. First competition; secondly, diffidence; thirdly, glory. [Hobbes n.d.: 81]

The most persistent objection to liberal political theory has been to its individualism. Liberalism's critics often invoke the idea of community when taking it to task, partly because they wish to reject what they see as the liberal understanding of persons as separate and self-contained atoms, sharing certain formal rights – pre-eminent among these, the right to be left splendidly isolated.

Michael Sandel, for example, criticizes Rawls for advancing a political theory giving primacy to justice, and presupposing that justice is a virtue of a society peopled by separate individuals whose goals and values are as independent of society as they are. This typically liberal stance, for Sandel, is mistaken because it does not appreciate the extent to which individual selves – and their desires – are not separate from, but are constituted by, the community into which they are born. The idea of a separate self is not merely unreal; it is incoherent (Sandel 1982). Similarly, Benjamin Barber objects to liberal theory's constructions because they presume that people are little more than consumers, pursuing their private desires, and incapable of valuing society (and politics) as intrinsic goods. Its assumptions about the atomistic character of persons thus lead to conclusions which are insensitive to the values of community, and which seem to affirm little other than the pursuit of self-interest (Barber 1984).

The flaw in liberalism, according to such views, is to be found not in the ideas it advocates but in its social ontology. The problem stems not from its vision of the way the world should be (though this in itself is troubling), but from its understanding of the way the world is to begin with (see also Taylor 1989).

In the work of Iris Young, however, we find a critique of liberalism which agrees that it rests on a flawed social ontology, but rejects the dichotomy between individualism and community. Liberal individualism and communitarianism, for Young, both stand condemned for denying 'difference'. 'Each entails a denial of difference and a desire to bring multiplicity and heterogeneity into unity, though in opposing ways' (1990: 229). Thus there is a 'common logic' underlying the polarity of individualism and community which enables them to define each other negatively.

> Liberal individualism denies difference by positing the self as a solid, self-sufficient unity, not defined by anything or anyone other than itself. Its formalistic ethic of rights also denies difference by bringing all such separated individuals under a common measure of rights. Proponents of community, on the other hand, deny difference by positing fusion rather than separation as the social ideal. They conceive the social subject as a relation of unity of mutuality composed by identification and symmetry among individuals within a totality. Communitarianism represents an urge to see persons in unity with one another in a shared whole. [Young 1990: 229]

According to Young's critique, then, liberal politics, in pursuing the ideals of an individualist egalitarianism, is essentially assimilationist in spirit. Its granting of rights offers little protection to minorities, who find themselves oppressed less by the deliberate denial of their rights than by the more subtle denial of the worth of their aspirations in the construction of a dominant cultural and political structure. Attending to these concerns, Young seeks to show, requires a turn towards a 'politics of difference', and away from liberal pluralism – upon whose ontological foundations nothing secure can be built.

It is this powerful critique of liberalism which is the subject of this chapter, whose aim is to defend liberalism from the attack by advocates of the politics of difference. My objective is to show that liberal pluralism is superior not only in the way in which it accounts for and handles 'difference' in society, but also in large part because it rests on sounder ontological foundations than its critics have allowed. In this regard this chapter offers an unashamedly individualist defence of liberalism. At the same time, however, I do not aim simply to restate the liberal position. There are numerous accounts of liberalism available, and I wish not only to add to the number on offer but also to make clear the strength of my own version. Furthermore, I propose to offer this account by taking seriously the claims and arguments of proponents of the politics of difference, such as Iris Young – and particularly their arguments that in today's multicultural societies there are important issues of oppression, domination and subordination at stake. Indeed, I propose to give careful consideration to the claim, advanced by Young, that liberal social ontology 'has no place for a concept of social groups', and that this is a serious – if not fatal – flaw in liberalism generally.

To complete this task, the rest of this chapter is organized in the following way. I will first sketch an outline of a liberal theory of multiculturalism, making clear this liberalism's attitude to the question of oppression. I then offer a detailed account of the critique offered from the perspective of the 'politics of difference', focusing on the arguments advanced by Young. This is followed by a critique of Young's 'politics of difference'. This opens the way for a consideration, in the final section of the chapter, of the ontological basis of liberalism.

A Liberal Theory of Multiculturalism

Liberalism is fundamentally a theory of multiculturalism. It is, in other words, a philosophical response to the fact of moral, religious and cultural diversity. Its recommendation is that diversity be accommodated and that differences be tolerated. It also argues that a form of social unity characterized by a uniform and common culture, integrating and harmonizing the interests of individual and community, is both unattainable and undesirable. Division, conflict, and competition will always be features of human society; the task of political institutions, according to liberal theory, is to palliate this condition, rather than to attempt a cure. Political institutions would be liberal ones if they left people free to pursue their own ends, whether separately or in concert with others, under the rule of law. By implication, people should therefore be left free to worship (or not worship) as they please, to dissociate from those whose ways they cannot abide, and to live by their own preferred cultural standards – provided that their doing so does not threaten the legal and political order which allows for peaceful coexistence.

Of course, any historically nuanced account of liberalism has to recognize that the story of its development is really a story of many 'liberalisms'. Liberal arguments have been identified in the works of thinkers ranging from Hobbes, Locke, Rousseau and Hume, to Kant, Hegel, Mill, T. H. Green and Berlin. An account of liberalism which leaves out, or denies membership to, any of these thinkers (to name only a few) is therefore bound to be controversial. Nonetheless, the version of liberalism presented here cannot accommodate all of these figures. How far what is being defended is really liberalism – or the best understanding of liberalism – is thus debatable. My concern here, however, is not to engage in this debate. It is to defend the liberalism which has been challenged, and to defend it not by changing its fundamental premises but by embracing them. These premises are the individualist premises its critics – both old and new – have found so objectionable, and which its recent critics have argued leave liberalism insensitive to the fact that society is composed of groups. This chapter is most explicitly a reply to the modern critics; in addition, it is implicitly a reply to the older critics and also to those liberals who would modify or abandon the individualism which lies at the heart of liberal thinking.

What does liberalism have to say, then, about the groups that are to be found in a multicultural society? According to the interpretation of liberalism being offered here, it says very little; for it takes no interest in the associations individuals form. Liberalism is indifferent to the groups of which individuals may be members. It recognizes the freedom of individuals to join or form groups, or to continue to belong to groups into which they may have been born – but it takes no interest in the interests or attachments (whether cultural or religious or ethnic) which people might have. Liberalism promotes no collective projects, expresses no group preferences, and privileges no particular individuals or individual interests. Its only concern is to uphold the framework of law within which individuals and groups can coexist in peace. This is not, of course, to deny that upholding the rule of law may sometimes require intervention in the affairs of individuals and groups; but liberal politics is not concerned with these affairs in themselves. Because it is indifferent to these matters, liberalism could be described as the politics of indifference (Kukathas 1997, forthcoming).

Is liberalism also indifferent to the existence of oppression, or dominance and subordination, or inequality in society? The answer to this question is: no; but the liberal attitude towards the issues involved needs to be spelt out more carefully. Oppression, domination, subordination, and, indeed, inequality, will always be features of human society – even though the extent to which they will be manifest will vary. The liberal outlook suggests not that the various forms of oppression can be eliminated, but only that they should not be entrenched through the recognition of the forms which might give them shape and substance. Thus it does not recognize (or privilege) groups, or traditions, or particular forms of social organization. It is not pro-business (any more than it is anti-labour); nor does it advocate (any particular version of) the family or family values; and it is neither for nor against the existence of particular groups or cultural communities or nations to which individuals may wish to continue to belong. It recognizes that any of these sorts of associations may be oppressive, or may – to varying degrees – allow some people systematically to dominate others. For this reason it refuses to see anything sacred or immutable about these forms of association, preferring to leave open the possibility that they will be abandoned by members who find them oppressive – or useless or irrelevant or unattractive.

Equally, liberalism recognizes – and accepts – that often human associations persist even when they are oppressive. This may be because even the oppressed members accept this as part of the trade-off involved in keeping the group or association going. Or it may be that the oppressed think that the risk or the cost of abandoning the organization or community in question to be too high to be worth considering. It may even be that the oppressed consider their lot a part of the natural order of things, and cannot conceive that things might be otherwise. In this regard, while liberalism maintains that individuals should be free to dissociate from any form of social organization in which they find themselves entangled, it does not say anything about the worth of the association itself, or about how individuals might be rescued from its clutches. It offers a theory of liberty, but (necessarily) not a theory of liberation.

In some circumstances, however, groups may be the victims, rather than the perpetrators, of oppression. They may be preyed upon by other, stronger, groups in society, for not all groups are equal economically or politically. Or they may be oppressed because they are minorities in a dominant culture they are unable to resist. However much they reject the ways of the larger society, they may find their own traditions and practices – indeed, their very identities – eroded as they are assimilated into the body social as well as the body politic. As Iris Young explains it, some groups might find themselves victims of 'cultural imperialism'. To experience cultural imperialism means 'to experience how the dominant meanings of a society render the particular perspective of one's own group invisible at the same time as they stereotype one's group and mark it out as the Other'. Cultural imperialism thus involves the 'universalization of a dominant group's experience and culture, and its establishment as the norm' (Young 1990: 58–9; see also Kukathas 1996: 98–9).

Liberalism's attitude to this is, first, to say that the norms or traditions or culture of the larger (or imperial) society have no special moral standing. That these prevailing traditions or norms are dominant counts for nothing when the question at hand is whether or not minorities should conform to them (although there may be *other* reasons why they should abide by some of the dominant norms). Moreover, liberalism is generally distrustful of the state, which, in the name of the interests of society, is often quick to dismiss the concerns of minorities which do not see the world in the same way as it does. This is a point powerfully made by James Scott, who, in his analysis of 'state simplifications' observes that

> *the modern state, through its officials, attempts – with varying success – to create a population with precisely those standardized characteristics which will be easier to monitor, count, assess and manage.* The utopian (immanent) tendency of the modern state, continually frustrated, is to reduce the chaotic, disorderly, constantly changing social reality beneath it to something more closely resembling the administrative grid of its observations. [1995: 230, emphasis in original]

In liberalism's book, there is nothing superior about the state's-eye view of the world. For one thing, it may not reflect the thinking of the majority (or even a plurality) of the population, but, rather, the dominance of particular interests or elites (Kukathas 1996: 99). But even if it did reflect the outlook of the majority, this in no way implies that dissenting perspectives may rightly be forced to conform to the dominant attitude. Where the majority of Australians see a mineral-rich valley, local Aborigines may see only a religious site. From a liberal point of view, there is no reason for those Aborigines to be made to see things differently – or to give up the land if it is theirs.

Yet at the same time, liberalism does not maintain that assimilation is in itself unacceptable or that the overwhelming of one (minority) tradition by another is wrong. Assimilation, no less than differentiation, is a part of the way of the world. If people elect to abandon their ways, or their communities, in order to enter others or to slip into the mainstream of social life, that has simply to be accepted. It is accepted by liberalism even if it means the disappearance of communities that cannot survive defections. And it is accepted even though the defectors leave reluctantly: because the costs or pressures of minority life are too great. The individuals have every right to leave their associations; but they have no right to be kept able to remain, and the associations have no right to be sustained.

It might be thought that this is acceptable from a liberal point of view because this process is not oppressive. But, clearly, this is not the case. Communities do die out because they find themselves marginalized, or because they are economically weak, or because they cannot withstand the force of the dominant ideology. It may not be easy – if possible at all – to raise a Christian family in a secular (although tolerant) community; or to sustain Aboriginal traditions if the majority of society see them as faintly ridiculous. It may not be possible even to sustain particular medical traditions (such as homeopathy) if there are not enough subscribers to make up a viable insurance pool, and the dominant medical elites dismiss them as quackery.

Groups are not equal in a liberal – or, indeed, in any – society. And liberalism does not aspire to making them equal. Nor does it hope to eradicate the oppression that often comes with this inequality. At the same time, however, it is not true to say that liberalism allows no place for social groups, or that liberal society is peculiarly oppressive. To understand why, however, we need to look more closely at the arguments of those who maintain otherwise.

The Politics of Difference and Multiculturalism

According to Iris Young, the 'politics of difference . . . promotes a notion of group solidarity against the individualism of liberal humanism' (1990: 166). She concedes that the free society envisaged by liberalism is certainly pluralistic: in it 'persons can affiliate with whomever they choose; liberty encourages a proliferation of life styles, activities, and associations'. Nevertheless, its vision does not touch on the important issues which give rise to the politics of difference (168). In her account, liberalism appeals to 'an ideal of justice that defines liberation as the transcendence of group difference', and which she refers to as an ideal of 'assimilation' (157). 'Liberal humanism treats each person as an individual, ignoring differences of race, sex, religion, and ethnicity', maintaining that each person 'should be evaluated only according to her or his individual efforts and achievements' (166).

The fundamental problem with this 'vision of liberation as the transcendence of group difference' is that it 'seeks to abolish the public and political significance of group difference, while retaining and promoting both individual and group diversity in private, or nonpolitical, social contexts' (Young 1990: 168). What is wrong with this, Young argues, is that the distinguishing of public and private spheres, where the public represents universal citizenship and the private individual differences, generally results in the exclusion of particular groups. 'Public life is supposed to be "blind" to sex, race, age, and so on, and all persons are supposed to enter the public and its discussion on identical terms. This conception of the public has resulted in the exclusion of persons from public life' (120). Thus the liberal view tends to allow certain kinds of persons or activities – homosexuality, for example – to exist only for so long as they remain confined to the private realm.

What is wrong with this, in Young's theory, is that it is oppressive. While ignoring difference may appear to be liberating, it is in fact severely oppressive in several ways. First, blindness to difference disadvantages groups whose experience, culture and socialized capacities differ from those of privileged groups. At best, it assimilates excluded groups into the mainstream; but the problem with assimilation is that those who are assimilated come into the game after it has already begun, after the rules and standards have already been set, and so have to prove themselves according to those rules and standards. Generally, this keeps the assimilated at a disadvantage (164).

One further problem with the ideal of universal humanity without group differences is that 'it allows privileged groups to ignore their own group specificity' (165). Here blindness to difference perpetuates 'cultural imperialism' by allowing the norms of the privileged groups to be presented as neutral and universal. The oppressed groups, however, are marked with particularity and objectified as the 'others' (165). Claims that all are treated *impartially* serve simply to mask the oppression, for it is no more than another means by which the privileged group presents its own particular norms as universal. Indeed, 'the propensity to universalize the particular reinforces that oppression' (116). Far from serving the interests of minorities, the commitment to an ideal of impartiality 'makes it difficult to expose the partiality of the supposedly general standpoint, and to claim a voice for the oppressed' (116). When their voices are heard, and the experiences of the minority groups are found to differ from those of the dominant groups, the former are simply represented as deviant and inferior.

An unhappy consequence of this, Young continues, is that the denigration of 'deviant' groups 'often produces an internalized devaluation by members of those groups themselves'. The denigrated become ashamed of themselves. 'The aspiration to assimilate helps produce the self-loathing and double consciousness characteristic of oppression' (165). While there are some conceptions of assimilation which are more subtle and sensitive to the circumstances of the deviant group, the assimilationist ideal fundamentally denies that group difference can be positive and desirable: 'thus any form of the ideal of assimilation constructs group difference as a liability or disadvantage' (166).

The problem with the assimilationist view that lies at the heart of liberal individualism is that it associates group-based difference with assertions of group differences as such: 'eliminating group oppression such as racism, then, implies eliminating group differences' (Young 1993: 131). At best, this view simply does not conform to experience. Many who are disadvantaged because of their group identity nevertheless find much of value – friendship, social solidarity, an aesthetic satisfaction – in their group-based lives (1993: 132). Furthermore, the assimilationist ideal also mistakenly presumes a conception of the individual self as transcending or prior to social context – implying that the authentic self is one that has voluntarily assumed all aspects of his or her life and identity. This understanding of the self, Young argues, is neither realistic, nor desirable, nor necessary. 'We cannot say that someone experiences injustice or coercion simply by finding themselves in social relationships they have not chosen. If unchosen relationships do not produce systematic group inequality and oppression, and also allow individuals considerable personal liberty of action, then they are not unjust' (1993: 132). At its worst, however, Young proclaims, 'an assimilationist ideal amounts to genocide' (1990: 182).

What is therefore needed to attend to the interests of oppressed groups in society is not a politics of assimiliation but a 'politics of group assertion': one which 'takes as a basic principle that members of oppressed groups need separate organizations that exclude others, especially those from more privileged groups' (Young 1990: 167). 'The oppressions of cultural imperialism that stereotype a group and simultaneously render its own experience invisible', she argues, 'can be remedied only by explicit attention to and expression of that group's specificity.' Group-conscious policies may thus be needed in order to 'affirm the solidarity of groups' and also to 'allow them to affirm their group affinities without suffering disadvantage in the wider society' (1990: 174).

In positive terms, Young recommends the following principle: 'a democratic public should provide mechanisms for the effective recognition and representation of the distinct voices and perspectives of those of its constituent groups that are oppressed or disadvantaged' (1990: 184). Specific representation for oppressed groups in a democracy would better promote justice, both procedurally and substantively. First, it would better assure procedural fairness in setting the public agenda; second, giving a voice to the oppressed would make it more likely that all the needs and interests in the public will be recognized in democratic deliberations; and, third, group representation promotes just outcomes by maximizing social knowledge and so furthering practical wisdom (1990: 185–6).

Democracy is of crucial importance in this argument. For Young, democracy is an element of justice, and one which is of particular importance because it minimizes domination. It thus has both instrumental and intrinsic value (1990: 92). Young's alternative to liberalism is essentially what she calls 'democratic cultural pluralism' (163). A 'thorough social and political democracy', she argues, 'is the opposite of domination' (38). In a society marked by the politics of difference, however, all people would be 'empowered' to discuss the ends and means of collective life. And empowerment, in this understanding, means 'at minimum, expanding the range of decisions that are made through democratic processes'. And it is quite clear that this view envisions a considerable expansion of the scope of democracy: 'The principle is simple: wherever actions affect a plurality of agents in the ways I have specified, all those agents should participate in deciding the actions and their conditions' (Young 1990: 251).

Young's argument for extending the scope of democracy, while sympathetic to the views of democratic theorists like Benjamin Barber, differs from these earlier theories because of the emphasis it places on 'difference', and her critique of the idea of social unity. Many of these writers, including Barber, she argues, call for the institution of a democratic public in which citizens transcend their particular contexts, needs and interests to address the common good. However, 'such a desire for political unity will suppress difference, and tend to exclude some voices and perspectives from the public, because their greater privilege and dominant position allows some groups to articulate the "common good" in terms influenced by their particular perspective and interests' (Young 1990: 118). In this regard, she rejects interest-group pluralism not because it is plural and particular but, rather, because it is 'privatized'. It 'institutionalizes and encourages an egoist, self-regarding view of the political process', in which each party competes with others for its own gain, and does not consider listening or responding to the claims of others. What Young seeks is a 'politics of inclusion': a form of participatory democracy that promotes the ideal of a heterogeneous public, 'in which persons stand forth with their differences acknowledged and respected, though not perhaps completely understood, by others' (1990: 118–19).

Young's critique of liberalism is a comprehensive one. It not only attacks liberalism's fundamental assumptions, but also presents a substantial alternative which marks out more clearly what she sees as the deficiencies of the liberal view of politics. The question which needs now to be addressed, however, is whether Young's politics of difference suffers from deficiencies of its own.

A Critique of the Politics of Difference

The power of Young's critique of liberalism stems from her focus on the problems of oppression and domination as these are manifest and lived through and around group differences. In most societies in which there are group differences of sex, race, ethnicity, and religion, she maintains, there are dominant and subordinate groups, and there are ideologies of group superiority which help to perpetuate that dominance. The politics of difference, for her, is how subordinated, oppressed, disadvantaged groups can, and ought to, obtain greater equality *vis-à-vis* the dominant groups. The problem with liberal humanism is that it turns out to be an ideology which – perhaps unintentionally – perpetuates the existing patterns of dominance. In the name of individual liberty, and justice as impartiality, it suppresses difference, by assimilating the deviant and the less powerful – and keeping them at a disadvantage. Under a liberal regime these people will remain oppressed because their condition will be one of economic and social domination and, so, political domination. This is a case which liberalism needs to answer. But it can be answered. While Young's challenge is a demanding one, its critique of liberalism is, in the end, unsound. This is, in part, because it is mistaken in its claim that liberalism is hostile or unsympathetic to difference. But it is also because her theory of oppression is flawed, and because her alternative social philosophy – the politics of difference – is inferior to the liberal approach to the problems posed by social diversity, resting as it does on less plausible ontological foundations than those supporting liberalism.

Liberalism is not hostile to difference because its response to the fact of diversity is to recommend toleration of the different groups, or cultures, or associations which might be found within society (see Kukathas 1992; 1996a). It does not, as Young and other critics of liberalism (such as Van Dyke 1985) have suggested, argue for – or even particularly favour – assimilation. Yet neither is it opposed to assimilation. While liberalism is perfectly prepared to accept that some communities or cultures or traditions reject the modern world or the dominant society, or simply wish to hold on to their distinctive identity, it is indifferent to whether or not they do so. It does not explicitly recognize the different groups of which individuals might be members because it takes no interest in them, and does not presume to make judgments about them – about their worth or their standing. Its outlook is culture-blind.

Iris Young's contention, however, is that this attitude is, in effect, one which favours assimilation; and that this assimilation is what lies at the heart of oppression. Yet on both counts she is mistaken. She is mistaken to think that assimilation is favoured because the understanding of assimilation she offers presents only a partial – and, indeed, a misleading – account of the complex interactions that take place when a minority (individual or group) comes face to face with mainstream society. At the very least, such a minority is confronted with two options: to enter mainstream society and to play the game as it exists; or to stay out of it altogether, either by leaving for another place (which may not be easy, even if at all possible) or by remaining in the vicinity but not embracing the ways which are dominant in the mainstream. Thus, for example, an Indian family coming to live in London might decide to become like the English in all important respects (that is, to assimilate), bringing up their children ignorant of their mother tongue, and unaware of the marital traditions, caste prejudices, and the community standards they left behind. Alternatively, they might opt to 'assimilate' into English society as much as they need to in order to prosper economically, but try to preserve their language, and to bring up their children in accordance with some of the standards they brought with them, and which they find lacking in English society. They might, in this regard, try to ensure that their children do not marry 'outsiders', since this would, in the end, dilute – or corrupt altogether – the identity of their particular race or culture or community. Or they might go further still, and gather with others of similar background in ethnic enclaves, not only surrounding themselves with the physical trappings of their societies of origin but also building up around them the moral structures which keep out the influences of the world beyond. Or they might find even this not enough, and head back 'home'.

The first point being made here is that all of these courses of action except the last amount to assimilation – so that assimilation is a matter of degree. A person may be assimilated in some respects, but not in others. Even a person who enters mainstream society as a migrant, but decides to form or join a political organization dedicated to furthering the interests of the group (in a society which gives explicit recognition to that group), is in a sense assimilated. (Arguably, nothing forces individuals and groups to assimilate more quickly than politics, in which success demands an appeal to the lowest common denominator.) The second point is that assimilation involves trade-offs. Some people assimilate readily because the gains outweigh the losses – retaining a mother tongue may matter less than getting job; some assimilate reluctantly – perhaps no job is worth losing a mother tongue. The third point is that, even in the most favourable circumstances, the individual and the group have very little control over the processes of assimilation, not least because to have control of one's identity requires having control over others. Parents must have control over children, for example; or husbands over wives, or elders over the young, or leaders over a community. This is, perhaps, not always desirable either; often it is simply not possible. Even those immigrants who choose to return home cannot return unchanged, however short their encounter with the new society may have been. The most important cause of assimilation is propinquity.

Assimilation is a complex and variable matter which has been described as a compound social process (Gordon 1964). The assimilation of immigrant groups might involve not only 'structural assimilation', but also 'cultural assimilation'. Yet it might involve one but not the other. In the development of American cities in the early part of this century, 'those of the migrant generation, and especially their American-born children, experienced rapid cultural assimilation as they adopted the language and forms of American life, but they experienced only limited structural assimilation' (Ward 1989: 176). This was because the primary group relationships remained concentrated in the ethnic community. At the same time, however, inter-group relationships, even when these extended to ethnic intermarriage, did not always result in the abandonment of ethnic identities. Again, studies of the development of ethnic immigrant communities in American cities reveal that, contrary to the notion that acculturation precedes assimilation, 'considerable residues of ethnic culture can remain among socially assimilated individuals' (Ward 1989: 176).

Given the complexity of assimilation not only as a sociological but also as a moral phenomenon, it should be unsurprising that the liberal attitude towards it is one of indifference – or neutrality – rather than favour. To come down in favour of assimilation would require some kind of account of the desirable extent of assimilation, which would be morally hazardous. But to come down against assimilation would be no less problematic, since that would involve recommending that obstacles – whether in the form of incentives or disincentives – be put in the way of those who do wish to assimilate. Ramesh Thakur, for example, has argued against the Canadian ideal of the 'mosaic', as compared with the American model of society as 'melting pot', ultimately, that it is one which demeans those immigrants who want to become members of society and not live out their days as 'expatriates'. 'By being officially hostile to assimilation, Canada forces newcomers to be expatriates rather than immigrants. The mosaic becomes a subtle policy instrument in the hands of "true blood" Canadians for maintaining their distance from the new pretenders' (1993: 131). It is clearly possible to make it easier for people not to assimilate; but this is not unlike – indeed, it is troublingly close to – making it harder for them to succeed in assimilating. And this point holds whether the minority in question is an immigrant or an aboriginal.

Young has argued, however, not only that liberalism implicitly favours assimilation, but also that assimilation is one of the ways in which the oppression of minorities becomes manifest under liberalism. This oppression is evident not only in the pressure put upon people to assimilate, but also in their unequal position after they have assimilated. To some extent, Young has a point: the pressures she mentions, and the shame and 'self-loathing' they are thought to provoke, undoubtedly exist. But here it has to be asked, first, how far this is avoidable. The pressure to conform is one of the most powerful pressures to which humans might be submitted – and it is powerful precisely because it is capable of producing self-doubt. This holds true in the academy no less than in the school playground. As John Stuart Mill observed, 'to extend the bounds of what may be called moral police, until it encroaches on the most unquestionably legitimate liberty of the individual, is one of the most universal of all human propensities' (1985: 216). Alas, this form of oppression is not only universal but also ineradicable. It is certainly not peculiar to liberal regimes. Yet while liberalism realizes that those who are different will invariably suffer the slights, the sniggers and the curses of the multitude, it also refuses to grant the multitude any standing, or to lessen – or elevate – the standing of the minority. And this is surely the wisest course to take; for to go further to strengthen the hands of the minority is dangerous, since every multitude is nothing more than a collection of minorities.

It should also be asked, secondly, how far it is the aspiration to assimilate itself which produces the 'self-loathing and double-consciousness characteristic of oppression'. Certainly the aspiration to assimilate may sometimes reflect such resignation. Yet it may equally reflect a very different attitude: a self-confidence which is manifest in the desire to make it in the bigger, hostile, and more dangerous world. (If this is so, it may well be that, while the denigration of deviant groups sometimes produces self-devaluation, it also produces the opposite.) In fact, the motives to assimilate are various – and numerous. People might assimilate (to different degrees) for economic gain, for prestige or status, for love, or for friendship; or out of fear, or greed, or spite, or simply indifference.

As for Young's point that, however subtle or sensitive the conception of assimilation, the assimilationist ideal constructs group difference as a liability or disadvantage, it ought to be asked whether this is indeed always so. And when it is so, it should also be asked whether or not this is because there is an element of truth in the assertion that difference is a disadvantage. Often it is. Thus parents may choose assimilation in order that their children will not suffer disadvantages in the future. (Sometimes, in the case of immigrants, the decision is made long in advance of setting foot on foreign soil.) They know that, while they will suffer a loss, it is a loss that their children need never feel. 'Given the negligible proportion of New Zealanders who are Hindi-speaking,' Thakur remarks, 'I do not expect the state to provide the opportunity of learning Hindi in the school system. . . . It would give me much joy to be able to speak to my children in my mother tongue. It will bring me more lasting satisfaction to see them gainfully employed.' As he observes even more tellingly, 'We do not live in an ideal world. In the real world, educational choices entail opportunity costs' (1993: 136).

This point may be generalized further: many of the sufferings that minorities endure are the consequence not of oppression but simply of inescapable opportunity costs. When Mr Ahmad, a teacher with the Inner London Educational Authority, discovered that his new-found employment did not offer him the time to attend Friday afternoon prayers at the mosque, he had to bear the consequences of his beliefs himself, and either miss prayers or lose his job. It was not possible to have the school bear the consequences of his need for a different sabbath. The problem in this, as in many other similar situations, is not oppression but opportunity cost (see Jones 1994). What liberalism calls for in such circumstances is not that the disadvantaged be dismissed but that they be given a fair hearing: that they or their case be considered impartially, and without prejudice founded on their race or sex or on other circumstances irrelevant to the matter of justice.

Yet here Young has another important argument to make: that impartiality is an inadequate standard for addressing the claims of groups. 'Impartiality' does not serve justice; rather, it serves simply to mask oppression. Her complaint is that claims about impartiality can turn out to be a means by which the privileged group presents its own particular norms as universal, and to that extent her point is sound. The argument that 'it's the same for everyone' is clearly fraudulent when the rule is systematically and unjustifiably biased against some. After all, the Nazis persecuted *anyone* with Jewish blood. Nonetheless, this only demonstrates that even impartiality can, on occasion, be turned to unjust purposes; it does not show that the problem lies with the aspiration to impartiality. At most, it shows that claims about impartiality are contestable. The response here should not be to jettison impartiality, but to take seriously any challenge that an apparently impartial, or neutral and universal, requirement is simply a partial one in disguise. (It is, of course, worth bearing in mind that a similarly sceptical attitude should be taken towards the challenger, since it is often those who would replace impartial standards with their own who are most vociferous in their opposition to prevailing standards.)

All this said, however, it would not do to deny that there is oppression in liberal societies – and always will be under a liberal regime. This is so not only because some groups are stronger than others and try to take advantage of them, but also because the minority cultures within it experience 'cultural imperialism'. While liberalism refuses further to entrench such standards by giving them explicit recognition, it does not claim to be able to eliminate them. There is no solution to this problem. Iris Young, however, suggests that there is, since she thinks that a 'politics of difference' will at least ameliorate the condition of the oppressed. Yet the democratic solution is, in the end, no solution at all because it makes no difference to the problem of oppression, and also brings with it other evils of its own.

It should be said at the outset that it is far from clear how the democratic principles Young enunciates would work in practice. In her argument for the extension of the scope of democracy, she suggests the 'simple' principle that all the agents affected by an action should participate in deciding the actions and their conditions. Yet given the extent of our interdependence, this would give most of us a right to a say in the affairs of innumerable public and private organizations. Australian farmers would have to have a say in the formulation of US agricultural policy, since the American Export Enhancement Program affects them more directly (and severely) than it does most citizens of the United States. But even within the USA it would mean giving business the right to participate in union meetings of the major labour unions; and labour and business and various other groups the right to participate in the decision-making processes of Harvard, Stanford and Berkeley. In Australia, it would give miners the right to take part in the decision-making processes of the various Aboriginal Land Councils. Even if, in all these cases, participation were made less direct and intrusive, participation would entail a substantial loss of autonomy for all kinds of associations.

Leaving this problem aside, however, the trouble is that the extension of democracy makes no difference to the extent of oppression. At best, it transfers some of the practice of oppression into the political realm. First, a system which recognizes difference politically or publicly does not necessarily confer advantages on the differentiated group. It may make the group more visible, but it does not make it more powerful – particularly if it is a small minority. It may even weaken the group, partly since enormous resources are needed to play the game of politics, but also because to play that game the group has to enter a game which is already going on, in which it is at a marked disadvantage. Perhaps more importantly still, to play the game of politics the group – or its leaders – have to become involved in the mainstream society in ways which have a significant bearing on the identity of the group. There is no quicker path to assimilation than political assimilation.

This last point should not be exaggerated. It may well be that, in engaging in political activity, it is not the group but its leaders who run the risk of being assimilated and losing their identity. But this brings out a second disadvantage of politics for the group: it may, in the end, benefit the elites rather than the group as a whole. The more the elites of the group associate with their political counterparts in mainstream society, the more likely their thinking (and their interests) are to diverge from that of the group. There is no doubt that elites sometimes use their political powers to further their personal ends, in some cases manipulating the sentiments of the group to further their own careers (Horowitz 1985: ch. 5; Kukathas 1992: 113–14).

Even when elites are not acting self-interestedly, they often want to pull the community in a different direction, and against the wishes of the majority of the group. The problem here is not simply that this may move the group in the direction of assimilation under the leadership of elites who share more with the dominant society than with their communities of origin. (Sometimes, it is the group that wants to assimilate while the leadership wants to withdraw into further isolation.) What may also result is the division of the group, or the exacerbation of existing conflicts within it. For example, an Aboriginal tribal community may wish to accept an offer from a mining company of substantial royalties in exchange for permission to mine on Aboriginal territory, while its most politically adept leaders may work to thwart the exchange because they do not want the changes this would bring to the society. (This is one interpretation of the 1996 conflict involving the Aborigines of North Queensland and the miners of Century Zinc, and of the role of the 23-year-old Aboriginal activist, Murandoo Yanner.) To some extent, politics may be unavoidable in such circumstances: groups are political entities regardless of whether they are recognized in the democratic processes of mainstream societies. But there is no reason to think that further politicization would benefit the cultural minority, rather than prove destructive of its ways, or even of the community as a whole. (See, for example, the case of the Salish community: Anderson 1987. For further arguments against politicization see Kukathas 1991.)

Engagement by minority groups in democratic politics has a further disadvantage: it not only pits minorities against the mainstream society but also brings them into conflict with each other. Even among groups with plenty of shared interests there is scope for sharp disagreement. Among Australian Aborigines there are divisions between urban and rural Aborigines, 'full-bloods' and 'part-Aborigines', and also between Aborigines of different 'tribes'. But there are also conflicts of interest between Aborigines and immigrants, with Aborigines resenting the concessions migrants receive for the protection of their cultures, and migrants sensitive to charges that they, as part of the mainstream, owe duties to Aborigines because of the society's history of past injustice. The politics of difference, while it may give these different groups recognition, also fuels their resentments and senses of grievance. Further fuel is added when politics fails to deliver – and it invariably fails, since it generates expectations faster than it can satisfy them.

Whether this is escapable is, however, another matter. Once groups have mobilized in politics there may be no alternative but for others to do likewise. The politics of group conflict, once certain players and structures are in place, may turn out to be a prisoners' dilemma game in which the strategic behaviour of each is governed by the competitive situation of all. In this circumstance, there may be good reason for policy to constrain freedom of association in order to prevent a tragedy of the (cultural) commons. Against this, however, it has to be said that often it is the state which is the cause of the tragedy that occurs when it turns the strategic structure from one of co-operation to one of competition for rents. This was clearly the case among ethnic groups in Australia, for example, when attempts by political parties to buy the ethnic vote with funding promises turned the relationships among ethnic communities into competitive conflicts. In the absence of such promises, the different groups had more to gain by co-operation; but the existence of rents to be gained turned the game into a prisoners' dilemma in which defection was the dominant strategy. (On this see Sestito 1982.)

At best, the politics of difference do nothing to reduce the levels of oppression in society, while serving further to divide one group from another, and further alienating many of them from the mainstream of society. Policies of affirmative action – indeed, preferential policies generally – provoke resentment against minorities. Perversely, they discredit even benign or harmless forms of affirmative action practised informally by individuals and organizations. For the politics of difference is a politics, not of the 'peaceable kingdom' of the painting alluded to by Will Kymlicka (1995), but of the 'Bonfire of the Vanities', painted in the lurid prose of Tom Wolfe.

Without doubt, there will be oppression in society when minorities find themselves in a dominant culture whose ways and outlook force upon them the harsh choice of assimilation or marginalization. This may happen even if no violation of rights takes place – if the political institutions are tolerant enough to allow dissenters to go their own way. In showing that oppression may take a number of forms, and manifest itself with subtlety as well as violence, Iris Young has pointed out an important feature of the moral landscape of modern society (1990: ch. 2). One might disagree with her understanding of the prevalence of oppression, since her categories of oppressed groups are nothing if not inclusive (excluding only able-bodied, heterosexual, young adult, white males), as Kymlicka among others has pointed out (1995: 145). But one can still agree with the point that oppression is manifest in various ways. The flaw in Young's theory of oppression lies in the contention that politics holds out the hope that oppression might be reduced, if not entirely overcome. For in this theory, 'Thorough social and political democracy is the opposite of domination' (1990: 36). But this neglects the fact that domination and oppression can take place through social democratic processes, particularly when so much of the energy of the participants in those processes is devoted to the capture of the most powerful instrument of oppression and domination we have known: the state.

In the end, the weakness of the perspective of the politics of difference lies in its hastiness to embrace a politics of group therapy. The problem is not to be solved by ministering directly to the needs of groups. The politics of difference does not recognize this because, in the end, it rests on too rosy a view of politics, which is underpinned by a faulty social ontology. The surer appreciation of politics, and of the limits of what may be accomplished, comes only if we view the world through the lens adopted by liberal individualism.

The Ontology of Liberalism

I began this chapter with the claim that the ontology implicit in liberalism, far from being the weakness that its critics said it was, is really its strength. The conclusion of the argument should, then, make good on this claim.

In *Bosnia: A Short History*, Noel Malcolm introduces his study with this observation:

> Racial history is the bane of the Balkans. As anyone who has lived or travelled in that part of Europe will know, there is no such thing as a racially homogeneous province there, let alone a racially homogeneous state. Few individuals in the entire Balkan peninsula could honestly claim a racially pure ancestry for themselves. And yet, at many times during the last two centuries, bogus theories of racial-ethnic identity had dominated the national politics of the Balkan lands. One reason for studying the early history of the region is that it enables us to see that even if it were right to conduct modern politics in terms of ancient racial origins, it would simply not be possible. [1996: 1]

The lesson drawn here may sensibly be generalized further, for we should be wary of the politics of identity. We should be wary of it because that is precisely what it is: a *politics* of identity. The most seductive and dangerous move in that politics asserts that identity is *not* political but, somehow, natural or original. But identity is not natural, or original, or permanent, or even necessarily particularly enduring. It is fluid, ever-changing (to varying degrees), and inescapably political. Any social ontology which begins with the assumption that the basic units of social reality are groups is fundamentally disabled – or at least disables any political theory which depends upon it. It is disabled because it cannot account for the politics of group life, which is the story not only of the interactions among groups but also of the creation of groups out of units more fundamental still.

This is why the individualist standpoint is to be preferred. It is not because individuals are somehow natural or original. It is rather because this stance recognizes that the identity of groups – no less than the identity of individuals themselves – is the product of the interaction of individuals. Now, to assert this is not to accuse the critics of individualism of reifying collectivities – Young, for one, is quite clear that groups 'are real not as substances, but as forms of social relations' (1990: 44). Rather, it is to acknowledge that, in order to understand groups as forms of social relations, those relations must be seen as relations among individuals. This does not require wholly denying that a 'person's particular sense of history, affinity, and separateness, even the person's mode of reasoning, evaluating, and expressing feeling, are constituted partly by her or his group affinities' (1990: 45). It does, however, require denying that groups '*constitute* individuals' (1990: 45, emphasis added). Groups affect the nature of individuals; but they do so because in groups individuals affect one another, whether directly through personal contact, or indirectly through the influence of the forms – the language, the art, the religion, the physical and moral landscape – they have created or sustained. Whether and how they continue to do so depends upon the actions of individuals – both within and beyond the group.

A group, in other words, is an *association*. It is an association of individuals. This is, however, the understanding of groups that Young wishes to reject: for her a 'group' is different not only from an 'aggregate' but also from an 'association'. An association, for her, is something which is constituted by individuals who come together as already formed persons; and the relationship of persons to associations is usually voluntary (1990: 44). The trouble with this model, she argues, is that it relies on a conception of the subject as something of autonomous origin, and of consciousness as something 'outside of and prior to language and the context of social interaction' (1990: 45). It may account for formally organized institutions such as clubs and churches – but not for groups. But the trouble with this objection is that it depends upon a *non sequitur:* the claim that to see a group as something constituted by already formed persons is to see it as constituted by a subject of autonomous origin, and existing outside the context of social interaction. Yet there is no need for an individualist to make any such assumption, even while agreeing that an association is indeed constituted of already formed persons. The individualist need not deny that the subject was itself formed by its (earlier) social context. But to understand *this*, current, form of association we need to understand it in terms of the individuals whose interactions make it what it is, and has become.

The critical assumption made by the individualist here is not that the individuals who make up the group-as-association are autonomous, or pre-social, but rather that they are *actors*. The social landscape, in the social ontology in which this is a crucial assumption, is made up of actors. To the extent that there are other features on the social landscape, they are either aggregates of actors or else epiphenomena. The sum of red-haired people in society is an aggregate; the *class* of red-haired people (should someone assert the existence of such a thing) is epiphenomenal. An association of individuals is not merely an aggregate of persons, because the association is understandable only in terms of the relations among the *actors* who comprise it. A morgueful of musicians is not an association, let alone an orchestra. Of course, individuals are not the only actors in society. Associations can themselves be actors. 'An actor is a locus of decision and action, where the decision is in some sense a consequence of the actor's decisions' (Hindess 1987: 110). But associations can be made up only of actors. Society is, in the end, made up only of actors.

In this regard, there are no groups in society, unless they are associations. For if they are not associations, they cannot act; and if they cannot act, they have no place in any plausible social ontology, except as epiphenomena. There are, in the end, only actors; and this means that there are only individuals, or associations of individuals. Any reference to other kinds of collectivities as actors 'would be allegorical at best, presenting us with a complex story in the guise of something simpler, and at worst thoroughly misleading' (Hindess 1987: 111). (This does not mean we have to deny the operation of things like crowds or mobs, for example; we have only to maintain that, since they lack loci of decision, they are not actors, and that their behaviour has to be accounted for in terms of individual interaction.)

All this matters for politics. If we fail to recognize that groups in any sense other than associations do not exist, it is tempting not only to reify them but also to accord them a standing they do not warrant. We are tempted to see them in the ways that many have tried to describe some of them in the past – as entities which are purer, or nobler, or more worthy than they really are. For groups, like individuals, are more calculating about their identity than we might assume – since there is much to be gained, economically and socially, by that choice.

The most important strength of the liberal individualist approach to politics, however, is something which its critics see as a weakness. According to Iris Young, this 'atomistic conception generates a political theory that presumes conflict and competition as characteristic modes of interaction' (1990: 228). Whether or not it is 'atomistic', liberal political theory certainly does make this presumption. The human condition is one of conflict. There is nothing in history that suggests that it has ever been otherwise; and there is no plausible social theory that explains how it might ever be different in the future. If that is so, the task of political institutions is to palliate a condition it cannot cure. And political theorists concerned about oppression in human society should learn to set their sights a little lower, aiming at a theory not of liberation, but of peace.

Note

Earlier versions of this chapter were presented to audiences at the Department of Politics, Flinders University, and the School of Politics, Australian Defence Force Academy. I would like to thank participants for some helpful comment and criticism. Thanks for comments on the paper are also due to Rick de Angelis, Robert Goodin, and Andrew Vincent, even though I was unable (or unwilling) to attend to all of their many helpful suggestions.

References

Anderson, Michael R. 1987. 'Law and the Protection of Cultural Communities: The Case of Native American Fishing Rights', *Law and Policy*, 9.
Barber, Benjamin. 1984. *Strong Democracy*. Berkeley: University of California Press.
Fraser, Nancy. 1995. 'Recognition or Redistribution? A Critical Reading of Iris Young's *Justice and the Politics of Difference*', *Journal of Political Philosophy*, 3.
Gordon, Milton. 1964. *Assimilation in American Life: The Role of Race, Religion and National Origins*. New York: Oxford University Press.
Hindess, Barry. 1987. *Politics and Class Analysis*. Oxford: Blackwell.
Hobbes, Thomas. n.d. *Leviathan*. Oxford: Blackwell.
Horowitz, Donald. 1985. *Ethnic Groups in Conflict*. Berkeley: University of California Press.
Jones, Peter. 1994. 'Bearing the Consequences of Belief', *Journal of Political Philosophy*, 2.
Kukathas, Chandran. 1991. *The Fraternal Conceit: Individualist versus Collectivist Ideas of Community*. St Leonards: Centre for Independent Studies.
Kukathas, Chandran. 1992. 'Are There Any Cultural Rights?', *Political Theory*, 20.
Kukathas, Chandran. 1996. 'Liberalism, Communitarianism, and Political Community', *Social Philosophy and Policy*, 13, no. 1.
Kukathas, Chandran. 1997. 'Cultural Toleration', in Will Kymlicka and Ian Shapiro, eds, *Ethnicity and Group Rights*. NOMOS XXXIX, New York: New York University Press.
Kukathas, Chandran. Forthcoming, 1997. 'Liberalism and Multiculturalism: The Politics of Indifference', *Political Theory*.
Kymlicka, Will. 1995. *Multicultural Citizenship*. Oxford: Oxford University Press.
Malcolm, Noel. 1996. *Bosnia. A Short History*, rev. edn. London: Macmillan.
Mill, John Stuart. 1985. *On Liberty*, in *Utilitarianism; On Liberty; Essay on Bentham*, ed. Mary Warnock. London: Fontana Press.
Oakeshott, Michael. n.d. 'Introduction', in Hobbes, *Leviathan*, pp. vii–lxvi.
Sandel, Michael. 1982. *Liberalism and the Limits of Justice*. Cambridge: Cambridge University Press.
Scott, James C. 1995. 'State Simplifications: Nature, Space and People', *Journal of Political Philosophy*, 3.
Sestito, Raymond. 1982. *The Politics of Multiculturalism*. St Leonards, NSW: Centre for Independent Studies.
Taylor, Charles. 1989. 'Cross Purposes: the Liberal–Communitarian Debate', in Nancy Rosenblum, ed., *Liberalism and the Moral Life*. Cambridge, Mass.: Harvard University Press.
Thakur, Ramesh, 1993. 'From the Mosaic to the Melting Pot: Cross-National Reflections on Multiculturalism', in Chandran Kukathas, ed., *Multicultural Citizens. The Philosophy and Politics of Identity*. St Leonards, NSW: Centre for Independent Studies.
Van Dyke, Vernon. 1985. *Human Rights, Ethnicity and Discrimination*. Westport and London: Greenwood Press.
Ward, David. 1989. *Poverty, Ethnicity, and the American City, 1840–1925: Changing Conceptions of the Slum and the Ghetto*. Cambridge: Cambridge University Press.
Young, Iris Marion. 1990. *Justice and the Politics of Difference*. Princeton: Princeton University Press.
Young, Iris Marion. 1993. 'Together in Difference: Transforming the Logic of Group Political Conflict', in Judith Squires, ed., *Principled Positions. Postmodernism and the Rediscovery of Value*. London: Lawrence and Wishart.

CHAPTER 7

Postcolonialism and Political Theory

Duncan Ivison

What does contemporary political theory have to learn from the recent outpouring of postcolonial writing? What aspects of the normative apparatus of contemporary liberal political theory, for example, are brought into focus and into question by postcolonial concerns and approaches? Despite the sometimes wilful obscurantism of postcolonial theorists, and a tendency to reduce complex arguments and traditions in political theory to easy slogans, I want to claim that there are enormously important and relevant issues at play in their work that deserve careful attention. They speak to some of the most pressing and distressing issues of our day. Namely, they are relevant to an understanding of the 'politics of recognition'; the 'bewildering landscape' of demands for cultural recognition in late-modern political societies *everywhere* – north, south, east and west (Tully 1995: 2; Taylor et al. 1992; Young 1990; Kymlicka 1995). The demand for recognition is linked to questions of identity, whether on the part of an individual or a group. Identity is partially shaped, as well as misshaped, by recognition (or its absence) by others. The specific differences that are recognized (or not), and the particular ways in which they are, have very real consequences – political, economic and cultural – for the parties involved. Postcolonial theory, in part, attempts to map and make sense of the interdependencies and asymmetries between these differences and identities.

I begin with a discussion of some general themes in postcolonial theory. I then turn to a central issue in contemporary political theory – the idea of public reason – as a way of fleshing out some of the concerns expressed by postcolonial writers about liberal political theory in general. Finally I turn to a real and important set of postcolonial issues confronting countries such as Australia and Canada – the claims of aboriginal people concerning land and self-government. How are these distinctive claims understood, given liberal assumptions about the reasoning of free and equal citizens in the public sphere?

Themes of Postcolonial Theory

I shall begin with a general sketch of postcolonial theory.[1] This is a somewhat paradoxical exercise, in so far as postcolonialism privileges the localized and specific over the general and global. Moreover, the discontinuities and differences between the various historical patterns of colonialism and imperialism make it extremely difficult to establish a general sense of postcolonialism, since it means different things to different people with different histories (Dirlik 1994; Ahmad 1992). Nevertheless, theorists persist in speaking of it as a general category of discourse, or at least, as consisting of a distinctive set of thematic, methodological and political commitments.

Gyan Prakash, for example, suggests a neat question to which post-colonial (and 'post-Orientalist') work is an answer: how does the 'Third World' write its own history? (1992: 383; Said 1978). For Prakash (and others) it must do so in a radically anti-foundationalist and anti-essentialist manner: 'It requires the rejection of those modes of thinking which configure the third world in such irreducible essences as religiosity, underdevelopment, poverty, nationhood, non-Westernness' (1990: 384). Postcolonial criticism seeks to:

> undo the Eurocentrism produced by the institution of the west's trajectory, its appropriation of the other as History. It does so, however, with the acute realization that postcoloniality is not born and nurtured in a panoptic distance from history. The postcolonial exists as an aftermath, as an after – after being worked over by colonialism. Criticism formed in this process of the enunciation of discourses of domination occupies a space that is neither inside nor outside the history of western domination but in a tangential relation to it. [Prakash 1992: 8]

Thus the 'meta-narratives' told by nationalist, Marxist and liberal histories and theories are tinged by Eurocentrism, the tendency to assume that history is founded upon and 'representable through some identity – individual, class, or structure – which resists further decomposition into heterogeneity' (Prakash 1990: 397). Postcolonialism focuses on this radical heterogeneity, or in the now famous phrase, on this *subalternity*.[2]

The concept of subalternity is difficult to summarize since it combines Marxist, structuralist, post-structuralist and 'post-foundationalist' historical and theoretical influences. It is probably best understood through a patient consideration of the impressive historical work produced under the banner of *Subaltern Studies* (Guha 1983; Guha and Spivak 1988; O'Hanlon 1988). However, we can isolate two key characteristics that connect with the comments of Prakash cited above. The first concerns the object of postcolonial concerns, and the second the account of human and political agency implied therein.

First, subaltern studies focuses attention on 'the dispossessed' – the particular forms of agency, subjectivity and modes of sociality (such as customary laws and practices) ignored or 'subjugated' by colonial and imperialist institutions, as well as by the universalizing and legitimating modes of historiography and political theory that accompanied them. Dipesh Chakrabarty, for example, takes the public/private distinction that lies at the heart of liberal conceptions of citizenship and is deployed in nationalist and liberal interpretations of Indian politics and history; he argues that it displaces and suppresses the distinctive ways in which various Indian subaltern communities challenged and contested liberal conceptions of 'domestic space' and negative liberty. He claims these 'voices' and communities are denied a place in a history driven by a European model of nation-state development and its attendant distinctions between public/private, citizenship/communalism, and tradition/modernity (1992: 10–12; cf. Das 1989; Guha 1982; Bhabha 1994: 6).

Some of the core assumptions of liberal political theory therefore render it incapable of capturing the complex, overlapping and ambivalent mode of subaltern agency. Homi Bhabha refers to its 'hybridity'; identities constituted by 'inbetweenness' and movement – 'the overlap and displacement of domains of difference' (1994: 2). It refers to the way the civilizing mission of colonialism, for example, was partly undone through the appropriation of the language and practices of civility by the natives. What was returned, as one missionary put it, was a 'sly civility', a 'mimicry' that was 'almost the same but not quite . . . at once resemblance and menace' (1994: 99, 86; cf. Thomas 1994: 53–65). However much colonialism dominates and subjugates the subaltern, he or she can still speak; hybridity disrupts colonial domination. From this a distinctive (and ethicized) concept of self emerges, one that operates in the 'interstitial passage between fixed identifications [and which] opens up the possibility of a cultural hybridity that entertains difference without an assumed or imposed hierarchy' (Bhabha 1994: 4).

A set of distinctive political commitments follows as well. Bhabha, for example, argues that the 'postcolonial perspective (in resisting holistic forms of social explanation) forces a recognition of the more complex cultural and political boundaries that exist on the cusp of these often opposed political spheres' (i.e. between First and Third Worlds).

> [It] forces us to rethink the profound limitations of a consensual and collusive 'liberal' sense of cultural community. It insists that cultural and political identity are constructed through a process of alterity . . . The time for 'assimilating' minorities to holistic and organic notions of cultural value has

dramatically passed. The very language of cultural community needs to be rethought from the postcolonial perspective, in a move similar to the language of sexuality, the self and cultural community, effected by feminists in the 1970s and the gay community in the 1980s. [Bhabha 1994: 175][3]

Equally, Chakrabarty calls for a 'radical critique and transcendence of liberalism', where 'liberalism' is taken to be 'the bureaucratic construction of citizenship, modern state, and bourgeois privacy that classical political philosophy has produced' (1992: 20). So some of the core ideas of liberalism – of citizenship, civil society and negative freedom – are categories 'whose global currency' can no longer be taken for granted in so far as they have been deployed in the 'colonial theatre' in aid of dubious projects aimed at 'civilizing' the natives or encouraging their 'development'.[4] The native or subaltern who is incapable of being a sovereign self-legislating subject (because of savagery, 'traditionalism', inarticulacy, unruliness or poverty) cannot participate in the public political space of *civil* society (cf. O'Hanlon 1988: 220–1). For it is within civil society that the liberty and welfare of the individual is secured by preserving both a 'private' domestic sphere of family life and personal interests free from the gaze of the political, and a public political space made up of diverse cultural, economic and political institutions and practices within which these 'free citizens' participate and which they help define.

Liberalism's narratives of citizenship thus have played a part in assimilating to the projects of the modern state 'all other possibilities of human solidarity' (Chakrabarty 1992: 23). Liberal diversity is too narrow (Parekh 1995). However inevitable this process may have been historically, argues Chakrabarty, what still needs to be mapped is what 'resists and escapes the best human effort at translation across cultural and other semiotic systems, so that the world may . . . be imagined as radically heterogeneous'. This means exploring other 'narratives of human connection' which are defined neither by the rituals of liberal citizenship nor the 'nightmare of "tradition" that "modernity" creates' (23; cf. Bhabha's discussion of a 'postcolonial contra-modernity', 1994: 6).

The focus on the subaltern then connects with a critique of, or at least antipathy towards, liberalism, particularly the way it links citizenship to conceptions of individual autonomy and rationality, and draws boundaries between the public and the private in the various conceptions of state and civil society. There are complex issues and problems to do with the alternative vision of subaltern agency which is sometimes explicitly contrasted with the liberal (as well as nationalist and Marxist) account. In recovering the subjectivity of the colonized – the 'autonomy' of the domain of the subaltern as Guha (1983) puts it – the danger is simply to reinstate a reconfigured version of the sovereign self-legislating figure of Western political theory. If not, then it is not clear exactly *who* or what is resisting or engaging in sly civility, especially given the way many of these studies emphasize the extraordinary reach and complexity of colonial domination. There is, I believe, a coherent response to these important questions hinted at in Bhabha's notion of hybridity, but it is never fully developed. The choice is certainly not between method- ological individualism and a blunt structuralism, though I cannot develop this here.[5]

There are also important issues to do with the extent to which 'post- colonialism', as a general category of cultural and political critique, lumps together incredibly disparate historical, social, geographical and political phenomena to do with the aftermath of colonialism. For example, as Thomas points out, it is not the case that colonial discourse everywhere sought to diminish or disavow difference through assimil- ation. It was sometimes concerned just as much to deny similarity. This was done either through the assertion of hierarchical differences (citizen/savage), or allowing only an 'authenticated' or official form of difference linked with, for example, exaggerated and demeaning accounts of exoticism and primitivism (Thomas 1994: 53). It is crucial to establish the context and historical specificity of the various forms of colonial governmental practices and discourses in order to understand what it was that indigenous people or 'subalterns' were (are) enmeshed within and resisting against. The difference between, for example, the colonialism of the British empire in nineteenth-century India and the settler-colonialism of seventeenth- and eighteenth-century Australia or Canada is significant. They cannot be reduced to a singular colonial logic that subsequently generates a global postcolonial project.

Postcolonialism and Liberal Theory

Let us look more closely at the postcolonial critique of liberalism. In particular, I want to use an example, the claims of indigenous people in countries such as Australia and Canada, to unpack the concern ex- pressed above about how liberal ideals of public space and citizenship marginalize and exclude subaltern and indigenous people.

Bhabha writes of the need for the whole idea of a 'cultural com- munity', as expressed in liberal political theory, to be radically rethought. In many ways this is precisely what has been occurring in relation to 'the politics of recognition' mentioned above. More concretely, the chal- lenges and questions posed by postcolonial theorists are being con- fronted in postcolonial countries struggling to accommodate and recognize cultural difference in their constitutions and core political institutions and norms. Aboriginal people in Canada and Australia, for example, are seeking recognition and affirmation of their claims to land and self-government. These matters are immediately complicated by the fact that such claims are not easily translatable into familiar categories of liberal self-determination, nationalist anti-colonial and anti-imperial movements, or communitarianism. Nor are the particular aboriginal conceptions of property and self-rule easily compatible with those in a generally liberal constitutionalist tradition.

So how are aboriginal claims handled, and where? Historically they have been fought out in wars between settlers and indigenous people, including forced removals from tribal lands, genocide and coerced assimilation. More recently, domestic and international courtrooms have become forums for confrontation, as indigenous people have struggled to protect their customs and lands by appealing to non-indigenous conceptions of justice and equality. And now legislatures too are confronted with these claims, as important legal decisions have to be given statutory effect, and current practices and norms have to be changed to meet new (judicially imposed) standards. Direct political action by indigenous people, whether through protests or land occupations or other forms of campaigning, has also forced politicians and the general public to confront these issues. The renaissance and popularity of indigenous art and culture has provided another entry point for these issues into mainstream society. These different domains interact and overlap with each other to form a complex web of sites within which indigenous claims are pressed and heard.

This web of sites can be described as forming, when linked, a meta-public sphere (including other domains and activities I have not mentioned, such as various forms of media, etc.). In so far as a public sphere can be defined generally as a common space within which members of a society 'meet' – if only virtually – to discuss matters of common interest, then clearly indigenous claims are at least *prima facie* eligible to be included, just in being made in these various contexts. But if the conception of public space is developed further, and we begin to see what it would mean to do justice to the claims of indigenous people, complications arise. The complaints of postcolonial writers – of marginality and exclusion and the concomitant assumptions of cultural homogeneity (or at least sharply limited diversity) – are relevant here. The challenges raised by indigenous appeals to non-liberal conceptions of property and self-rule provide a contemporary context to test these concerns.

The meta-public sphere in liberal political theory is a moralized conception, and not simply a neutral descriptive claim about the way citizens interact in (any) society generally. For the opinions and judgments that people form in the public sphere have normative significance. Namely, the government ought to listen to these views. First, because they are (or should be) reflective and deliberative, and not simply a bald declaration of preferences. And second, because if 'the people' are sovereign, than the government is morally bound to pay heed to them anyway (Taylor 1995: 262–5; Habermas 1989; Fraser 1992: 134–5). So ideally, in the public sphere, citizens debate and form rational views that are meant to guide the conduct of government. The legitimacy of the government in large measure depends upon its coercive power being exercised in accordance with these rational views (i.e. being justified in relation to them).

The public sphere provides a framework within which a particular (liberal) mode of public expression or dialogue occurs. Following recent discussions in contemporary political philosophy, we can label this particular mode of expression in the public sphere a form of *public reason*. Citizens engage in public reason when they reflect upon and debate issues to do with the exercise of the coercive power of the government, and with its legitimacy generally. We need to examine this idea of public reason more closely, since it sets the boundaries as to what counts as a genuine contribution to this dialogue of legitimacy. We can then return to the question as to how indigenous claims for self-rule, for example, are handled, given this concept of the public sphere and the account of public reason circulating within it.

Public Reason

Given deep diversity about conceptions of the good and the best way to live, the only way people can live together in complex societies is to find some way of living with each other's difference. For liberals such as Rawls, this entails finding some way of justifying the legitimacy of political institutions and regulative norms of justice in terms that all (or at least the vast majority) can accept, given 'reasonable pluralism' (1995; Barry 1995a).[6] Establishing the requirements of legitimacy, that is, the permissibility of using the coercive powers of the state, is not the same as constructing agreement on relatively specific rules of justice (see Rawls 1993: 226; 1995: 175–6; Estlund 1996). We concentrate on the former here, since this is what postcolonial critics seem mainly to be concerned with, as well as what the indigenous claims refer to in so far as they question the legitimacy of a constitution or political system that does not recognize their cultural distinctiveness.

For Rawls, legitimacy is closely bound up with the idea of public reason. The 'liberal principle of legitimacy' states that 'our exercise of political power is fully proper only when it is exercised in accordance with a constitution the essentials of which all citizens as free and equal may reasonably be expected to endorse in light of principles and ideals acceptable to their common human reason' (1993: 137). 'Common human reason' alone, however, does not converge on the necessary principles. It has to be focused on a specific set of questions and grounded in a specific conception and ethos of citizenship. Hence the account of public reason.

> Public reason is characteristic of a democratic people: it is the reason of its citizens, of those sharing the status of equal citizenship. The subject of their reason is the good of the public: what the political conception of justice requires of society's basic structure of institutions, and of the purposes and ends they are to serve . . . Public reason is the reason of equal citizens who, as a collective body, exercise final political and coercive power over one another in enacting laws and in amending their constitution. [212–14]

Public reason, then, is a mode of reasoning specific to political questions, which might include criteria for the use and/or validity of certain arguments and information in the political sphere. (Much rests on elaborating just what is meant by 'political'.) They are meant as reasons to be shared in the sense that they are reasons for each in virtue of being reasons for all (Postema 1995: 69–71). The scope of public reasons is crucial; they are distinct from 'non-public' reasons in so far as they invoke reasons acceptable to all and not just to a particular group or class. In recent liberal political argument, they tend to be principles that can be shared and, sometimes, shared in the same way. Indeed, the legitimacy (and stability) of liberal-democratic regimes is said to derive largely from agreement on such fundamental principles.

Public reason includes a 'set of guidelines of inquiry that specify ways of reasoning and criteria for the kinds of information relevant for political questions' (Rawls 1993: 223). These guidelines specify the modes of reasoning that may be used, and the types of considerations that may be appealed to, in discussing political questions. But public reason has 'special subjects'. It does not apply to the specifics of tax legislation, or the regulation of the environment, or the funding of the arts, but only to 'constitutional essentials' and questions of basic justice. This is not to say that we do not, in our 'personal deliberations', reason on the grounds of a whole range of 'background' philosophical, moral, religious, political, and cultural beliefs. But in the 'public forum', whether as members of political parties, as candidates, or as citizens, when discussing (or voting on) matters to do with constitutional essentials, the limits of public reason must be observed. We should not appeal to what we see as the truth of a particular philosophy, religion, or other 'comprehensive doctrine', but instead confine ourselves to 'plain truths, now widely accepted, or available, to citizens generally' (250–4). There is a distinction between what we may believe to be a superior conception of the good, and what can reasonably be advanced as a foundation for society's basic political institutions (see Rawls 1995: 140).

It is unreasonable to appeal to a 'nonpolitical value' in the course of establishing the proper exercise of political power, because it proposes a view about constitutional essentials that citizens, given the 'burdens of judgment', are bound to disagree over. The burdens of judgment are the sources of disagreement between reasonable people, the different manner in which people weigh, value and assess evidence (Rawls 1993: 54–8). These burdens remain even in the course of the most free and open discussion. Thus the 'burdens of judgment are of first significance for a democratic idea of toleration' (58).

Convergence on this principle of public reason is part of the process of converging on the two principles of justice.[7] Rawlsian citizens must exercise 'epistemological restraint' (or adopt a moderate scepticism) with regard to their conception of the good when deliberating about regulative political institutions (Barry 1995a: 177–83). For Rawls, no configuration of institutional devices or 'invisible hand' mechanisms can conjure such a convergence, and so he proposes an ideal of citizenship that derives from his conception of the moral person as a citizen – the 'political conception of citizens as free and equal' (and reasonable and rational). Co-operation involves a moral 'duty of civility', a willingness to 'listen to others, and a fairmindedness in deciding when accommodations to their views should reasonably be made' (1993: 217). Such 'fairmindedness' is exhibited towards world-views which accept the burdens of judgment and seek agreement on principles that do not go 'beyond the political' (1995: 145). This is connected to Rawls's conception of the person as having two moral powers. One is the 'capacity to form, revise, and rationally pursue a theory of the good' (the rational), and the other is a capacity for an effective sense of justice (the reasonable) (1993: 48–54). This includes the willingness to 'propose fair terms of cooperation that others as free equals also might endorse'; to act on these terms provided others do ('even contrary to one's own interest'); and to recognize the burdens of judgment (1995: 134).

So why should citizens honour the limits of public reason? Part of Rawls's response is that the requirement to act in accord with public reason is grounded in the fact that people are reasonable – that they have a higher-order motivation to act for public reasons (i.e. to suggest and comply with 'fair political ideals', the second moral power). He assumes that reasonable people have a higher-order interest in forming, revising and rationally pursuing a conception of the good (1993: 30). The concept of the person, in other words, presupposes the particular form of practical reason required.[8] This hardly helps *justify* the priority of the right – the acceptance of public reasons as defined – to those who do not have the higher-order desire in the first place. Moreover, there might be very different accounts of where the boundaries between public and non-public reasons can be drawn, even accepting that abstracting from particular standpoints is necessary for any kind of social co-operation, given deep pluralism.[9] It is not a case of having to justify it to those who reject *any* form of reasonableness whatsoever, but rather to those who reject, for example, the particular distinction between public and non-public at the heart of Rawlsian reasonableness.[10]

Rawls's conception of the political is closely related to consensus and thus restricted to topics which reasonable people can agree on, given a plurality of comprehensive doctrines. This is, at the very least, a controversial sense of the political. Take his contrast between the political conception of justice and a *modus vivendi* – which is '*political in the wrong way*' (1993: 39–40). Rawls presents the idea of a *modus vivendi* as an analogy to relations between two hostile nation-states. A *modus vivendi* is akin to an equilibrium point between the two; it is like a treaty that neither party has an interest in violating, given certain circumstances (roughly equal power, etc.), but will violate if the opportunity arises. This is similar, Rawls claims, to a social consensus founded exclusively on political bargaining: 'social unity is only apparent, as its stability is contingent on circumstances remaining such as not to upset the fortunate convergence of interests' (a *modus vivendi* can only ever be a stage along the way to a 'well-ordered society'; 1993: 147, 158–68). If society is to be a fair system of co-operation, a pragmatic balance between different moral and political views will not do.

But given deep diversity, a rational convergence on a single standard of public reason appears remote. This is not a claim that it is unlikely that *anything* can be agreed upon save for some vague Oakeshottian 'civil association' or theory of the 'rule of law' *à la* Hayek.[11] Rather, if it is unlikely to expect convergence from or upon a single public standpoint or standard, we should expect to find a mix of different levels of agreement and points of convergence. Some will be more justified and fleshed out than others, but all could be seen as part of the working out of a diverse and fluid public sphere containing *plural* public reasons.[12]

The greater the limits of public reason, the narrower the range of possible interpretations of principles admissible to the public sphere. And yet late modern politics is increasingly characterized by demands for the expansion of this space, and for the recognition of diverse modes of political identification and thus diverse modes of public justification. This presses directly against strategies that rely upon the implicit 'fixed points' of a bounded political culture as premises to be worked up into a consensus on regulative first principles. In these circumstances, it might be that it is Rawls's theory that is political in the wrong way, or at least controversial in ways it thinks it avoids.

Benhabib (1992), for example, argues that Rawls's account mis-
construes democratic politics in so far as he associates it with an
essentially juridical model of public space that emphasizes conversational
restraint based on a *prior* distinction between public and non-public
reason (see also Bohman 1995; Tully 1995).[13] Her account of democratic
politics is very different: it is about challenging, redefining, and
renegotiating the divisions between 'the good and just, the moral and
the legal, the private and the public' (Benhabib 1992: 99–100, 106–7;
Fraser 1992). The kind of reasoning described by Rawls is less exemplary
of robust democratic deliberation, argues Benhabib, and more akin to
the reasoning of a parliamentary committee or federal agency (102).
Actually, the image Rawls provides is more precise. We are to imagine
ourselves as providing reasons in a manner similar to the way Supreme
Court justices are constrained to develop and express their judgments
publicly on complex constitutional issues (1993: 235–40).[14] For Benhabib, it is important to point out what is lost in this picture
of democratic deliberation; all 'contestatory, rhetorical, affective, im-
passioned elements of public discourse, with all their excesses and
virtues' (1992: 102; cf. Gutmann and Thompson 1995: 101–3). Allowing
for the development of a more 'critical public sphere' with an agenda
that is 'radically open' has its dangers too.[15] But Benhabib argues that
such a public sphere, if properly construed and constructed, is in reality
more true to the democratic pedigree that informs any plausible account
of legitimacy in conditions of deep social and political diversity.

The crucial thing to note is that for Rawls, whatever the diversity of the
background culture of a society, there is 'but one public reason' based
on common human reason (1993: 220). Legitimacy depends upon our
being able to justify to each other (as free and equal citizens) the
coercive exercise of political power in terms that all (or a significant
majority) can accept. For Benhabib, given the radical openness of the
agenda of the public sphere and a proliferation of sub-publics other than
those of formal political institutions, there might be any number of
different forms of public reason. That is, there is more than one norm of
reasonableness in play. Reasonable epistemic diversity follows from
reasonable moral diversity. Legitimacy thus depends upon an openness
to the questioning of any normative assumptions or distinctions –
including those between the right and the good, public and non-public
– by all those affected by their actual or foreseeable consequences. It
follows from the existence of plural public reasons that there will not be
a *single* impartial standard or mode of justification upon which legitimacy
can be grounded. The difficult question then is exactly how the different
public reasons can be co-ordinated in such a way that a lack of consensus
does not engender an unwillingness on the part of citizens and groups

to co-operate and negotiate, despite their often radical differences and disagreements.

Indigenous Claims and the Public Sphere

Let us return to the example of indigenous claims in order to flesh out these issues in more concrete terms, and to reconnect the discussion more explicitly to the postcolonial critique of liberal political theory discussed above.

A recent landmark High Court case in Australia has thrust these issues into the centre of that country's public sphere. In *Mabo v. State of Queensland* (No. 2),[16] a majority of the court held that the people of the Murray Islands (Mer) retained native title to their land which was not extinguished by the annexation of the islands to the colony of Queensland in 1879, nor by subsequent legislation.[17] The significance of the decision was that the court abandoned the previously regulative doctrine of *terra nullius*. As is well known, this doctrine enabled British colonizers to apply the laws of England to newly settled areas where there was not a recognizable set of laws already in place. It presumed, in other words, that the territory was literally empty before their arrival. This was enlarged to include settlement of lands inhabited by 'backward' or 'barbarous' peoples, whose laws or customs simply did not count as law. In overturning this assumption, the court rejected the claim that the acquisition of sovereignty by the Crown made it the universal and absolute beneficial owner of all land in the territory. If this were true, Aboriginal people would be made 'intruders in their own homes', as Brennan J. put it in his lead judgment. 'Judged by any civilized standard,' argued Brennan, 'such a law is unjust and its claim to be part of the common law to be applied in contemporary Australia must be questioned.' The common law cannot be 'frozen in an age of racial discrimination'.

The basic formula for the recognition of native title in *Mabo* was: 'Native title has its origin in and is given its content by the traditional laws acknowledged by and the traditional customs observed by the indigenous inhabitants of a territory. The nature and incidents of native title must be ascertained as a matter of fact by reference to those laws and customs.'[18] As one Aboriginal commentator has argued, the gist of this claim is the recognition of an 'inherent right – an original right that does not need to be granted by the Crown because it arises out of Aboriginal law and custom'. Thus, 'Aboriginal law and custom is now a source of law in [Australia]'.[19]

The implications for self-determination and self-government, then, are clear. If native title arises out of Aboriginal law and custom, then that law and custom apply to other activities on that land. And if inherent rights to land exist, then why not inherent rights to self-government? Note that self-government is meant to refer to a whole range of possibilities, and is not exhausted by assumptions of international law about sovereignty being necessarily related to independent statehood.[20] Aboriginal government might be considered as one strand of a larger web of entities and institutional actors exercising discrete forms of sovereignty over territories and peoples within Australia – which has a federal system anyway.[21] But these possibilities are generally dampened by the court's reasoning and, by extension, lend credence to those who deny such possibilities in more overtly political spheres.

In an earlier decision, Mason CJ., quoting another justice, argued that Aboriginal people have

> no legislative, executive, or judicial organs by which sovereignty may be exercised. If such organs existed, they would have no powers, except such as the law of the Commonwealth, or of a State or Territory, might confer upon them. The contention that there is in Australia an aboriginal nation exercising sovereignty, even of a limited kind, is quite impossible in law to maintain.[22]

The relevant point for our discussion is to note the assumption that legislative and judicial organs do not exist save as those that would be granted by the Commonwealth. As well, that sovereignty is only associable with European-style 'legislative, executive [and] judicial' organs.

This last assumption follows a long tradition in colonial jurisprudence and political theory. Defining the possession of sovereignty as hinging on the existence of a particular form of civil and political society neatly excludes any consideration of Aboriginal institutions and norms, and thus any reasonable consideration of their claims. Indeed it was invoked by Locke, amongst others, to justify the expansion of British colonization in the Americas (Tully 1993: 137–76; 1995: 70–8). Are the democratic goods of participation and self-rule realizable only in terms of conceptions of sovereignty (and popular sovereignty) derived ultimately from Hobbes, Locke and international law? Could there be a form of self-government for Aboriginal people that was neither imposed from above nor merely ornamental? What about the distinctive constitutional norms and practices of Aboriginal people themselves – norms and practices that were in fact part of the intercultural context within which the common law and constitutional law of settler-states developed (Slattery 1991; Tully 1995: 116–39)?

So here is one example of Chakrabarty's point. Key concepts in Western political theory, and the institutions shaped in their image – such as property, in the case of *terra nullius*, and sovereignty, in Mason's opinion – can obscure the specific nature of subaltern or indigenous claims, and thus constrain the possibilities for giving them their proper due. Reinforced in constitutional jurisprudence and common law precedent, two crucial strands of the meta-public sphere, these concepts and assumptions have only recently come under critical inspection through the prompting of indigenous political activism and a related radical revaluation and rethinking of the history of settler–native relations.[23] The reshaping of normative conceptions of sovereignty and property by contemporary political theory surely needs to follow – hence the value of the postcolonial challenge.

More positively, we can catch a glimpse of how a postcolonial sensibility might add to a richer and more complex understanding of the public sphere and public reason examined above. In Canada, the Supreme Court has recently established a justificatory threshold (in *R v. Sparrow*)[24] which governments must meet in order to modify 'existing' aboriginal rights (which have been recognized in the Canadian Constitution). This might result in a different interpretation of the distribution of sovereignty in Canada, where it has been assumed that provincial and federal governments always have supremacy over aboriginal laws and customs (Macklem 1993). The 'Sparrow test' signals to legislators the manner in which legislation affecting aboriginal rights will be interpreted by the courts, including the conventions, principles, and sources that will be appealed to. The justificatory payoff is this: any legislation regulating these rights is justifiable if and only if it passes a justificatory test with reference to the customs and laws of aboriginal people, and the recognition of an 'inherent theory of aboriginal rights' (Tennant 1991: 372–86). This has important consequences for the legitimacy of any legislation that might affect aboriginal interests. A different practice of justification is now in place; the onus shifts from the aboriginal claimant to the Crown. More to the point, it changes the nature of what counts as a 'public reason' to which aboriginal people can appeal, and the kinds of concerns and arguments which non-aboriginal courts and legislatures – and the public sphere generally – must engage with and take seriously. It adds another dimension to a public sphere previously unable (or unwilling) to recognize such claims and standards of justification. Indeed, it changes its very shape, and thus the way in which citizens understand themselves and each other in relation to it.

Postcolonial theory prompts critical reflection on the ways in which political theory claims to give proper care and consideration to the 'strange multiplicity' of demands for recognition in late-modern multinational and multicultural states. Given what is at stake in countries around the world where such demands are the daily stuff of politics, this is a significant contribution. To find answers to the questions it poses, we must discover new lands in the often under-explored conceptual world of normative political theory.

Notes

I am grateful to Andrew Vincent for his encouragement, as well as to Paul Patton, Barry Hindess, Philip Pettit, Will Sanders, Caroline West, Robert Goodin, Alex Callinicos, and T. V. Sathyamurthy for valuable discussions, comments and help.

1 For more comprehensive reviews see Thomas 1994; O'Hanlon 1988; Chakrabarty 1992; Dirlik 1994; Guha 1982; Guha and Spivak 1988.

2 Gramsci is one source of this concept of subaltern: '(not simply an oppressed group) but lacking autonomy, subjected to the influence or hegemony of another social group, not possessing one's own hegemonic position' (in Bhabha 1994: 59).

3 The invocation of an affinity with feminist critiques of liberalism is striking; Bhabha (1994: 10) and Chakrabarty (1992: 20), for example, refer admiringly to the work of Carole Pateman.

4 Aside from Mill's extensive writings on India, see the impressive recent work on the relationship between Locke's political theory and the dispossession of Ameri-Indian lands in North America (Tully 1993), and on theories of dispossession and conquest generally (Pagden 1988; 1995).

5 See O'Hanlon (1988) for a review of these issues and further references; O'Hanlon and Washbrook (1992) claim postcolonial theory offers 'methodological individualism' as an alternative to especially Marxist accounts of postcolonialism. This seems a gross distortion of what Prakash, Chakrabarty and Bhabha intend, even given the imprecision of their arguments. Cf. Thomas 1994: 59–65 and his interesting use of Bourdieu. On political identification generally, and especially the perverse effects of successful collective action around identification, see Hardin (1995).

6 I adapt some of what follows from Ivison 1997, forthcoming.

7 Despite Rawls's explicit statement that *Political Liberalism* abandons none of the elements of justice as fairness outlined in *A Theory of Justice* (1993: 7), some have argued that he in fact does, or at least the logic of his account of political legitimacy undermines the basis for the second principle dealing with social and economic inequalities. See Barry 1995b: 874–915; cf. Estlund 1996: 68–78; and Rawls 1995: 171–5.

8 Cf. Rawls (1995: 148): 'No sensible view can possibly get by without the reasonable and rational as I use them.'

9 Rawls insists that there is 'but one public reason' (1993: 220). But note (226) that 'accepting the idea of public reason and its principle of legitimacy emphatically does not mean . . . accepting a particular liberal conception of justice down to the last details . . .'

10 For example, Habermas (1995: 129–30).

11 Cf. Gray (1993).

12 See the discussion of the conditions for legitimate political deliberation which does not rely upon an assumption of an ultimate rational convergence of views in Bohman and Rehg (1996: 79–99).

13 Note that public/non-public is not strictly analogous with the public/private distinction, since Rawls is concerned with the nature of reason; there is no such thing as 'private reason'. Non-public reason is what we find in the 'background culture' of society; the reason of 'associations of all kinds: churches and universities, scientific societies and professional groups'. There is also a form of 'domestic reason'; the reason of families as small

groups in society, that contrasts with both public and non-public reason (1993: 220 and n. 7).

14 Consider also the image of practical reasoning in *A Theory of Justice*; we are to imagine ourselves as delegates to a constitutional convention trying to design institutions and procedures to accord with the two principles of justice we have agreed to from the perspective of the original position.

15 See Holmes (1995: 202–35).

16 (1992) 66 ALJR 408.

17 There is now a huge literature on *Mabo* and its consequences for Australia generally. For a good introduction and background, see Brennan (1995); Goot and Rowse (1994).

18 *Mabo*, p. 429.

19 Pearson in Goot and Rowse (1994: 180–1).

20 For a comprehensive discussion in relation to the United States and Canada, see Macklem (1993: 1311–67).

21 Ibid., 1347.

22 *Isabel Coe on Behalf of the Wiradjuri Tribe v. The Commonwealth of Australia and the State of New South Wales* (1993) 118 ALR 193 (quoting Gibbs J., *Coe v. Commonwealth* (1979) 53 ALJR 403. In *Milirrpum v. Nabalco Pty Ltd* (1971) 17 FLR at 267, Blackburn J., though denying the existence of native title, did remark that his findings of fact led him to conclude that Aboriginal communities were characterized by 'a government of laws, and not of men'.

23 What is missing from this brief discussion is a theory about exactly how legal decisions influence and mould discussions in the public sphere. Crudely, given the limited opportunities historically and practically that aboriginal people have had to make their views heard in overtly political forums such as parliament or Congress, the courts of settler-states have been the focus of aboriginal efforts. Governments (and public opinion) in Australia, Canada and the United States have tended to respond to indigenous claims – if at all – only at the prompting of major legal decisions (especially ones with serious consequences for industries such as mining and natural resources).

24 (1990) 1 SCR 1075.

References

Ahmed, A. 1992. *In Theory: Classes, Nations, Literatures*. London: Verso.

Barry, B. 1995a. *Justice as Impartiality*. Oxford: Oxford University Press.

Barry, B. 1995b. 'John Rawls and the Search for Stability', *Ethics*, 105.

Benhabib, S. 1992. *Situating the Self: Gender, Community and Postmodernism in Contemporary Ethics*. Cambridge: Polity Press.

Bhabha, H. 1994. *The Location of Culture*. London: Routledge.

Bohman, J. 1995. 'Public Reason and Cultural Pluralism: Political Liberalism and the Problem of Moral Conflict', *Political Theory*, 23.

Bohman, J., and Rehg, W. 1996. 'Discourse and Democracy: The Formal and Informal Bases of Legitimacy in Habermas' *Faktizitat und Geltung*', *Journal of Political Philosophy*, 4.

Brennan, F. 1995. *One Land, One Nation*. St Lucia: University of Queensland Press.

Chakrabarty, D. 1992. 'Postcoloniality and the Artifice of History: Who Speaks for "Indian Pasts"?', *Representations*, 37.

Das, V. 1989. 'Subaltern as Perspective', in R. Guha, ed., *Subaltern Studies VI.* Delhi: Oxford University Press.

Dirlik, A. 1994. 'The Postcolonial Aura: Third World Criticism in the Age of Global Capitalism', *Critical Inquiry*, 20.

Estlund, D. 1996. 'The Survival of Egalitarian Justice in John Rawls's Political Liberalism', *Journal of Political Philosophy*, 4.

Fraser, N. 1992. 'Rethinking the Public Sphere: A Contribution to the Critique of Actually Existing Democracy', in C. Calhoun, ed., *Habermas and the Public Sphere.* Cambridge, Mass.: MIT Press.

Goot, M., and Rowse, T. 1994. *Make a Better Offer: The Politics of Mabo.* Sydney: Pluto Press.

Gray, J. 1993. *Postliberalism: Studies in Political Thought.* New York: Routledge.

Guha, R. 1982. *Subaltern Studies: Writings on South Asian History and Society.* Delhi: Oxford University Press.

Guha, R. 1983. *Elementary Elements of Peasant Insurgency in Colonial India.* Delhi: Oxford University Press.

Guha, R., and Spivak, C. 1988. *Selected Subaltern Studies.* New York: Oxford University Press.

Gutmann, A., and Thompson, D. 1995. 'Moral Disagreement in a Democracy', *Social Philosophy and Policy*, 12.

Habermas, J. 1989. *Structural Transformation of the Public Sphere*, trans. T. Burger. Cambridge, Mass.: MIT Press.

Habermas, J. 1995. 'Reconciliation through the Public Use of Reason: Remarks on John Rawls's Political Liberalism', *Journal of Philosophy*, 92.

Hardin, R. 1995. *One for All: The Logic of Group Conflict.* Princeton: Princeton University Press.

Holmes, S. 1995. *Passions and Constraints: On the Theory of Liberal Democracy.* Chicago: University of Chicago Press.

Ivison, D. Forthcoming, 1997. 'The Secret History of Public Reason', *History of Political Thought*, 18.

Kymlikca, W. 1995. *Multicultural Citizenship: A Liberal Theory of Minority Rights.* Oxford: Oxford University Press.

Macklem, P. 1993. 'Distributing Sovereignty: Indian Nations and Equality of Peoples', *Stanford Law Review*, 45.

O'Hanlon, R. 1988. 'Recovering the Subject: Subaltern Studies and Histories of Resistance in Colonial South Asia', *Modern Asian Studies*, 22.

O'Hanlon, R., and Washbrook, D. 1992. 'After Orientalism: Culture, Criticism, and Politics in the Third World', *Comparative Studies in Society and History*, 34.

Pagden, A. 1988. *The Fall of Natural Man: The American Indian and the Origins of Comparative Ethnology.* Cambridge: Cambridge University Press.

Pagden, A. 1995. *Lords of All the World: Ideologies of Empire in Spain, Britain, and France c.1500–1800.* New Haven: Yale University Press.

Parekh, B. 1995. 'Liberalism and Colonialism', in J. Pieterse and B. Parekh, eds, *The Decolonization of the Imagination: Culture, Knowledge, Power.* London: Zed Books.

Postema, G. 1995. 'Public Practical Reason: An Archaeology', *Social Philosophy and Policy*, 12.

Prakash, G. 1990. 'Writing Post-Orientalist Histories of the Third World: Perspectives from Indian Historiography', *Comparative Studies in Society and History*, 32.

Prakash, G. 1992. 'Postcolonial Criticism and Indian Historiography', *Social Text*, 31–32.
Rawls, J. 1993. *Political Liberalism*. New York: Columbia University Press.
Rawls, J. 1995. 'Reply to Habermas', *Journal of Philosophy*, 92.
Said, E. 1978. *Orientalism*. London: Penguin.
Slattery, B. 1991. 'Aboriginal Sovereignty and Imperial Claims', *Osgoode Hall Law Journal*, 29.
Taylor, C. 1995. *Philosophical Arguments*. Cambridge, Mass.: Harvard University Press.
Taylor, C., et al. 1992. *Multiculturalism and the Politics of Recognition*. Princeton: Princeton University Press.
Tennant, C. 1991. 'Justification and Cultural Authority in s. 35(1) of the Constitution Act 1982: *Regina v Sparrow*', *Dalhousie Law Journal*, 14.
Thomas, N. 1994. *Colonialism's Culture: Anthropology, Travel and Government*. Cambridge: Polity Press.
Tully, J. 1993. *An Approach to Political Philosophy: Locke in Contexts*. Cambridge: Cambridge University Press.
Tully, J. 1995. *Strange Multiplicity: Constitutionalism in an Age of Diversity*. Cambridge: Cambridge University Press.
Young, I. 1990. *Justice and the Politics of Difference*. Princeton: Princeton University Press.

CHAPTER 8

Legal Positivism and Political Power

Tom D. Campbell

This chapter presents a thesis about Legal Positivism and political power, to the effect that positivism is a defensible theory which is addressed to both the facilitation and the proper limitation of power in society. More particularly, it is argued that Ethical Positivism, identified as an ethically normative mode of Legal Positivism (Campbell 1996), is required to give point and purpose to the constitutional doctrine of the separation of powers. To articulate this broad thesis, some analytical work is undertaken concerning varieties of power which is of general relevance to the heartland of political theory. The object of this analysis is to identify the sort of power that judges can exercise, and to work out how we might distinguish between legitimate and illegitimate uses of judicial power. The chapter concludes that, in an adequately functioning democratic system, acceptable rationales for the doctrine of the separation of powers imply that judges should not exercise political power.

The current critical orthodoxy is that Legal Positivism is a doctrine which latently supports the mythological autonomy of law and hence, it is argued, underpins the often hidden political power of judges and lawyers (Cotterrell 1989: 216–35). The consensus is that Legal Positivism is a lawyers' theory which falsely legitimizes the role of judges and enables them to exercise extensive political power without appearing to do so (Hutchinson and Monohan 1986). Magisterially above the political fracas, judges pronounce on what the law is; in fact, what they are doing is deciding cases in accordance with their own individual or group political judgment. This deception enhances judges' political power by making their decisions unchallengeable outside the legal sphere. Secure from political criticism or electoral pressure, the higher echelons of judicial establishments wield substantial political power without any accountability beyond the acquiescence of their peers.

This scenario does not require us to impute conspiratorial designs or calculated agendas to a group of persons who may be naive politically and generally lacking in political *mens rea*. The assumed common sense is that judges are a narrow and internally socialized collectivity largely unaware of the political contestability of their social and economic assumptions; this is quite enough to fit the system which Legal Realists and Critical Legal scholars seek to render visible. On the other hand, the critical analysis is compatible with the situation where politically aware and calculating judicial officers make decisions that serve their own ends or their own view of the public interest, while prudently disguising their objectives behind the citation of precedent and fulsome verbal deference to legal principle.

Legal Positivism is standardly implicated in this charade, despite the fact that the manifest function of the theory is to provide a basis for sharply distinguishing law-making and law-application, a distinction which positivists use to underpin the separation of legislative and judicial power. The critical thesis is that the distinction between making and applying law collapses, both in philosophical theory and in legal practice, but that the public appearance of independence in judicial reasoning gives it a political acceptability which it would not otherwise enjoy. Countering the critical analysis of judicial reasoning as an ideology of judicial power, which amounts to little more than *post hoc* rationalisation of decisions taken on other grounds, this chapter argues that Legal Positivism, in its prescriptive forms at least, is a doctrine which can help to limit the political power of courts and lawyers. The thesis is that Legal Positivism can be a theoretical basis for effectively curbing the power of courts and enhancing that of elected legislatures and democratic politics in general, as well as protecting the liberty and equality of citizens as individuals or groups. This type of Legal Positivism does not exclude the historical realities which critical Realism exposes. It is clearly a superb basis for the exercise of political power when those affected do not realize that it is being exercised. Legal Positivism has indeed often served to cloak judicial skulduggery and maintain entrenched class dominance. Nevertheless, positivism can still be utilized in good faith to provide the wise and virtuous judge with a theory that maximizes democratic accountability and gives substance to the ideal of the rule of law.

In debating the proprieties of the exercise of judicial power, Legal Positivism confronts, not only the empirical critiques of Legal Realism and Critical Legal Studies, but also its historical rival, Natural Law theory. The current resurgence of Natural Law is in part a counter to the Realist contention that judges are not bound either by existing law or external morality, and that whatever courts decide has the authority of law. A question left largely unanswered by Legal Realism relates to the way in which judges ought to make their decisions. This doctrinal void may be filled by many different political approaches. Thus, the economic analysis of law, in its normative forms, urges judges to decide cases on the basis of some model of economic rationality (Posner 1977). Legal Realists themselves suggest a form of economic pragmatism. Other theorists provide a framework for judicial decision-making from some form of Natural Law that posits basic and universal moral imperatives for the general guidance of judicial determinations as well as citizen conduct (Finnis 1980). Ethical Positivism, in contrast, seeks to locate the required substantial moral choice in the realm of the political process in so far as it is directed towards legislative outcomes; the ethics of legal process is confined to the manner in which the politically determined law is to be interpreted and applied.

As a general analytical and descriptive theory, Legal Positivism has lost much of its credibility, and hence its ideological force. Many contemporary judges and most commentators take it to be evident that judges make law, rather than simply interpret and apply it; they assume this as a premise with which to justify quite radical judicial amendments of current law and increasingly bold political uses of broad constitutional provisions. Creative law-making used to be regarded as a *prima facie* abuse of judicial power. Now it no longer needs to be hidden behind lip-service to a judicial ethic that confines legal judgment to the application of legal criteria, with legislatures as the sole ultimate legitimate source of new law. Politicized judicial practice has been deftly unmasked by Legal Realists and Critical Legal theorists; it is now the unashamed basis for asserting the inevitability, and hence (fallaciously) the acceptability, of judicial legislation. The constitutional consequence is a noticeable shift of political power from legislatures to courts.

The effectiveness of the ideological role of Legal Positivism, as identified by the critics, is contingent upon its descriptive credibility. If the political neutrality of judges is not given credence, then the exercise of political power behind the mask of that neutrality is weakened. Legal Positivism is now verging on the threshold of losing that credibility as a descriptive theory of judicial practice. Moreover, by default and association with its discredited descriptive variant, Legal Positivism is also underrated as a constitutional ideal that can and should be cultivated. The confidence trick is collapsing. Hence judicial loyalties are moving from orthodoxies of Legal Positivism to the pragmatics of Legal Realism or the moralism of Natural Law. Neither alternative is, however, a stable rationale for the exercise of judicial political power. Legal Realism, as the theory that the law simply is what courts tend to decide, lacks both a sense of direction and the means to block the demand for political accountability. Natural Law, as the theory that judges have a duty to apply universal moral principles, accords ill with the pluralism of current moral outlooks. Moreover, the overt politicizing of judicial roles that is involved in both tactics brings corollaries: the right of others to make political criticism of judicial decisions; the demand for elected judges; the pressure on judges to follow accepted social and political norms, to be educated, to be questioned, to be pilloried and reduced to the status of mere politicians. If to resort to law is simply to engage in politics by other means, the protected status of the legally skilled but politically neutral judge is undermined.

All this has some way to run, as yet. In Europe and Australasia judiciaries are flexing their constitutional muscles, resuscitating nineteenth-century versions of the common law (Allan 1993) or importing globalized rights rhetoric for selective implementation, often on the model of US constitutional jurisprudence. This makes it an exciting time to be involved with legal philosophy and constitutional law, disciplines that are heading for amalgamated intellectual dominance as the rout of black-letter law continues. New forms of constitutional interpretation are gaining ground; they offer suggestions as to how judiciaries might go about selecting an interpretative approach on which to ground their now accepted political role. Only rarely do we come across a contemporary political philosophy which seeks to depoliticize judiciaries in the cause of effective democratic government.

If we are to counter these trends, the first task is not one of normative political philosophy but of analytical political theory, the discipline which is directed to the analysis and understanding of politics rather than its reform. To arrive at any norms and strategies for the deployment and control of political power, we require an initial analysis of judicial power in contrast to political power. This analysis may then be used in the formulation of a normative philosophy concerning the proper methods and functions of judicial office.

Powers

When lawyers talk of judicial powers, they mean the legal capacities of the judicial organs of government in accordance with adjectival or 'power-conferring' (that is, facilitative) rules. In particular, judicial power is the legal capacity to hear and decide cases and make determinations which are binding on the parties concerned. Thus, when judicial power is vested by the Constitution in the High Court of Australia, the court has the legal capacity to adjudicate such particular disputes as are brought before it within its allotted jurisdiction, that is, the geographical area and type of law for which it has the legal capacity to hear and decide cases (Zines 1992: 151–84). As legal powers, these are *de jure* and by definition legitimate within the legal system. In so far as they are viewed externally to the legal system, judicial powers may be viewed also as political rights requiring moral justification.

Whether or not constitutions may be said to give judiciaries *de jure* political power, however, is dependent on their content. Any *de facto* political power deriving therefrom depends on the extent to which their decisions are complied with. Thus, a *de jure* adjudicative 'power', if its content is such as to permit or require judges to decide cases as they please, gives judges *de jure* political power; if respected, it gives them *de facto* political power as well. On the other hand, a *de jure* power, or legal right, to decide a case in accordance with a specific set of consistent comprehensive and specific rules supplied to the judiciary, even if respected, does not give *de jure* or *de facto* political power.

To explicate this analysis, it is necessary to relate lawyers' talk of powers to the language of power in the discourse of political theory. Lawyers are interested in the legal capacity to alter the legal status of particular others. Political theorists are concerned with the autonomous or independent intentional control of the conduct of others in ways which may be contrary to the wishes and/or the interests of those others. Power, in the social sciences, is something that enables the holder to make a difference in other people's lives whether they like it or not (Dahl 1957: 203; Lukes 1974: 26), and to do so autonomously – on their own account, as it were – rather than as mere instruments of yet other people.

The dimension of autonomy is a necessary feature of political, but not of legal, power. However, if we enquire a little closer and ask what makes political power *political*, as distinct from economic or religious, then political and legal powers are less readily distinguishable in other respects. The concepts 'power' and 'political' power are both strongly contested. A large part of what is meant by political power – where it is contrasted with, for instance, bribery or brute force – is control exercised through the possession of authority, that is, the ability to be accepted as having the right to command or permit within a non-native system, political or legal. The struggle for political power is in part the quest for such authoritative control over others as is exercised through the medium of the mutual recognition of the right to rule by rulers and ruled. The right to legislate is a formidable and important form of political – as distinct from, say, economic – power. It can be argued that authority of this sort is continuous with the capacity to communicate and persuade with respect to social behaviour (Habermas 1984; Foucault 1980).

Evidently, the exercise of political power also involves an element of coercion, as one means of controlling others without obtaining their consent. Indeed, the right to use force in such a way is characteristic, and perhaps definitive, of political authority (Weber 1947: 132). However, since political power has a necessary ingredient of *authority* to command (perhaps coercively), it cannot be said that legal powers are *de jure* and political powers *de facto*. There is some truth in this contrast: political power that is not *de facto*, in the sense of being effective, ceases to be regarded as political power because it lack the property of actually controlling others. But only that *de facto* control of (perhaps unwilling) others that involves the possession of *de jure* power is actually *political* power. This analysis also has application to legal powers. When theorists explicate legal validity, they deal in norms that enable people, especially judges, to recognize the rules that are authoritative in that jurisdiction; but they must do so in relation to effective systems, that is systems in which the rules identified by judiciaries are acknowledged and adhered to in practice. In H. L. A. Hart's terms, validity presupposes efficacy; that is, there cannot be a valid law unless a given population, and particularly legal officials, generally adhere to the system of which they are a part (Hart 1961: 100–1). The connection may be stronger to the point of conceptual necessity in the case of political power, but the contrast with legal power is only a matter of degree.

The significant difference between political and legal power is, therefore, with respect to autonomy: a necessary feature of political, but not legal, power. The relative independence that is a necessary feature of political power, its identification with the source of control, is not a necessary feature of legal power. Decision-making within a legal system may be circumscribed in ways that lead us to say that the actors involved do not exercise the autonomous *de jure* capacity to impose their will on others, but still exercise legal power. On the other hand, the legal power to legislate does have such *de jure* power and normally a measure of *de facto* power as well (unless a legislature is entirely controlled externally). The same *may* hold of adjudication, if this is defined broadly as deciding particular cases, for this can be an open-ended *de jure* power allowing immense *de facto* power in relation to particular cases. But, in contrast to political power, adjudication can be circumscribed to the point where it lacks any significant autonomy and consequently is not, in that case, an instance of political power. Indeed, it may be said that the more circumscribed the power, the more distinctively legal it is.

This approach does not conceptualize power in an old-fashioned positivist model as a commodity or substance which can be hoarded and spent, and even located in one supreme sovereign (Austin 1954). It is understood that political power is a set of psychological and sociological, as well as physical, relationships; these relationships produce certain patterns of the distribution of benefits and burdens, in part through the normatively accepted hierarchy of command. Moreover, political power, so conceived, is not confined to the self-conscious attainment of such distributions. Political power could be attributed to those who get their way in competition with others even if it is not their intention to do so.

However, getting your own way may be regarded as twofold: intentional, in so far as the conduct of the power-holders is directed at achieving their own objectives; and, at the same time, non-intentional, with respect to overriding the wills and interests of others who may be adversely affected by the manner in which the power-holders obtain their objectives. The adverse impact on others is, in the latter case, something that just happens, an unintended side-effect. Much social power is of this nature, and it is to be distinguished from political power in a narrower sense, which is the direct intention to exercise and control. Majority or elite attitudes often prevail without in any way being overtly directed at overriding the attitudes of minorities or majorities. We may speak of societal power as this capacity to obtain desired benefits, irrespective of the opposition or the lack of acquiescence of others, without seeking authority to command others. Societal power constitutes the background social reality which more self-conscious politics seeks to redirect. It is a significant part of the context of intentional political power. Most of what happens in a society is not in any strong sense intended, and may be ascribed to the operation of unchosen social, economic and material factors. Politics, as popularly conceived, operates as an overt struggle for position and influence; its effects are greatly exaggerated, and it operates in a relatively non-malleable social field in the causal interstices of human conduct. Conceptually, it is helpful to be stipulative here and take politics to be the conscious struggle for control over others; we speak of 'societal power' when referring to the capacity unwittingly to affect others to their detriment.

To attribute political power to judges is to imply that their role in the legal process is such that their values and outlooks produce coercive outcomes for the lives of others, even although their intention may be no more than to apply the rules previously determined by legislatures. In this case we have an illustration of societal as distinct from (intentional) political power. It is generally agreed that, in a democratic society incorporating the idea of the rule of law, judges should not be involved in overt and intentional political activity and should not exercise political power as I have defined it. The deeper issue is whether the societal power exercised by judges through the legal process, by virtue of the fact that their values and outlooks have a significant effect on adjudicative outcomes, can and should be controlled by overtly political process.

Where we go to from this point is dependent on the issues that are in contention. The notion of political power, with its ingredients of authority and force, points us to fundamental normative questions relating to the justification of its existence, its distribution and its control. Even if we regard all force as *prima facie* undesirable or wrong, given its multiple uses in relation to evidently laudable goals, we may not wish to argue that the exercise of power is necessarily an evil phenomenon. As a means it may be tainted; it may be regarded as at best inferior to harmonious agreement and at worst entirely unacceptable (Campbell 1986). These are matters which give us reason for resisting power, or at least reason for allocating power only to those whom we can hold accountable. We may require that such allocations be justified in relation to their outcomes, in terms of efficiency in the attainment of the objects that justify the political organisation in question. Much political philosophy has to do with the task of identifying those purposes which legitimate the exercise of force, and the proper limits to impose on its use.

No political philosophy has come up with a satisfactory answer to the problem of how to utilize and control political power within acceptable perimeters. The tragic paradox of politics is that societies need organized political power for many legitimate purposes, but the very existence of organized and centralized power is an inherent danger to social well-being due to its inherent potential to be used for purposes other than those which justify its existence. This unhappy conjunction of the need for, and vulnerability to, political power enables us to appreciate the nature of Ethical Positivism as a theory: it articulates how and why we can ameliorate the evil effects of political power and at the same time direct its legitimate functions in a humane and effective manner. Hence the tensions between political and legal powers.

Where legal powers are seen as contributing to political power, this may be as part of an attempt to create channels for the effective exercise of political power originating outside the legal system; or the legal powers themselves may be an exercise of autonomous political power. Ethical Positivism takes the former approach, favouring an analysis of legal power which commends it as a channel for the political power of others, including political power directed to the control of the societal power of judges. Thus judicial power is not an independent source of authoritative coercion. At the same time, however, the request that political power be exercised via the medium of general yet specific rules is seen as a potentially significant check on political power. It is in this context of the ambiguous interconnections of law and politics that this chapter proposes an analysis of political power which makes a degree of autonomy, in conjunction with effective claims to exercise binding authority, one of its defining features. Thus it clears the way for the discussion of politics-free legal process as a feasible ideal.

Ethical Positivism

The legal theory of Ethical Positivism (LEP) sets out the importance of precise, clear rules as the medium for the implementation of political power (Campbell 1996). LEP is in the tradition of Legal Positivism in two areas: its identification of valid law as the outcome of empirically identifiable actions; and its insistence that legal rules be empirically applicable, in that it is possible to see whether or not actual conduct is in accordance with such rules without at the same time making value judgments about the conduct or situation in question. One ethical aspect of LEP is that the orthodox positivist image of law is to be taken not as an attempt to describe actual legal systems but as a picture of an ideal towards which actual systems may approximate. As a model, it calls for an ethical rationale to justify the practices that constitute a positivist legal system. Moreover, according to the theory, the model of positivist law is ethical for another reason: this ideal picture cannot be realized unless the legal establishment is sufficiently committed to adhere to procedural and methodological requirements without being legally obliged to do so.

Current readings of Legal Positivism often assume that positivism goes along with the liberal assumption that there can be a set of substantive legal rules that are politically neutral; but this is not a tenet either of traditional positivism or of LEP. On the contrary, laws are taken to be the expressions of a particular political will, whose justification lies not in its inherent neutrality as between different social groups, but in the (usually democratic) credentials of its origins. However, given the empirical basis for the understanding and application of laws that meet positivist standards, formally good laws can be known and administered by officials who understand but do not accept their substance; this does involve a degree of procedural neutrality as a positivist objective. Such a procedural neutrality does not extend to the substance of law.

While traditional Legal Positivism has its own (usually utilitarian) specific value commitments, the theory itself is normally presented as a mixture of abstract analysis of legal concepts and empirical claims about the operation of actual legal systems. LEP, on the other hand, stresses the significance of the ideal over the actual in the positivist model. Government through empirically applicable rules is justified by its provision of the possibility of the effective, fair, limited and predictable use of political power (Campbell 1996: 49–58). It is also claimed that the positivist model facilitates meaningful democratic decision-making. This aspirational ideal of a political system focused on the choice and impartial implementation of empirically applicable rules is the backcloth against which we can identify certain types of bias and oppression.

The core concept within LEP is the notion of general rules (Schauer 1991). Rules lay down what must or may be done or not done. They are prescriptive and mandatory, removing or opening up certain choices for the individuals and groups to whom they apply (Raz 1975: 35–45). Rules carry the intrinsic prescriptive notion that what they require must or may be done without any calculation of the consequences of so doing other than those provided for in the rule or accepted overriding rules. Rules, at least as they feature in Legal Positivism, are hard-and-fast requirements or permissions, rather than simply guidelines or rules of thumb. LEP defines and defends the moral and practical priority of such rules within a polity.

The most common liberal defence of government through rules is that rules enable individuals to protect their liberty, or freedom of action. Empirically applicable substantive rules, promulgated in advance of the application, may limit freedom in the sense of a person's right to act as they please. It follows that liberals, in general, support the minimalization of law. Just as important for liberty is the fact that prescriptive rules, when they are known in advance, enable individuals to avoid breaking them and thus incurring the sanctions which follow from the contravention of these rules. We may call this the *liberty advantage* of rule governance (Campbell 1996: 52). An associated factor, also valued by liberalism, is that the prior enactment of clear and empirically applicable rules makes it reasonable to blame individuals for the harmful consequences of violating those rules.

Legal Positivism does not favour the enforcement of moral rules as such, but equally, it does not seek conduct which is thought to be immoral. While particular rules may be morally either good or bad, the fact that they are rules – that is, are general in form with respect to types of conduct – makes them candidates for moral approval. They are suited to realizing the ideal that rules ought to require conduct which is morally acceptable. This *moral-form advantage* of rules does not provide moral justification for any particular rule; but it does mean that the power exercised through such rules is in a form which renders it open to moral assessment. Morality has to do with the qualities of acts as a type of conduct in specified types of situation. Laws are formulated in similarly general terms and can therefore be readily assessed in moral terms.

Further, when government is conducted through the adoption and enforcement of rules, there are efficiency gains: the same questions do not have to be revisited on each occasion of choice, and the mutual interaction of decisions binding on groups can be foreseen and assessed in the light of their objectives. This *efficacious-choice advantage* of rule governance directs our attention to the benefits, rather than the dangers, of political power, and serves as a pragmatic justification for the rule of law (Campbell 1996: 60).

A bureaucratic element of efficacious choice is the use of rules to set down the legal powers of public officials. This can limit as well as empower, since, by implication, officials may act only within their powers. Additional political advantages accrue from government-through-rules when the government is democratic in form, for majorities have more power when they can establish general ongoing rules rather than seeking to make a long series of *ad hoc* decisions. Moreover, it is evident that majorities can exercise more extensive power through enacting general rules than they can merely through electing officials.

This brief survey of some of the alleged advantages of adopting a system of government via general rules illustrates the sorts of argument which are relevant to the justification of LEP. Some of these considerations relate to the facilitation of political power, others to its limitation. All require some separation of law-making from the implementation of law, for rules must have a relatively permanent existence and effect if any of the advantages outlined above are to apply. On this basis, the power we might want to give to judges is the power required for the implementation of rules; not the power to determine the content of these rules, or the power to decide cases on their perceived merits in relation to background economic or moral goals. In summary, the division of functions (law-making and law application) is not simply a matter of expertise: it is a necessary feature of the rule governance on which the claimed benefits depend. Government-through-rules has structural frameworks in place which prevent legislatures from making *ad hoc* political decisions in unprincipled ways, and which limit justiciaries in the exercise of their societal powers in relation to individual cases.

The Limits of Legal Powers

The legal theory of Ethical Positivism works well for ordinary law. It is more flakey in relation to constitutional matters, if only because a legislature's *de jure* capacity as law-maker is dependent on constitutional rules that are not themselves the creation of that legislature. Legislatures cannot be constitutionally self-regulating without threatening the demise of constitutional government. Or so it is standardly asserted, for instance in *R v. Kirby, Ex Parte The Boilermakers' Society of Australia* (1956: 268). Constitutional courts, it is said, must be ultimately responsible for determining the constitutionality of the activities of law-making bodies. Basic principles of rule governance exclude any body from assessing the propriety of its own conduct in relation to its constitutive rules.

Unfortunately for this thesis, the same principles appear to prevent courts from assessing the constitutionality of their own activities. This takes us to a constitutional form of the tragic paradox of politics. An ultimate adjudicative authority is necessary for a political system, but no individual or body ought to be a judge in its own cause. The conundrum is how to give courts such ultimate constitutional judicial power, without at the same time handing to them unwarranted *de facto* political power. Systems to minimize and provide remedies for the abuse of judicial office are inherently problematic, for such systems themselves lack accountability.

There are difficulties in gaining even a theoretical foothold in the determination of what amounts to misuse of judicial power. While the idea of the abuse of judicial office is constitutionally indispensable, there is no neutral site from which to identify what does and what does not count as abuse. The idea of judicial abuse cannot without circularity be captured in law, for it is the source of law that is contested. Ultimately, judicial legitimacy must be a matter of political, philosophical or judicial ethics. Further, the content of judicial ethics with respect to such matters as interpretive method or interstitial discretionary powers is also extensively contested. One theorist's idea of abuse is another theorist's ideal, and we are all theorists on such matters. Reasonable people may reasonably disagree about the proper role and methodology of judicial powers within a polity, and therefore on the propriety of the different ways in which judicial power may be exercised. There can be no constitutionally decisive way of determining these issues as a matter of theory.

One way in which we may seek such objectivity as is attainable in such matters is by drawing out the implications of the separation of powers doctrine as explicated and as justified by LEP. LEP does not embrace the sort of conceptualism that deduces interpretive methods from such notions as representative government or the concept of discursive democracy, or from judicial power itself. Choosing a method for the interpretation of a constitution is similar in character to choosing a system of government. Who should properly make that choice is practically insoluble as a matter of legal and political process, but it is possible to construct an ethics which has application to the conduct of those who are charged with the task of administering whatever governmental system is adopted. Thus, while courts may have to have, in any federal system, the ultimate say as to the interpretation of constitutional provisions that are authoritative in their society, they should not therefore have ethically free rein with respect to their interpretive methods. The impossibility of solving the classic riddle of guarding the guardians may entail that judges have the *de facto* as well as the *de jure* power to decide such matters in any way that they can get away with, but we need not accept that they have the moral right to rewrite constitutions through expansive interpretive methodologies. Judicial conduct in this regard cannot be legally, and perhaps also politically, overridden; nor is it, *ex hypothesi*, justiciable in some higher court. But it does not follow that the judicial *de jure* powers of constitutional interpretation cannot be described as being abused. A constitutional court with the final say on constitutional matters has real opportunities to wield constitutionally unwarranted political power. Nevertheless, because of its constitutional ultimacy, the only legitimate checks on its activities are self-administered ethical ones.

In this manifestation of the paradox of politics, we are denied the benefits of a legal system without incurring the disadvantages of constant

vulnerability to judicial impropriety. In the necessary absence of legitimate remedies for judicial abuse of *de jure* interpretive power, constitutional courts are bound to have considerable *de facto* political power,
which is a measure of the gravity of their ethical responsibilities. That
said, it is not entirely clear that courts cannot in principle be, with
propriety, controlled by other branches of government when they step
outside their judicial functions. Thus, the Australian Constitution
confines the exercise of Commonwealth judicial power to the High
Court and other federal courts. Uncontroversially, this means that the
Parliament cannot act as a court and cannot tell courts how they must go
about their business in a particular case: 'Commonwealth legislation
proposing to direct a court exercising federal jurisdiction as to the
manner in which it should decide a particular case would be invalid as
an interference with the judicial power of the Commonwealth'
(Winterton 1994: 198). Certainly, legislatures cannot usurp judicial
power, but can courts usurp legislative power? The other side of the
constitutional warrant of exclusive judicial power could be that this
power is limited to judicial matters, as indeed was determined in the
Boilermakers' case (*Attorney-General (Cth) v. the Queen; Ex Parte The Boilermakers Society of Australia*, 1957).

This judgment leaves unresolved what constitutes a judicial matter.
The principle that 'the legislature makes, the executive executes, and the
judiciary construes the law' (Marshall CJ in *Wayman v. Southard*, 1825) is
used to prevent the legislature construing laws (*New South Wales v. The
Commonwealth*, 1915). It could as easily be used to exclude the judiciary
from legislating. It has been held that 'section I [of the Constitution],
which vests legislative power in a Federal Parliament at the same time
negates such power being vested in any other body' (*Attorney-General
(Cth) v. The Queen*, 1957: 311).

Further, it is possible to give positivist substance to the traditional view
that judges are bound to decide the cases that come before them in accordance with existing law. Thus Deane, Dawson, Gaudron and McHugh JJ. in
Brandy v. Human Rights and Equal Opportunity Commission (1995: 16):
'Another important element which distinguishes a judicial decision is that
it determines existing rights and duties and does so according to law. That
is to say, it does so in relation to pre-existing standards rather than by the
formulation of policy or the exercise of an administrative discretion.' On
these lines, LEP asks that judicial development of law be tightly restricted;
we should not, for instance, be content with laws that utilize very general
standards, such as 'oppressive' and 'unjust', whose application requires
political judgment. Thus Windeyer in *R. v. Trade Practices Tribunal; Ex Parte
Tasmanian Breweries Pty Ltd* (1970: 399) contends that 'the public interest is
a concept which attracts indefinite considerations of policy that are more

appropriate to law-making than to adjudication according to existing law
. . . an exercise of the legislative or administrative function of government
rather than of judicial power'.

The orthodox position on the separation of legislative and judicial
power is that, while the Australian Constitution clearly reserves Commonwealth judicial power exclusively for the appropriate courts, this
does not exclude courts from exercising legislative or 'law-making'
power. This is unsurprising within a common-law jurisdiction. Yet there
are strong arguments against this position where it goes beyond filling in
gaps in existing law pending legislative action. First, legislative power is
explicitly given to the Parliament and, as a matter of constitutional interpretation, it could be taken as understood that this is an exclusive right.
If not explicitly provided for in the written Constitution itself, it is a
convention of the Constitution derived from its British sources that the
Parliament is the legislative sovereign, and this can be taken to involve all
law-making. Historically, this may be countered by citing the continuing
role of the common law as a subordinate but judicially developing source
of new law, but even if this tradition is not rejected as outmoded in a
democratic society, it evidently does not apply in the sphere of constitutional law. Here we can draw on Brennan CJ's distinction, to be found in
Theophanous v. The Herald Weekly Times Ltd (1994: 124–6), between the
power to make common law and the power to make constitutional law;
the former, but not the latter, is a valid exercise of judicial power,
although it can be overridden.

The implicit denial of law-making power to courts, particularly with
respect to constitutional matters, is not a fanciful constitutional doctrine in
a field where the practice of drawing implications is common. A
developing list of Australian cases imply that judicial power must be
exercised in line with proper judicial process, as delineated in the rules of
natural justice or due process; we might extrapolate from this and draw the
conclusion that the substantive legal rules relevant to this process are the
pre-existing authoritative rules emanating from the legislature. It can be
further argued that it is an abuse of due process for courts to make up the
substantive rules as they go along. If federal judicial power must be
exercised 'in accordance with the judicial process', as Brennan, Deane and
Dawson JJ. all insist in *Chu Kheng Lim v. Minister for Immigration, Local
Government and Ethnic Affairs* (1992: 27), then, on this implication, it must
be exercised in accordance with existing substantive law.

Currently, legal argument rages around whether *substantive* due
process is implied in judicial power. *Leeth v. The Commonwealth* (1992:
493) toys with the prospect, enunciated by Gaudron J., that courts may
decide that substantive inequality is a basis for legal invalidity whenever
the challenged law does not involve what the court believes to be relevant

distinctions. Also, Deane and Toohey JJ. hold that it is 'the duty of the court to extend to the parties before it equal justice, that is to say, to treat them fairly and impartially as equals before the law and to refrain from discrimination on irrelevant or irrational grounds'. This appears to come close to the assertion of substantive due process by Gaudron J. Such dicta open up the remarkable prospect that judicial opinion – as to substantive equality or as to the relevance of distinctions embodied in legislation – could be used as the basis for judicial review of enacted legislation.

Equally, however, these opinions may themselves be regarded as unconstitutional, on the grounds that they are incompatible with the separation of powers in so far as this involves the exclusive or superior right of the Parliament to make law. In that case, we can argue from implied due process to a conclusion different from that enunciated by Gaudron, Deane and Toohey JJ., namely, that the courts must apply existing law. This means that there could be an implied constitutional right to Ethical Positivism.

Against this conclusion stands the judgment of Mason CJ. in *Polyukovich v. The Queen* (1991: 532). There, Mason CJ. argues that the presumption against retrospective legislation 'does not require that the rule or standard should have been ascertained precisely before the determination is made in the exercise of judicial power'. Yet a measure of precision in law-making is required for the prohibition on retrospectivity to have any bite, for otherwise unspecific laws can be used to create unforeseeable legal obligations. It can also be argued that considerable precision is desirable, particularly in criminal matters, for reasons that bear on the liberty advantage and other values that justify the ideal of rule governance. Similar arguments can be deployed to prevent courts using interpretive methods that free them from adherence to the rules in question by enabling them to rewrite existing law when it seems contrary to their view of current social values.

These considerations may be regarded as a retreat from a discussion within political theory to an analysis of the constitutional law of a particular jurisdiction, thereby evading appropriate philosophical argument for establishing a satisfactory view of judicial power. One philosophical issue at stake here is the shaky distinction between law-making and law interpretation. To deploy the language of abuse in relation to judicial practice, and to make sense of claims to an implied constitutional right to Ethical Positivism, we need an agreed working distinction between the interpretation of existing rules and the creation of different or new rules. LEP argues that the first activity, rule interpretation, and the way in which it is carried out, are part of judicial legal power, and need not be exercised politically; whereas the second activity, rule change, is a matter of legislative power and is necessarily political.

To sketch a positivist position on this issue, we may distinguish between three possible species of 'interpretation': interpretation as comprehension, interpretation as bounded selection, and creative interpretation (see Wroblewski 1992). Interpretation as understanding is part of the capacity for meaningful language use (Davidson 1984: 141), but this does not equate grasping meaning with interpretation in its other senses (Dummett 1986: 484). Indeed, the idea of interpretation as comprehension is an enlarged and misleading conception of interpretation: it confuses and diffuses the standard discourse of interpretation so that it unhelpfully denotes all language-based understanding. Interpretation as bounded selection, on the other hand, is a conception that encapsulates the familiar practice of choosing between alternative meanings of a text, both or all of which are feasible within the linguistic community in question. This may be regarded, perhaps stipulatively in this context, as genuine interpretation (Perelman 1980: 143–4). Finally, creative interpretation is a conception which denotes more expansive developments of texts, such as filling in gaps in the coverage of the text, altering contextually evident meanings to give more desirable outcomes, and in other ways going beyond textual understanding and clarification to develop the text for some further purpose beyond understanding and the resolution of ambiguity (Hart 1961: 138–44; Dworkin 1986: 52). While creative interpretation is often appropriate in such fields as artistic performance and literary criticism, in the legal sphere it can be regarded as an unwarranted and confusing extension of judicial method.

Following this scheme of interpretation types, we can articulate a position: courts may go beyond interpretation as understanding (which is not really interpretation at all), and use such methods as are approved of to settle matters requiring bounded interpretation (their indispensable role), while stopping short of changing contextually evident, plain meanings for ulterior purposes (which may be classified as a *prima facie* abuse of judicial power). However, even if we can make sense of this ideal of judicial practice, this does not show it to be the preferable theory. These are matters on which we can all have views and on which there is little agreement. The choices between so-called literalism and purposive styles, or between formalism and teleology, or between rights-directed and utilitarian tests, are all controversial. Yet a great deal of the distribution of political power in a society depends on the outcome of the struggle for theoretical supremacy on these matters in so far as this affects the practice of courts. The *de jure* power to determine the interpretive style of courts, limited as it may be in legal doctrine and open as it may be in general to political criticism, cannot be restricted by institutions; in practice, it confers potentially substantial political power.

Legal Realists stress the truism that the rules that matter to those involved are the rules applied by courts, and therefore the understanding of the rules arrived at by courts is what counts. Those whose understandings of the rules are adopted by courts are those who determine much of the outcome of the case and therefore the distribution of the contested resources. More broadly, the capacity to determine what interpretive method is deployed by courts affects the distributive pattern of disputed resources. Thus, a strict adherence by courts to contextually clear meanings of a written constitution may ensure a measure of political power in a legislature, while an open-ended, purposive approach to a constitution gives extensive power to judiciaries who are able to come to their own ideas as to what purposes are at stake and how they are best realized.

In the context of the thesis that non-rule-based theories of legal interpretation are unacceptable, legally or politically, it is interesting to explore the role of legislatures in relation to the interpretation of their own laws. Constitutional experts might argue that a parliament must be able to determine how, in general, its laws are to be interpreted. The Australian Parliament, in the *Acts Interpretation Act 1901*, lays down certain principles of interpretation, including provisions that permit or enjoin courts to have regard to the stated purposes of an Act when they have a problem of interpretation. This Act in fact says that judges should depart from the clear meaning of a rule if this will further the purposes of the Act (s. 15AA).

The specific exhortation to follow purposes rather than rules is not, of course, compatible with LEP, for it enables courts to unmake law by reducing the rules to mere guidelines. As we have seen, it is part of the idea of a real rule, as distinct from a rule of thumb, that it cannot be departed from because of consequences not allowed for in the rule; otherwise we have not a rule, but simply an injunction to do what is best to reach a particular goal. It follows that any parliamentary right there may be to determine interpretive method cannot be permitted to undermine the rule-based nature of legitimate governance. And yet we may accept a legislature's right to decide how its own rules are to be interpreted, without agreeing that this power can extend to requiring that its rules be ignored if they do not have the desired outcomes in particular cases.

In practice, Australian courts have generally avoided paying explicit notice to this provision of the *Acts Interpretation Act*. It may be that they think it a constitutional impropriety for the Parliament to interfere in the exercise of judicial legal power to this extent. It may be that the purposive requirement is judged to be in conflict with judicial process as set out by LEP. But if the High Court is able to adopt whatever interpretive method it pleases, however 'liberal' or policy-oriented it may be, then the

Constitution's position on the separation of powers has been effectively amended in a way that is not provided for in the Constitution.

Who, then, should decide what is to be the authoritative interpretive method of courts? The answer is not self-evident. If courts must determine constitutionality, it might seem that courts must choose their method of constitutional interpretation. On the other hand, parliaments have the right to make the rules; if the rules are not applied as the Parliament intended because of some unforeseen or unpredictable styles of 'interpretation', then the Parliament must have the right to change the rules in the light of what the courts make of them, so that they are more likely to have the outcomes the Parliament desires. In this case, legislatures should be able to establish how their rules are to be understood and interpreted as a necessary part of their legislative power. Legislating is a means of communication as to what must or may be done or not done, and the purposes of the communicators can claim priority in relation to how law ought to be understood.

It may only be in the case of constitutions that we have serious doubts about the interpretive sovereignty of legislatures within their sphere of competence, for constitutions are not usually the creatures of the parliaments they legitimate. The role of a constitution is, *inter alia*, to keep parliamentarians in line with the model of government established in the constitution. And yet this power of constitutional interpretation could be used to undermine the parliament's right to legislate generally, by making it a matter of constitutional right for judiciaries to adopt whatever interpretive method they please. Ethical Positivism, stressing as it does that government must be via specific general rules, acknowledges that there are problems in giving the power of determining constitutional interpretive method to legislatures. On the other hand, giving the courts an unrestricted capacity in this respect licenses an unbounded and unlimitable acquisition of power by courts at the expense of legislatures.

The LEP solution to this stand-off is to give the choice of interpretive theory to courts, but to seek to establish political guidelines for the exercise of that choice, adherence to which is a matter of judicial ethics. That ethical system may be derived from a political philosophy, including particular views of democracy, the separation of powers and the rule of law. The substantive proposal of LEP with respect to the ethic of judicial power over interpretive method is this: interpretation should be guided by the disinterested search for clear contextual meanings that resolve ambiguities and obscurities by transparent devices that promote predictable selection between the alternative contextual meanings of a text. It follows that legal change in general, and constitutional amendment in particular, should be pursued through the avenues established within that constitution. The argument that constitutions must be adapted to changing circumstances, and that such changes may be read into existing text by judges, sounds plausible; but it undermines the normative control of constitutions in the same way as loose purposive interpretations undermine the intentions of ordinary legislation.

Back in the real world, we know, of course, that courts are not presented with good positive law: clear, unambiguous, comprehensive and consistent. Legal Positivists have always recognized that we need some delegated legislation by judges to fill these gaps, to resolve these inconsistencies, and perhaps to make needed developments in areas where legislatures have not the time, inclination or political will to venture.

Resort to the notion of delegated legislation is a neat way of preserving the integrity of democracy, but in political terms it is suspect. Delegated legislative power in the hands of courts undermines those arguments for the separation of powers that rest on their perceived and actual independence. Further, it brings with it the danger of abuse of such delegated power, as when clear and consistent law is ignored because in the opinion of the court it is substantively ineffective or unjust. Also, delegated legislation provides a new legal status quo, whose alteration requires effort and the exercise of political power that may not be available at any given time; therefore it may be, in effect, impossible to override it. Delegated legislative powers bestow a substantial measure of societal power, because it is usually more difficult to undo legislation than not to do it in the first place. The burden of inertia, and the potential unpopularity of any change in the law, give political advantage to judicial innovations. Delegated legislation changes the political scene. It not only sets a new agenda: it captures the high ground of established law, which is particularly powerful when popular opinion is against major legislative amendment of recent judicially developed law.

Nevertheless, in both constitutional and ordinary law, there is no evident mechanism for dealing with the paradox of creating, while controlling, ultimate decision-making power in a society; if this is the case, we have little choice but to explicitly acknowledge the necessity for a powerful judicial ethic, involving self-restraint and interpretive integrity. In practice, there is little that can legitimately be done, except public criticism, when judicial office is abused and subverted in terms of the norms of LEP. Perhaps only the desperate rely on the ethics of others. But democratic rule governance is a desperate business, and we may have no choice but to trust judiciaries with respect to the model of judicial power they adopt.

The legal theory of Ethical Positivism sets out to circumscribe the power of both politicians and judges, and to locate this circumscribed political power in the hands of the former. But theories carry no clout unless they are accepted as models and guides by political participants, including judicial ones. The *de facto* political power of judiciaries lies in the legally unrestrictable, and in this sense legally legitimate, opportunities that judges have to adopt creative interpretations in and of their roles. However, LEP holds to the political view that the interpretive methods adopted should minimize the elements of political power that, in the normal course of events, accrue to those who exercise judicial power.

References

Allan, T. R. S. 1993. *Law, Liberty and Justice: Legal Foundations of British Constitutionalism.* Oxford: Clarendon Press.
Attorney-General (Cth) v. The Queen; Ex Parte The Boilermakers' Society of Australia (1957) 95 CLR 529.
Austin, J. 1954. *The Province of Jurisprudence Determined,* ed. H. L. A. Hart. London: Weidenfeld and Nicolson.
Brandy v. Human Rights and Equal Opportunity Commission (1995) 127 ALR 1.
Campbell, T. D. 1986. 'Power and Resistance: a Legal Perspective', *Societas Ethica Jahresbericht.* 29–51.
Campbell, T. D. 1996. *The Legal Theory of Ethical Positivism.* Aldershot: Dartmouth.
Chu Kheng Lim v. Minister for Immigration, Local Government and Ethnic Affairs (1992) 176 CLR 1.
Cotterrell, R. 1989. *The Politics of Jurisprudence.* London and Edinburgh: Butterworths.
Dahl, R. 1957. 'The Concept of Power', *Behavioural Science,* 1.
Davidson, D. 1984. *Inquiries into Truth and Interpretation.* Oxford: Clarendon Press.
Dummett, M. A. E. 1986. 'A Nice Derangement of Epitaphs: Some Comments on Davidson and Hacking', in E. LePore, ed., *Truth and Interpretation.* Oxford: Blackwell.
Dworkin, R. M. 1986. *Law's Empire.* London: Fontana.
Finnis, J. 1980. *Natural Law and Natural Rights.* Oxford: Clarendon Press.
Foucault, M. 1980. *Power-Knowledge.* New York: Pantheon.
Habermas, J. 1984. *The Theory of Communicative Action.* Boston: Beacon Press.
Hart, H. L. A. 1961. *The Concept of Law.* Oxford: Clarendon Press.
Hutchinson, A. C., and Monohan, P. 1986. *The Rule of Law: Ideal or Ideology?* Toronto: Toronto University Press.
Kairys, D. 1984. 'Law and Politics', 52 *George Washington Law Review,* 243.
Leeth v. The Commonwealth (1992) 174 CLR 455.
Lukes, S. 1974. *Power: A Radical View.* London: Macmillan.
New South Wales v. The Commonwealth (Wheat Case) (1915) 20 CLR 54.
Perelman, C. 1980. *Justice, Law and Argument.* Dordrecht: Kluwer.
Polyukovich v. The Queen (1991) 172 CLR 501.
Posner, R. 1977. *The Economic Analysis of Law.* Boston: Little, Brown.
R. v. Kirby, Ex Parte The Boilermakers' Society of Australia (1956) 94 CLR 254.
R. v. Trade Practices Tribunal, Ex Parte Tasmanian Breweries Pty Ltd (1970) 123 CLR 361.

Raz, J. 1975. *Practical Reason and Norms*. London: Hutchinson.

Schauer, F. 1991. *Playing by the Rules: A Philosophical Examination of Rule-Based Decision-Making*. Oxford: Clarendon Press.

Theophanous v. The Herald Weekly Times Ltd (1994) 68 ALJR 104.

Wayman v. Southard, 23 US, 10 Wheaton I at 46 (1825) 1.

Weber, M. 1947. *The Theory of Social and Economic Organisation*. Glencoe, Ill.: Free Press.

Winterton, G. 1994. 'The Separation of Judicial Power as an Implied Bill of Rights', in G. Lindell, ed., *Future Directions in Australian Constitutional Law*. Sydney: Federation Press.

Wroblewski, J. 1992. *The Judicial Application of Law*. Dordrecht: Kluwer.

Zines, L. 1992. *The High Court and the Constitution*, 3rd edn. Sydney: Butterworths.

CHAPTER 9

Political Theory, International Theory, and the Political Theory of International Relations

David Boucher

Theories of international relations, in both their behaviouralist and anti-behaviouralist forms – that dominated the sub-discipline for sixty years or so – self-consciously rejected political theory in an attempt to establish their own intellectual credentials. Although subject to similar pressures, international theory rejected the option taken by political theory of defining itself in terms of its illustrious past, and missed the opportunity of firmly anchoring itself on sound philosophical foundations. Para-doxically, the 'English School', represented by Wight and Bull, far from strengthening the intellectual heritage, undermined it: they failed to employ discriminating criteria to differentiate genuinely philosophical contributions from the merely polemical. The emphasis upon taxonomy averted the gaze from the quality of argument. However, political theory and international relations theory become genuinely united in focusing upon the issue of identity, that is, the answers to the question 'Who am I?' The consequent politics of recognition, inclusion and exclusion bring into focus not only the politics of the nation, state and cosmopolitanism, but also of gender, race, religion and ethnicity. All these forms of identity are answers to the question 'Who am I?', and all are integral to a multi-dimensional approach to the political theory of international relations. I conclude by suggesting that much of the newly generated normative political theory of international relations, from whatever intellectual perspective, is directly addressing the key question long ago identified by T. H. Green, and that is the ethical status of one's community and how to extend it to become more and more inclusive of a wider range of people we are prepared to regard as our neighbours.

The Politics of Indifference

The sub-disciplines of political theory and international relations theory, within the discipline of politics in the twentieth century, have tended to go their separate ways. To a large extent international relations, and its theoretically oriented practitioners, pronounced a unilateral declaration of independence in order to establish its credentials as a worthwhile and relevant academic activity. Political theory, traditionally conceived, and international relations theory were deemed to inhabit two distinct universes of discourse (Aron 1967).[1] Three examples from the post-1945 period will serve to illustrate three tendencies in the process of differentiation. On the one hand, the assault by David Easton (1951) upon traditional political theory and his redefinition of the term to refer to the formulation of hypotheses for empirical testing was also carried forward in international relations. Kenneth N. Waltz, more sympathetic than most to classical political theory, has rightly pointed out that the term 'theory' is used loosely among specialists in international relations, often referring to any work that rises above mere description and which includes some analysis. Rarely does it 'refer only to work that meets philosophy-of-science-standards' (1979: 1). The criterion of what constitutes good theory betrays a prevalent belief among theorists of international relations that explanation must aim to approximate the achievements of natural science. Theories, in Waltz's view, aim to explain why associations or laws obtain. He complains that 'much of traditional political theory . . . is concerned more with philosophic interpretation than with theoretical explanation' (6).[2]

The fostering of a dichotomy between political theory and international relations theory was particularly pronounced in the work of Martin Wight, the doyen of the English school. Unlike Waltz, he was vehemently anti-behaviouralist. Political theory, he argued, is mainly preoccupied with speculation about the state, whereas international theory concerns itself with the international community of nations. Understood in these terms, there is no body of theory in international relations comparable with the classic texts in political theory (Wight 1966: 18). By using such a narrowly stipulative definition of political theory, Wight cuts international theory off from a rich source of stimulus. 'International Theory', Wight tells us, 'can be discerned existing dimly, obscured and moreover partitioned, partly on the fringe or margin of ordinary political philosophy and partly in the province of international law' (1991: 1). Despite his protests that international theory approximates not to natural science, but to philosophy, Wight engages in an activity that looks more like pre-Darwinian biology than philosophy. Having stipulatively defined the rare genus international theory, he sets about classifying its species and sub-species. Wight describes his adventures in theory as 'an experiment in classification, in typology, and . . . an exploration of continuity and recurrence, a study in the uniformity of political thought: and its leading premiss is that political ideas do not change much, and the range of ideas is limited' (1991: 5).

A second form of anti-behaviouralist theory in international relations brought the sub-discipline no closer to a reconciliation with political philosophy. There was a wide range of fashionable, short-lived attempts theoretically to reorient the discipline; from among them emerged the activity of constructing models, or perspectives, to act as tools of analysis in explaining international relations. The perspectives were Realism, with its emphasis upon power and security; Pluralism, with its focus upon interdependence and transnational relations; and Structuralism, with its central themes of dominance and dependence. These offered ready-made theoretical frameworks which could be refined and applied for value-free, post-behavioural social scientific explanation.[3] Mervyn Frost argues that all of the dominant approaches, including the so-called classical approach of Wight, Bull, Vincent and others, give epistemological priority to the facts. This is what he has called the bias towards 'objective explanation' in the sub-discipline, and is the main reason why normative political theory has been largely neglected (Frost 1996: 12, 18–19).

The point of the chapter title will by now have become apparent. Political theory and international theory are quite different things, and where there is a superficial resemblance or point of contact the inferiority complex is so overwhelming that it serves to stultify original and philosophically rigorous thought about international relations. The result, in Chris Brown's words, is 'an undertheorized and limited conception of international relations' (1993: 83). His view is that international relations theory has to be seen as embedded in the broader project of social and political theory. The growing acknowledgement that there is a need for reconciliation is evident. Howard Williams, to cite one of numerous examples, has gone as far as to suggest that in many ways 'the study of political theory is the study of international relations' (1992: x).

Political theory as it emerged at the beginning of the twentieth century defined itself in terms of its past. This reflected to some extent its disciplinary origins, but also the dominance of philosophical idealism, which contended that philosophy was indistinguishable from the history of philosophy. Political theory constructed a canon of texts which served as its legitimizing pedigree. Since World War II, positivism has dominated the discipline of politics, privileging inductive and deductive knowledge – empirical observation and analytic statements – over the opinion of values. The emphasis upon the analysis and explanation of ordinary language, made popular by Wittgenstein and Austin in philosophy, led to the near-death of normative political theory in the 1950s.[4] While Logical Positivism exacted its toll on normative political philosophy, it did not succeed in displacing the great texts in the history of political thought from their central place in the discipline of politics.[5] David Easton and his followers charged that the reliance of political theory upon the classics was now redundant, except for the formulation of hypotheses that could be empirically tested. Nevertheless, Leo Strauss, Sheldon Wolin, Hanna Arendt, Eric Vöegelin, Isaiah Berlin and John Plamenatz drew heavily upon past thinkers in order to make contemporary political points.

Unlike political theory, international relations theory allied itself much more closely with law, and particularly with international law. World War I generated a considerable impetus for understanding the conditions of world peace, and for exploring the means of establishing and sustaining them. The improvement of the condition of humanity by means of 'scientific study' (meaning scholarly and systematic study) and the application of scientific methods to social problems were the primary goals of the sub-discipline. Euphoria accompanied the establishment of the League of Nations and a consensus developed around the idea of liberal internationalism during the 1920s. These generated a widespread belief that reason and rationality, given the appropriate conditions, would lead to the shared values of liberal democracies becoming manifest in international agreements for the fostering of a shared harmony of interests and the establishment of permanent peace and security. Such a strong belief in the power and efficacy of reason was necessarily premised on the belief that education in international affairs would lead to progress in world understanding and co-operation. Along with the chairs founded at the University College of Wales, Aberystwyth, by David Davies in 1919 and at the University of London by the Cassel Trustees in 1923 came the conscious attempt to establish a canon of classic texts relating to the origin and development of the law of nations. In the most ambitious and significant publishing venture in the history of thought in international relations, the Carnegie Institution of Washington undertook to republish a large number of texts in Latin or vernacular languages, with English translations, in order to disseminate the knowledge they contained to scholars and the interested public in all countries of the world. Under the auspices of the Carnegie Endowment for International Peace, the works of Ayala, Belli, Bynershoek, Gentili, Grotius, Legnano, Pufendorf, Rachel, Suaréz, Textor, Vattel, Vitoria, Wheaton, Wolff, and Zouche were published. With the failure of the League of Nations, the ideals for which these texts stood were largely rejected by international relations theorists.

Since 1945 most writers interested in the political theory of international relations have been happy to concur with Martin Wight's observation that – with the exception of Thucydides' *History of the Peloponnesian War*, which is not a work of philosophy at all – there are no classic texts in the philosophy of international relations. Even Linklater, who has done a great deal to revive interest in some of the classic thinkers, drives a wedge between the political theory of international relations and political theory proper, by suggesting that the former considers issues that the latter does not. International political theory questions the legitimacy of the division of humanity into states, and the assumed primacy of obligations to the state over those to humanity. This, however, is a stipulative definition; it is just as stipulative as Wight's definition that political theory is speculation about internal matters of state and international theory is speculation about relations among states.

  This is not to say that political theorists of international relations believe that there is no heritage in the history of thought in international relations. In fact they believe that there is a considerable heritage scattered throughout a vast variety of literature. The reluctance to acknowledge, or to establish, a canon has had a regrettable consequence. This consequence I call intellectual egalitarianism. Because international relations theory is first defined as an exceedingly rare and rather shy creature, anyone of any degree of fame in whatever area of achievement who happens to have said something on the subject has a right to be heard. The quality of theorizing is secondary to the fact of theorizing. The obvious need to expand the traditional classic canon of political theory to incorporate international theorists has resulted in a failure to apply appropriate qualitative criteria in discriminating who should and who should not be included. Invoked alongside the great political philosophers such as Hobbes, Rousseau and Hegel, are the international jurists Grotius, Pufendorf and Vattel; polemicists such as Cobden, Bright and Hobson; writers of distinction such as Tolstoy, Wells and Huxley; along with distinguished statesmen such as Lincoln, Bismarck, Gladstone and Churchill.

  Until the beginning of the 1990s there was little interest in, or recognition of, the place of ethical and political theory in international relations, nor in the contribution which the history of thought or contemporary normative theory might have to make to understanding and responding to the ethical and political dilemmas of the modern world. The four decades following 1950 have aptly been christened the forty years' detour, in which, for the most part, values might permissibly be allowed a role in the choice of issue to be investigated, but not in its analysis (Smith 1992).

  The publication of John Rawls's *A Theory of Justice* in 1970 served to stimulate a return to grand theory. The repercussions were taken up in international relations theory by Charles Beitz, Michael Walzer, Terry

Nardin and Mervyn Frost. While the works of these writers often draw
upon the classic theorists, the tendency is much more pronounced in
John Vincent, Michael Donelan, Andrew Linklater, Justin Rosenburg,
Janna Thompson and Chris Brown. The mistake that theorists of
international relations made was to cut themselves adrift from the
mainstream of political theory in order to develop their own theories
and concepts. The consequence was to deprive themselves of the
powerful background theories in which to embed their own thought.
The acknowledgement that many of the pressing world issues of today
are at once political and ethical, and that the answers to them need to be
firmly anchored in a systematic and comprehensive political theory, has
led a number of theorists to explore the viability of various background
theories. Thompson (1992) and Brown (1993), for instance, investigate
the value of 'cosmopolitanism' and 'communitarianism' in their various
guises and their capacities to generate and sustain answers to international issues of justice and rights. Frost (1996) follows Ronald
Dworkin's method of drawing up a list of settled norms in international
relations, and then interrogates background theories that are candidates
for sustaining them; utilitarian, contractarian, and rights-based justifications. Frost's own theory is a version of communitarianism, or what
he calls a constitutive theory, derived from Hegel. Brown also subscribes
to this constitutive theory which refuses to privilege individuals over
communities (1994: 167). Nardin's approach, while not normative in the
sense of justifying or recommending states' conduct, looks at the nature
of the association that gives rise to the law and morality of the international community.[6] Adapting Oakeshott's distinction between civil and
enterprise association, with their respective non-instrumental and instrumental rules, Nardin (1983) suggests that the international community is
best understood as a form of civil association which he calls practical, and
in which the rules are constraints upon the actions of states with different
values, cultures, interests and beliefs. The rules are not instrumental in
achieving substantive goals and purposes, but instead provide the framework in the context of which the various goals pursued by independent
states can be pursued.

Increasingly political theorists, such as John Rawls, David Miller and
Brian Barry, have come to acknowledge that the concerns of international relations are a continuation of, and indistinguishable from, the
traditional issues of political obligation, sovereignty, citizenship and distributive justice. Critical Theorists such as Habermas (1993), Cox (1981)
and Linklater (1990a; b); anti-foundationalist postmodernist political
theorists of international relations, such as James Der Derian (1987),
R. B. J. Walker (1993) and Jim George (1994); and postmodernist
political theorists, such as William Connelly (1988) and Richard Rorty

(1993) all have explored the implications of postmodernism for the dominant approaches to international relations, particularly realism, and for the issue of human rights.

Reconciliations

There has, then, been something of a renaissance in the political theory of international relations. How is this activity related to political theory itself? The fundamental question that links political theory and the political theory of international relations is 'Who are you?' or, self-referentially, 'Who am I?' In other words, the question of identity. This is not simply a question of boundaries under a different guise at which authority and legitimacy begin and end. Identities are not necessarily territorially bound, although they may in some instances (such as national identity) seek to be so; when they are, they may become integral to the identity of competing national groups, as for example in Palestine and the former Yugoslavia (O'Neill 1994: 77).

The question of identity is not perennial and transhistorical. It is relational, not relative, in that it is asked in a context of conventions which endows it with a point. If one gets the point of the question, then in the terms of J. L. Austin (1962), one gains uptake. We live our lives, as Mervyn Frost (1996) suggests, in the context of social institutions which are constitutive of our identity. Who we are is bound up with what we do and who we do it with.

The question of attachments and self-identity is complicated by factors which go beyond self-perception. Self-identification is of little value without recognition: recognition by those with whom one wishes to be associated, and externally by those whose acknowledgement of one's identity is deemed important. Recognition comes in all sorts of ways, and the lack of it may have all sorts of consequences. In order for a nation to qualify as a state, for example, to take the criteria proposed by Northedge (1976), it is not enough that its leaders deem it to be so because it has a physical identity and possesses internal sovereignty. It must also have external sovereignty, that is, recognition by the community of states. It must be welcomed into the club of the United Nations. Such issues are related, of course, to the politics of inclusion and exclusion in which all societies engage, and which critics, opposed to the notion of cosmo-politanism, invoke as evidence of a deep-seated need for individuals to 'belong' in and be anchored to historically identifiable communities. Walzer (1985), for example, contends that it is always a matter of priority that societies establish rules that define membership. States themselves are the classic expression of these patterns with their systems of inclusion and exclusion relating to ideas on sovereignty, citizenship and territoriality

(Linklater 1992: 82; Walker 1993: 179). Both R. B. J. Walker and Andrew
Linklater remark that the patterns of inclusion and exclusion that are
currently taken for granted are historically contingent. This point, of
course, cuts little ice with those empirical theorists of international
relations who are not interested in the origins or causes of current patterns
but are more concerned with their consequences (Mayall 1994: 183).

Our selves, then, are multi-faceted and a whole array of social institutions are constitutive of our identities. Consequently, the calls upon our
loyalty and commitment, the factors that shape us and the demands we
make upon others, come from a diversity of directions; they are often in
the form of legal obligations, or strictly defined organizational norms,
but often in the form of conventional or moral claims arising in the
context of our participation in a practice. This is what Walzer calls the
divided self, divisible into interests and roles, identities, and the subject
and object of self-criticism (1994: 85–6). We stand, as Dilthey (1976)
suggested, at the centre of a system of interactions.

The state has traditionally in the modern period been the sustainer of
this constellation of values. The basic structural security to which all our
social institutions look for support has to be sustained. The modern state
is, of course, historically contingent; much modern political theory of
international relations is critical of its centrality, and its privileged
position especially in realist theories which still dominate the discipline.
The fact remains, however, that as the sustainer of all our cultural, social
and political institutions and practices it is the agent through which
citizens are collective actors on the world scene. Whatever the trend may
be towards alternative ways of responding to the major crises of our age
– nuclear proliferation, the hunger and poverty of 20 per cent of the
world's population, the imbalance in the ecosystem, and increasingly
repressive regimes and the systematic violation of human rights (Ekins
1992) – we continue to look in times of crises to the acknowledged and
legitimate authority of the state to act as a deliberative agent in setting
goals and devising plans to attain them. But what is the source of identity
that is able to act through the state?

Although national identity is a historically contingent fact of social life,
one can envisage other foci of social cohesiveness, such as religion,
gender, colour or class, being just as strong or stronger on certain issues.
To be a member of Christendom, a woman, black or working-class, all
have made strong claims to transcend nationality as the source of one's
primary loyalty and identity. National identity has, however, predomi-
nated. Even Marx's and Engel's internationalism eventually had to
accommodate the nation-state by suggesting that the revolution required
the working class first to come to terms with their own national bour-
geoisie. Yet, national identity is also too large and abstract an entity to

generate the sort of unconditional loyalty that at times of emergency it demands. The idea of nationality has to be sustained by more concrete and immediate attachments. National consciousness, Janna Thompson argues, rests on the foundation of the overlapping social relations that sustain the groups and communities that individuals value (1992: 175). Conflicts of interest may frequently occur between the obligations of the various identities one shares, but which identities are primary at any particular time depends not only upon the contingencies of the circumstances, but also upon the kind of person I happen to be. Principles are always mediated by persons: when translated into the special circumstances of each, what one person regards as a duty may for another person be outweighed by other obligations.

It is when the source of dignity and pride is threatened that national identity takes on the more pernicious aspects of nationalism. However, the unacceptable face of nationalism has tended to be that presented as its typical manifestation (Kedourie 1993; Minogue 1967), and, when understood in such pejorative terms, Hobsbawm (1990) may have had some justification for suggesting that the age of nationalism was over, only to be immediately proved wrong with a vengeance. The resurgence of nationalism in Eastern Europe, and especially its identification with ethnicity and ethnic cleansing – the modern euphemism for genocide – has demonstrated the continuing destructive force of harnessing the strong emotional ties of national identity to the ideals of political liberation.

Elshtain has argued that nationalism is neither intrinsically good or bad: it is possible for it to be both (1995: 271). Both political theory and international theory have been described as impoverished because they fail to theorize adequately about nationalism (Seth 1993: 76). In relation to matters of international justice, in particular, 'it is above all important to determine whether nationalist ideas have any validity from a moral point of view: whether it is true that people ought to identify with their nation and defend it, and if so, what this means as far as international relations are concerned' (Thompson 1992: 127). Nevertheless, much normative political theory of international relations conceptualizes the last two hundred years in terms of the rights and obligations of the citizen, and their relation to the rights and obligations of humanity, characterized in terms of citizens versus people, communitarianism versus cosmopolitanism, nationality versus universality, or cultural relativism versus human rights. The attempts to ground our rights and duties come from two categorially distinct standpoints. What is at issue between the contending approaches is the source of our claims and obligations.

On the one hand the community, often assumed synonymous with the self-determining nation, is identified as the context within which rules and conventions emerge, and which give rise to our special moral rights and duties towards our fellow citizens, and which have priority over any we might have to humanity as a whole. Indeed, those duties towards humanity to which the community subscribes, by being party to conventions on human rights, are mediated by the political apparatus of the community or nation, namely the state. As Miller reminds us, we must not fall into the trap of using nation as a synonym for state. A nation is a community of people with an aspiration to be politically self-determining, and the state is the set of political institutions that they aspire to achieve (Miller 1995: 18–19). This community-generated morality is maintained and sustained, both formally, by being codified in law, and informally, by being embedded in social practices. Vincent sees this as a form of cultural relativism not invented by post-imperialist nationalist movements, but certainly popularized by them (1986: 37).

On the other hand, the source of our rights and duties is identified outside the national community, in a higher law, or as a dictate of reason. In order to avoid cultural imperialism (the imposition of a dominant state's standards upon less powerful states) and cultural relativism (the denial that there can be any transcultural standards), the moral basis for judging the actions of states, it is argued, must rest on the assumption that there is a community of humankind. This is what Michael Donelan calls the 'primordial community of mankind' (1978: 90). It is presupposed that moral discourse cannot proceed without some basic shared values. The problem here, as Vincent suggests, is to reconcile the idea that there are human rights that everyone should enjoy by virtue of being human, and at the same time to acknowledge that their content and importance are subject to contention (1986: 56). Natural Law theorists, of course, acknowledge this problem. They are aware that the basic abstract principles governing the primordial community, when translated into human positive laws governing specific communities, vary in their application and interpretation. They contend that there are self-evident goods which all communities hold in common, and which are presupposed in our relations with each other. In John Finnis's view, these goods are life, sociability, being practically reasonable, delight in art and literature, aesthetic experience, a desire for knowledge, and some form of religious experience. These goods are pursued in different ways (1980). The way that we seek knowledge, and indeed what is regarded as knowledge, has changed considerably over time. Nevertheless, people pursue knowledge by different processes of reasoning, and even the sceptic is making a claim to knowledge in denying that there can be certainty in these matters; this demonstrates a commitment to the value of knowledge.

The historicist, of course, argues that when the pursuit of what is claimed to be the same value over space and time is contextualized, it strains credulity to think of it as in any fundamental sense the same value. And even if there is a coincidence of values at a very abstract level, in what way can this be said to constitute a moral community which has claims on us as individuals? A resemblance of attributes, whether moral or physical, may be sufficient for the purposes of classification, identifying us as human beings or certain types of human beings, but something more is required to designate something as a society or community, a collection of people with which we feel a certain solidarity. Rorty, for example, argues that our sense of solidarity – our sense of others being 'one of us', with its associated beliefs – is historically specific and does not transcend time and institutions. Such beliefs, even when those who hold them are conscious of their contingency, are capable of regulating action, and even of inspiring people to die for them. He denies that a sense of identity centred on humanity as the relevant focus can have the same power to move an individual as solidarity with co-religionists, co-nationals, revolutionary comrades, etc. He argues that 'our sense of solidarity is strongest when those with whom solidarity is expressed are thought of as "one of us," where "us" means something smaller and more local than the human race. That is why "because she is a human being" is a weak, unconvincing explanation of a generous action' (Rorty 1989: 191).

The idea of national identity, and of the nation as a source of moral obligation, and even as the foundation of obligation to one's co-nationals, is not incompatible with the idea of universal human rights and of duties to humanity. But the idea of compatibility can be expressed in different ways. The real issue is the relative moral standing of the state and global society: when the obligations they dictate are in conflict, which has priority?

First, we have the view that human rights move upwards, from the community to the self-determining nation, and through the nation find expression in the international community. This is the point that Walzer is making when he argues that maximal morality, the type embedded in our societies and social practices, precedes universal minimal morality, which is in fact abstracted from the former (1994: 13). Eleanor Roosevelt was well aware of the role of the community in upholding and sustaining human rights when she asked: 'Where, after all, do universal human rights begin? In small places, close to home . . .' (MacKinnon 1993: 83). A sense of national identity embraces universal concepts, such as natural rights and the right to self-determination (Elshtain 1995: 271). The United Nations Covenants on Civil and Political Rights, and on Economic, Social and Cultural Rights maintain self-determination as a fundamental right of all peoples. This was asserted as a human right in 1960 when the General Assembly adopted the Declaration on the Granting of Independence to Colonial Countries and Peoples (Resolution 1514, XV). Effectively this is an assertion of the rights of individuals within national groups, and an acknowledgement that national self-determination is the condition for enjoying other human rights. Freedom of the nation precedes freedom of the individual. Bernard Bosanquet (1997) argued nearly eighty years ago that patriotism was perfectly compatible with humanitarianism, and indeed the source and sustainer of all that has been elevated to the status of universal principles. In this he was following T. H. Green's example in believing that human progress has consisted in a consciousness of a good which the person holds in common with others.[7] My well-being is not transitory and is held in common with a group of people whose well-being is taken to be the same as my own, and in which I am interested by the very fact that I am interested in myself. In other words, my well-being and that of the group are almost inextricable. Any duties that I have to humanity arise because of a gradual extension or widening conception of those people I regard as included in the common good. It is the recognition of more and more people as our neighbours and their inclusion in the moral community that gives rise to our obligations towards them. As Green says, 'It is not the sense of duty to a neighbour, but the practical answer to the question Who is my neighbour? that has varied' (Green 1899: 247; Boucher 1994).

The cosmopolitan, on the other hand, who takes the individual as the subject of a universal moral law – what Beitz calls moral or ethical cosmopolitanism – is not thereby committed to an institutional cosmopolitanism (1994: 124–5). The key idea here, as Pogge suggests, 'is that every human being has a global stature as an ultimate unit of moral concern' (1994: 90). The idea of a global moral community of humanity does not logically preclude the division of the world into smaller, administratively manageable units in whatever political form may be deemed most appropriate; states, federations, empires. Typically in the modern era that unit has been the sovereign state, often coinciding with a desire on the part of a community for national self-determination. The points that the Natural Law theorist makes are that the division is not absolute, and that states are merely more convenient administrative apparatuses to sustain the common good of the communities they serve. Together these states in co-operation with each other serve the common good of humanity. In such a view there is an overlaying of responsibilities, laws, rights and obligations, and at some point a conflict of duties may arise between one's obligations as a citizen and as a person.[8]

Where the state is seen as the basic unit in international relations, this does not preclude the idea of an international morality. Such views are expressed in terms of an international society of states which, in their relations with each other, have both moral rights and responsibilities. Sovereign states are the subjects of international law, and individuals are its objects. To uphold a principle of intervention opens the way for interference by foreign states in the domestic affairs of others on the most tenuous of moral pretexts. One may call this the legal sceptical consequentialist or prudential justification of an international system based on states. Alternatively, the acknowledgement of sovereignty may entail mutual respect for each other's natural rights as 'moral individuals', and a subscription to the principle of non-intervention is an expression of respect for these rights. The ground of the moral obligation is typically Natural Law in such classic thinkers as Pufendorf, Wolff and Vattel. But one may take the system of states itself, and not the universal moral community of humanity, as the society of shared values from which moral argument can proceed.

What emerges from the above discussion is a much less distinct division between cosmopolitanism and communitarianism than much of the literature tries to project. The focus upon identity reveals that an emphasis upon universalism does not preclude recognizing the value of the nation, the state, and other particularistic institutions, as agents of justice. The particularistic moralities are derived from the universal principles. On the other hand, an emphasis upon the constitutive nature of the nation does not preclude universalism, but the universal morality is, to use the terms of Walzer (1994), a thin universalism derived from a thick particularism. In other words, there is a common recognition of the moral significance of particularistic associations, and not even among the constitutive theorists is there a commitment to the immutable validity of the nation-state as it currently exists. There is a common recognition of the possibility, and even the desirability (with different degrees of enthusiasm), of extending the moral community beyond the state.

States and Beyond

I want in this section to illustrate that, whether from a so-called cosmopolitan or communitarian starting-point, the same end is desired: namely, an extension of the moral community that posits a certain degree of universalism, while at the same time preserving difference and respect for diverse identities. However, it is the mechanism by which the extension takes place which remains at issue: whether, for example, the means is Held's cosmopolitan democracy or Rorty's sad sentimental stories. I will begin by looking at Mervyn Frost's constitutive theory, which he uses to ground currently accepted international norms. Those norms, in themselves, embody elements, such as respect for human rights, which have a universalist component. I then go on to discuss Walzer's attempt to show how thin universalism develops out of thick particularism. Finally, from Linklater's critical theory perspective and Rorty's postmodernism, I show how they both emphasize the historicity of identities, and the desirability of transcending those that currently hold sway by more inclusive communities held together by a strengthened sense of human solidarity.

Mervyn Frost (1996) is committed to the state as the basic unit in international relations. He takes the international system as given, and tries to identify the settled norms associated with it and largely accepted by its members. He then seeks to establish a background theory which can be used to justify these norms and give some guidance in the difficult ethical cases in international relations. Frost maintains that, despite the absence of the kind of foundations for ethical theory of which philosophers once dreamed, moral argument can still take place, and moral conclusions can still be reached, by reasoning from the premises that we hold in common. Like the Natural Law theorist, he believes that a community of shared values must be presupposed in order for moral argument to take place. He differs, however, in believing that, far from the community of values being independent of the modernizing state system, it is this system itself which provides 'the idiom within which normative argument takes place' (1996: 85). Whatever proposals are made for a modification of the international system have to be made in the modern idiom of the state, the discourse that already provides the vocabulary for discussion. For Frost, recognition of one's state within the international system of states is constitutive of one's freedom. Frost's whole approach thus assumes that there is an international community beyond the state.

Walzer (1983) refuses to ground our ordinary notions of justice in such fundamental principles as equal treatment, desert or inalienable rights. We should, he contends, see justice as the product of particular political communities at identifiable times, and our accounts of justice should be constructed within the terms of reference dictated by these communities. Within any society, particularly liberal societies, there is a variety of social goods whose distribution is governed by different criteria in their respective spheres of activity. However, the well-known communitarian (an attribution which he renounces) in his famous book on international relations begins by positing a minimal content to human rights, the universal rights of life and liberty (Walzer 1992: 136). These rights, irrespective of how we ground them, whether natural or invented, are part of what we mean by being human. They are irredeemably a feature of our moral world. The authority of the state rests upon the consent of those who have authorized it to act in the interests of protecting their rights. The state is the sustainer of a common way of life, which it protects against outside interference. In so far as it fulfils its purpose as a state, it is worthy of moral status. This entails the state itself acquiring a persona and bearing the same rights of life and liberty against other states who might without adequate constraints attempt to impose their collective ways of life upon it. States have value and worth, not because they are like individuals, but because they provide collectively for the pursuit of individuals' purposes. If states possess rights, as individuals do, then it is possible to envisage a society of states, just as there are societies comprised of individuals (Walzer 1992: 53–60).[9] From the priority of rights-bearing individuals who construct political communities, the priority shifts to these communities themselves (1992: 254).[10]

Elsewhere, Walzer has suggested that there is a minimal code of universal morality constituting cross-cultural requirements of justice, such as the expectation not to be deceived, treated with gross cruelty, or murdered (1988: 22). Walzer, in fact, posits the idea of an international society which he grounds, not on a natural or a hypothetical contract in a Rawlsian original position, but on ideals and principles that have become commonly accepted by leaders of states and their citizens. This is because he wants to endorse difference while at the same time subscribe to a 'thin' universalism. As suggested earlier, the universalism in Walzer is not prior to, but instead a distillation of, the 'thick' morality associated with communities. This is not what he calls 'covering law universalism', which gives priority to a way of life as uniquely right, and which can be used as the basis for imperialist arguments. Instead, his universalism is reiterative, acknowledging that, subject to minimal universal constraints, there are many different and valuable ways of life that have equal rights to flourish in their respective locations, and deserve equal respect to our own (Walzer 1990b).

The same Hegelian source which gives Frost inspiration also serves to generate a more critical political theory of international relations. It takes as its premise a philosophical history that has at its core the idea of the development of human freedom. The development is an ideal one in which the individual's feelings of estrangement and powerlessness are overcome in more and more adequate social and international arrangements. This is a philosophical history, inspired by Kant, Hegel, Marx and Collingwood, which comprises a scale of forms, the essence of which is the Kantian idea of the contribution made by various human associations to the achievement of world citizenship. The current condition of international relations, as defined by Realists, is, in Linklater's view, at a point where states are inadequately conscious of their ability to overcome the structural systemic forces in the international system which they deem to be out of their control. The task of Critical Theory is to provide an account of ways of acting in the international environment that would enable people to circumvent international systemic constraints and take control of their history (Linklater 1990b: 14). Linklater's philosophical history acknowledges that social and inter-societal relations are historical creations which reveal people's capacity to create forms of life capable of breaking down inter-societal estrangements which are barriers to personal development. The account he gives does not depend upon historical verification because it is an ideal characterization of the development of human freedom. The ideality of it does, however, depend upon the acceptance of the initial premises. Like Marx, he assumes that there is a human essence, or species being, from which individuals are alienated in the smaller restrictive associations in which they are trapped. The human formations, identified as tribes and states, do constitute types of estrangement and powerlessness, and the larger associations, including the universal community, contribute to greater individual freedom. Implicit in the whole account is the idea that forms of attachment and obligation that arise from particularistic associations (such as the family, tribe or nation) are primitive, imperfect and even irrational in comparison with the ideal end of a global community, in which obligations are owed to each other as individuals and not as members of lesser associations. Progress is defined by Linklater as the process of ascending to the level of ethical universalism. It is by no means clear, however, what value would be placed on cultural diversity at this level at which a Western liberal conception of freedom predominates. Linklater himself has recently recognized that it is untenable to dismiss these attachments, and has acknowledged the universal prevalence of the politics of inclusion and exclusion.

This is a project which brings up to date the Idealist aspiration of extending the moral community to include people we are willing to acknowledge as our neighbours. The Idealist aspiration, however, had its dangers. Idealists tended to be what Walzer calls 'covering law universalists'. Taking the ideas of freedom and individual choice as central to human development, from the vantage-point of the present, and viewing any impediments to self-realization as regressive historical tendencies, they were able, despite being communitarians, to eschew relativism. But in doing so, they were affirming a way of life as right and desirable for world moral progress. Many of the British Idealists justified imperialism on the grounds that the more civilized nations had a duty to raise the lower nations to be capable of self-government.

Contemporary theorists who acknowledge that particularistic communities and the nation (but not necessarily the state) have to be accommodated in any theory of cosmopolitanism seek to avoid the implications of the Idealist path. Linklater's later position suggests that what is needed is a balance between the need to identify transnational values and respect for cultural differences (1992: 84). The task of a Critical Theory of international relations, he tells us, is to go beyond Marxism and develop a more adequate theory in which to anchor the state than that tradition has provided. Following from this, Critical Theory 'must regard the practical project of extending community beyond the nation-state as its most important problem – and not just as a backdrop to the allegedly more basic struggle between antagonistic social classes' (Linklater 1990b: 171; cf. 1992: 93). From the point of view of international justice, Janna Thompson, for example, sees her idea of overlapping consensus among overlapping or interlocking communities, the consciousness of which is the basis of the ethical life of the nation, extending beyond state boundaries. She shares with cosmopolitan democracy theorists the idea that there is nothing inviolable about nation-states (Archibugi and Held 1995; Held 1995). States themselves often comprise more than one nation, and nations could in principle form the basis of cosmopolitan schemes. Indeed, many interlocking and overlapping communities, such as religions, social movements, learned societies etc., are already transnational. The conditions of justice in an ever-increasing association of interlocking communities will be freedom of association and the openness of communities (Thompson 1992: ch. 9).

This differs from the Natural Law foundation to the community of humankind in positing a historical identity to the moral obligations incurred, first to the family, the tribe, the nation, the state, and then to humanity. The broadening of the community within which the common good prevails brings with it an extension of the obligations owed to a larger number of people and eventually to humanity as a whole. Curiously this is a position Rorty also advocates. He urges that we should extend our sense of 'we' to include those whom we have previously regarded as 'they': 'The right way to take the slogan "We have obligations to human beings simply as such" is as a means of reminding ourselves to keep trying to expand our sense of "us" as far as we can' (Rorty 1989: 192, 196). From the Natural Law perspective, this sentiment to treat everyone as part of a world moral community is there from the outset. The obligations to humanity, far from having a historical basis, are innate: whether we recognize and act upon them or not makes no difference to the fact that they exist. And if we come to acknowledge them at a later time it does not alter the fact that they were there from the beginning (Donelan 1990: 10–11).

Notes

1 Raymond Aron complained that 'theory' has become a much over-used and abused word, particularly in the field of international relations where the most banal observations are dressed-up under the guise of theory.

2 Twenty years earlier Waltz had developed his famous analysis of war in terms of three images – the internal psychology of man, the internal structure of the state, and the structure of the world state system – by drawing upon the insights of classical political theorists, tempered nevertheless by the assumptions of contemporary social science. See Waltz (1959).

3 This characterization became widely accepted, and it still acts as a useful
   heuristic device for teaching international relations to students. The most
   influential perpetrators of what has been called the inter-paradigm debate
   are Little and Smith (1991). The list of what passes as theory in the field of
   international relations could be extended considerably, but it would not add
   anything to the point that international theory has, on the whole, developed
   independently of political philosophy, to the detriment of the former, and I
   may add to the latter. For surveys of the various 'theories' of international
   relations see Holsti 1987; Smith and Booth 1995; Groom and Light 1994.
4 In criticizing contemporary political philosophers, A. H. Hanson argued
   that they have abandoned the claim to offer any practical guidance and
   'remain content with the intellectually exciting but politically sterile task of
   teasing out linguistic puzzles' (1956: 7).
5 Chris Brown attributes the parting of the ways largely to the demise of
   normative moral philosophy following World War I (1993: 84–9). This does
   not explain why international theorists did not take the route of political
   theorists and define themselves in terms of their pedigree.
6 Following Oakeshott, Nardin takes the task of philosophy to be the identification and examination of the postulates that sustain and constitute given
   human practices. See Michael Oakeshott (1933; 1975).
7 Of recent political theorists of international relations, Michael Walzer and
   Andrew Linklater explicitly acknowledge his influence (Walzer 1992: 28,
   n. 28; Linklater 1990a: 25–7, 30–2; Linklater 1993: 320–1).
8 Kant's cosmopolitanism, for instance, is fully cognizant of the existence of a
   primordial community of humankind and of the impracticality of a world
   state. The best that could be hoped for was a peaceful federation of states.
   The world order for him rests on three types of right: constitutional right,
   that is ideally a republican form of government in each state; international
   right, the rights of states; and cosmopolitan right, the rights of individuals
   in relation to each other. His criterion of morality, however, is universal. The
   modern Kantian ethical cosmopolitan Onora O'Neill fully acknowledges
   that nationality and other forms of community have an importance, and that
   securing a national state may be instrumental in achieving justice for some:
   for example, this looks to be the case with the Kurds. On the other hand, the
   achievement of a national state may be just as likely to be the instrument of
   injustice to others, as the nationality problem in the former Soviet Union
   testifies (1994: 78–9).
9 Charles Beitz (1979) challenges similar assumptions. He argues that the
   state is not autonomous in the way that the principle of non-intervention
   requires. Modern states are heavily interdependent and unlike individuals
   they do not have personalities that have to be respected. The moral worth of
   a state cannot be attributed to its autonomy. Its value has to be assessed on
   the arrangements it supports for contributing to the well-being of its citizens
   and humanity as a whole.
10 He denies that he is a communitarian in Walzer (1990).

References

Archibugi, Daniele, and Held, David, eds. 1995. *Cosmopolitan Democracy: An
   Agenda for a New World Order.* Cambridge: Polity Press.

Aron, Raymond. 1967. 'What is a Theory of International Relations', *Journal of International Affairs*, 21.
Austin, J. L. 1962. *How to Do Things with Words*. Oxford: Clarendon Press.
Beitz, Charles R. 1979. *Political Theory and International Relations*. Princeton: Princeton University Press.
Beitz, Charles R. 1994. 'Cosmopolitan Liberalism and the States System', in Chris Brown, ed., *Political Restructuring in Europe*. London: Routledge.
Bosanquet, Bernard. 1997. 'The Function of the State in Promoting the Unity of Mankind', in D. Boucher, ed., *The British Idealists*. Cambridge: Cambridge University Press.
Boucher, David. 1994. 'British Idealism, the State, and International Relations', *Journal of the History of Ideas*, 55.
Brown, Chris. 1993. *International Relations Theory: New Normative Approaches*. London: Harvester Wheatsheaf.
Brown, Chris. 1994. 'The Ethics of Political Restructuring in Europe', in Brown, ed., *Political Restructuring in Europe*. London: Routledge.
Connolly, William. 1989. 'Identity and Difference in Global Politics', in James Der Derrian and Michael Schapiro, eds, *International/Intertextual Relations: Postmodern Readings in World Politics*. Lexington: Lexington Books.
Cox, R. W. 1981. 'Social Forces, States and World Orders: Beyond International Relations Theory', *Millennium*, 10.
Der Derrian, James. 1987. *On Diplomacy: A Genealogy of Western Estrangement*. Oxford: Blackwell.
Dilthey, William, 1976. *Selected Writings*, ed. H. P. Rickman. Cambridge: Cambridge University Press.
Donelan, Michael. 1978. 'The Political Theorists and International Theory', in Donelan, ed., *The Reason of States*. London: Allen and Unwin.
Donelan, Michael. 1990. *Elements of International Political Theory*. Oxford: Clarendon Press.
Easton, David. 1951. 'The Decline of Modern Political Theory', *Journal of Politics*, 13.
Ekins, Paul. 1992. *A New World Order: Grassroots Movements for Global Change*. London: Routledge.
Elshtain, Jean Bethke. 1992. 'Reflections on War and Political Discourse: Realism, Just War, and Feminism in a Nuclear Age', in Elshtain, ed., *Just War Theory*. Oxford: Blackwell.
Elshtain, Jean Bethke. 1995. 'International Politics and Political Theory', in Ken Booth and Steve Smith, eds, *International Relations Theory Today*. Cambridge: Polity.
Finnis, John. 1980. *Natural Law and Natural Rights*. Oxford: Oxford University Press.
Frost, Mervyn. 1996. *Ethics in International Relations: A Constitutive Theory*. Cambridge: Cambridge University Press.
Green, T. H. 1899. *Prolegomena to Ethics*, 4th edn. Oxford: Clarendon Press.
Greenfield, Liah. 1992. *Nationalism: Five Roads to Modernity*. Cambridge, Mass.: Harvard University Press.
Groom, A. J. R. and Light, Margot, eds. 1994. *Contemporary International Relations: A Guide to Theory*. London: Pinter.
Habermas, J. 1993. *Justification and Application: Remarks on Discourse Ethics*. Cambridge: Cambridge University Press.
Hanson, A. H. 1956. *Political Philosophy or Political Science: An Inaugural Lecture*. Cambridge: Leeds University Press.

Held, David. 1995. *Democracy and the Global Order: From the Modern State to Cosmopolitan Governance*. Cambridge: Polity Press.

Hobsbawm, E. J. 1990. *Nations and Nationalism since 1780*. Cambridge: Cambridge University Press.

Holsti, K. J. 1987. *The Dividing Discipline*. London: Allen and Unwin.

Kedourie, Elie. 1993. *Nationalism*. Oxford: Blackwell.

Linklater, Andrew. 1990a. *Men and Citizens in the Theory of International Relations*, 2nd edn. London: Macmillan.

Linklater, Andrew. 1990b. *Beyond Realism and Marxism*. London: Macmillan.

Linklater, Andrew. 1992. 'The Question of the Next Stage in International Relations Theory: A Critical-Theoretical Point of View', *Millennium*, 21.

Linklater, Andrew. 1993. 'Men and Citizens in International Relations', in Howard Williams, Moorhead Wright, and Tony Evans, eds, *International Relations and Political Theory*. Buckingham: Open University Press.

Little, Richard, and Smith, Michael. 1991. *Perspectives on World Politics*, 2nd edn. London: Routledge.

MacKinnon, Catharine A. 1993. 'Crimes of War, Crimes of Peace', in Stephen Shute and Susan Hurley, eds, *On Human Rights*. New York: Basic Books.

Mayall, James. 1994. 'Nationalism in the Study of International Relations', in A. J. R. Groom and Margot Light, eds, *Contemporary International Relations: A Guide to Theory*. London: Pinter.

Miller, David. 1995. *On Nationality*. Oxford: Clarendon Press.

Miller, David, and Walzer, Michael. 1995. *Pluralism, Justice and Equality*. Oxford: Oxford University Press.

Minogue, Kenneth. 1967. *Nationalism*. London: Batsford.

Nardin, Terry. 1983. *Law, Morality, and the Relations of States*. Princeton: Princeton University Press.

Northedge, F. S. 1976. *The International Political System*. London: Faber.

Oakeshott, Michael. 1933. *Experience and its Modes*. Cambridge: Cambridge University Press.

Oakeshott, Michael. 1975. *On Human Conduct*. Oxford: Clarendon Press.

O'Neill, Onora. 1994. 'Justice and Boundaries', in Chris Brown, ed., *Political Restructuring in Europe*. London: Routledge.

Pogge, Thomas. 1994. 'Cosmopolitanism and Sovereignty', in Chris Brown, ed., *Political Restructuring in Europe*. London: Routledge.

Rawls, John. 1993. 'The Law of Peoples', in Stephen Shute and Susan Hurley, eds, *On Human Rights*. New York: Basic Books.

Rorty, Richard. 1989. *Contingency, Irony and Solidarity*. Cambridge: Cambridge University Press.

Rorty, Richard. 1993. 'Human Rights, Rationality, and Sentimentality', in Stephen Shute and Susan Hurley, eds, *On Human Rights*. New York: HarperCollins.

Seth, Sanjay. 1993. 'Political Theory in the Age of Nationalism', *Ethics and International Affairs*, 7.

Smith, Steve. 1992. 'The Forty Years' Detour: The Resurgence of Normative Theory in International Relations', *Millenium*, 21.

Smith, Steve, and Booth, Ken, eds. 1995. *International Relations Theory Today*. Cambridge: Polity Press.

Thompson, Janna. 1992. *Justice and World Order*. London: Routledge.

Vincent, R. J. 1986. *Human Rights and International Relations*. Cambridge: Cambridge University Press.

Walker, R. B. J. 1993. *Inside/Outside: International Relations as Political Theory*. Cambridge: Cambridge University Press.

Waltz, Kenneth N. 1959. *Man, the State and War: A Theoretical Analysis*. New York: Columbia University Press.

Waltz, Kenneth N. 1979. *Theory of International Politics*. New York: McGraw-Hill.

Walzer, Michael. 1983. *Spheres of Justice*. New York: Basic Books.

Walzer, Michael. 1988. 'Interpretation and Social Criticism', in S. M. McMurrin, ed., *The Tanner Lectures on Human Values*, vol 7. Salt Lake City: University of Utah Press.

Walzer, Michael. 1990a. 'The Communitarian Critique of Liberalism', *Political Theory*, 8.

Walzer, Michael. 1990b. 'Nation and Universe', in G. B. Peterson, ed., *The Tanner Lectures on Human Values*, vol. 11. Salt Lake City: University of Utah Press.

Walzer, Michael. 1992. *Just and Unjust Wars: A Moral Argument with Historical Illustrations*, 2nd edn. New York: HarperCollins.

Walzer, Michael. 1994. *Thick and Thin: Moral Arguments at Home and Abroad*. Indiana: University of Notre Dame.

Walzer, Michael. 1995. *Spheres of Justice: A Defence of Pluralism and Equality*. Oxford: Basil Blackwell.

Wight, Martin. 1966. 'Why is There No International Theory?', in H. Butterfield and M. Wight, eds, *Diplomatic Investigations*. London: Allen and Unwin.

Wight, Martin. 1991. *International Theory: The Three Traditions*. London and Leicester: University of Leicester Press.

Williams, Howard. 1992. *International Relations in Political Theory*. Buckingham: Open University.

CHAPTER 10

Method Matters:
Feminism, Interpretation and Politics

Elizabeth Frazer

I want to consider a particularly interesting and significant strand of
feminist political theory. It consists of two threads, and each thread
consists of separable fibres. The first thread is the commitment to *interdisciplinarity*. This embodies the eclecticism necessary to achieve a
rounded view of an object like gender, which can be studied from the
perspective of psychology, literature, biology, political science. This
should perhaps be labelled 'multidisciplinarity'. 'Interdisciplinarity'
prompts us to look at competing constructions of an object or phenomenon. Disciplinary perspectives might subtract from each other as much
as add. This perception of the tensions between disciplines possibly has
much to do with feminist women's uneasy relationship with the
academies. It is difficult to believe, as many academics and scientists have
believed, that any one discipline can offer an adequate account of its
objects. For the purposes of this chapter, there is reason to be sceptical
about the pretensions of political studies (or political science) in two
areas: *picking out* objects of analysis (politics, political institutions,
political relationships) which are uniquely its own; and *explaining* those
objects itself, entirely from its own resources.

The second thread is the *centrality of interpretive method*. 'Interpretivism'
encompasses the interpretation both of texts proper (films, books, the
life's work of an author or group), and of text analogues (social events
and social practices). It can refer to conceptual analysis, theory formation, or the construction of social reality as interpretation. Interpretivism
can be a strong commitment – underpinned by a principle such as that
the world is a text or is for social scientific and theoretic purposes like a
text. This might imply scepticism about causal analysis in social science,
or about deontological ethics. More weakly, interpretation (here it is
appropriate to drop the aggrandizing suffix '-ism') can be construed as a

214

necessary first step in explanation or criticism. More weakly still, interpretation is treated as just one of a range of analytic methods. My argument that this is a significant strand in feminist political theory itself emerges, of course, from an interpretive reading – the theme has not been articulated very explicitly in that literature.

One purpose I have is to restate the principle that method matters. It is not just what you do in political theory, as in the conduct of social relations: it's the way that you do it. Of course, plenty of others have agreed with this – the thousands of words within political theory about 'interpretation' testify to that. But feminist contributions add something specific to debates about the interpreter's position, and thence to debates about the process of interpretation. This brings me to another concern I wish to address.

In anglophone political theory, in the era of the 'liberal-communitarian debates', the threads of interdisciplinarity and interpretivism have often been twisted together with a third: communitarianism. This also consists of a number of separable fibres. To begin with, there is the commitment to *community as a causally significant social relation*, more significant than the individual, or the larger social entities of nation or state (although sometimes these are construed as communities). Then, there is the commitment to *community as a valuable thing*, and the associated commitment to a series of values which maintain, enhance or constitute community – such as solidarity and reciprocity. Finally, there is *political communitarianism*, which has two aspects. First is the idea that the community is the, or one, correct locus for political action (by which I mean, action and practices that are relevant to the power to govern – pursuing it, contesting it, resisting it, influencing governors). Second is the idea that a primary political (not simply moral) objective should be the building, maintenance and enhancement of communities and life in community for individuals.

Within the communitarian literature there is a good deal of warrant for linking interpretivism with communitarianism (Walzer 1983: xiv; 1987; Taylor 1985a; 1985b; MacIntyre 1981). In what follows I want to argue that we should untwist this 'communitarian' thread. We should retain some of its fibres, and discard others – notably a number of communitarianism's implicit and explicit sociological theses. Interpretivism introduces into social analysis an interpreter whose social identity and epistemic standpoint cannot be effaced or glossed over so easily as can that of the theorist or philosopher responsible for some other kinds of analysis. The problem is that the category 'community' mystifies this standpoint just as much as does the putative 'view from nowhere' or 'Archimedean point' that is a characteristic of the universalist and deontological ethics the communitarians attack.

Feminism and Interpretation

Interpretation has its place in feminist political theory at a number of levels. First, an important strand consists of a research program devoted to the *rereading and reinterpretation of the texts* of political theory (for instance, Shanley and Pateman 1991). The feminist interpretation of texts challenges traditional readings and the deployment of traditional strategies to cope with the question of gender. One such has been to acknowledge that particular conceptualizations of marriage, femininity, household and so on are present in texts, but to argue (mostly with unusual brevity) that these are irrelevant to the important questions about governance, state, society and individual, liberty and equality. Another is to ignore conceptualizations and arguments about gender altogether. Feminist interpretation brings the treatment of these phenomena and concepts to the centre, revealing the relations between concepts of gender and sexual difference and others – polity, political relations, equality, freedom and democracy. This interpretive process is focused on the surface of texts: passages traditionally said to be insignificant are brought to the reader's attention. In the process, concepts like politics, state and equality are re-presented – shown to have a gender component.

Second, feminists have conducted *critique of texts*. This means something specific – the elucidation of the unspoken or tacit assumptions, the conceptualizations (of key terms and phenomena like subject, society and individual) which must underpin the argument, if the text is to make sense. A notable example of this is Pateman's reading of the social contract tradition. She points to the absence of women from the social contract, their irrelevance in the processes of construction of state, civil society and laws that are described; this can only be accounted for if we presume that the question of the oppression of women has been dealt with before the story begins, so to speak, in a sexual contract which is hinted at in various ways in the social contract texts (Pateman 1988). Here we have a closer reading of the text – one that notices rather than ignores questions about marriage and sexual relations. Moreover, we have a reading process where what is said licenses inference about what is not said. In critique, the interpretive process delves deep 'beneath the surface' of the text. Although authors do not explicitly address the questions that are on the agenda of their readers and critics, we can nevertheless enquire what the author would have said, had they addressed the issue explicitly, or in the form the critic poses it.

Third, *texts are interpreted as political texts*, given feminist conceptualizations of key terms. For instance, feminists argue that the terms 'politics' and 'governance' apply in interpersonal relations, within the putatively private or personal arena of kinship, family and household, and in relations and practices that are usually considered to be cultural. This means that relations of domination and power in household and in culture are susceptible to exactly the same kinds of questions of legitimacy as are relations of domination and power in the state, and involve similar processes. It also means that relations of power in these contexts are causally connected with relations of power at the level of state and inter-state relations, and the competition for the power to govern states. Thus, feminists challenge the canon of political theory, which has excluded texts like Mary Wollstonecraft's *Vindication of the Rights of Woman*, Virginia Woolf's *Three Guineas*, and *A Room of One's Own*, and Simone de Beauvoir's *Second Sex*. These texts precisely address questions of governance and the competition for the power to govern. Note that the usual criteria for canonical status are not themselves challenged at this stage. This is not the same argument, as has been made by Quentin Skinner and others, about the relevance of popular and genre works, letters, diaries and speeches, to our interpretation and understanding of political theory, although there may be independent reasons why feminist theorists would advance that line of argument (Skinner 1978).

A separate interpretive strand in feminist political theory focuses on 'facts'. If ever there has been a class of facts and body of knowledge that vividly demonstrates, first, the interpretive basis of facts, and, second, the need to continue to reinterpret facts and evidence, it is that of gender. Facts about sexual difference frequently reveal that sexual difference is *a priori*: a set of presumptions, in the light of which particular characteristics are discerned and labelled sexual. It is not just sexual difference that is *a priori*, but, rather sexual hierarchy. Concepts are prior to observation and are an ingredient in interpretation – this seems to be the best way to understand how 'prejudice' and 'bias' work (Tuana 1989).

Feminist method also calls for the *interpretation of practices*. The relationship between normative bodies of ideas, the world we inhabit, and individuals' actions and interactions, cannot be presumed. Any exploration involves the scrutiny of mundane practices as well as arcane and specialized ones. Critical analyses of practice go on to explore the importance of action structured by norms in the maintenance of unequal power relations. They argue that one important aspect of critical political action is to interpret and challenge these practices (not simply the norms, not simply the actions) (Frazer and Lacey 1994: 268–73). This inevitably involves interpretation. People who act in the light of available normative justifications perforce interpret those norms; the critic or scientist who studies what they do similarly has to interpret what they are doing. Another way of putting this is to say that we need to scrutinize the 'gender sub-text of our societies' (Benhabib and Cornell 1987: 7, 11).

If we put it this way, we are making plain the hermeneutic principle that all kinds of phenomena can and should, for the purposes of social analysis, be conceptualized as text analogues, to be read.

Finally, we can also see *conceptual analysis itself as a species of interpretation*. Consider three common ways of thinking about concepts. First, some think of concepts as bounded entities, with a clear and determinate relationship with their referents. In this case, the analyst's job is to delineate for the benefit of others the exact boundary, the relation between the concept and relevant others, and the exact content of the concept. This position tends to imply that philosophy offers us the tools for the identification of the concept as distinct from the various conceptions met with in ordinary discourse and argument. Second, concepts can be thought of as having open frontiers, boundaries that are only drawn by specific language users or social actors for specific purposes (Wittgenstein 1958: s. 69). In this case, the analyst's job is perhaps to interpret for the benefit of others where the boundaries have been drawn: to detail for them by whom, under what circumstances, with what success. It might be argued here that we should retreat from the idea of 'concept' to that of 'term' or something similar. A good deal of recent political theory deploys a third way of thinking about concepts or categories: it sets out to show that concepts (certainly many of those of interest and importance to political theorists, like 'woman' or 'equality') are unstable and perhaps (rightly) unsustainable (Butler 1990: 1–13). The method by which this is shown is frequently performative or exemplary, rather than deductive or demonstrative. It is also shown by examining the concepts in use, in texts. Hence, here, conceptual analysis is intimately bound up with textual analysis.

Arguably, whichever of these three ways of conceptualizing 'concept' we accept, the process of analysis begins, at least, with interpretation. The object of analysis – the concept or term or category, its boundaries, its stability from instance to instance of use – is not obvious. Concepts do not come with their reference, implications, and elements clear and apparent, written on their faces. Their appearance is, so to speak, incomplete and partial – their fullness must be the outcome of a process of interpretation.

If it is accepted that conceptual analysis itself is interpretive, then interpretation runs very deep – deeper than if we accept the less controversial claims that the conduct of interpersonal relations or the apprehension of facts is interpretive. There are, of course, other important threads in feminist political theory – for instance, hypothesis, conceptualization, poetics and the exploration of meaning by exploration of the echoes of language, the semantic effects of the juxtaposition of terms. It might be argued that interpretivism is fundamental – that we cannot think any of these without acknowledging the place of interpretation. For example, philosophers of science argue that there must be an interpretive moment prior to measurement, or prior to the hypothesis or identification of causal relations (Taylor 1985a: 29–31; Giddens 1976: 158ff.). Some argue that, because the 'objects' of social science are themselves interpreters – of themselves and others – causal explanation of human action fails (Winch 1990). Similarly, we meet strong interpretive claims in ethics, such as Walzer's argument that invented and discovered moralities alike are really interpretations of what we already possess (1987: 19). In any exploration of concepts by juxtaposition or poetics, interpretation is fundamental. But all this begs the question – what is interpretation?

A Model of Interpretation

There is, of course, a vast and complex literature on interpretation, and there is no space in a chapter like this, nor much to be gained, from an analytic discussion focused on varying approaches to interpretation and, among other things, the disputes between them. Instead, I propose to begin by constructing a model of interpretation.[1] To be more precise, I shall set out the elements and relations of a bare-bones model (Figure 1), and this will enable me to indicate the points that are subject to controversy and briefly discuss what the bones of contention are. Obviously, this model is very minimal. But it is not minimal enough to be quite uncontentious. For instance, discussions of interpretation frequently omit the audience at this stage (Taylor 1985a: 15–16).

1. A good deal of confusion about interpretation can stem from theorists and philosophers focusing on different kinds of Thing Interpreted. The Thing might be a perception or a sense impression, an utterance, an action or behaviour (discrete or continuous), a sign, a word/phrase/sentence, a text or discourse, an event, a state of affairs.

2. Debates about the relevance of Authors' or Actors' intentions can be made more complex by cases where the nature of the subject of authorship is contested (for instance, holy writings) or where the very existence of an Author or Actor is contested (for instance, such signs as thunderbolts, plagues, mountains; and indeed conventional gestures in mundane social life).

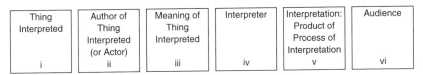

Thing Interpreted	Author of Thing Interpreted (or Actor)	Meaning of Thing Interpreted	Interpreter	Interpretation: Product of Process of Interpretation	Audience
i	ii	iii	iv	v	vi

Figure 1   The elements of interpretation

3. The Actor or Author might be a writer or producer of another text or text analogue, deploying technology (say a photographer); a participant in mundane social interaction and thereby a producer of signs; a contested abstraction like God, or 'nature'; a dog or an amoeba.

4. Interpreter and Audience may be the same human individual. I may, as it were, say to myself, 'Whatever does that mean?' and then, having engaged in interpretation, respond 'Oh, it means . . .'. But they are equally likely to be different individuals. Both cases raise interesting problems about the status of interpretations.

5. Meaning, of course, is analysed in many ways.

- The simplest view, and one that will not detain us long, is that meaning is intrinsic to, or just attached to, the Thing. We could depict this diagrammatically by superimposing box iii on box i.

- A second equally abstract possibility is that the meaning of the Thing is just what the Author intends it to mean. Diagrammatically, this would involve superimposing box iii on box i and across some section of box ii that represents the Author's intentions. The Interpreter, in this theory, has recourse to the intentions of the Author in determining what the Thing means, and the Audience, for their part, will make reference to both the Thing, and the Actor's intentions, when they assess the goodness of the Interpretation.

- More often, theorists and philosophers consider the meaning of the Thing to inhere somewhere and somehow in the space of relations between the Thing, the Author's intentions, the Interpreter's process of Interpretation, and the Audience. That is, meaning depends on the relation between Things and social subjects (interpreters, observers, interested parties).

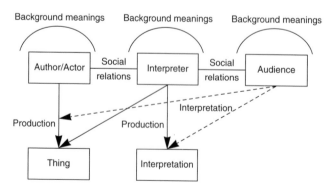

Figure 2   The relations of interpretation

In Figure 2 I have added a new element: for each subject a background or penumbra of already accepted or taken-for-granted meanings (Background Meanings) into which interpretations of new things must be assimilated, and in light of which new things will be interpreted or new interpretations accepted. This introduces into the model the 'hermeneutic circle' of appeal to prior understandings and accepted meanings which are themselves the outcome of earlier interpretations. Note that the Audience is an audience of two kinds of objects: first, the production of the Thing itself; second, the production of the Interpretation by the Interpreter. Different theorists will locate the meaning of the Thing differently on this diagram. For some it might be represented by a box, encompassing and probably cutting in some untidy way across all the boxes in the top half of the diagram. For others, given certain kinds of Thing (historical texts of political theory, perhaps), the box would still mainly take into account the Author's intentions and Background Meanings.

6. Many controversies in the philosophy and theory of interpretation are, of course, focused on the location of Background Meanings in a model like this. In Figure 2 I depict these as differentiated: the logic of showing the Interpreter as having their own penumbra of accepted meanings and understandings is that each Audience member also has their own. Most interpretivist theorists would prefer a model like that in Figure 3. Here, Interpreter and Audience, and indeed Author, are participants in a shared universe of meaning represented by arcs A–B or A–C. The social relations between Interpreter, Actor and Audience are

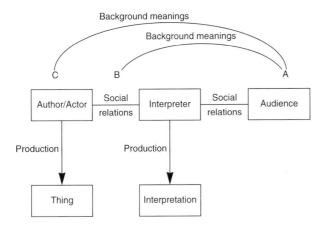

Figure 3   Social relations, shared meanings and interpretation

presumed to feature, among other things, shared language, understandings and meanings.

7. The consideration that Things typically do not come with their
meaning written plain upon their faces, together with consideration of
the complex set of relations that contribute to the production of interpretation, makes clear the possibility that different Interpreters might
produce different Interpretations. This, of course, raises the problem of
adjudication between competing Interpretations. The fact that Things
do not come with their meaning plainly displayed could imply that the
meaning is obscured, or it could imply that the Thing in question does
not have a determinate meaning. Even if it is not possible to pinpoint *the*
meaning of an object, we certainly should accept that some interpretations might be in error or might prove false (Wittgenstein 1958:
212).

8. Consideration of the social relations between interpreter and
audience shows how an interpretation (in its 'product' sense) can shift
modality from the status of interpretation proper, to that of 'fact' or
'accepted as true', or even 'commonsensical' or 'authoritative'. In this
process, audiences can lose sight of the interpretive status of interpretations! They can become sedimented: to all intents and purposes, as
brute a set of facts as one could wish to meet. On the other hand, the
riposte 'That's just your interpretation' is an unambiguous declaration
of doubt, scepticism, or dissent.

It seems clear that social power is a relevant factor in the acceptance or
sedimentation of interpretations. If the Interpreter is a 'big cheese', their
interpretation 'That Thing is x' when articulated and promulgated to an
audience, will prompt the thought ' "The Thing is x" is true', and thence
'T is x.' If the Interpreter is a 'little cheese', the outcome might be rather
different. Of course, a significant development here might be a split in
the audience (Figure 4).

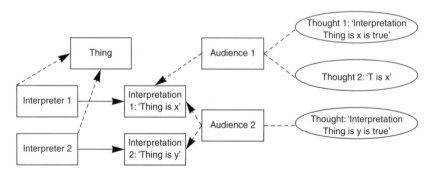

Figure 4   Rival interpretations and split audience

Here is an example: Rousseau's conception of gender has, in recent textbooks and other scholarly works, been glossed over or ignored; where it has been addressed, interpreters have presented it as worthy of only passing note, irrelevant to our consideration about Rousseau's and others' conceptions of state, society, government, etc. It is fair to say that most well-meaning scholars and teachers would take the line, 'Of course Rousseau's conception of political rule and participation excluded women among others – this aspect of his work is shared by diverse eighteenth-century thinkers.' Having noted and perhaps lamented this, we can pass on to thinking about the general will and the common good on their (gender-neutral) merits. Let us call this Interpretation 1. There is an alternative view: that the very notions of political rule and governance themselves depend upon a conception and theory of gender, upon a rejection of the feminine; and that therefore we are forced to pay attention to the meaning of gender when we try to conceptualize and articulate a theory of politics for us. Let us call this Interpretation 2; it has not become part of the academic and pedagogic mainstream. We do, though, in political theory as in other disciplines, now have a split audience. Why is this? It might be argued that feminist readers of Rousseau are just wrong; although, interestingly, I have never seen this argument explicitly made out. The more plausible argument is that dominant readings of the Western political tradition, as gender-neutral, really (despite the overt misogyny within them) are just that – dominant. Doubtless, this dominance in turn can be accounted for by a range of complex interests – interests both in the weaker sense of what people are interested in and curious about, and in the stronger sense of what states of affairs it is in people's material interests to maintain.

A different kind of example is also salient. Feminist politics in the last twenty-five years has focused largely, deliberately, on challenging and changing mundane practices, especially but not only those in which the sex of the protagonists is, broadly speaking, relevant. One result of this emphasis has been an explosion of conflict about what particular words, gestures, classes of actions, and so on mean: that is, what they signify, what connotations they have, what they do in the contested space of relations between the sexes. Consider a mundane case in which an Actor considers their gestures and words to have just a polite interrogative meaning, such as 'May I buy you a drink?' An interlocutor may interpret them as having the evaluative content of deliberate bad manners and impoliteness, and take them to be an insult. Other members of the Audience, knowing the relative social status of the two protagonists, may consider that the Actor has severely misjudged the social context and is behaving with the wrong degree of familiarity.

Doubt is cast, when we consider both these examples, on the principle that interpretations should be adjudicated, as Taylor puts it, by reference to 'our understanding' (1985a: 17). Of course, 'our understanding' might yield to us an appreciation of the range of possible ways in which these gestures, in this context, might be interpreted by a variety of kinds of social actor. But 'our understanding' does not get us very far in adjudicating between these competing interpretations. If we take the view that all of these competing understandings are justified, as it were, we raise the spectre of idiosyncratic and subjective multiplication of interpretations between which adjudication is well-nigh impossible (Warnke 1992: 10).

Walzer attempts to steer a middle course between subjectivism and objectivism. He characterizes the interpretative task in ethics and political theory as the retrieval of the understandings a community has of itself, its values, and the world: 'to interpret to one's fellow citizens the world of meanings that we share' (1983: xiv). But he also emphasizes the critical role of the interpreter. Shared meanings and everyday practices might be incoherent, there might be contradiction between principles and practices; the best reading might be a new reading (1987: 29–30). Critics can exploit the larger meanings of key terms to reveal weaknesses in conventional usage (1987: 43). But Walzer, like other interpretive political theorists, underestimates conflict over meaning and interpretation, the political nature of this conflict, and the associated normative questions of responsibility. For instance, it may be culpably ignorant of an agent not to understand, say, the sexual meanings that are for certain social subjects pressingly implied by certain kinds of familiarity with others.

To insist upon this, of course, prevents us from sitting on the fence regarding a theory of meaning and a normative theory of interpretation. This approach accepts that the meaning of a word, utterance, sentence or gesture is a matter of convention. But conventions are, by their very nature, susceptible to shifts over time and across contexts, and susceptible to dispute. Further, there are connotations, echoes, traces of suppressed or almost abandoned reference, traces of old or superseded or potential performances; these form a shadowy and elusive aura around any use of a word. This is also a site of contestation. Meaning is indeterminate and interpretation is unavoidable. Moreover, protestations of innocence in the deployment of word or gesture become bad faith – the protestations of someone who does not understand how language in its broadest sense works, and therefore lacks social know-how which ought to be non-optional.

Consequently, we cannot reserve the term 'interpretation', as Wittgenstein recommends, for cases of conscious confrontation of something not understood, and a conscious process of classification, slotting it into a particular place in one's understood world (1958 II: xi; Searle 1995: 134). Rather, this analysis suggests that all understanding (even of simple referential terms) is interpretive; all deployment of terms, all linguistic and conceptual choice likewise, whether it is fully conscious and deliberate, habitual and unreflective, or wholly unconscious. Of course, this does not preclude the apprehension of others' utterances and texts, and one's own choice of words, being careless, reckless, mistaken, ignorant or unhappy.

How then, can we conceptualize and theorize the background meanings by reference to which new things are interpreted and understood, and which constrain these interpretations? This emphasis on the elusive, on the partially disclosed and half-remembered, on the shifting and coming into articulation of new meanings in new contexts, clearly militates against us thinking of this as anything like a straightforward corpus of definitions. There is no dictionary of meanings to which all speakers have in principle the same access, as though the background or universe of shared meanings just is the *Oxford English Dictionary*. Although some words do have widely agreed core meanings, no core meaning is entirely resistant to change or contestation. Most interesting words – abstract nouns, theoretical terms – either lack such core meaning, or consist just in partially overlapping, imperfectly convergent use.

Social Standpoints

My discussion so far hints that what might generate new interpretations of meaning is new or newly understood social positions. The example of conflicting readings of political theory, for instance, is based on the emergence within the academy (or incursion into it, depending on your politics) of a distinctive strand of feminist theory and scholarship. The example of conflicting interpretations of mundane gestures, words and practices problematizes above all *social position*.

Interpretivism, *per se*, thinks of the interpreter as positioned in language, within a range of concepts and meanings. These meanings inevitably constitute the ingredients by means of which the interpreter can get to grips with an object of interpretation, and then constitute the points of reference that can be brought to bear in judging the success or acceptability of the interpretation. This idea of a *linguistic position* is also extended to the interpreter's audience, or those for whom the objects are interpreted. In a good deal of feminist theory, and elsewhere, we find the insistence that these subjects are not only linguistic, and epistemic, but social. Subjects inevitably occupy a *social standpoint*, and this social standpoint is every bit as important as, and indeed systematically connected with, their linguistic and epistemic standpoint (Hartsock 1983; Harding 1986: 141–53).

This insight has generated the huge corpus of feminist interpretation of the meaning of texts from a social standpoint which takes gender to be important; of practices, from a social standpoint which cannot take for granted that masculinities are epistemically, ethically or politically neutral; of terms, utterances, and concepts from a social standpoint which is sensitive to implications for sexual relations.

A good deal of this work is *sociologically commonsensical*. For instance, Baier spells out an interpretation of liberal individualism from the point of view of a woman – that is to say, a person who cannot avoid the issues of how to give children loving care, or who should take responsibility for reproductive decisions (1994: 7). I say this is 'commonsensical', not pejoratively, but meaning that, given the distribution of responsibilities, burdens and benefits in industrial societies, it is difficult to dissent from the sociological judgment that a creature with these particular charac- teristics is very much more likely to be a woman than a man. Others have proceeded from the standpoint of a 'mother' or a 'parent', and have asked how we can then interpret social contract theory, or the liberal ethical tradition, or conventional understandings of political priorities (Held 1990; Ruddick 1984). Nel Noddings (1984) takes the standpoint of 'teacher' as a starting-point for judging some conventional ethical approaches. Some have argued that the standpoint of the oppressed is peculiarly epistemically privileged: the person who stands in this place sees more, understands more, develops better social skills, than the dominator (Matsuda 1986; Smith 1987).

Debates about the relative merits and demerits of these projects can focus on a variety of issues. For instance, notwithstanding the failure of many philosophers to abstract themselves away from their social, specif- ically their gender, standpoint, it should nevertheless be an enduring aim of philosophy to do this. To substitute the standpoint of teacher, or woman, for that of detached man, is not to further this philosophical project. Philosophy, unlike social life, should not consist of competition and conflict between social positions. I shall return to this below. For now, it is important to notice that to argue that specific social standpoints creep into philosophical analysis and interpretation is not to imply that we lack the tools to analyse just this. A separate debate focuses on how strategically helpful, as well as morally valid, it is to elaborate the stand- point of 'mother' or 'woman' as the vantage-point for the development of philosophy and theory.

Consideration of this last question takes me to a discussion of the deployment of standpoint theory which is *sociologically critical* rather than commonsensical. If the social positions of woman or mother are them- selves the outcome of unequal power struggles, or of the sedimentation of the authoritative interpretations of priests, philosophers and judges, or of the use of material and symbolic force, it is a grievous mistake for women now to embrace them (Dietz 1985). Yet another tendency in feminist interpretation has been based on *sociological and philosophical irony*. The most notable proponent of this is Luce Irigaray, who takes up the standpoint of 'woman' as constructed in masculine texts. She turns the philosopher's concept of femininity as formless, undifferentiated, and unbounded against him; this mimesis provokes in the archetypically masculine reader precisely the fears that generate the negative category of woman in the first place. The writing brings the reader to read sexual difference as such (Irigaray 1991).

Irony, or something like it, is an important element elsewhere in feminist interpretation. In the encounter with the text and authoritative interpretations, not much more is needed than a simple reading – preferably out loud – of the relevant passages. The interpretation (the process) is done in the shared laughter; it barely has to be articulated else. Disgust, outrage, and genuine mirth are contained in this laughter, the laughter of the audience; it is these that adjudicate the interpretation (the product) as 'successful'. Laughter de-authorizes dominant interpretations. Perhaps the price of making an interpretation authoritative is that it is not funny; once it is funny, it perforce loses its authority with those who find it so. But paradoxically, feminist laughter also de-authorizes (in the eyes of their enemies) the feminist interpretation: feminist interpretation will be contested for the foreseeable future. A gladiatorial contest is set up here, of laughing interpreters and their supportive audience against dominant interpreters and theirs.

The anger in such mirth is an impetus to political action. There are, of course, disputes within feminist politics about strategies. The explosion of theory, the insistence upon the blurring of any sharp distinction between theory and practice, and the politicization already mentioned of mundane micro-relations have in turn led to a recent reaction which seeks to redefine the distinctions between these forms of political action, and action in the public sphere (Dietz 1985; Mouffe 1993). In the course of these debates, doubt has been expressed about the capacity of rhetorical strategies, like laughter, irony or textual redefinition, to dislodge dominant conceptions. Where interpretations are institutionalized, the battle has to be fought, in other words, on the terrain of those very institutions. Nevertheless, the terrain in which laughter and anger and reinterpretation proceed – the pages of journals, in theatre, in the seminar room and elsewhere – is also a properly political terrain.

Finally, and relatedly, a significant strand of feminist interpretation is *sociologically utopian*, although I hasten to add that these utopias – conceptions of how the world might be – are highly constrained by conceptions, interpretations, of how the world is. The answer to the question how the world is is a matter of interpretation. Whether an episode of child care is an episode of 'work'; whether a gesture is an insult, or an expression of structural power; whether a good is needed; whether a constraint is political – no amount of conceptual analysis settles the question of what counts as what in the real world. All of these, and countless other phenomena of social life, are the subjects of contested interpretations. By pinpointing the extent to which particular interpretations are consistent with widely accepted understandings, parties to these contests gain ground. By exploiting ambiguities of meaning, interpreters can redefine and resignify.

In so doing, interpreters and theorists can construct visions of how the world might be (Benhabib 1986). These utopian visions are quite explicitly grounded, though, in extant fragments of ways of life, extant meanings and understandings. Just as critique of texts articulates meanings that are suppressed, but present by implication, so this critique of social arrangements articulates possibilities that are already present.

Interpretivism and Communitarianism

We have met the fear that, because an interpreter has an idiosyncratic and unique position within discourse, and is in command of a unique set of concepts and understandings, interpretations are correspondingly subjectivist and incorrigible (Warnke 1992: 10). Most theorists, though, emphasize that interpretations are corrigible and acceptable by reference to conventional understandings (Skinner 1974: 284–5). The successful interpreter exploits their membership of, or at any rate, close acquaintanceship with, a group – the group whose members constitute the audience for their interpretations.

The question I wish now to address is: what is the nature of this group? And the answer to that question that I wish particularly to oppose is that it is a community.

According to Taylor, where there are shared meanings – and that meanings are shared is itself understood by those who share them – the relevant individuals are tied together by the special relationship of community. Common meanings, in this sense, are the basis of community (Taylor 1985a: 39). When we ask whose understandings must be appealed to in order to judge interpretations, we answer, the community's. But we should note the equivocation here: are common meanings constitutive of community? or are they a condition of community? We meet the same ambiguity in Sandel's discussion: common meanings – a common vocabulary and a background of implicit practices and understandings – constitute community. A spirit of benevolence, shared aims and particular values are not sufficient for community in this sense (Sandel 1982: 172). Whether this means that shared meanings are a necessary, or a sufficient, constituent of community is unclear from this and related passages in Sandel's argument. At this point I do not complain that these theorists interpret the concept community in a way that attributes to it a minimal content (although I want to take issue on this point too). My complaint is that the concept is analysed in a way that fails to address this equivocation, let alone resolve its ambiguity.

Of course, the concept of community is under-theorized and under-analysed, as well as ubiquitous, in political philosophy (Plant 1978). Theorists tend to invoke it, give examples of it, and illustrate the kind of conduct we might expect to find within it, but they rarely analyse it except very sketchily. It seems to me we can identify a clear fallacy here: the inference from shared meanings to some kind of collective, association or consociation seems reasonable; the inference to community does not.

It is commonly remarked that the concept community slips between a *descriptive* usage and a prescriptive or *evaluative* usage. It is also remark-able, but unremarked, that within the descriptive category, we find a good deal of slippage between community as *a relation*, and community as *an entity*. It seems to me that the very grammatical possibility of this slippage is partly responsible for the peculiar attractiveness of the term – compare 'community' with related terms like 'solidarity' and 'recip-rocity'. In speaking of community, theorists seem to be speaking of a concrete social formation or entity; and this seems to add substance to theory. In my view, this slippage is best seen, then, as part of a further element of the concept: community as above all a term that generates *rhetorical echoes* (Lacey 1996a: 112).

On the whole, analyses of community within political theory attend to the quality and kind of the relation between the putative members, and attempt to be noncommittal about the exact shape of the social entity. For instance, Mouffe characterizes community as an ethical relationship – the political community is constituted by an ethico-political bond which binds the participants (1994: 66–7). G. A. Cohen characterizes com-munity as a context in which we serve and are served, and our service responds to the needs of others (1994: 9–10). Obviously, both these characterizations add a good deal to Taylor's minimal conception focused on common meanings, although Mouffe adds that membership of political community requires the acceptance of a specific language of civil intercourse (1994: 67). In the context of legal theory, Dworkin conceptualizes the 'community of principle', which comes as close as is possible in the modern world to a true community (1986: 206–15). Although it is not always spelled out, these characterizations go beyond the putative facts of shared language, meanings or interpretations; they also carry an implication of members' *commitment* to continued common life. It is certainly made clear by serious sociological communitarians –

Murray Bookchin, for instance, emphasizes people's own economic power and their own 'institutionalization of the grass roots' (1995: 222). This takes us closer to the ordinary-language usage in such contexts as community action, community work, religious community and locality. Usually, sociological research reveals, people deploy the term 'community' (for instance, in talking about their local area) declaratively – they are declaring their own commitment to furthering common life – and persuasively – they are hoping that others will join them (Farrar 1995). That is, some actually existing social formation (a locality or neighbourhood, even a workplace or an interest group) is *described* as community with an explicitly *prescriptive* intent. The use of the term 'community', rather than 'neighbourhood', or 'locality', or 'network', and the appendage of the suffix community to 'gay', 'black', 'Protestant' and so on, also has another inescapable (although hardly ever articulated) connotation: that of transcendence. It is unwise to ignore the etymological relationship between community and 'communion': here we have the slippage from relationship to entity within the concept of a transcendent association of souls (Fraser 1987).

These two aspects, of commitment and of transcendence, give the term community its peculiarly powerful character. Just as 'community' is invoked in pursuit of commitment, so it is also invoked in pursuit of a sense of transcendent connectedness one with another. But the two aspects also make community, as a social entity, difficult to realize. Where people do build and sustain community, they need, on the one hand, to secure commitment and assent from members in some way, and on the other to enact – usually through the use of symbols, and the periodic enactment of ritual – the transcendence. This experience of transcendence is typically fleeting, although real enough. But it does not substitute for solid social relationships and practices as the foundation for social change and new ways of living. In addition, it is precisely these symbolic and ritual aspects of community that engender the dissent and resistance that is felt from, for instance, gay people who contest the inclusivity that such practices express. Of course, that communities are fragile does not make them less real, nor less worthy of our hopes. For the purposes of this chapter, though, my main point is that shared meanings, or shared interpretations, seem barely to warrant the epithet 'community'.

In any case, interpretation and the challenge of reinterpretations, the interrogation of concepts, the refusal to accept accepted meanings – all these disrupt any cohesion that might exist within the population of persons who share a natural language, or a set of meanings. Shared meanings are clearly a necessary threshold for any kind of interaction, including antagonism, dispute, argument: anything more than the most wordless physical violence. But the existence of a threshold tells us nothing about the quality or nature of the social relationships and collectivities that lie beyond it. Shared meaning, as the history of feminist and other political and social movements shows, can underpin unstable coalitions, fragile alliances, social groups of many degrees of robustness, enmities and antagonisms. Similarly, alliances and coalitions can be made across differences of meaning. Indeed, given any theory of meaning which is the least bit sceptical about meaning being fixed independent of context, then we had better be able to do this.

Feminism, Interdisciplinarity and Politics

I have argued that the view that interpretations can be validated (or not) by 'the community' is methodologically unhelpful. This does not mean that groups or populations of persons who share meanings and existing interpretations are not significant for the acceptance of interpretations: it seems almost trivial to say that this must be so.

I have also argued that interpretivism, or interpretation at least, is central in political theory and, indeed, in political practice. Disputes about meanings are important political disputes. Feminist theorists and activists then face the problem of how to validate, and secure acceptance of, their reinterpretations.

Undoubtedly, at moments when material relations are changing (as for instance the present period of entry of women into changing waged labour markets, the decline of traditional male occupations, and the reconfiguring of patterns of relationships within workplaces), it is easier to secure rather widespread acceptance of changes in meaning. The newly perceived importance of traditionally women's ways of relating to colleagues makes it easier to redefine as offensive certain patterns of relations that feminists, and women more generally, have always found offensive. But this is not to say that meaning change follows passively on material change – rather, the particular interpretations of material change that become widespread themselves depend on prior efforts to redefine material relations. Similarly, in so far as there is any hope of altering the norms and procedures of politics and public life in polities, it is important to have on the agenda, to have articulated, feminist interpretations of what politics means, and has meant, to and for women. It is important to have articulated feminist critique of the conduct of politics, and to have pulled out of present practices what is widely acceptable (albeit perhaps not dominant) and what is dominant (but not acceptable to the critics). It is only by building on existing normative fragments that we can realize utopias.

Like other social actors, feminists are both interpreters and the audience for interpretations. Acceptance or rejection of existing interpretations involves, in part, considering the social identities of the producer of the interpretation and the audience addressed – the conventional and shared meanings the interpreter was banking on in his efforts to have the interpretation accepted. Production of reinterpretations involves considering the social identities of the relevant audience(s), and partaking of (or exploiting) common meanings. Acceptance of feminist interpretations and reinterpretations requires shared understandings – shared, that is, across alliances or coalitions; or shared by those who stand on a threshold of agreement about values and understandings. But it is important that, at the same time as this is an appeal to or deployment of shared meanings, it is also a rejection of, dissent from, some accepted meanings. Feminist politics, for instance, refuses to share 'accepted' conceptions of the good or proper way to organize governance and work; it refuses to concede to the dominant diagnosis of how power is exercised, and who is oppressed in what respects.

If such dissent from shared meanings is to make any progress at all with the individuals who maintain the shared understanding, there must be a moment, a threshold, over which communication occurs. This is likely to be a slow and possibly painful process. It relies on difficult dialogue within shifting coalitions of interlocutors. Within these alliances, coalitions and conversations it is important for individuals to be aware of who their fellows are, if they are to make reliable judgments about assent to or dissent from interpretations.

This kind of insight is more apparent in feminist work than elsewhere. This is mainly because feminist research and theory has made plain the complexity of 'femininity' – and *ipso facto* of masculinity. Indeed, much work on gender casts doubt on the idea that here we have any determinate set of traits and social phenomena that actually constitute an internally consistent category.

In many discourses 'femininity' has no particular content apart from its difference from 'masculinity' – women are everything that men are not. Obviously, this does not constitute a possible identity to live up to. And gendered life is so replete with mimicry, ironic performance, and socially grounded attempts to instantiate specific gendered attributes, that the social critic is faced with a cacophonous pantomime of gender identities (Butler 1990). Other strands of political theory make assumptions, implicit or explicit, of what women will or might do. Theorists, like Baier, point out that liberal philosophers can ignore questions of the body and its reproduction, the care of children, and so on, only because they can reasonably presume that women will undertake certain tasks – theory, that is, exploits culturally encouraged traits and habits (1994: 7).

All this means that, in attending to the social standpoint of an interpreter or members of the audience for our own interpretations, we have to attend not only to people's material position, but also to their sense of who they are and with whom they feel allegiance and alliance. Here I am identifying a reflexively political aspect to interpretation itself. There is also an implication here for both political activity and political studies and theory. Political theory has an inevitably hypothetical element: it must contain propositions about what people will do under certain circumstances. In so far as it is prescriptive, it must exploit culturally encouraged traits and habits. Both of these aspects lock political scientists and theorists into interaction with practitioners of other disciplines. The whole interpretive approach commits the political theorist to an acknowledgement of the social basis of meaning, and the importance of practices.

This commitment to interdisciplinarity determinedly avoids any tendency to reduce politics, political phenomena and events to something else. It does not reduce politics to economics, whether exchange (as some liberalism does) or production (as in a good deal of Marxism); nor to 'culture' as some communitarians tend to. Neither does it, proscriptively, attempt to eliminate political relations in favour of traditional social stability – as in some varieties of conservatism.

Feminists have shared many of the antipathies to politics found in liberalism, Marxism, and elsewhere – although with a distinct inflection. They have insisted upon the political relevance and political nature (that is the relevance for rule and governance and relationships of power and authority) of personal conduct in private and domestic settings; they have included our organization of such homely events as meetings, and the running of projects and organizations, and the production and circulation of cultural artefacts – images, texts, performances. As I have emphasized, they have been aware of the power involved in making meanings stick, and the importance of authority in establishing interpretations. These tendencies have been coupled with suspicion of state power, and scepticism about the efficacy of legislation and, therefore, party and parliamentary strategies. On one hand, this has led to a correct identification of a political aspect to most social contexts and events; on another, there is an obvious danger of losing the specificity, and specific importance, of political relations.

In this connection, it is possible to identify the specifically political aspects of the vast range of social phenomena, events and relationships, without thereby committing ourselves to saying that the relevant event is, through and through, political. So, for instance, the authoritive interpretation of some behaviour as innocent mateyness, as against the dissenting interpretation of the same behaviour as an oppressive expression of social domination, has a political aspect, as well as linguistic, moral, social, psychological and doubtless other aspects. It is part of the task of political studies to conceptualize and study specifically political relationships and their connection with other – moral, economic and psychological – relationships between persons. But if we acknowledge that 'political' entities, institutions, relations and events are not *purely* political; if we acknowledge that there is no discrete chunk of the world (state capitals or city halls) where we can look and find just political things, then we are committed to interdisciplinarity.

Note

1 I consulted the following texts prior to working out this 'model': Hartsock 1983; MacIntyre 1981; Searle 1995; Skinner 1974, 1978, 1996; Taylor 1985a, 1985b; Walzer 1983, 1987; Warnke 1992; Winch 1990; Wittgenstein 1958.

References

Baier, Annette 1994. *Moral Prejudices: Essays on Ethics.* Cambridge, Mass.: Harvard University Press.

Beauvoir, Simone de. 1953. *The Second Sex.* London: Jonathan Cape.

Benhabib, Seyla. 1986. *Critique, Norm and Utopia.* New York: Columbia University Press.

Benhabib, Seyla, and Cornell, Drucilla, eds. 1987. *Feminism as Critique: Essays on the Politics of Gender in Late Capitalist Societies.* Cambridge: Polity Press.

Bookchin, M. 1995. *From Urbanization to Cities: Towards a New Politics of Citizenship,* rev. edn. London: Cassell.

Butler, Judith. 1990. *Gender Trouble: Feminism and the Subversion of Identity.* New York: Routledge.

Cohen, G. H. 1994. 'Back to Socialist Basics', *New Left Review,* 207, 3–16.

Coole, Diana. 1993. *Women in Political Theory: From Ancient Misogyny to Contemporary Feminism* 2nd edn. Hemel Hempstead: Harvester Wheatsheaf.

Dietz, Mary. 1985. 'Citizenship with a Feminist Face: The Problem with Maternal Thinking', *Political Theory,* 13.

Dworkin, Ronald. 1986. *Law's Empire.* London: Fontana.

Farrar, Max. 1995. 'Agency, Metaphor and Double Consciousness: Black Community Action in Leeds, 1970–95', Conference paper delivered to 'Ideas of Community', University of West of England, September 1995.

Fraser, John. 1987. 'Community, the Private and the Individual', *Sociological Review,* 35.

Frazer, Elizabeth, and Lacey, Nicola. 1993. *The Politics of Community: A Feminist Critique of the Liberal Communitarian Debate.* Hemel Hempstead: Harvester Wheatsheaf.

Frazer, Elizabeth, and Lacey, Nicola. 1994. 'Feminism, MacIntyre and the Concept of Practice', in John Horton and Susan Mendus, eds, *After MacIntyre: Critical Perspectives on the Work of Alisdair MacIntyre.* Oxford: Polity Press.

Giddens, A. 1976. *New Rules of Sociological Method.* London: Hutchinson.

Harding, Sandra. 1986. *The Science Question in Feminism*. Milton Keynes: Open University Press.

Hartsock, Nancy. 1983. 'The Feminist Standpoint: Developing the Ground for a Specifically Feminist Historical Materialism', in Sandra Harding and Merrill Hintikka, eds, *Discovering Reality: Feminist Perspectives on Epistemology, Metaphysics, Methodology and the Philosophy of Science*. Dordrecht: Reidel.

Held, Virginia. 1990. 'Mothering Versus Contract', in Jane Mansbridge, ed., *Beyond Self Interest*. Chicago: Chicago University Press.

Heyes, Cressida J. Forthcoming. 'Back to the Rough Ground: Wittgenstein, Essentialism and Feminist Methodologies', in Naomi Scheman, ed., *Rereading the Canon: Feminist Interpretations of Ludwig Wittgenstein*. Philadelphia: Penn State Press.

Irigaray, Luce. 1991. *Marine Lover of Friedrich Nietzsche* trans. Gillian C. Gill and Amante Marine. Paris: Les Editions de Minuit; New York: Columbia University Press.

Lacey, Nicola. 1996a. 'Community in Legal Theory: Idea, Ideal or Ideology', *Studies in Law, Politics and Society*, 15.

Lacey, Nicola. 1996b. 'Normative Reconstruction in Socio-Legal Theory', *Social and Legal Studies*, 5.

MacIntyre, Alasdair. 1981. *After Virtue*. London: Duckworth.

Matsuda, Mari. 1986. 'Liberal Jurisprudence and Abstracted Visions of Human Nature', *New Mexico Law Review*, 16.

Mouffe, Chantal. 1993. *The Return of the Political*. London: Verso.

Noddings, Nel. 1984. *Caring: A Feminine Approach to Ethics and Moral Education*. Berkeley: University of California Press.

Pateman, Carole. 1988. *The Sexual Contract*. Oxford: Polity Press.

Pateman, Carole. '"God Hath Ordained to Man a Helper": Hobbes, Patriarchy and Conjugal Right', in Mary Lyndon Shanley and Carole Pateman, eds, *Feminist Interpretations and Political Theory*. Cambridge: Polity Press.

Plant, Raymond. 1978. 'Community: Concept, Conception and Ideology', *Politics and Society*, 8.

Ruddick, Sara. 1984. *Maternal Thinking: Towards a Politics of Peace*. London: Women's Press.

Sandel, Michael. 1982. *Liberalism and the Limits of Justice*. Cambridge: Cambridge University Press.

Searle, John R. 1995. *The Construction of Social Reality*. Harmondsworth, Mddx: Penguin.

Shanley, Mary Lyndon, and Pateman, Carole, eds. 1991. *Feminist Interpretations and Political Theory*. Oxford: Polity Press.

Skinner, Quentin. 1974. 'Some Problems in the Analysis of Political Thought and Action', *Political Theory*, 2.

Skinner, Quentin. 1978. *The Foundations of Modern Political Thought*, 2 vols. Cambridge: Cambridge University Press.

Skinner, Quentin. 1996. 'From Hume's Intentions to Deconstruction and Back', *Journal of Political Philosophy*, 4.

Smith, Dorothy. 1987. 'A Sociology for Women', in Sandra Harding, ed., *Feminism and Methodology*. Milton Keynes: Open University Press.

Taylor, Charles. 1985a. 'Interpretation and the Sciences of Man', in *Philosophy and the Human Sciences*. Cambridge: Cambridge University Press.

Taylor, Charles. 1985b 'Self-Interpreting Animals', in *Human Agency and Language*. Cambridge: Cambridge University Press.

Tuana, Nancy, ed. 1989. *Feminism and Science*, Bloomington: Indiana University Press.

Walzer, Michael. 1983. *Spheres of Justice*. New York: Basic Books.

Walzer, Michael. 1987. *Interpretation and Social Criticism*. Cambridge Mass.: Harvard University Press.

Warnke, Georgia 1992. *Justice and Interpretation*. Oxford: Polity Press.

Winch, Peter. 1990 [1958]. *The Idea of a Social Science and its Relation to Philosophy* 2nd edn. London: Routledge.

Wittgenstein, Ludwig. 1958. *Philosophical Investigations*, trans. G. E. M. Anscombe. Oxford: Blackwell.

Wollstonecraft, Mary. 1792 [1929]. *A Vindication of the Rights of Woman*, London: Dent.

Woolf, Virginia. 1984. *A Room of One's Own* [1929] and *Three Guineas* [1938] ed. Hermione Lee. London: Chatto and Windus.

CHAPTER 11

The Political Philosophy of Deleuze and Guattari

Paul Patton

It is difficult to read poststructuralist philosophers as political theorists, since their work does not appear to engage with the problems and normative commitments of mainstream political theory. In the case of Deleuze and Guattari, this difficulty is compounded by their own highly idiosyncratic terminology: when they discuss politics, it is in terms of machinic assemblages, becomings, nomadism, forms of capture, processes of reterritorialization and deterritorialization, and the like. The concept of deterritorialization is particularly important and will be discussed further below. To illustrate its role in Deleuze and Guattari's political theory, and its relation to other concepts, consider the section of *A Thousand Plateaus* entitled 'Micropolitics and Segmentarity', in which they take up the concept of segmentation of social space as developed by anthropologists. They argue that the social fabric of modern capitalist society is segmented in a variety of ways, in its economic and political organization no less than in its language and its organization of desire. Different types of segmentation result in different kinds of line through social space: molar lines, which correspond to the forms of rigid segmentation found in bureaucratic and hierarchical institutions; molecular lines, which correspond to the fluid or overlapping forms of division characteristic of 'primitive' territoriality; and finally, lines of flight or deterritorialization, which are the paths along which things change or become transformed into something else.

As individuals and as collectivities, Deleuze and Guattari argue, we are composed of different kinds of lines. What they call 'micro-politics', 'schizoanalysis' or social 'cartography' may be understood as the study of these different lines and their interactions in a given social field. While lines of flight are associated with 'absolute deterritorialization', molar and molecular lines are associated with distinct kinds of territoriality.

237

These correspond to different ways of organizing or occupying social space. In the sections dealing with nomadism and the state-form in *A Thousand Plateaus*, Deleuze and Guattari contrast sedentary or state-governed social space with a nomadic relation to space. Although they sometimes contrast macro-politics and micro-politics with reference to these kinds of segmentation of social space, they insist that the distinction is not a matter of scale; nor is it a matter of material, as opposed to psychological, levels of social reality. It is a qualitative distinction between kinds of social space, rather than a numerical distinction between different spaces. Even the most rigidly hierarchical institution also has its molecular forms of association, its informal and unstable channels of influence and communication.

It is possible to translate some of this terminology into the language of anglophone political theory, and to find in the work of Deleuze and Guattari conceptions of freedom, power and domination, or even theories of the state and revolution (Patton 1994). But there is always a remainder that does not translate, a point at which the normative dimensions of their work do not map onto those of mainstream political theory. For example, they appear to be unconcerned with issues of political community; they are more interested in ways in which society is differentiated or divided than in ways in which it is held together. In their social theory, as well as in their account of individual subjectivity, Deleuze and Guattari privilege the processes of creative transformation and the lines of flight along which individuals or groups are transformed into something different to what they were before. It is possible to find in their work a conception of freedom, but one which corresponds neither to negative nor to positive freedom. The capacity to attain one's deepest goals, and the capacity to act without hindrance in accordance with one's desires, both imply a degree of stability in the assemblages of desire which define subjects of freedom. The work of Deleuze and Guattari points to the ways in which individuals or societies may undergo radical transformation in connection with a given line of flight, and suggests that freedom consists in the capacity to undertake or to withstand such ruptures. Their ideal of freedom is closer to Nietzsche's ideal of self-overcoming, with all that this implies regarding the loss of the self that has been overcome.

Political Orientations

In everyday political terms, the sympathies of Deleuze and Guattari were those of the post-1968 libertarian French left. Their public intellectual activity did not distinguish them from a variety of other neo-Marxist, existentialist, anarchist or left-liberal intellectuals who signed the same

petitions and took part in the same demonstrations. They were associated with a number of causes, such as the rights of prisoners and immigrant workers, support for Italian intellectuals accused of complicity with
terrorism, opposition to the French nuclear strike force and to the Gulf
War, to name but a few. They shared many of the political and theoretical
orientations common to this milieu: a concern for the micro-politics of
social life, for the political effectivity of desire, and for the unconscious
investments which play a part in macro-political movements. While they
were neither semioticians nor theorists of 'discourse' in Foucault's sense
of the term, they acknowledged the importance of language and its pragmatic dimension for modern political life. While they were not Marxists
in any traditional sense, an anti-capitalist thematic pervades all their
writings, up to and including their final collaboration, *What is Philosophy?*
(1994). In an interview with Antonio Negri first published in 1990,
Deleuze reaffirms his view that any political philosophy must take
account of the nature and evolution of capitalism, which he describes as
a fantastic system for the fabrication of great wealth and great suffering.
He goes on to point out that what they found most useful in Marx was
'his analysis of capitalism as an immanent system that's constantly over-
coming its own limitations, and then coming up against them once more
in broader form, because its fundamental limit is Capital itself' (Deleuze
1995: 171). In *Anti-Oedipus* and *A Thousand Plateaus*, they develop their
own account of capitalism as a unique mode of co-ordination and regulation which is immanent rather than transcendent to the social field, in
contrast to earlier forms of empire which operated by transcendence and
by the 'overcoding' or capture of existing social and economic processes.
Whereas earlier forms of empire extracted rent or other forms of
obligatory payment, Deleuze and Guattari argue that capital functions in
the manner of an axiomatic system which is indifferent to the content of
the propositions it connects: it operates by means of the axiomatic
conjugation of decoded flows of labour, money, commodities and,
increasingly, of information.

Although Deleuze and Guattari accept aspects of Marx's social and
economic theory, there are significant points at which their conceptual
and normative commitments do not map onto traditional Marxist views.
They reject the Marxist philosophy of history in favour of a differential
typology of the macro and micro assemblages which determine the
character of social life. They reject the idea that contradiction is the
motor of historical progress: for them, a society is defined less by its
contradictions than its lines of flight (1987: 216). On their account,
capitalism is a deterritorializing process as well as a reterritorializing one;
hence the importance of the idea mentioned above, that capitalism
continually pushes back its own limits. Capitalist economic organization

may indeed constitute an axiomatic system inseparable from the fabric of modern social life, but it does not follow that particular axioms cannot be removed or replaced by others. Deleuze and Guattari do not envisage global revolution at the level of molar economic and political institutions; rather, they advocate a process of experimentation that amounts to permanent revolution at the molecular level. They provide a conceptual language in which to describe the impact of social movements that impose new political demands upon the qualitative or cultural dimensions of social life.

What is important, in their view, is a 'revolutionary becoming' which is in principle open to anyone (Deleuze and Parnet 1987: 147). What they mean by this is not simply resistance to the mechanisms of capture and reterritorialization which define forms of the state, but the invention of new forms of subjectivity (feminist, ecological, queer) and new forms of connection between these deterritorialized elements of political life. Recent examples might include alliances such as those forged between a women's movement and a peace movement, or between a politics of indigenous land claims and an environmental politics. It is not the capture of state power which interests them, but rather the forms of social change which take place alongside or beneath any given form of state, and the manner in which these changes react upon political institutions themselves. More generally, they contrast the dynamism of such forms of social nomadism with the essentially parasitic and reactive character of state power. They point to examples from logic and computational theory, as well as the natural world, to show that centralized control mechanisms are not essential to the functioning of complex systems (Deleuze and Guattari 1987: 15–18). Does this mean that Deleuze and Guattari should be considered a new species of anarchist?

Todd May has suggested that the political perspective which they share with some other poststructuralists may be considered an offshoot of the anarchist tradition: 'This new anarchism retains the ideas of intersecting and irreducible local struggles, of a wariness about representation, of the political as investing the entire field of social relationships, and of the social as a network rather than a closed holism, a concentric field, or a hierarchy' (1994: 85). However, May also notes that these poststructuralist thinkers abandon several key assumptions of classical anarchist thought, such as the repressive conception of power, and a belief in the essentially benign and co-operative character of human nature. While their poststructuralist politics does share the anarchist suspicion of political representation, it is no less suspicious of attempts to turn the principles of non-coercive and non-hierarchical organization into a blueprint for society as a whole. As May points out, it remains a tactical rather than a strategic style of political thought, directed at particular or local forms of revolutionary-becoming rather than wholesale social change.

Up to this point, I have emphasized the terminological inventiveness of Deleuze and Guattari and their normative commitments; my intention is to suggest that they represent a novel political perspective, shared perhaps by others such as Lyotard and Foucault. I now want to consider the sense in which, by creating new concepts and new means for the expression of this political perspective, they are engaged in political philosophy of a thoroughly conventional kind. I shall do this first by considering the meta-philosophical reflections set out in *What is Philosophy?* Second, I will argue that the concepts they put forward are as important for their normative content as for their descriptive value. Finally, I will return to the concept of deterritorialization in order to demonstrate the peculiar normativity of their political philosophy. Deleuze and Guattari outline a conception of philosophy which in many respects parallels Foucault's description of his genealogical approach as a form of critical engagement with current limits to thought and action. Like Foucault, they consider philosophy to be inherently political, a form of critical reflection upon the present. While they have no illusions about the efficacy of philosophy alone, they argue that it does and should have a utopian vocation. Despite their reservations about the term 'utopia', they suggest that 'it is with utopia that philosophy becomes political and takes the criticism of its own time to its highest point' (Deleuze and Guattari 1994: 99).

In their own philosophy of nature as well as their political philosophy, it is the concept of deterritorialization which bears the weight of the utopian aspirations of Deleuze and Guattari. They invent this concept in *Anti-Oedipus*, then refine and extend it in *A Thousand Plateaus* before applying it to thought itself in *What is Philosophy?*[1] They use it to describe social and economic processes such as those which Marx described in *Capital* in his chapter on primitive accumulation: in their terms, Marx recounts the deterritorialization of money from the sphere of exchange which occurs once it can circulate as capital, along with the deterritorialization of rural workers which occurred as a result of the Enclosure Acts, and the consequent reterritorialization of labour in the early forms of capitalist industry. Fundamental to the concept of deterritorialization is the contrast between earth and territory (*terre* and *territoire*): like Spinoza's *natura naturans* and *natura naturata*, earth and territory are the two components or dimensions of nature. Territory is in the first instance territorialized earth, but it produces its own movements of deterritorialization; conversely, earth gives rise to processes of reterritorialization and the constitution of new territories. Deleuze and Guattari align philosophy with the creative aspect of this complex process, describing it as utopian in a sense that involves the absolute deterritorialization of the present and therefore the possibility of creating new forms of individual and collective identity. By its very nature, they argue, philosophy summons forth 'a new earth and a people that does not yet exist' (1994: 108).

Philosophy, Concepts and Events

In an interview published at the same time as *A Thousand Plateaus*, Deleuze described his work with Guattari as 'philosophy, nothing but philosophy, in the traditional sense of the word' (Deleuze 1980: 99). By philosophy, he means the invention or fabrication of concepts. In some respects, this is an uncontroversial idea: political philosophy provides many examples of conceptual invention, from Plato's *Republic* to modern concepts of civil society, justice, power and community. The novelty of Deleuze's conception of philosophy emerges only when his concept of 'concept' is examined more closely. *What is Philosophy?* elaborates the constructivist conception of philosophy which had been more or less explicit throughout Deleuze's earlier work. This conception is summed up in Nietzsche's comment that philosophers 'must no longer accept concepts as a gift, nor merely purify and polish them, but first *make* and create them, present them and make them convincing' (1968: 220). Such a conception implies an object peculiar to philosophy as well as a particular skill, namely the ability to bring out the 'potentiality of the concept'. The philosopher is 'expert in concepts and in the lack of them': the philosopher knows which are not viable because they are arbitrary or inconsistent, and which ones are well formed, consistent and therefore likely to be effective (Deleuze and Guattari 1994: 3). I propose to illustrate their claims about the nature of philosophical concepts, and the constructivism of this account, using the concept of the social contract as an example.

A primary thesis is that concepts are singularities: 'Every creation is singular, and the concept as a specifically philosophical creation is always a singularity' (Deleuze and Guattari 1994: 7). But a concept is always a complex singularity: concepts are always a matter of articulation, of establishing certain kinds of linkage between components. Thus in the case of Hobbes's social contract, there are a number of component concepts, each with its own history and internal complexity. These include the state of nature, the restless desire for power, human reason, and the sovereign or Leviathan which results from the compact. A change in one of more of these elements changes the nature of the contract. This occurs in Locke, when the parties to the contract are characterized not as subjects of a relentless will to power but as property owners subject to natural laws; and in Rousseau, with the introduction of the concept of the general will. Rawls's contractarianism involves the altogether different concept of a hypothetical original position in which rational agents choose principles of social justice behind a veil of ignorance as to their own social position and fortunes. In each case, the concept of a social contract is singular, and its singularity is determined by the complex relations between its components.

Concepts also have a history, which may include their history as components of other concepts and their relations to particular problems: 'A concept lacks meaning to the extent that it is not connected to other concepts and is not linked to a problem that it resolves or helps to resolve' (Deleuze and Guattari 1994: 79). The concept of contract has a long history in political thought prior to Hobbes. It is transformed in part by virtue of the specific problem to which he relates it, namely the constitution and legitimation of civil authority. Because concepts are always created in relation to particular problems, and because different problems themselves may be interconnected, any given concept is located in a particular nexus of problems, and hence, in a series of virtual relations to other concepts. The concept may be modified or recast by being brought into relation to a new problem and new concepts. The history of a given concept is not linear but may zig-zag through a variety of different problems: 'In any concept, there are usually bits or components that come from other concepts, which correspond to other problems' (Deleuze and Guattari 1994:18).

Deleuze and Guattari thus conceive of concepts as open-ended totalities which contain the potential for links to other concepts. In this respect, their conception resembles Wittgenstein's notion of open concepts, which was once used to support the thesis of the 'essential contestability' of political concepts. However, Deleuze and Guattari are concerned less with the undecidability of particular concepts than with the manner in which virtual relations with other concepts constitute the 'becoming' of the concept in question. This refers to the particular paths along which the concept might be transformed into something else. These paths derive from the manner in which components of a given concept may enter into proximity with those of other concepts, zones in which the elements of one concept cannot be discerned from those of another. Consider the concept of power which informs Hobbes's social contract: his argument – that individuals in the state of nature become caught up in a competitive drive for ever more power – appears to anticipate Nietzsche's will to power. In fact, it is not the same concept of power in each case. From the Nietzschean perspective of power as an active force, Hobbes's conception of power is reactive; his social contract amounts to the institution of a community of slaves, whose only remedy for the inability to keep promises is to establish a power sufficient to compel observance by fear of punishment. Hobbes does canvass, only to put aside as implausible, another basis upon which people might be held to their contracts: namely, the moral strength of those individuals whose pride does not permit them to break their word. By contrast, Nietzsche invokes precisely this noble character type in envisaging the possibility of a sovereign individual 'who has the right to make a promise' (1994: 40). Nietzsche is commonly criticized for his individualism and his lack of any concept of political community. Yet by retracing this path from a reactive, towards an active, modality of power, which must be regarded as a potential inherent in Nietzsche's concept, we can envisage a transformation in the concept of political community which is the outcome of the social contract (Patton 1993: 158–9).

The components of a concept are not like individual terms falling under a given concept as in the set theoretical model of concepts as extensional classes. Rather, they are intensive elements, pure singularities such as the individual subject of power, natural law, the state of nature and so on. Unlike the situation in science, where concepts are extensive and hierarchized, Deleuze and Guattari argue that philosophical concepts have 'neither constants nor variables but pure and simple variations'; these are internally ordered according to the zones or thresholds of interconnection that make up the internal consistency of a particular concept (1994: 20). Concepts may therefore be understood as a certain kind of 'rendering consistent' of their components. The components and their consistency in a particular concept are two distinct dimensions of the concept, but they are related in that the consistency is established only by means of the existence of a certain 'communication' between the components. For example, in Hobbes, the relative weakness of human beings, combined with their rationality, ensures acceptance of the rational precepts or laws of nature that lead to the compact with the sovereign. On this account, a philosophical concept has as much in common with a film or a piece of music as it does with a demonstrative statement. Like a concept, a film represents nothing. Rather, it creates its own universe: it has a plane of consistency, characters and a style of composition, which are like so many intensive features of the film as a whole. Just as we might say that a film does not exist apart from its components (its shots, sequences, its assemblages of sound and image), so Deleuze and Guattari describe the concept as the intensive and variable unity of all its components: in these terms, a concept is 'the point of coincidence, condensation or accumulation of its own components' (1994: 20).

Deleuze and Guattari insist upon the creativity of philosophy and upon the importance of creating new concepts; this suggests both affinities with, and differences from, other intellectual activities. They allow that not all forms of creative thought need produce concepts. On the contrary, they use the term 'concept' to distinguish the object and materials of philosophy from those of science and art, suggesting that 'only philosophy creates concepts in the strict sense' (1994: 5). Science aims at the representation of states of affairs by means of mathematical or propositional functions; art does not aim at representation at all, but at the capture and expression in a given medium of the objective content of particular sensations. Philosophy's exclusive right to concept creation means that it has a distinct object and vocation, but no 'pre-eminence or privilege' with regard to these other activities. Art, science and philosophy each construct their own distinctive planes as a means of imposing order upon chaos: art constructs planes of composition, just as science continually reconstitutes its planes of reference, and philosophy transforms its planes of immanence.

Philosophy shares certain characteristics with each of its neighbouring forms of thought. It is like art, especially modern art, in that it does not refer to or represent independently existing objects or states of affairs; but it is like science in that it fulfils a cognitive rather than an affective function. Science provides knowledge of states of affairs, things and processes that are defined as external to its functions. By contrast, philosophical concepts do not refer to objects or states of affairs but express events. The concept is knowledge of a particular kind, Deleuze and Guattari argue, but 'what it knows is the pure event' (1994: 33). There is thus a twofold semantic difference between philosophical and scientific statements, which encompasses both the nature of their respective objects and their relation to those objects: scientific statements refer to bodies and states of affairs, while philosophical statements express events. It follows that philosophy does not provide discursive knowledge of the kind provided by the sciences. It does not provide proof of its claims in a manner that may be disputed from the standpoint of the facts. Concepts are not like scientific propositions, which are defined by their reference; concepts are like works of art, which do not refer to objects or states of affairs outside them. Concepts are autopoetic, self-positing entities, defined not by their relations to things or states of affairs but by their internal and external consistency, by the relations between their elements as well as by their relations to other concepts. In this sense, Deleuze and Guattari argue, the concept 'has no *reference*: it is self-referential, it posits itself and its object at the same time as it is created' (1994: 22).

In part, what is at issue here is a distinction between thinking and knowing. This distinction may be traced back to Kant's distinction between concepts of understanding and ideas of reason, and it resonates throughout Deleuze's defence of non-representational conceptions of thought in his earlier work. In *Difference and Repetition*, with explicit reference to Kant's transcendental Ideas, Deleuze developed a conception of Ideas as the specific objects of thought in terms that closely resemble the later account of concepts. For Kant, however, philosophy provides a non-empirical knowledge of the transcendental conditions of empirical, moral and aesthetic judgment; for Deleuze and Guattari, in contrast, philosophy provides a non-empirical knowledge of pure events. These are incorporeal entities that subsist over and above their empirical actualizations, in the sense that the social contract is the pure event of the incorporation of political society under a rule of law; it cannot be reduced to its actualization in different societies at particular moments. In a material sense, Deleuze and Guattari allow that events are indistinguishable from the bodies and states of affairs in which they are actualized, but the specific task of philosophy is to extract events from the ongoing encounters between bodies and states of affairs: 'Every concept shapes and reshapes the event in its own way. The greatness of a philosophy is measured by the nature of the events to which its concepts summon us or that it enables us to release in concepts' (1994: 34).

Moreover, it is not just any event which philosophy seeks to extract but those hitherto unconceptualized events that shape our present and future reality: philosophy creates new concepts, and when it extracts an event from bodies and states of affairs the task is 'always to give them a *new* event' (Deleuze and Guattari 1994: 33). Deleuze always aligned his conception of philosophy with that of Nietzsche on two points: opposition to those whose ultimate aim is the recognition of what exists; and preference for an untimely thought which seeks to invent new possibilities for life. Foucault invokes a similar conception of thought in his introduction to *The Use of Pleasure*, when he suggests that philosophy consists in 'the critical work that thought brings to bear on itself'. He asks rhetorically: 'In what does it consist, if not the endeavour to know how and to what extent it might be possible to think differently, instead of legitimating what is already known?' (1985: 9). Similarly, when Deleuze and Guattari suggest that philosophy is a vector of absolute deterritorialization, they mean that it is a form of experimentation, a means of acting upon present social reality. Obviously, philosophy as the creation of concepts cannot by itself bring about or actualize what its concepts express (political society under a rule of law, justice, equality between the sexes), but it contributes to this process. The characterization of a new event affords new means of description and action. It may enable us to become conscious of the dynamics in which we are engaged, and to act in awareness of the becomings to which we are subject. In these terms, philosophy's utopian vocation is achieved when the events to which a philosophy gives expression are those which are at work in the present and which point towards a different future: 'the concept is the contour, the configuration, the constellation of an event to come' (Deleuze and Guattari 1994: 32–3). In *Difference and Repetition*, Deleuze described the act of thought as a dice-throw, meaning that thinking is a form of experimentation. For the same reason, Deleuze and Guattari comment: 'Philosophy does not consist in knowing and is not inspired by truth. Rather, it is categories like Interesting, Remarkable or Important that determine success or failure' (1994: 82). The Interesting, Remarkable or Important concepts are those which summon 'a new earth and a new people', those which act upon the present for the benefit of a different future.

However, it is not for philosophy itself to decide which concepts express events of this kind. Deleuze and Guattari link their account of the utopian vocation of philosophy to a pragmatic response to the question of the value of particular philosophical concepts. While philosophy involves the determination of events and their attribution to bodies and states of affairs, the value of such thought lies outside itself. Philosophy can offer guidelines for well-formed, as opposed to flimsy, concepts; but it cannot offer criteria for judging the importance of events, nor rules for the attribution of events to states of affairs. One of the advantages of this pragmatic constructivism is that it enables us to understand why philosophical criticism alone is largely ineffective. A concept such as the social contract cannot be disproved by reference to the facts, or even by another concept of the origin of political community; it can only be displaced. For example, the contractarian tradition might be discredited by drawing attention to the implicit sexual contract on which the social contract is founded (Pateman 1988). Alternatively, the classical conception of a uniform citizenry subject to a single body of law, upon which the contract is founded, might be challenged by drawing attention to the requirements of social justice for indigenous populations in postcolonial societies (Tully 1995).

Deleuze and Guattari give a constructivist account of philosophy, which appears to raise a problem for the apparent descriptiveness of much of their writing. Their account of capitalism as an immanent axiomatic system, mentioned above, provides one example of an obvious descriptive claim. Deleuze also published under his own name a short 'Postscript on Control Societies'. In it he sought to supplement Foucault's analysis of disciplinary power in *Discipline and Punish* by arguing that new mechanisms of control had displaced the techniques of power that Foucault described (Deleuze 1995: 177–82). What are we to make of such apparently empirical claims? Negri sees in them a kind of neo-Marxist social science concerned to trace the evolution of capitalism and its forms of economic, social and political regulation. He finds in *A Thousand Plateaus* 'the fundamental elements of the renewal of historical materialism, in function of the new dimensions of capitalistic development' and sees the book as providing 'a perfectly operational phenomenology of the present' (Negri 1995: 104, 108).[2] Granted that concepts play a significant descriptive role in the social theory of Deleuze and Guattari, comments such as these seem to miss something essential. The primary concern is not empirical social science, but normative political philosophy. The descriptive function of their concepts is subordinate to the ethical function served by giving expression to particular events. In effect, in describing concepts as non-referential, Deleuze and Guattari say no more and no less than Foucault does when he claims that political philosophy (his own included) produces fictions.[3] The concept of the social contract is acknowledged, even by its defenders, to be a fiction. Its function is not to represent an actual state of affairs, but to sustain a larger fiction about the nature of modern political societies: namely, that they are in principle composed of more or less autonomous, and more or less rational, individual subjects. This fiction serves to legitimate the existence of centralized government by suggesting that the free consent of those subjects is the ultimate moral foundation of government. Deleuze and Guattari, in their account of philosophical concepts, give a precise sense in which such concepts are fictions. Moreover, they spell out a sense in which philosophical fictions can nevertheless produce effects of truth and, as Foucault says, 'fiction' or help to bring into being something which does not exist.

Ethics of Deterritorialization

On the basis of this account of philosophy and the peculiar effectiveness of its concepts, we can assess more clearly the contribution of Deleuze and Guattari to political thought. Ultimately, this must be judged by reference to the particular concepts they have created. As suggested above, they propose concepts that do not map onto even the most enduring fictions of Western political thought. They are concerned with neither the legitimation of government, nor its delegitimation, but rather with the transformation of existing forms of government of self and others. Their social theory involves no reference to individual subjects of freedom or autonomy, much less to notions of contract or consent. It is couched entirely in non-subjectivist terms, and it refers only to abstract assemblages, lines and processes of various kinds. They propose concepts that express movements of individual or social differentiation as well as capture, individual self-overcoming as well as self-constitution. In all cases, the primary processes are the movements of transformation of existing identities. Deleuze and Guattari describe a world in which the overriding tendency is deterritorialization. Stable identities or territories are secondary formations upon the mobile earth. This ontology is an ethics in Spinoza's sense. Its normative commitments are immanent to its philosophy of nature as well as its social ontology. In all cases, it presents a world understood as a complex of interconnected assemblages (earth, territory, forms of deterritorialization and reterritorialization), where the overriding norm is that of absolute deterritorialization.

At the end of *A Thousand Plateaus*, the authors outline a normative typology of processes of deterritorialization; they distinguish three distinct types on the model of the three lines of social segmentation discussed at the beginning. The first is the case in which the deterritorialized element is immediately subjected to forms of reterritorialization which enclose or obstruct its line of flight. In this case, deterritorialization is negative. In the second case, deterritorialization is positive but goes nowhere because it fails to connect with other forces or lines of flight. In this case, deterritorialization remains relative. The third and most important case, from an ethical point of view, is that of absolute deterritorialization: 'Deterritorialization is absolute when it . . . brings about the creation of a new earth, in other words, when it connects lines of flight, raises them to the power of an abstract vital line . . .' (Deleuze and Guattari 1987: 510). This refers to a type of movement qualitatively different from relative, or merely quantitative, change. It has to do with the creation of new territories, and of new subjectivities which inhabit those territories in nomadic rather than sedentary fashion. While the molar dimension of individual or collective life can generate forms of relative deterritorialization, it is the molecular or nomadic planes of social existence which give rise to absolute deterritorialization.

Deterritorialization is defined with deceptive simplicity as the movement or process by which something escapes or departs from a given territory (Deleuze and Guattari 1987: 508). Yet it is a complex concept in a number of ways: first, because it forms a pair with the corresponding movement of reterritorialization; second, because each of these processes involves at least two elements, namely the territory which is being left behind or reconstituted and the deterritorializing element. A territory of any kind always includes 'vectors of de-territorialization', either because the territory itself is inhabited by dynamic movements or processes or because the assemblage which sustains it is connected to other assemblages. In the case of Marx's account of primitive accumulation, the development of commodity markets is one such vector of deterritorialization in relation to the social and economic space of feudal agriculture, encouraging the shift to large-scale commercial production. The conjugation of the stream of displaced labour with the flow of deterritorialized money capital provided the conditions under which capitalist industry could emerge. In this sense, Deleuze and Guattari point out, 'deterritorialization is never simple but always multiple and composite', as well as being 'inseparable from correlative reterritorializations' (1987: 508–9).

Reterritorialization does not mean returning to the original territory, but the different forms of reconnection or rebinding of a deterritorialized element in connection with some other assemblage. In this context, Deleuze and Guattari distinguish between the *connection* of deterritorialized flows, which refers to the ways in which distinct deterritorializations can interact to accelerate one another; and the *conjugation* of distinct flows, which refers to the ways in which one may incorporate or 'overcode' another, thereby effecting a relative blockage of its movement (1987: 220). This concept of conjugation opens up a 'zone of indiscernibility' through which the concept of reterritorialization may be connected to concepts of state and the forms of capture associated with historically distinct kinds of state. What they call the state-form is an abstract machine of capture; it includes among its specific actualizations the different kinds of imperial, ideological and monarchical capture effected by various kinds of political state. On their account, capital constitutes a novel form of capture because it conjugates the flows of money and commodities from within. As a result, it inverts the previous relationship between state and economic capture, since modern nation-states become 'models of realization' of this axiomatic system.

Deleuzian ethics is not prescriptive, but it does offer a conceptual language in which to describe different responses to processes of deterritorialization and reterritorialization. Depending upon the level of the analysis and the nature of the individual assemblages, these responses might be interpreted as moral attitudes, micro-political or macro-political tactics, or even principles of institutional design. Depending upon the subject position adopted within the complex dynamics of any such process, they might be used to characterize responses from the perspective of the deterritorializing or the deterritorialized assemblage. It may be helpful to conclude by suggesting some contemporary applications. Consider the event of colonization as this was replayed throughout the New World between the sixteenth and nineteenth centuries. As noted above, the fundamental opposition between earth and territory implies a contrast between a primary surface or field of potentiality, and the forms of organization, regulation or codification to which this is subjected. The occupation and clearing of land was a primary modality of colonial territorialization: it formed a basis on which the European institutions of property, law and government could subsequently impose their own secondary reterritorializations. William Connolly points out that '*territory* derives from *terrere*, meaning to frighten, to terrorize, to exclude' (1995: xxii). Certainly the terrorization and exclusion of indigenous peoples was a precondition of the formation of modern territorial states in many parts of the New World.

In Australia, this was accompanied by a legal reterritorialization which denied the existence of any form of indigenous title to land, on the grounds that the only peoples present were so lacking in social or political organization as to be incapable of such rights. In *Mabo v. Queensland* (1992), the Australian High Court recognized a form of native title at common law for the first time since colonization. Against the background of effective legal capture of the land, which was considered to be the status quo in Australian law prior to this judgment, this recognition of native title, and the admission that it could survive the Crown's claim to sovereignty, opened a path of legal and political deterritorialization. The judgment created legal grounds on which native title could be established, thus reclaiming a quantity of indigenous land from the mass of unalienated Crown land. In strictly legal terms, this was never more than a form of relative deterritorialization of the legal status quo, since the overriding right of the Crown to annul such title by grants of land remained in place. Even so, in political and economic terms, it amounted to a line of flight that threatened to disrupt important state interests, notably mining investment and pastoral property values. The government of the day was therefore impelled to undertake a secondary reterritorialization by legislative means: it passed the *Native Title Act 1993*, which served to validate mining and other leases, and to regulate the procedure by which native title claims could be made. Over and above the immediate economic and political interests at stake, this response amounts to the reaffirmation of the integrity of a colonial society founded upon a primary territorialization and exclusion. A more generous response might have exemplified what Connolly calls 'an *ethos of critical responsiveness* to social movements seeking to redefine their relational identities' (1995: xvi). Connolly finds in such an ethos the basis for a far-reaching revision in the political imaginary of contemporary democratic societies. In the present case, such an ethos might have expressed a capacity to accommodate the indigenous population's right to land, along with a capacity to accept the revision of the moral and legal boundaries of the colonial society.

On the other hand, consider the possible responses to this postcolonial line of flight from the standpoint of the indigenous land rights movement. One response might seek to resist any secondary reterritorialization, and to maintain as far as possible a legally and politically open space in which native title claims might be pursued. This would be to maintain a space of becoming in which as many options as possible were kept open.[4] In Deleuzian terms, this corresponds to a purely negative deterritorialization. Creative reterritorialization is absent. A different response might seek to pursue the legal and political lines of flight, but always with a view to establishing and maintaining productive connections with other political forces. The example of an alliance between indigenous landowners and Greens serves to illustrate what is meant by the connection, as opposed to the conjugation, of relative deterritorializations. The possibility of further connection between such creative political initiatives and a responsive national polity might lead to the emergence of 'a new earth and a new people'. In other words, the creation of new forms of economic and cultural independence for indigenous communities, along with new boundaries to the self-conception and power of the national community in relation to them, would be a form of absolute deterritorialization of the colonial polity.

Notes

I am grateful to Andrew Vincent and especially Moira Gatens for their helpful comments on earlier drafts of this chapter.

1   The term derives from Lacan's use of 'territorialization' to refer to the imprint of maternal care and nourishment on the child's libido, and the resultant formation of part-objects and erogenous zones out of the conjugation of particular organs and orifices such as mouth–breast. In *Anti-Oedipus*, Deleuze and Guattari used 'deterritorialization' in this psychoanalytic context to refer to the freeing of the 'schizophrenic' libido from such pre-established objects of investment (Holland 1991: 57). In *A Thousand Plateaus*, the concept is further developed and applied in a variety of contexts, to musical as well as social 'territories', to animal behaviour as well as language.

2   In similar fashion, Best and Kellner read *Anti-Oedipus* as 'a materialist, historically grounded, Foucauldian-inspired critique of modernity with a focus on capitalism, the family and psychoanalysis' (1991: 85).

3   'I am well aware that I have never written anything but fictions. I do not mean to say, however, that truth is therefore absent. It seems to me that the possibility exists for fiction to function in truth, for a fictional discourse to induce effects of truth, and for bringing it about that a true discourse engenders or manufactures something that does not as yet exist, that is, "fictions" it' (Foucault 1980:193).

4   Such a refusal of closure would correspond to the critical gesture of deconstruction in so far as this is modelled upon the proliferation of the signifying relation. Thereby every sign defers to another sign and meaning is disseminated in the constant deferral from sign to sign (Deleuze and Guattari 1987: 112).

References

Best, Steven, and Kellner, Douglas. 1991. *Postmodern Theory: Critical Interrogations.* New York: Guildford Press.

Connolly, William E. 1995. *The Ethos of Pluralization.* Minneapolis: University of Minnesota Press.

Deleuze, Gilles. 1980. 'Entretien 1980' (with Catherine Clement), *L'Arc*, 49 (rev. edn).

Deleuze, Gilles. *Difference and Repetition*, trans. Paul Patton. London: Athlone Press; New York: Columbia University Press.

Deleuze, Gilles. 1995. *Negotiations, 1972–1990*, trans. Martin Joughin. New York: Columbia University Press.

Deleuze, Gilles, and Guattari, Felix. 1987. *A Thousand Plateaus*, trans. Brian Massumi. Minneapolis: University of Minnesota Press.

Deleuze, Gilles, and Guattari, Felix. 1994. *What is Philosophy?*, trans. Hugh Tomlinson and Graham Burchell. New York: Columbia University Press.

Deleuze, Gilles, and Parnet, Claire. 1987. *Dialogues*, trans. Hugh Tomlinson and Barbara Habberjam. London: Athlone Press; New York: Columbia University Press.

Foucault, Michel. 1980. *Power/Knowledge: Selected Interviews and Other Writings, 1972–1977*, ed. Colin Gordon. Brighton: Harvester.

Foucault, Michel. 1984. 'What is Enlightenment?', *The Foucault Reader* ed. Paul Rabinow. New York: Pantheon.

Foucault, Michel. 1985. *The Use of Pleasure: Volume 2 of The History of Sexuality*, trans. Robert Hurley. New York: Pantheon.

Gatens, Moira. 1996. 'Through a Spinozist Lens: Ethology, Difference, Power', in Paul Patton, ed., *Deleuze: A Critical Reader*. Oxford and Cambridge, Mass.: Blackwell.

Holland, Eugene W. 1991. 'Deterritorializing "Deterritorialization" – From the *Anti-Oedipus* to *A Thousand Plateaus*', *Substance*, 66.

May, Todd. 1994. *The Political Philosophy of Poststructuralist Anarchism.* University Park: Pennsylvania State University Press.

Negri, Antonio. 1995. 'On Gilles Deleuze and Felix Guattari, *A Thousand Plateaus*', *Graduate Faculty Philosophy Journal*, 18, no. 1.

Nietzsche, Friedrich. 1968. *The Will to Power*, trans. W. Kaufmann and R. J. Hollingdale. New York: Random House, Vintage Books.

Nietzsche, Friedrich. 1994. *On the Genealogy of Morality*, ed. Keith Ansell-Pearson. Cambridge: Cambridge University Press.

Pateman, Carole. 1988. *The Sexual Contract.* Cambridge: Polity Press.

Patton, Paul. 1993. 'Politics and the Concept of Power in Hobbes and Nietzsche', in Patton, ed., *Nietzsche, Feminism and Political Theory*. London and New York: Routledge.

Patton, Paul. 1994. 'Metamorpho-logic: Bodies and Powers in *A Thousand Plateaus*', *Journal of the British Society for Phenomenology*, 25, no. 2, May.

Patton, Paul. 1995. 'Mabo, Freedom and the Politics of Difference', *Australian Journal of Political Science*, 30, no. 1, March.

Patton, Paul. 1996. 'Concept and event', *Man and World*, 29, no. 3, July.

Tully, James. 1995. *Strange Multiplicity: Constitutionalism in an Age of Diversity.* Cambridge: Cambridge University Press.

CHAPTER 12

The Object of Political Theory

Barry Hindess

My title can be understood in two rather different senses. In the first, the object of political theory is, quite simply, politics itself. Accordingly, this chapter could reasonably be expected to explore the diverse ways in which 'politics' and related terms have been understood. In fact, I have addressed this issue elsewhere (1995c; 1996). I have argued that most, if not all, contemporary understandings of politics can be seen as based upon (or descended from) diverse metaphorical elaborations of the idea of politics as attending to the affairs of the *polis* or to the *res publica*. That is, they can be seen as variously derived from idealized representations of the public life of the cities of classical antiquity. What these idealizations share is an image of politics as the government of a community of citizens: a community consisting, at least in part, of autonomous political actors. Such an image of politics implies a corresponding view of a non-political domain, but the precise distinction between the two domains has always been open to dispute; the various boundaries that have been proposed have invariably been regarded as somewhat insecure. As a result, the political or governmental sphere is usually thought to be in danger of corruption – if not in fact as already and inescapably corrupted – by the invasions of concerns that properly belong elsewhere, while the non-political domain is thought to be in danger from the tyrannical reach of government. These twin threats lie at the heart of the problem of 'institutional design', which has been a major theme of political theory in the modern period.

This chapter focuses on the second understanding of my title, in which 'object' is taken in the sense of aim, purpose or objective. In this sense the object of political theory is commonly understood as being to make normative recommendations about matters of political concern. Political theory, in other words, is a distinctly normative enterprise; it is distinct from, say, positive theories of politics whose aim is to provide a scientific account of how politics can be understood in relation to other aspects of social life. The greater part of this chapter examines the normative presumptions of political theory and the grounds on which they rest. I argue that the enterprise of political theory presupposes a view of the political theorist as speaking to (and speaking for) a presumed community of reasonable persons. In the modern period this imaginary community has itself often been seen as standing for a substantially larger whole – for humanity, the West, or particular nations within the West. While this view of the political theorist is clearly fanciful, it nevertheless plays an important part in what has come to be known as political theory. If political theory is not what it pretends to be, this chapter considers how its pretensions are to be understood.

Usages of Theory

The *Journal of Political Philosophy* advertises itself as being 'devoted to the study of theoretical issues arising out of moral, legal and political life'. If political theory is understood in this broad sense, then it may take a considerable variety of forms, and there is nothing of any general significance to be said about its aim, purpose or objective. However, there are also more specific usages. One of them is clearly represented in Arnold Brecht's programmatic entry on 'Political Theory' in the *International Encyclopedia of the Social Sciences*; it is a product of the behavioural putsch in American political science. It identifies theory with scientific theory, and 'political theory' with that faction's narrowly sectarian view of what a positive, scientific theory of politics should be. Since a positive account of politics must resolve the contentious boundary issue noted above, it is clear that this or any other candidate for a positive theory of politics will be congenial to some political agendas and uncongenial to others. If only for this reason, distinctions between positive and normative theories of politics are never as clear as their supporters would prefer.

A second, more specific usage of 'political theory', and one which most concerns me here, understands it as a distinctly normative enterprise. Even this usage covers a considerable variety of understandings, but what is of particular interest to this chapter is not so much the differences between them as the common ground on which they rest. As a provisional demarcation of this territory, consider David Held's introduction to his *Political Theory Today*. Held's book includes contributions from a wide range of intellectual standpoints, and his introductory discussion aims to provide a concise survey of the field. Held notes that, in spite of considerable disagreements, his contributors share a view of the project of political theory as comprising a number of distinct tasks:

'first, the philosophical – concerned, above all, with the conceptual and normative; second, the empirical-analytical – concerned, above all, with the problems of understanding and explanation; and third, the strategic – concerned, above all, with an account of the feasibility of moving from where we are to where we might like to be' (1991: 20). It is the explicit (rather than surreptitious) inclusion of the first and third of these tasks which distinguishes this understanding of political theory from the sectarian, scientistic understanding noted above.

I return to the normative and strategic character of political theory in a moment, but first there is a further demarcation to be made. As Andrew Vincent notes in his introduction to this collection, the modern usage of the term 'political theory' is of comparatively recent vintage. Nevertheless, while the term may be new, political theorists commonly write as if the thing itself has been around for some time. The explicit or implicit invocation of tradition – stretching back at least to David Hume, if not to the supposed birth of politics and democracy in the cities of classical antiquity – is an aspect of the contemporary understanding of political theory that deserves more attention than I can give it here. For the moment, let me just say that the invention of tradition is as much a feature of political theory as it is, say, of contemporary nationalisms. The traditions invoked in such cases are retrospective constructions; they make use of real or imagined continuities with the past as the means of representing what are said to be essential characteristics of the present. In the case of political theory, the treatment of, say, Hume, Augustine or Aristotle as if they too were participating in what is now the academic discipline of political theory risks both the anachronistic reading of their work and a corresponding misunderstanding of the distinctive features of contemporary political theory itself.

With these strictures in mind, this chapter focuses on the character of contemporary political theory. Although, as we shall see, it makes considerable use of the past on which political theory claims to draw, it makes no claim that the dead white males of the tradition should be regarded as political theorists in the modern sense. As a normative enterprise, political theory involves an account of how things should be, often together with some kind of acknowledgement that this is not how things are. The appearance of a gap between ideal and mundane reality, then, provides the impetus for liberal projects of institutional design and for numerous styles of critical political theory. However, there is considerably more to political theory than the fact that its practitioners each have a view of how the world should be: this characteristic hardly distinguishes political theorists from many of their contemporaries.

The distinctive feature here is that political theorists commonly treat the question of how things should be as the starting-point of a certain kind of theoretical enterprise. In this section I characterize the enterprise of political theory in terms of its political, disciplinary and ethical qualities before turning to the significance which political theorists especially tend to claim for it.

The Political Quality of Political Theory

At the beginning of *Between Philosophy and Politics*, John Gunnell refers to the myth 'that academic discourse about politics is equivalent to political discourse' (1986: 1). The academic discourse in question here is that of contemporary political theory, and Gunnell's remark is clearly directed against what he regards as the pretensions of its mainstream practitioners. Many readers no doubt sympathize with Gunnell's position on this point. Nevertheless, it should be noted that his description of this presumption as a myth is misleading for at least two reasons. First, it supposes that we know what political discourse is, and that the general run of academic discourse about politics is obviously not part of it. The problem with this supposition is not that it misrepresents the political significance of academic discourse, but rather that it turns on a definitive resolution of boundary issues, which, as I noted in my opening paragraph, are more properly seen as indeterminate.

The second, and more serious, problem concerns the suggestion that normative political theory is 'about politics'. If we adopt the view of 'politics' that seems to be entailed in Gunnell's understanding of 'political discourse' – as concerning the current practices of, and major influences on, governments, parties and leading figures within them – we have to say not only that contemporary political theory has little direct impact on politics, but also that much of political theory is not about politics at all. In fact, the term 'political' does not qualify political theory in the way that, say, 'genetic' or 'literary' might be said to qualify genetic or literary theory. Political theory has a 'political' quality not primarily because it examines 'political' institutions and practices (although it often does), but rather because the normative issues it considers are presented as if they were (or should be) pertinent to political decision. Indeed, in spite of its limited political impact, it is only a little misleading to say that the primary mode of normative political theory takes the form of advice to the Prince – a figure which, like Hobbes's sovereign, may be thought of as an individual or an 'Assembly of men' (Hobbes 1968: 227).

To say that this representation of political theory is even a little misleading is also to say that there are certain respects in which it has to be qualified. First, the advice given by political theory is often provided at one or more removes from the practical matters on which the Prince may have to decide. Political theory, in other words, often addresses

issues which (or so it maintains) should be considered in the preparation
of such advice – thereby leaving the political pamphlet, memorandum or
position paper to be put together by someone else. John Rawls's *A Theory
of Justice*, for example, would not normally be regarded as a manual of
practical advice on government. But, suitably interpreted by Raymond
Plant, the principles set out in Rawls's work reappeared in Roy
Hattersley's *Choose Freedom: The Future for Democratic Socialism*, a piece of
(unheeded) advice to the Prince written by the then deputy leader of the
British Labour Party.

Second, while the more influential styles of political theory recommend principles which ought to be implemented in governmental
practice, there is an alternative style which recommends quiescence or
resignation. This often takes the form of conservative or liberal advice
insisting, albeit for rather different reasons, on the limits to what politics
can achieve. Alternatively, expecting little from even the best of Princes,
it takes the form of a Straussian word to the wise, a therapeutic discourse
in which perceptive readers are advised to adjust their hopes and
expectations to a somewhat unpromising reality.

Third, 'the Prince' stands for a variety of governmental functions
which, even in the most dictatorial political regimes, are rarely brought
together into the hands of a single individual or assembly. In fact, some
important governmental functions are often thought to be very widely
dispersed. An influential early example of this view appears in Locke's
discussion of the 'Law of Opinion and Reputation', which he presents as
playing a major role in the formation and maintenance of public
morality. Locke invokes the image of a mode of governing individual
behaviour that operates through everyday interactions within a substantial moral community (1957, II, ch. 28). In our liberal and democratic
polities, what I have called advice to the Prince may well be addressed (at
some remove) to political leaders, to public officials in specialized fields
of administration, to the judiciary, or to what is thought to be a broader
moral community of reasonable persons. This last mode of address has
an important place in the history of political thought, and it constitutes
perhaps the most influential form of academic political theory in the
West today. Thus, when contemporary political theorists refer to 'our'
moral intuitions, beliefs or interests, the presumed addressees normally
include substantially more than the theorists concerned and their actual
readers. The presumption is that political theory speaks to, and speaks
for, a national (or larger) moral community consisting mostly of persons
who are not themselves political theorists.

Finally, it is important to recognize cases in which the rule of the Prince
(or the dominant moral community) might be perceived as illegitimate.
A significant body of political writing takes the form of advice, not to an

established Prince, but rather to his challenger: advice, in other words, to the Pretender. Locke's *Two Treatises* was certainly read in this way in much of continental Europe (Koselleck 1988). Here too, in our liberal and democratic polities, the more influential challengers are those who seek a compromise with the Prince, rather than his abdication or the overthrow of princely rule. It is in this spirit, for example, that 'politics of difference' theorists (Phillips 1991; Yeatman 1994; Young 1990) urge the incorporation of those who currently find themselves excluded from the dominant moral communities of contemporary societies.

Much of what I have said here about political theory as advice to the Prince applies equally to contemporary economics (which, unlike political theory, has an undeniable impact on politics) and to its predecessor, political economy. Both of these might be described as governmental discourses of a rather specialized kind – and even, in certain respects, a rigorous kind.[1] In order to identify the distinctive character of political theory's advice, we must also take account of its particular focus on principles or values, that is, of its disciplinary and ethical qualities which I consider below.

The Disciplinary Quality of Political Theory

Paul Patton's contribution to this collection outlines Gilles Deleuze's view of philosophy – and of political theory in so far as it can be seen as a branch of philosophy – as 'the fabrication of concepts'.[2] This is Deleuze's version of a misleading, but all too common, view of the discipline as a romantic and heroic enterprise whose history is essentially a history of great names and the achievements (the new concepts) for which they are famous. To say that this is misleading is not to deny the reality of either great names or the appearance of new concepts (although it seems odd to suggest that the fabrication of the latter is the distinctive province of philosophy) – or even of intellectual progress in certain limited respects. My point rather is that this romantic view hides substantially more than it reveals; in particular, it obscures (and Deleuze may intend it to overcome) the character of philosophy – and of modern political theory – as a disciplinary enterprise.

Philosophy is a disciplinary enterprise most obviously in the sense that the greater part of the practice of philosophy consists in the training (of oneself or of others) to be able to rehearse certain kinds of argument and to apply them in what are thought to be appropriate contexts. To study philosophy is to work on oneself, and to work, in particular, on one's habits of thought and argument. At least in its modern Western forms, philosophy is a spiritual exercise of a distinctly intellectual kind. Bodily techniques, such as fasting, recitation, or the use of drugs, play no significant part in philosophical training; unlike training in dance or music, both of which have a significant spiritual component, philosophical training is not concerned with mastery of bodily technique.

Readers familiar with Pierre Hadot's studies of Greek and Hellenistic philosophy (Hadot 1995) will recognize several elements of this brief characterization of the disciplinary quality of philosophy – a quality that it shares with academic political theory and, indeed, with much of the humanities and social sciences academy. Hadot argues that ancient philosophy should be seen as a way of life, or rather, as a number of ways of life which share certain distinctive characteristics. In particular, the discipline of philosophy aimed to develop in each of its practitioners an inner attitude of wisdom and serenity in the face of the world. It was, as Martha Nussbaum presents it, a discipline of spiritual therapy.[3] To insist on its therapeutic character is not to deny the importance of demonstration and proof, say, in ancient physics or mathematics; but it is to maintain that the advancement of knowledge was not the primary concern of ancient philosophy. On the contrary, reason and argument were valued primarily because of their role in the spiritual formation of the initiates. This subordination of argument and demonstration to the requirements of spiritual formation accounts for the extraordinary longevity of the main Hellenistic schools of philosophy.

As Hadot (1995) presents it, then, the principal significance of philosophical discourse among the ancients was as an aid towards, and a training in, the practice of philosophy as a way of life. Innovation within that discourse was valued primarily to the extent that it served those functions. In the modern period, on the other hand, while the idea of philosophy as a way of life still has a considerable appeal, philosophy is nevertheless identified primarily with philosophical discourse – and with the 'fabrication of new concepts' within that discourse. Hadot suggests that the emergence of this more constrained view of philosophy can be attributed to the victory of Christianity in the late Roman world. As a result, philosophical discourse was subordinated to the requirements of theology, and thence to the maintenance of Christianity (rather than philosophy itself) as a way of life. In the modern period philosophy has broken away from many of its theological shackles, but the primacy of philosophical discourse over the practice of philosophy as a way of life has nevertheless remained.

Hadot clearly regards this modern understanding of philosophy as unfortunate, and in its place he favours a return to what he sees as the fuller understanding of philosophy as a way of life. I leave this aspect of his argument to one side for the purposes of the present discussion. What matters here are two other issues. First, in spite of the considerable changes that he notes, Hadot nevertheless writes as if there were a

substantial degree of continuity between ancient and modern philosophy. This suggests that much of the disciplinary character of the earlier
practice of philosophy remains, albeit in a somewhat attenuated form.
In particular, competing schools of thought play a major role in the
contemporary practice of philosophy. As a result, the demonstrative
functions of argument coexist with, and are sometimes dominated by, its
function as rehearsal or elaboration of the standpoint of one or other
school; its aim is the spiritual formation of the neophyte and the spiritual
progression of firm adherents as much as, if not more than, the conver-
sion of members of other persuasions.

Second, alongside the increased significance of philosophical discourse in the modern period, there are a number of other changes
which play no part in Hadot's discussion. One, which I alluded to above,
concerns the proliferation of disciplines, with the result that much of
what might once have been seen as philosophy is conducted under other
disciplinary labels. There has been a corresponding narrowing of the
disciplinary focus of what is now regarded as philosophy itself. The
phenomena of competing schools can also be found in political theory,
and all the other academic disciplines which have emerged from what
Kant (and many others) once saw as the province of the philosophy
faculty.[4] The more important change for our purposes concerns the
character of 'philosophical' discourse itself – including here the
theoretical discourses of the humanities and scientific disciplines. As
Hadot presents it, the philosophical discourse of the ancients aimed to
induce an inner attitude of wisdom and serenity in the face of the world;
in contrast, the corresponding discourses of the moderns frequently
have a distinctly activist or interventionist pretension. This pretension is
clearly encapsulated in Marx's eleventh thesis on Feuerbach: 'The
philosophers have only interpreted the world . . . ; the point, however, is
to change it.'

What is at issue here may be variously described: as the rise of the
world view of modern science, with its fusion of activist and contem-
plative aspirations; as what Weber and Critical Theory call the rationaliza-
tion of the modern world and the domination within it of instrumental
reason; or as the emergence of the orientation that Heidegger (1978)
identifies as 'the essence of technology'. Heidegger's description seems
to me the most useful, in part because it is also the most abstract and
general. The technological orientation sees the world as consisting of
forces which, at least in principle, can be identified and harnessed to
human purposes. On this view, all natural phenomena, including human
individuals and aggregates, can be seen as a standing reserve of energy
which could be put to use once the relevant forces had been properly
identified.

This last point might seem to have taken us a long way from the disciplinary quality of political theory. I have stressed it here because the phenomena of spiritual formation and reinforcement that are associated with the existence of competing schools of thought now both coexist and compete with the rather different functions of argument and reason that arise from a technological orientation.[5] Alongside the view that our desires should be adjusted to the world, philosophy, and political theory in particular, now teaches that the world should also be adjusted to our desires – at least if we ensure that the latter are suitably realistic. We should, of course, expect that the relationships between spiritual formation and technological orientation will vary in different areas of intellectual activity, with competing schools playing a major role in some cases and a relatively minor role in others. In the case of a normative enterprise like political theory, where competing schools have an undeniable importance, the technological orientation which assumes that the world can and should be adapted to our purposes appears in two of the three tasks set out in David Held's characterization of the discipline with which I began this section. First, there is the 'empirical-analytical' task, requiring at least a gestural recognition that normative recommendations furnished by political theory should take account of the relevant scientific knowledge of society.[6] The other task is 'strategic': consideration of specifically normative issues frequently seems to aim not only at inducing an inner attitude of serenity and wisdom but also – if somewhat abstractly – at the activist's question of what is to be done. This combination brings us to the ethical quality of political theory.

The Ethical Quality of Political Theory

The distinctive ethical quality of contemporary political theory is not a matter of its character as a predominantly academic discipline – that is, of operating in terms of professional standards and a professional academic ethos – since, with only minor variations, it shares that character with other academic disciplines. Nor is it to be found in the fact that political theory deals with ethical materials such as values and principles, since this is also true of certain kinds of empirical social scientific enquiry. Max Weber's studies of the economic ethos of the world religions provide a particularly notable example.

In addition to these features, political theory is presented (at least by its practitioners) as if it had a distinctive moral value of its own, not only for the practitioners themselves and for their pupils but also for the wider community to which they belong. This is something that one would not necessarily expect to find, say, in the enquiries of sociologists or political scientists into the values which exist in a particular community and the practices to which they give rise. While such enquiries may well result in recommendations, these normally take a conditional form: 'If you wish to obtain X, then our findings suggest that you must do . . .'. Political theorists frequently make recommendations of that kind, of course, but they also go further to recommend the values or principles which we *should* aim to implement. Where the responsibility of the empirical social scientist is to aim at a certain kind of value-freedom, the responsibility of the political theorist is to affirm a commitment to particular values.

As I noted earlier, this last feature is seen to be desirable not only as a moral quality of the political theorist as a person, but also as a central moral component of the political theory which that person elaborates: political theory is to be both dispassionate in the style of its argument, and morally committed in its substance. This expectation accounts for what can only be called the moral impatience exhibited by many political theorists in their treatment of those who, while clearly having commitments of their own and elaborating theoretical arguments of a politically relevant kind, refuse to provide their commitments with an appropriate theoretical foundation. The most obvious recent examples of such impatience are the treatment of Foucault, Lyotard and other French poststructuralists by Taylor (1986), Habermas (1989) and numerous others sympathetic to the claims of Critical Theory. The complaint in such cases is not that the former are amoral in their personal conduct, but rather that, where their theories should present dispassionate arguments offering moral guidance, they manifestly fail to do so. The significance of this complaint is a consequence of the peculiar disciplinary and ethical qualities of political theory and, in particular, of two assumptions: first, that the spiritual formation of initiates is an important part of the argumentative practice of political theory; and second, that the spiritual formation in this case should promote an orientation to the world which is both moral and instrumental. A theory that rejects the second assumption will be seen as inducing a spiritual formation which is morally incomplete, if not in fact destructive: it threatens the corruption of academic youth.

Political Theory and the Modern Problem of Government

It would not be difficult to imagine something like a modern Western society in which political theory of the kind outlined above had no significant presence. Political issues would still be addressed in such a society, and many of them would be subject to dispute, but they would be addressed in ways that were not much affected by the specialized concerns of academic political theory. Indeed, the fear that we might be approaching, or already be in, such a condition is a significant feature of the work of many contemporary political theorists. Why does it matter? Why, in other words, do political theorists themselves, and (at least a few) others in universities, the law, politics and government, treat as important political theory's distinctive kind of advice to the Prince? And why does the Prince to whom that advice is addressed so often take the form of a presumed moral community?

Such questions can be answered in a number of ways, most directly perhaps in terms of the self-sustaining character of the discipline itself. Political theorists have had extensive training of a formal or informal kind in the practices of the discipline, and their intellectual personae have acquired certain characteristics as a result: they have learned, in particular, to value the spiritual consolations offered by political theory, and especially by the rehearsal and elaboration of the styles of argument with which they are most comfortable. Many more, who are not professional political theorists, have been exposed to its practices, and some at least of them have learned to appreciate what it has to offer. Like MacIntyre's 'practices',[7] spiritual disciplines are valued in part for rewards that are strictly internal to the disciplines themselves. In this respect, political theory is no different from, say, chamber music, white-water rafting or fox-hunting: it is valued by those who have learned to value what it has to offer, and viewed with indifference or distaste by those who have not.

While there is much to be said for such an answer, it is certainly incomplete. Apart from the motivations that arise from the comforts which political theory provides for adherents, it is also necessary to enquire into the conceptual conditions of its particular ethical and political pretensions. What assumptions must be made about the Prince, and the community over which he rules or has designs, if political theory is to appear to be worthwhile in a more general sense? In other words, how are the rewards of political theory to be valued, not only as the contingent outcome of their own cultivation, but also as the due rewards of virtue itself? I cannot hope to deal here with all of the issues raised by this question but, as a partial and preliminary response, I will suggest that political theory of the kind outlined above is predicated on, and should be seen as one of the responses to, what might be called the modern problem of government.

Briefly, the modern problem of government has three fundamental features: first, a view of the governed as a population consisting largely of autonomous persons; second, the belief that there is a rationality of government that is independent of sectional interests and values; and third, the existence of a state in the modern sense, that is, of a distinctive institutional structure independent of the person or persons of the ruler.[8] The third feature distinguishes the modern problem of government from the otherwise similar problem that arises with regard to governing the citizen populations of relatively small independent cities (Hindess 1995c; 1996). Oversimplifying some complex lines of development, the view of the governed as a population of autonomous persons can be seen as resulting from the gradual dissolution of the medieval view that individuals were essentially subordinate to others – to fathers, husbands and masters, to lords and princes, both secular and spiritual, and through them ultimately to God. In its place, we find an emerging view that individuals (or, at least in the first instance, those who are the heads of substantial households) should be seen as governing themselves or else as failing to do so. This in turn raises two obvious questions. First, if appreciable numbers of individuals are not subordinated to others, then how is ordered social life possible at all? Second, where ordered social life does exist, what should be done with those who cannot or will not behave themselves – a category which, until recently, was seen by most writers on government (including liberals) to contain a clear majority of the population?

As to the first question, if the orderly interactions of large numbers of individuals are not to be explained by the subordination of each of them to a superior external authority, it seems that the explanation must lie in sources of control that are internal. The dissolution of the old order in the West is also the period of the development and refinement of a moral psychology concerned precisely with identifying (and making use of) 'internal' sources of behaviour: on the one hand there are values, interests and passions, and on the other there are the faculties of will and reason.[9] To the extent that the latter are able to impose some order on the impact of the former, individuals will be endowed with what Nietzsche calls 'the right to make promises' (1967, essay II, s. 2): that is, they can be regarded as capable of controlling their present and future behaviour, and therefore as able to take on obligations and, by and large, to satisfy them. On this view, what makes the orderly interaction of many individuals possible is, first, internal motivations, many of which are shared or complementary although many are also in conflict. Second, there are agreements of various kinds, which, for the most part, such individuals can be relied on to honour and which allow them to defuse the potentially destructive consequences of their disagreements. Third, there is a central reserve of force which functions as a back-up, both to strengthen individuals' motivations in favour of fulfilling their obligations and to put down those who nevertheless insist on breaking them. The moral psychology which seems to tell us how autonomous individuals can nevertheless interact in a relatively peaceful and orderly fashion, also provides the means of dealing with the second question: those who cannot or will not behave themselves can be trained in suitably reasonable habits of thought and behaviour, while those who cannot even be trained in those habits must be locked away and kept down by force.

Since, with minor variations, this is still how the major academic and political discourses of the West tend to present things, it is worth noting that there is nothing inevitable about this picture of human individuals and therefore of the character of the interactions between them.[10] For the moment, let me suggest that, in addition to our habituation in its usage, this individualistic picture is persuasive for two reasons: first, it develops the individualizing elements in earlier Christian thought; and second, it fills the gap left by the secular loss of faith in the efficacy of the supra-individual networks that were once thought to hold Christian communities together.

The second feature of the modern problem of government is constituted by the belief that there is a rationality of government which is autonomous in the sense of being independent of merely sectional interests and values.[11] Versions of this belief can be found in the republican and absolutist thought of the early modern period. However, it will be most familiar to contemporary readers in the form developed by the liberal or proto-liberal critics of absolutism: they represented the community as a collection of free individuals, and regarded absolute rulers and their minions as having sectional interests of their own, which should play no part in the proper work of government. In this last form, the belief that there is a rationality of government independent of sectional interests and values leads to the ubiquitous liberal problem of institutional design: how to arrange a government of free persons so that it will not be dominated by factions? A faction is defined as a group of citizens united by a common purpose that is, as Madison et al. (1987) put it, 'adverse to the rights of other citizens, or to *the permanent and aggregate interests of the community*' (emphasis added).

This belief in an autonomous rationality of government continues to play a major part in the political life of Western societies, and I have discussed some of its vicissitudes elsewhere (Hindess 1996). What should be noted here is that, while it clearly depends on the individualistic model of human interaction noted above, it is not a necessary consequence of that model. Thus, it is entirely possible to accept some version of the individualistic model of human interaction while regarding the idea of an autonomous rationality of government as a fiction. On this view, the governmental invocation of a general or common interest represents at best a certain kind of pragmatic accommodation amongst influential players – an accommodation rendered no less pragmatic by the belief of some participants that there is an autonomous rationality of government.

Many readers will be able to convince themselves that the government of a political community should represent something more than the maintenance of an ongoing accommodation. For them, it is easy to see the attractions of a view of political community as twofold: first as a moral community, constituted in part by widely shared norms and values; and second as reflecting a number of society-wide (and narrower) agreements, especially the agreement to form or to recognize a government and to obey its legitimate instructions. The most prominent addressees of political theory are individuals who are regarded as members of such an imagined political community and the ethical specialists who claim to advise them. This point provides the answer to the question with which I began this section. It is the role attributed to shared values and to real or presumed agreements in the maintenance of a political community of that kind which establishes the central importance of the work of political theory in clarifying those values and agreements and in working through their implications.

Conclusion

What I have called the modern problem of government represents the most influential view, at least in contemporary Western societies, of what political communities are, and therefore of the materials with which the government of such communities has to deal. I have argued that political theory can be seen as a response to that problem which suggests, not only that societies are constituted on the basis of shared values, agreements and the laws (and penalties for their infringement) which arise in consequence of those agreements, but also that these values and agreements are the principal means by which societies can and should be governed.

I conclude by noting some of the limitations of that response. Perhaps the most serious limitations are those that arise from the terms of the problem itself. I have already suggested that the idea of an autonomous rationality of government is a fiction, albeit one which has been remarkably influential in the history of the modern West. Widespread recognition of this fictional character can be expected to have substantial consequences for perceptions of the legitimacy of government, and also for the efficacy of laws and other instruments of government that rely on the invocation of a presumed sense of personal obligation (Hindess 1996).

I have also suggested that there is nothing inevitable about the manner in which the problem of orderly social interaction has been posed in the modern West – that is, in terms of elements internal to each of the participants. It has been posed in this way, I suggest, largely as a response to the breakdown of conditions in which the issues here were addressed in other ways. However, granted that the problem of government has in fact been posed in such terms, political theory's solution in terms of shared values and agreements still provides a remarkably limited view of the modern Western practice of government. This last point has been extensively discussed elsewhere,[12] and it is sufficient here to note two considerations. First, since no one imagines that the capacities required for the exercise of a 'right to make promises' are properly developed at birth, the idea that adult members of society may be governed by means of those capacities clearly requires that they be subjected to training and other processes of character formation. A society which is thought to be governed by values and agreement must also be seen as governed in other ways – for example, by paternalism, civil society and the market. Second, while there may be a sense in which the personal obligations arising from agreement could be seen as enabling governments to regulate the actions of each of their subjects, it is clear that the invocation of such obligations are not themselves sufficient to co-ordinate activities within a large and diverse population. Governments must therefore rely also on other means of regulating the behaviour of their subjects. These include, on the one hand, what Bentham calls 'indirect legislation'; and on the other, the more direct reliance on bureaucracy and independent self-governing associations of various kinds.

Why then do common values on the one hand, and real or presumed agreements on the other, occupy such a prominent place in the discourse of political theory? Largely, I suspect, for the reason suggested by Foucault: their prominence confuses the political problem of legitimacy with a political problem of a very different kind, namely, the problem of how large populations can in fact be governed. It is as if, once we assume that individuals are endowed with the 'right to make promises', then the fact of their real or presumed agreement can be regarded as giving their government not only the *right*, but also, through its invocation of obligations which arise from that agreement, the *capacity* to govern their behaviour.[13] But this answer still leaves us with something of a puzzle, since the agreement–obligation nexus clearly does little to resolve the governmental problems involved in co-ordinating the actions of large numbers of individuals. Part of the explanation for the significance that political theorists attribute to values and agreements surely lies in the institutional development of political theory as a university specialism. My point is not the familiar, and often misleading, complaint about the remoteness of academic life from the practical problems of government. The more significant issue here is that political theorists more than, say, specialists in public policy, are likely to be infected by the modern, liberal image of the role of the university, and especially of the humanities, in the moral development of the more intelligent and active members of society (Hindess 1995b). For those who see the university in this way, the focus on values and the spiritual formation of initiates is simply part of their job.

Notes

1 They are governmental in the sense of focusing especially on conceptualizing what is involved in, and developing practical recipes for, managing aspects of the conduct of large numbers of actors. For this understanding of government, see the references in note 8 below.

2 See especially Deleuze and Guattari (1994).

3 Nussbaum (1994). Where Hadot presents ancient philosophy in general as a way of life (or rather, a number of competing and closely related ways of life), Nussbaum insists on the therapeutic character only of the major Hellenistic Schools (Epicureans, sceptics and stoics), distinguishing them, in particular, from Plato, Aristotle and the early Academy.

4 Kant (1979) and the discussion in Mary Gregor's useful Introduction. See also Hunter (1995).

5 I refer to coexistence and competition rather than to displacement here because, even in the most technological of intellectual disciplines, the spiritual formation of practitioners is commonly thought to be a condition of disciplinary integrity. On this point see Weber's 'Science as a Vocation' in Lassman et al. (1989).

6 Rawls, without going into the details of the 'general facts', 'principles', etc., in question, nevertheless assumes that the parties to his original position 'know the general facts about human society. They understand political affairs and the principles of economic theory; they know the basis of social organization and the laws of human psychology' (1972: 137).

7 MacIntyre (1981), especially chapter 14, and the discussions in Horton and Mendus (1994).

8 My treatment of this issue is based on the rethinking of early modern understandings of government inspired by the work of such diverse scholars as Foucault (1991) and Oestreich (1982). See, in particular, the essays by Burchell and Gordon in Burchell et al. (1991) and the discussions in Dean (1994) and Hindess (1995a).

9 See the somewhat different discussions in Hirschman (1977) and Holmes (1995), especially chapter 2, 'The Secret History of Self-Interest'.

10 This is a difficult issue to debate since many of the anthropological and historical studies to which we might turn in search of relevant evidence have themselves been informed by precisely this picture of the human individual. But see the various discussions in Carrithers et al. (1985), Foucault (1993), Strathern (1988) and Williams (1993).

11 See note 8 and my discussion of this presumption in Hindess (1996).

12 Burchell et al. (1991), Barry et al. (1996).

13 The confusion of power as right and power as capacity is endemic in modern political thought. See Hindess (1995a).

References

Barry, A., Osborne, T., and Rose, N. 1996. *Foucault and Political Reason: Liberalism, Neo-liberalism and Rationalities of Government*. London: University College London Press.

Burchell, G., Gordon, C., and Miller, P. 1991. *The Foucault Effect: Studies in Governmentality*. Chicago: University of Chicago Press.

Carrithers, M., Collins, S., and Lukes, S. 1985. *The Category of the Person: Anthropology, Philosophy, History*. Cambridge: Cambridge University Press.

Dean, M. 1994. *Critical and Effective Histories: Foucault's Methods and Historical Sociology*. London: Routledge.

Deleuze, G., and Guattari, F. 1994. *What is Philosophy?* London: Verso.

Foucault, M. 1991. 'Governmentality', in G. Burchell, C. Gordon, and P. Miller, eds, *The Foucault Effect*. Chicago: University of Chicago Press.

Foucault, M. 1993. 'About the Beginning of the Hermeneutics of the Self', *Political Theory*, 21, no. 2, 198–227.

Gunnell, John C. 1986. *Between Philosophy and Politics*. Amherst: University of Massachusetts Press.

Habermas, J. 1989. *The New Conservatism*. Cambridge, Mass.: MIT Press.

Hadot, P. 1995. *Philosophy as a Way of Life. Spiritual Exercises from Socrates to Foucault*, ed. Arnold I. Davidson. Oxford: Blackwell.

Hattersley, R. 1987. *Choose Freedom: The Future for Democratic Socialism*. Harmondsworth, Mddx: Penguin.

Heidegger, M. 1978. 'The Question Concerning Technology', in D. F. Krell, ed., *Martin Heidegger: Basic Writings*. London: Routledge and Kegan Paul.

Held, D. 1991. *Political Theory Today*. Oxford: Blackwell.

Hindess, B. 1995a. *Discourses of Power: From Hobbes to Foucault*. Oxford: Blackwell.

Hindess, B. 1995b. 'Great Expectations: Freedom and Authority in the Idea of a Modern University', *Oxford Literary Review*, 17.

Hindess, B. 1995c. '"The Greeks had a Word for It": The Polis as Political Metaphor', *Thesis Eleven*, 40, 119–32.

Hindess, B. 1996. 'Fears of Intrusion: Anti-political Motifs in Western Political Discourse', in A. Schedler, ed., *The End of Politics? Explorations into Modern Antipolitics*. Basingstoke: Macmillan.

Hirschman, A. O. 1977. *The Passions and the Interests*. Princeton: Princeton University Press.

Hobbes, T. 1968 [1651]. *Leviathan*. London: Penguin.

Holmes, S. 1995. *Passions and Constraints: On the Theory of Liberal Democracy*. Chicago: University of Chicago Press.

Horton, J., and Mendus, S. 1994. *After MacIntyre: Critical Perspectives on the Work of Alasdair MacIntyre*. Oxford: Blackwell.

Hunter, I. 1995. 'The Regimen of Reason: Kant's Defence of the Philosophy Faculty', *Oxford Literary Review*, 17, nos. 1–2.

Kant, I. 1979. *The Conflict of the Faculties*. Lincoln, Nebraska, and London: University of Nebraska Press.

Koselleck, R. 1988. *Critique and Crisis. Enlightenment and the Pathogenesis of Modern Society*. Oxford, New York and Hamburg: Berg.

Lassman, P., Velody, I., and Martins, H. 1989. *Max Weber's 'Science as a Vocation'*. London: Unwin Hyman.

Locke, J. 1957. *An Essay Concerning Human Understanding*. Oxford: Clarendon Press.

MacIntyre, A. 1981. *After Virtue*. London: Duckworth.

Madison, J., Hamilton, A., and Jay, J. 1987 [1788]. *The Federalist Papers*. Harmondsworth: Penguin.

Nietzsche, F. 1967. *On the Genealogy of Morals*. New York: Random House.

Nussbaum, M. C. 1994. *The Therapy of Desire: Theory and Practice in Hellenistic Ethics*. Princeton: Princeton University Press.

Oestreich, G. 1982. *Neo-stoicism and the Early Modern State*. Cambridge: Cambridge University Press.

Phillips, A. 1991. *Engendering Democracy*. Oxford: Polity Press.

Rawls, J. 1972. *A Theory of Justice*. Oxford: Oxford University Press.

Strathern, M. 1988. *The Gender of the Gift: Problems with Women and Problems with Society in Melanesia*. Berkeley: University of California Press.

Taylor, C. 1986. 'Foucault on Freedom and Truth', in D. Hoy, ed., *Foucault: A Critical Reader*. Oxford: Blackwell.

Williams, B. 1993. *Shame and Necessity*. Berkeley: University of California Press.

Yeatman, A. 1994. *Postmodern Revisionings of the Political*. New York and London: Routledge.

Young, I. M. 1990. *Justice and the Politics of Difference*. Princeton: Princeton University Press.

Index